TORAH
Queeries

TORAH
Queeries

Weekly Commentaries on the Hebrew Bible

Edited by
GREGG DRINKWATER, JOSHUA LESSER,
and DAVID SHNEER

Foreword by JUDITH PLASKOW

New York University Press
NEW YORK AND LONDON

NEW YORK UNIVERSITY PRESS
New York and London
www.nyupress.org

© 2009 by New York University
All rights reserved

Library of Congress Cataloging-in-Publication Data
Torah queeries : weekly commentaries on the Hebrew Bible / edited by Gregg
Drinkwater, Joshua Lesser, and David Shneer ; foreword by Judith Plaskow.
p. cm.   Includes index.
ISBN-13: 978-0-8147-2012-7   (cl : alk. paper)
ISBN-10: 0-8147-2012-9   (cl : alk. paper)
1. Bible. O.T. Pentateuch—Commentaries.   2. Homosexuality—Religious
aspects—Judaism.   3. Jewish gays.   4. Jewish lesbians.
I. Drinkwater, Gregg.   II. Lesser, Joshua.
III. Shneer, David, 1972–
BS1225.53.T677   2009
222'.10708664—dc22   2009016577

New York University Press books are printed on acid-free paper, and their
binding materials are chosen for strength and durability. We strive
to use environmentally responsible suppliers and materials
to the greatest extent possible in publishing our books.

Manufactured in the United States of America

10 9 8 7 6 5 4 3 2 1

Contents

Foreword

JUDITH PLASKOW

"Turn it and turn it again, for everything is in it." This Mishnaic statement about the Torah (*Pirke Avot,* 5:25) captures a fundamental Jewish attitude toward the first five books of the Bible, an attitude that has been elaborated over time: The Torah is eternally fruitful, a source of wisdom that is worthy of study in every generation. Its meanings are inexhaustible; there is no aspect of human experience that can't be illuminated by it. Just as each of the six hundred thousand souls who stood at Mount Sinai heard something distinctive in the Torah, so Jews of succeeding generations can delve into Torah and discover new facets of its message that have never been seen or appreciated before.

Given the centrality of Torah study and interpretation to Jewish self-understanding, it is not surprising that many contemporary Jews continue to grapple with Torah as a way of defining their Jewish identities. Whether they turn to Torah out of a simple desire to learn, deep commitment, puzzlement, or passionate anger and dissent, they continue to understand the acts of reading and interpretation as crucial to who they are. Over the past forty years, each new group that has wanted to claim a place for itself within some Jewish community has done so partly in relation to the text that stands at the center of Jewish life and that has shaped Jewish memory over the course of centuries. In the late 1960s and early '70s, when feminists began to explore and critique the marginalization of women within Judaism, they identified exclusion from Torah study as a key element in women's subordination. Because studying Torah is the heart and soul of traditional Judaism, barring women from such learning meant educating and marking them as peripheral Jews. The purpose of the feminist project was not simply to name women's exclusion but to bring them into the centuries-old process of commenting and elaborating on Torah, a process previously reserved for learned men. Feminist anthologies on various books of the Bible, commentaries on the Torah and Haftarah portions, and courses and institutions established for women's Torah learning sought to open the world of Torah to women and to enrich the Jewish community by bringing multiple women's perspectives to Jewish texts.

Torah Queeries builds on this history of feminist commentary by enlarging the circle of former outsiders who now claim the authority to participate in the process of expounding on Torah and by demonstrating the fruitfulness of reading through queer lenses for all those interested in challenging traditional readings of Torah. The volume constitutes an exciting contribution to the project of democratizing Jewish communities by highlighting perspectives that have previously been neglected or anathematized, whether those perspectives are developed by authors who define themselves as queer or by allies questioning the inequalities of power that heretofore have been justified by Torah texts. The approaches of the contributors to *Torah Queeries* are as diverse as the multiple meanings of queer, but all the authors seek to uncover new facets of Torah by bringing to it viewpoints and experiences that have been missing from the ongoing process of interpretation, by reading through a "bent lens." Some pieces use *queer* as synonymous with gay and lesbian rights; others use it as an umbrella term for lesbian, gay, bisexual, and transgender Jews. Still others use the concept in the broad sense of challenging the stability of all sexual identities and, beyond that, insisting on the fluidity of all seemingly fixed boundaries. The overall effect of these different voices is to make clear that not only does the Jewish community today include queers but that it has never been otherwise. Read with fresh eyes and new questions, the Torah emerges as a queer text, filled with fertile contradictions. It is replete with shifty and shifting characters who challenge norms that the text elsewhere seems to proclaim as absolute, sometimes policing boundaries that at other moments dissolve.

Why is it important to read Torah through queer lenses? I argue that the need of formerly marginalized groups to establish their Jewish legitimacy by linking themselves to Torah converges with the Jewish community's need to continually renew itself by discovering possible new meanings in Torah. The excellent mix of queer writers and allies in this volume demonstrates the mutually fruitful relationship between the process through which women, queers, and other outsiders define their Jewish identities by finding themselves in Jewish texts and the process through which Jewish tradition develops and unfolds. Just as feminist perspectives on Jewish texts opened to the whole Jewish community a new world of questions and categories for understanding Torah, so queer perspectives do the same.

The transformative potential of such new readings is very far reaching. A recent ad for a new women's Torah commentary notes that, throughout Jewish history, male-authored Torah commentaries have shaped our views of the text. "The Torah hasn't changed," it goes on to say, "the commentary has." But I think that the impact of new volumes such as *Torah Queeries* is greater than that ad allows. To be sure, Torah does not change in a material sense; the letters on the scroll that Jews read in the synagogue remain the same. But insofar as Jews have always appropriated Torah through midrash and interpretation, new collections of commentaries such as this one have the power to alter deeply what we bring to and take from the text. As emergent voices within the Jewish community turn Torah and turn it again, they shift and expand our sense of what it might mean to be Jewish and thus contribute to keeping Judaism evolving and alive.

Introduction

Interpreting the Bible through a Bent Lens

DAVID SHNEER

It is the world's longest running rerun, the best-selling book of all time, the foundational text of Western culture and the core of the Jewish religion. The Hebrew Bible, sacred to nearly half the world's population, infuses the myths, politics, literature, art, and daily language of billions of people across the globe.

Jews throughout the world gather in synagogues every Saturday, as they have been doing for two thousand years, to read together from the Hebrew Bible, what most Christians call the Old Testament. Indeed, reading the Hebrew Bible is one of the longest continuously running ritualized reading and performance of text in history. The Bible, known in some circles as "torah she-bikhtav," the learning that was written down, is traditionally considered to be the word of God as transmitted to Moses on Mount Sinai, making it one of the world's oldest divine texts.

Within the Hebrew Bible, however, there is a hierarchy of holiness. Jews divide the Bible, or Tanakh, into three main sections that more or less correspond to chronology. The last section is called "Writings," and contains such texts as the Book of Esther, read every Purim; the Book of Ruth, the classic text of Shavuot; and Psalms, traditionally understood to have been penned by the great kings of Israel. Preceding the Writings in both age and standardized textual order are the Prophets, the books whose stories form the main historical narrative of ancient Israel. From the judge Joshua to kings David and Solomon, this section of the Bible contains historical narratives and moralistic stories that continue to inform modern Jewish thought and Western culture generally.

Moving back in time, and higher in the hierarchy of authority, comes the Torah, known variously as the Five Books of Moses, the Chumash, or in Greek, the Pentateuch. These first five books of the Bible are the most well known, the most interpreted, the most often retold, and the most important texts in Judaism. Although all Judaism's sacred texts are open to commentary and analysis, none is more interpreted than the Torah.

To this day, the Torah is considered so divine that its material form, a scroll of parchment known as a *sefer Torah* that replicates the structure of ancient scrolls, and a particular version of the Biblical text (known as the Masoretic Text, preserved by the early Masoretes or rabbis concerned with fixing a particular text) has been passed down almost miraculously with the utmost care in copying. Every letter of every part of the text is precise, perfect, and most important *intended*. There are no extra words, nothing missing, with every letter, every space, every repetition or seeming inconsistency thus inviting interpretation, or exegesis.

The Torah has been interpreted and reinterpreted ever since it was canonized in the 6th to 5th centuries BCE. After the destruction of the Second Temple in 70 CE, Jews were scattered throughout the Mediterranean and away from their physical center, the Temple in Jerusalem. Without a physical home in which a class of priests could manage Jews' relationship to the divine, the text became the primary route to holiness. Rabbis in the first five centuries after the expulsion crafted a new religion, now known as Rabbinic Judaism, that used the Torah and other holy texts as the basis for laws and customs that would govern Jews' lives wherever they lived. Temple sacrifice and elaborate priestly rituals gave way to prayer, synagogue services, and textual interpretation.

That early heyday of Torah interpretation was so central to the future of Judaism that the interpretations and commentaries of these early sages were themselves canonized as the Talmud, the foundational text of Rabbinic Judaism. Such rabbinic interpretation of the text was so important that it earned the name *Torah she'bal peh*, the Oral Torah, thus elevating these rabbinic debates to a status just below the original *Torah she'bikhtav*. Although this moment of Torah exegesis became canonized, it did not mean the end of Torah interpretation. In fact, interpreting the interpretations of the interpretations became the primary way Jews adapted their rituals and customs in different times and different places.

The system of textual interpretation that formed the basis of Rabbinic Judaism reigned supreme for a thousand years in Europe and in much of the world. But modernity, the Enlightenment, and the rise of reason did a funny thing to the text. The text that was *Torah she'bikhtav*, the word of God as given to Moses, was suddenly put under a new microscope, as potentially just another text. If the divinity of the Torah, with its parchment scrolls, voluptuous drapery, and silver adornments, all stored in a special closet called an *aron kodesh*, was suddenly under question (okay, not so suddenly . . . the rise of reason and secularization took a long time), then what role would the Torah have? Should it form the basis of a modern, rational Judaism? Should Jews continue living by laws, based on interpretations of interpretations of interpretations of this book, if the book itself was no longer regarded by all Jews as the direct word of God?

Modern Jews have been wrestling with these questions for a few hundred years. And despite the rise of Reason, of seeing this book as just a fine piece of literature (as many contemporary scholars consider the Torah), Jews still read this text ritualistically around the world every Saturday of every week of every year. The text still has power, and Jews, those who continue to live their lives according to the tenets of Jewish law—known as *halacha*—as well as those who do not, continue to interpret the text.

If rabbis were the only Jews authorized to produce commentary on the Torah through the period of Rabbinic Judaism, in the modern era, when the printing press, vernacularization, and mass education for people of all genders democratized access to the Torah, a much wider range of people have the power to interpret the text. Rabbis still have moral and legal authority in many communities, but in the past one hundred years, other groups of people have claimed the right to interpretation and commentary. Most notably, scholars—people who are trained in a rationalist approach to text and who do not interpret the text for the sake of generating new laws and customs but for the sake of knowledge and a better understanding of the text— have become some of the most important interpreters of the Torah. The scholarly study of the Bible in general, and the Torah in particular, goes back to the mid-nineteenth century, when Protestant theologians began seeing the book as one needing to be situated in a particular historical context—the ancient Near East. Jewish scholars, especially in Germany, applied modern history and textual analysis to put the book that held so much sway over Jewish life into its Jewish context.

Some scholars went as far as to identify Biblical "authorship," with the idea, commonly known as the Documentary Hypothesis, that different parts of the Torah were penned at different times by different groups of people and later assembled into a coherent whole by a Redactor, a single editor or group of editors. The J, or Jahwist, source was theoretically written around 950 BCE. The E, or Elohist, source was written around 850 BCE. The D, or Deuteronomist, source was written around the 7th century BCE. And the P, or Priestly, source written around the 6th century BCE. This idea is a far cry from *Torah she-bikhtav* as given directly by God to Moses at Mount Sinai.

But all this close scrutiny of the text presumes that the Torah, even if its divinity comes under assault, is still central, foundational in fact, as a text, myth, and history for Jews, Christians, and Muslims and for much of Western society. God's word or not, as a literary text it still holds sway. It holds so much sway that the oldest fragments of a Torah text, some of which are now called the Dead Sea Scrolls, draw millions of visitors whenever they are exhibited. Clearly, even in the age of Reason, this book is not just another book. It is ritualized, sanctified, and elevated, even for many of those who see themselves as secular.

There was a time, under the influence of modernity, when some Jews and Christians tried to dismiss the power of the Bible. They argued that if the Hebrew Bible is just another old book, it should hold no more power over the laws and customs of a secular society than any other canonical old book, such as the Epic of Gilgamesh or ancient Greek myths. It could be read, enjoyed, and performed, but frankly, these critics argued, given its role in the creation of rigid and sometimes archaic religious systems, modern society would be better off if the Bible were relegated to the past. The impulse to take the Bible off its physical and metaphoric pedestal often came from liberal and progressive activists, who saw religion as an impediment to social justice in the modern era. Read in this way, the Bible is a text narrating the story of a vengeful God, of violent wars and conquests, proclaiming arcane laws and customs that frankly have little to do with modern life.

The origins of this impulse to set the Bible aside began during the Enlightenment with thinkers such as Baruch Spinoza, who questioned revelation, and Voltaire, who saw all forms of religious ritual as superstition. Karl Marx and Friedrich Engels took the idea even further, with Marx calling religion the "opiate of the masses," for what he considered its ability to blind people to their suffering in this world with the hope of redemption in the next—thus dulling what he felt was their impulse toward revolution.

From the late 19th century onward, Jewish intellectuals across the ideological spectrum, including socialists, Zionists, anarchists, liberal democrats, and others, saw a clear correlation between a decline in the power of religion and an improvement in society. Religion, in this view, was oppressive of the working classes, women, minorities, gays and lesbians, and the poor and should be cast off as society becomes more just. This powerful link between social justice and secularism dominated the 20th century and still largely holds sway over American and European societies today and is also powerful in modern Israel.

But a countertrend attempted to link religion and social justice, especially in the legacies of Liberation Theology and of Christian leaders, such as the Reverend Dr. Martin Luther King, and Jewish ones, such as Rabbi Abraham Joshua Heschel. These leaders saw social justice and religion as intimately linked and the Bible as a text of liberation, not oppression. Through their and other religious leaders' examples, progressives, especially in the United States, began to see new ways of approaching the ancient texts.

As the foreword by Judith Plaskow so eloquently articulates, feminism sparked the most powerful form of this textual revolution. Beginning most visibly in the 1960s, although relying on a much older tradition of feminist activism in Judaism, women challenged their exclusion from the religion, from the text, and from positions of authority. Women rabbis began to be ordained in each of the major American Jewish denominations, except for Orthodox Judaism, which maintains the traditional restriction on women's access to the rabbinate. Putting feminism in service of revolutionizing religion in general, and Judaism in particular, has had profound effects. For the first time in history, the largest Jewish denomination in the United States, the Reform movement, has more women studying for the rabbinate than men; women now hold positions of senior authority in the Conservative movement, the Reconstructionist movement, and in many areas of the Jewish world.

Feminism's challenge to Judaism meant women's access not only to Judaism, text, and power but also to the *way* Judaism was interpreted. A feminist Judaism meant broadening the access points into Judaism. It meant giving education, and therefore power, to more people over their Judaisms. Feminist Judaism also contributed to the individualizing of Jewish practices and the notion that one can create new rituals to honor contemporary realities.

Torah Queeries, then, follows a history of textual interpretation that is more than two thousand years old. Reading Torah through a bent lens opens up new insights and allows the text to liberate rather than oppress. As might seem obvious to many readers, lesbians, gays, bisexuals, and for other reasons transgender and intersex people have seen the text as a tool of oppression for as long as the text has been foundational to Western society. In Christianity, the notorious passage in Leviticus, "Thou shalt not lie with a man as with a woman," at least as the Jewish Publication Society translates it, has led priests, pastors, ministers, and other religious leaders to exclude gays, lesbians, and bisexuals from their communities—dismissing them as "sinners," excommunicating them, or in the most extreme cases, killing them. In some Muslim societies, because of the way these and other holy texts are read, homosexuality is still punishable by death.

In the Jewish tradition, those same Biblical passages function as the basis for a system of religious law that absolutely forbids homosexual relations, at least in the Orthodox, or traditional, view. In most traditional Jewish communities, homosexuality is anathema and leads to social opprobrium, making Judaism very much like its Christian and Muslim counterparts. Despite the stringency with which the traditional Jewish law regards gay sex, Jewish leaders rarely escalate to the same level of public vitriol seen among some of the more conservative Christian denominations. The Reverend Fred Phelps may be an admittedly extreme case and not representative of most evangelical or "fundamentalist" Christians, but regardless, his extremely public and violent "God hates fags" rhetoric is hard to imagine coming from a rabbi. The classic sermonic denunciations of gays by Jerry Falwell or Pat Robertson have no real Jewish counterparts. The closest example is the antigay rants of insular ultra-Orthodox leaders in Israel. However, it is rare to hear even the most conservative Jewish voice calling for the death of Jewish gays and lesbians. Perhaps in a post-Holocaust Jewish world, calling for death for any Jew seems anathema, unless of course it comes to the politics of Israel.

This is not to trumpet Jewish triumphalism but is instead to suggest that Judaism has textual interpretive traditions built into it that make *Torah Queeries* not just possible but *central* to conversations in Judaism writ large. There have been other queer commentaries on the Bible, written within Christian contexts or from an officially interfaith perspective that included a handful of Jewish voices.[1]

But *Torah Queeries* pushes in two directions to make this project unique. The editors have sought out the voices of transgender writers as well as scholars of gender to suggest that queer readings are not just about making space for gay and lesbian Jews. Some readers may consider the inclusion of so many trans voices radical, but in fact, one of the things these essays show is how old the notion of a complicated gender system is. In addition, *Torah Queeries* includes the voices of some of the most central figures in contemporary American Judaism today, from the rector of one of Conservative Judaism's seminaries to the president and dean of the Reform Movement's seminary and the president of a national rabbinical association, highlighting, in some ways, just how central the topic of lesbian, gay, bisexual, and transgender (LGBT) inclusion has become, at least in the American Jewish world.

In the process of gathering the writers for this book, more than one colleague suggested that perhaps all the contributors should be LGBT rabbis, implying that the lived experience of a committed gay or trans Jew is the most fruitful lens with which to approach such a project. Instead, a significant percentage of the contributors to this volume identify as "straight allies," and several do not personally identify as Jews but work within the scholarly circles of Judaic studies or Biblical studies. As much as the editors may celebrate the diversity of this book's contributors, that very diversity highlights the ways in which the topics of LGBT inclusion, gender, and sexuality have become frames of reference for all people, regardless of their particular identity politics or subject position.

On the American religious scene, established Jewish communities are wrestling with the issue of sexuality and homosexuality in fairly radical ways. The two largest Jewish denominations, Reform and Conservative Judaism, now ordain gays and lesbians as rabbis and allow their rabbis to perform same-sex weddings; and even Modern Orthodox communities in the United States are starting discreetly to make space for gay and lesbian Orthodox Jews. The equivalent in Christianity would be if the Episcopalian, Methodist, and Presbyterian denominations began freely ordaining and sanctifying the unions of gays and lesbians. Unlike the Episcopal Church, for example, there has been no official schism in Conservative Judaism, whose American rabbinic seminaries just opened their doors to openly gay and lesbian Jews in 2006.

What all this means is that actual gay and lesbian Jews have had more access to Judaism and the ability to live Jewishly rich lives for a longer period of time than members of other religions. There have been openly queer rabbis for thirty years. For this fact alone, Jews have had pressing reason to reread the Bible to make space for gay, lesbian, and bisexual Jews. This has been a social-justice issue that followed on the heels of the feminist revolution in Judaism, and the work has been profound.

More recently, transgender Jews have been creating space for more diverse expressions of gender in Judaism, and this effort has forced a reexamination not only of the Bible but of the history of Judaism's relationship to gender. Judaism has historically had a very strict gender system, prescribing roles for men and women, sex segregating Jewish public life, and at times even sex segregating Jewish private life, as in the laws of *niddah* (laws of ritual purity focused on women and the family). But just as feminism called for a reexamination of the gender system in Judaism, more recently transgender Jews have called for a reexamination of the very notion of fixed gender. One of the things found by people interested in complicating notions of gender is that the rabbis of the Talmud, so often brushed off as those who created the strict gender system in the first place, had a more complicated understanding of gender than we moderns do.

Reading the Bible through a bent lens, then, puts the nearly fifty authors in this book in a very long line of illustrious readers and interpreters of the Bible. In fact, most of the contributors to *Torah Queeries* rely on the most authoritative rabbinic source to make their point about queering the text. Names such as the Rambam (Maimonides), Ibn Ezra, and Rashi get dropped in nearly every essay. By wrestling with ancient text to illuminate modern concerns, these authors are in fact engaging in something incredibly traditional. Each generation has had its particular lens through which to look at the text. The very fact of this book suggests that people interested in things queer nonetheless have a deep investment in text and tradition, and in the way they are used to shape contemporary society.

But reading the Torah queerly also means doing something not very traditional. This book brings together scholars who are well trained in reading the Bible, like the traditional rabbinic elite, with scholars who are trained to read the Bible in very different ways. For some of these scholarly voices, the goal is to excavate the meaning of the Bible in its ancient Near Eastern context, rather than as it has been understood since medieval or in modern times. Others take the same historical approach for the Talmudic period and ask, "What did the rabbis, in their world, mean by this text?" These questions lead to some surprising conclusions.

And this book includes the voices of social-change activists, who fifty years ago would have probably run screaming from a project that asked them to wrestle with the "Holy Book" that, for many activists, has been the source of pain and oppression, not liberation. These writers focus on issues of social justice, rethinking community, and understanding power, and they are using rereadings of the Torah to make new commentaries on contemporary social reality. *Torah Queeries* brings all these voices together in one volume.

Readers have different kinds of "bent lenses" through which they read the text, and they understand the word *queer* in different ways. Some are highly trained in a body of literature known as "queer theory" that challenges norms, upends hierarchies, and trains people to read against the grain. These kinds of readings break down boundaries and make everything more complicated than it might seem. Others do not have this literary background and instead bring training as Bible interpreters to the table and read the text looking for ways to honor the lives of gays and lesbians. For these readers, boundaries may be useful, but they should be broadened to include gays and lesbians, bisexuals, and transgender people. For others, the text is a rallying cry to social action, and for others, the story of the Israelites is one of the world's most ancient coming-out stories, considering how many Biblical characters conceal parts of their identities to survive in a sometimes hostile world and the forty years of wandering in the desert before reaching the Promised Land. Because of this diversity of lenses, the authors often do not agree on how to read a particular portion. The famous story of Jacob and Esau, for example, gets two quite different queer readings.

Reading the Bible through a bent lens means, of course, rereading the texts that have traditionally been used to exclude queer people, such as the passages in Leviticus about men lying with other men or the Sodom and Gomorrah story, from which comes the modern word *sodomy*. Based on the two-thousand-year history of Jewish textual interpretation, the authors provide radical rereadings of these central texts. The authors also wrestle with seemingly mundane sections of the Torah, such as the detailed recounting of the building of the *Mishkan,* the holy dwelling place of God. The flamboyance of the *Mishkan*'s decoration—gold, precious stones, velvet—is read on the background of queer culture's flamboyance to render queer fabulousness holy, rather than simply campy. Others have taken on the main characters of the Biblical narrative—from Abraham, Isaac, Jacob, Sarah, Rebecca, Leah, and Rachel to the "queerest character in the whole Torah," Joseph—to show how a queer reading illuminates the personalities of these well-known characters.

Like the Biblical characters being reread, the authors also come from different backgrounds, have diverse identities—men, women, and trans—and identify as straight, gay, queer, gender queer, lesbian, bi, and other; some write in first person, others in a very scholarly third person. Most are deeply learned in Jewish tradition and Jewish text, but what they all bring to the table are unique *ways of reading and interpreting* that allow the Torah to speak to modern concerns. Interpretation means looking back at texts written thousands of years ago and simultaneously looking forward to new ways of seeing.

The book is organized in the way that Jews traditionally read Torah. Each week, one portion, or *parasha,* is read publicly from the *bimah* (stage) in the synagogue. On certain weeks, two portions are read (in order to account for the complexity of the ancient Jewish lunar calendar), and on Jewish holidays different texts are brought to the table. The book provides the reader with a *drash,* or interpretive reading, of each and every portion and most major holiday readings.

This book is a labor of intellectual rigor, social justice, and personal passions. The contributors have donated their time and intellect to this project, and the editors are putting any proceeds raised from the book back into the Torah Queeries project, launched online in 2006 by Jewish Mosaic: The National Center for Sexual and Gender Diversity. The editors thank all the contributors for their wisdom and time and the staff at Jewish Mosaic, especially Katie Roy and Noach Dzmura, who have built Torah Queeries from an online Torah-interpretation initiative into an important book. The editors are appreciative of the support of Congregation Bet Haverim and of Laurie D. Price for her assistance. Thanks to Judith Plaskow and Alison Schofield, two Bible scholars who read and critiqued the manuscript, to Michael Lee, the editors' research assistant and project manager, who saw the book through its final stages and to Shane Fountain for his proofreading of the final manuscript. The editors are grateful to Moshe ben Chacon for helping imagine and popularize the original online project and also for translating many of the Web essays into Spanish. The editors are especially thankful to the Kayden Fund at the University of Colorado at Boulder for supporting the publication of the book and to Jennifer Hammer, editor at New York University Press, who had the vision to see the transformative nature of this project and agreed to publish it as the beautiful book you hold in your hands.

NOTE

1. Some volumes that include substantive commentary on the Hebrew Bible or feature one or more contributions from Jewish studies scholars include *The Queer Bible Commentary,* edited by Deryn Guest, Robert E. Goss, Mona West, and Thomas Bohache (London: SCM, 2006); *Queer Commentary and the Hebrew Bible,* edited by Ken Stone (Cleveland: Pilgrim, 2001); *Take Back the Word: A Queer Reading of the Bible,* edited by Robert E. Goss and Mona West (Cleveland: Pilgrim, 2000); and Thomas W. Jennings, Jr., *Jacob's Wound: Homoerotic Narrative in the Literature of Ancient Israel* (New York: Continuum, 2005).

PART I

BERESHIT

The Book of Genesis

ONE

Male and Female God Created Them
Parashat Bereshit (Genesis 1:1–6:8)

MARGARET MOERS WENIG

"And God created the human being *b'tzalmo* in . . . [God's own] image" (Genesis 1:27a).[1] Perhaps no Biblical verse has meant more to gay people than this one. It confirms what LGBT people know in their hearts to be true: We too have been created in God's image. We too deserve respect as God's own handiwork. Our sexual orientation is part of creation's original design. We are as much a reflection of God as any straight person may claim to be. We are entitled to as much dignity, as many rights, and as much happiness as any other child of God.

This verse has challenged readers of Torah to reconsider their views of homosexuality and the place of gay and lesbian people in civic and religious life.

But the challenges of this verse do not end there. For the assertion that God created human beings in the divine image comprises only half of the verse. The verse continues with an equally challenging second half: "male and female [God] created them" (Gen. 1:27b). This assertion is a challenge of a different kind, for its simple statement appears, at least on its surface, to fly in the face of what many know to be true: that gender and gender identity cannot be neatly divided into immutable categories of "male" and "female."

Our Sages understood this complication as early as the 2nd century. The questions they asked and the questions we now ask lead us to a deeper understanding of the second half of this crucial verse.[2]

Challenge Number 1: Not All Human Beings Were Created Wholly Male or Female

Among even those who do not take the words of Genesis literally, most people do place great stock in the notion that human beings are either male or female. On a birth certificate, a driver's license, or a passport our society insists on knowing: is a person male or female? When we name a baby, call someone to the Torah as a bar or bat mitzvah, or write a *ketubah* (a Jewish wedding contract), we presume to know whether the infant, adolescent, or adult before us is male or female. Yet some scientists estimate that 1.7 percent of infants are born intersexed, with their chromosomes, internal reproductive organs, or external genitalia not consistently male or female but some combination of the two.

True stories:

"Beautiful . . . ," the doctor says. They place the baby on the mother's stomach, clamp the cord and hand the father a pair of slim scissors to cut it. The next day the doctor comes in and sits down and speaks softly: "Your baby will be fine," he says. The parents brace themselves. . . . "Somehow your baby's genitals haven't finished developing so we don't know quite what sex it is. We're going to run a couple of tests and we'll know very soon. . . . It may be that some cosmetic surgery is required. But don't worry. . . . This will be okay. We can solve this in just a few days. The sooner the better. . . ." This scene occurs about 2,000 times a year in hospitals all over America.[3]

At her birth, in suburban New Jersey, in 1956, baby Chase presented a case of "ambiguous genitalia." Instead of a penis and testicles there was a somewhat vagina-like opening behind her urethra and a phallic structure of a size and shape that could be described as either an enlarged clitoris or a micro penis. After three days . . . , the doctors told Chase's parents that their child should be reared as a boy. She was christened Charlie. But a year and a half later her parents . . . consulted . . . other . . . experts. They reassigned her as a girl. . . . Her parents changed her name . . . to Cheryl and the doctors removed her clitoris. Chase was raised without knowledge of her true birth status. She experienced childhood punctuated with mysterious unexplained surgeries and regular genital and rectal exams. She grew up confused about her sex. By age 19 Chase had done some of her own medical sleuthing and understood that she had been subjected to a clitorectomy as a child. . . . It took three years for her to find a physician willing to disclose medical records . . . then . . . Chase read that doctors had labeled her a true "hermaphrodite" a term that refers to people whose gonads possess both ovarian and testicular tissue.[4]

Challenge Number 2: Not All Human Beings Identify with the Gender in Which They Appear to Have Been "Created"

Some people who are born with consistently male genes and anatomy or with consistently female genes and anatomy are convinced in their innermost hearts that they are not the gender they appear to be, and they choose to live as the opposite sex.

True stories:

Lilly will never forget her seventh birthday party. The entire family gathered around to watch her blow out the candles. "Make a wish," her mother urged her. . . . Lilly blurted out, "My wish is to grow a penis before my next birthday."[5]

Many of these kids fall asleep at night praying, hoping, dreaming about waking up in the morning the "right" sex.[6]

Andy remembers contemplating suicide on a regular basis. "I had so much anger all through my growing-up years because of a situation that was not of my choosing. . . . My existence, my maleness, was a nightmare a purgatorial madness."[7]

And some people who identify as male derive a profound sense of "peace," "integration," and pleasure from dressing as women. And yet they face ridicule and physical danger for doing so.

A true story:

"I openly cross-dressed at home from my teens on, and although my mother grudgingly tolerated it, she was adamant about not letting the neighbors find out."[8] Once he cut his hand and had to be rushed to the hospital before he could change out of the dress he usually wore around the house. His mother insisted that he enter and exit the car through the garage so that no neighbors would see him.[9] "My mere presence was an embarrassment to her and she didn't want to be seen with me although in the hospital she had no choice. On the way home as soon as we got to our street she insisted that I scoot down on the seat until she pulled the car into the garage. I became so nauseous with self-loathing that I collapsed on the kitchen floor in a fetal position and couldn't move. I remember sobbing over and over: 'I am a person, not a thing. I have value and worth.'"[10]

Challenge Number 3: What Should Parents or Society Do When a Person's Gender Does Not Fall Neatly into the Categories "Male" or "Female"?

"If a child is born with two X chromosomes, with oviducts, ovaries, and a uterus on the inside but with a penis and scrotum on the outside,"[11] should the parents raise this child as a boy or as a girl? Should a surgeon remove the child's penis, open the scrotum to form two labia, and fashion a vagina that will have to be deepened through repeated surgeries as the child matures?[12] Or should the ovaries be removed so that at puberty this child with a penis does not develop breasts and a female form? Or should the child be allowed to grow up without sex-assignment surgery and be allowed to choose to identify as male, as female, or as neither?

How about an adult who had been born with XY chromosomes, undescended testes, and a vagina who developed breasts in puberty? And what of the person who has both an ovary and a testis or who has gonads with both ovarian and testicular tissue? Should a U.S. court consider this person a man or a woman? If 1.7 percent of the population is intersex, how absurd is it that the granting of marriage licenses is limited to couples that can be defined as a male and a female!

And what of a male-to-female transsexual: will the company she works for permit her to use the women's bathroom? May she legally marry a man? What if she is pre-operative or has no intention of having sexual-reassignment surgery? Is this person a man or a woman? Who gets to decide: the person or the courts?

And what if the husband in a heterosexual marriage turns out to be genetically female or decides to live as a woman? If the couple wants to stay together, may their marriage remain a legal marriage in a state that does not yet permit same-sex couples to marry? If they are Jewish and decide to separate, will a *bet din* (a Jewish religious court) require a *get* (a Jewish divorce)?

Until a few years ago, an intersexed child born with XY chromosomes whose penis at birth was under one-and-a-half centimeters most likely would have been surgically assigned female, castrated, and raised as a girl. An intersexed child born with XY chromosomes whose penis was larger than one-and-a-half centimeters would have been raised as a boy.

What if an intersexed child is born to members of a Jewish congregation, and they ask their rabbi, "What can the Torah teach us about how to raise our child?" What would you want the rabbi to say? What would you say to a little boy in your congregation who insists on wearing girls' clothes to religious school? What would you say to your own son?

Challenge Number 4: Do Genesis 1.27b and Others Prohibit Cross-Dressing and Transitioning from Male to Female or from Female to Male?

Jewish tradition has long understood that gender is more complicated than simply "male and female" and that some people might want to cross-dress and that others may not identify with the gender assigned to them at birth.

Although it appears as though *Parashat Ki Tetse*, discussed later in this book, prohibits a woman from wearing *kli gever* (man's apparel) and a man from wearing *simlat isha* (women's clothing),[13] there is, in fact, extensive debate in rabbinic literature about the meaning of this prohibition.[14]

Parashat Emor prohibits offering as a sacrifice any animal with a blemish including bruised, crushed, broken, or cut testicles.[15] The words *lo takrivu l'Adonai* (Don't sacrifice [such an animal] to God) are followed by *u'vartzechem lo taasu* (And in your Land, do not do [this]). The rabbis extended the Biblical prohibition against animal castration to human castration, but the Babylonian Talmud asks whether this prohibits only direct castration or sterilization by medicinal potion as well.[16]

Although liberal *poskim* (rabbinic authorities offering decisions in Jewish legal matters) permit sex-reassignment surgery for the mental health of the adult requesting it, most orthodox *poskim* prohibit it *l'hatchilah* (before the fact).[17] However, *b'diavad* (after the fact), even orthodox *poskim* have to address the status of a post-op transsexual: Can an Orthodox male-to-female (M to F) be married as a woman?[18] Can an Orthodox M to F give an ex-wife a *get*. Is a *get* even necessary?[19] Are Orthodox men permitted to listen to an M to F sing, or would that violate the prohibition against hearing a woman's voice (*kol isha*)?[20]

The responsa reflect a surprisingly diverse range of answers.[21] Rabbi Eliezer Waldenberg (a *posek* in Israel who has written volumes of responsa especially on medical issues) has even suggested thanking God for a sex change.[22]

A Response to Some of the Challenges Posed by Genesis 1:27b: Our Sages Were Well Aware of Gender Diversity in Human Kind

Rabbinic tradition, which obsessively separated men and women and assigned distinct roles to each, was remarkably appreciative of the fact that some people do not fit neatly into one category or another. Chapter 4 of Mishnah Bikkurim[23] discusses the *androginos,* about whom it says,

> *Yesh bo drachim shaveh l'anashim.*
> *Yesh bo drachim shaveh l'nashim.*
> *Yesh bo drachim shaveh l'anashim ul'nashim.*
> *Yesh bo drachim shaveh lo l'anashim vlo l'nashim.*

> (There are [legal] ways he is [treated] like men.
> There are ways he is like women.
> There are ways in which he is like men and women.
> There are ways he is like neither men nor women.)

For Rabbi Yose, the *androginos* belongs in none of the above categories but is *bifney atzmo hu,* a human being "unto itself."

Our tradition knows not only of the *androginos* (a hermaphrodite with both male and female sexual organs) but also of the *tumtum* (with hidden or undeveloped genitals), the *aylonit* (a masculine or infertile woman), and the *saris* (a feminine or infertile man).[24] So prevalent are these terms in tannaitic and amoraic literature that in the *Encyclopedia Talmudit,* the list of citations of *aylonit* fills five and a half columns, citations of *androginos* fill eleven columns, and citations of *tumtum* fill sixty-six columns, or thirty-three pages.

Aggadic literature imagines the main male character of the Purim story, Mordechai, suckling Esther when no wet nurse could be found[25] and imagines God changing the gender of a child even "on the birthing stool."[26] It imagines that when God first created "them" male and female, the creation known as "Adam" was one creature both male and female.[27] To the *saris* "who holds fast to the covenant," Isaiah promises "a place in God's house and *yad vashem,* a monument and a name, better than sons or daughters, an everlasting name which shall not perish."[28] Can we imagine a place in the Jewish community, in our synagogues and seminaries, for the intersexed and the transgendered?[29]

The Mishnah anticipated in its discussion of the *androginos* what scientists now understand nearly two millennia later. There are not two but five sexes, argues Anne Fausto-Sterling, an embryologist at Brown University. "In addition to males and females [there are] . . . true hermaphrodites born with a testes [sic] and an ovary [and those] born with testes and some aspect of female genitalia and . . . [those] born with ovaries and some aspect of male genitalia. . . . While male and female stand on the extreme ends of a biological continuum, there are many other bodies . . . that . . .

mix together anatomical components conventionally attributed to both males and fe-males."[30] Some scientists now speculate that *the brain* is actually the dominant sex organ in the body.[31] Add nonbiological factors into the mix of gender-shaping influ-ences and you may find a chromosomal, hormonal, and genital male with a female gender identity.

Rereading Genesis 1:27b

"*Zachar u'nikevah bara otam.*" Read not "God[32] created every single human being as *either* male *or* female" but "God created some humans male, some female, some who appear male but know themselves to be female, others who appear female but know themselves to be male, and others still who bear a mix of male and female characteristics." "*Zachar u'nikeva*" is, I believe, a merism, a common Biblical figure of speech in which a whole is alluded to by some of its parts. When the Biblical text says, "There was evening, there was morning, the first day," it means, of course, that there was evening, there was dawn, there was morning, there was noon time, there was afternoon, there was dusk in the first day. "Evening and morning" are used to encompass *all* the times of day, *all* the qualities of light that would be found over the course of one day. So, too, in the case of Genesis 1.27b, the whole diverse panoply of genders and gender identities is encompassed by only two words, "male" and "fe-male." Read not, therefore, "God created every human being as either male or female" but rather "God created human kind *zachar u'nikevah* male and female *and every combination in between.*"[33]

NOTES

1. Genesis 1:27 is the first of two Biblical accounts of the creation of human beings. In the second (Genesis 2:4–24), man is created first and woman only later, from man's rib. As much as Genesis 1:27 became a cornerstone in the argument for the equality of all human beings, the creation of woman from man's rib served, in a different era, as a cornerstone in argu-ments for the subordination of women. Phyllis Trible refutes that line of interpretation once and for all: "Man has no part in making woman. He exercises no control over her existence. He is neither participant nor spectator nor consultant at her birth. Like man, woman owes her life solely to God. To claim that the rib means inferiority or subordination is to assign the man qualities over the women which are not in the narrative itself. Superiority, strength, aggressiveness, dominance, and power do not characterize man in Genesis 2. By contrast he is formed from dirt; his life hangs by a breath which he does not control." From "Depatriar-chalization in Biblical Interpretation," *Journal of the American Academy of Religion* 41, no. 1 (March 1973): 30–48, quoted in Plaut's Torah Commentary, p. 33.

2. The Jewish material in this article was first gathered for a symposium I organized, at the invitation of Dean Aaron Panken, at Hebrew Union College–Jewish Institute of Religion (HUC-JIR) in New York entitled "Gender Identity, the Intersexed and Transsexuals: An In-troduction to Religious, Legal and Policy Issues," held on February 12, 2002, and repeated at the Reconstructionist Rabbinical College on February 11, 2003. I received extensive help from

Rabbis Ayelet Cohen, Sharon Kleinbaum, Benay Lappe, Tracy Nathan, and Roderick Young and from Ian Chesir-Teran, Dana Friedman, Gwynn Kessler, and Beth Orens. I gathered the first- and third-person testimonies in preparation for an April 10, 2005, workshop at Congregation Beth Simchat Torah in New York entitled "God Created Them Male and Female and Every Combination in Between." Reuben Zellman, who organized that workshop with me, helped select and edit the testimonies.

3. Amy Bloom, *Normal: Transsexual CEOs, Crossdressing Cops, and Hermaphrodites with Attitude* (New York: Random House, 2002), 101–102.

4. John Colapinto, *As Nature Made Him: The Boy Who Was Raised as a Girl* (New York: HarperCollins, 2001), 216–217.

5. Mildred L. Brown and Chloe Ann Rounsley, *True Selves: Understanding Transsexualism for Families, Friends, Co-workers and Helping Professionals,* (New York: Jossey-Bass, 2003), 36.

6. Ibid., 35.

7. Ibid., 76.

8. Ibid., 63.

9. Ibid.

10. Ibid., 64.

11. Anne Fausto-Sterling, *Myths of Gender: Biological Theories about Women and Men,* rev. ed. (New York: Basic Books, 1992), 5.

12. "When an infant or toddler receives vaginal surgery parents are taught to insert a dildo so that the newly built vagina won't close." Anne Fausto-Sterling, *Sexing the Body: Gender Politics and the Construction of Sexuality* (New York: Basic Books, 2000), 86. "Enlargement of the vaginal cavity is also maintained by metal dilators inserted by the parents daily for six months beginning two weeks postoperatively. Monthly dilation of the seven or eight year old continues into adolescence to prevent narrowing or closure of the vaginal cavity" (Bloom, *Normal,* 106).

13. Deut. 22:4.

14. Does the verse prohibit women from bearing arms and from wearing *tallit* and *tefillin*? Does it prohibit men from shaving their underarms and pubic hair? Does it prohibit cross-dressing as a form of sexual play? Does it prohibit men from taking estrogen and women from taking testosterone? Fortunately, there are responsa that issue a resounding "No!" to these questions. See "A Message from Rabbi Tilsen: Cross Dressing and Deuteronomy 22:5," Congregation Beth El-Keser Israel, available online at www.uscj.org/ctvlly/newhavcb/cross-dress.html; Beth Orens, "What Transgressions Are Involved in Changing Sex from Male to Female?" (unpublished manuscript); and the extensive discussion of this prohibition by Rabbi Eliot Kukla and Reuben Zellman later in *Torah Queeries.*

15. Lev. 22:24.

16. *Shabbat* 110b.

17. See, for example, J. David Bleich, "Survey of Recent Halachic Periodical Literature: Transsexual Surgery," *Tradition: A Journal of Orthodox Jewish Thought* 14, no. 3 (Spring 1974); Fred Rosner and J. David Bleich, eds., *Jewish Bioethics* (New York: Sanhedrin, 1979); J. David Bleich, "Transsexual Surgery and Ambiguous Genitalia," in *Judaism and Healing: Halachic Perspectives* (New York: Sanhedrin, 1981); and Fred Rosner and Rav Moshe Tendler, "Sex Change in Adults," in *Practical Medical Halacha* (Hoboken, NJ: Ktav, 1990).

18. Some *poskim* say that a transsexual may not contract a marriage either as a man or as a woman. A 1978 responsum from the Central Conference of American Rabbis permits the marriage of a post-op transsexual (whose new status is recognized by the state) as long

as it does not constitute a homosexual marriage. A 1990 responsum acknowledges that some rabbis would officiate even if it were a same-sex wedding. "In addition, Reform would also accept the findings of modern science which holds that external genitalia may not reflect the true identity of the individual." "Conversion and Marriage after Transsexual Surgery," CCAR Responsa 5750.8, www.ccarnet.org.

19. Both Yosef Palachi and Eliezer Waldenberg in their responsa (Yosef Et Echav 3:5 and Tzitz Eliezer X25:26, respectively) say no *get* is necessary. Their opinions are cited by Michael Broyde in "The Establishment of Maternity and Paternity in Jewish and American Law, Appendix: Sex Change Operations and Their Effect on Marital Status," www.jlaw.com.

20. Orthodoxy prohibits men from listening to the voice of a woman singing.

21. See, for example, the *teshuvah* written by Rabbi Mayer Rabinowitz (Rabbinical Assembly Law Committee), October 15, 2002, in response to the questions, "Is Sex Reassignment Surgery permissible? What is the sexual status of a person who has undergone SRS? Can SRS redefine the basic status of male and female?"

22. That is, instead of reciting among the daily morning blessings "*she lo asani isha*" (who has not made me a woman) or "*she asani kirtzono*" (who has made me according to His will), an male-to-female transsexual should recite "*shehafchani kirtzono*" (who has changed me according to His will) or, if female to male, "*shehafchani l'ish*" (who has changed me into a man). *Tzitz Eliezer* 10, no. 25.

23. Tosefta Bikkurim, chapter 2.

24. Maimonides's *Mishneh Torah*, Hilchot Ishut, chapter 2, including "A person who possesses neither a male sexual organ nor a female sexual organ but instead his genital area is a solid mass is called a *tumtum*. There is also doubt with regard [to this person's status]. If an operation is carried out and a male [organ is revealed] he is definitely considered to be a male. If a female organ [is revealed] she is definitely considered to be a female."

25. *Bereshit Rabbah* 1:1, 30:8, Babylonian Talmud, *Shabbat* 53b.

26. Jerusalem Talmud, *Berachot* 14a.

27. *Bereshit Rabbah* 8.

28. Isaiah 56:4ff.

29. In 2006, HUC-JIR ordained Eliot Kukla, the first rabbi who was admitted as a woman and ordained as a man. Reuben Zellman, the first to apply to a seminary as openly transgender, was admitted to HUC-JIR in spring 2003.

30. Fausto-Sterling, *Myths of Gender*, 31. See also Anne Fausto-Sterling, "The Five Sexes, Revisited," *Sciences* (New York Academy of Sciences) (July 2000); and Claudia Dreifus, "A Conversation with Anne Fausto-Sterling: Exploring What Makes Us Male or Female," *New York Times*, January 2, 2001.

31. Colapinto, *As Nature Made Him*, 271.

32. Some people would substitute "nature" for "God."

33. Cheryl Chase, founder of the Intersex Society of North America, wants to end the idea that "it's monstrous to be different" (quoted in Colapinto, *As Nature Made Him*, 220). "It's not complicated. We don't say: Celebrate that your kid has severe hypospadias or CAH [Congenital Adrenal Hyperplasia, which may cause "ambiguous genitalia" in females and "virilization" of females in adolescence]. We say: No unnecessary surgery, no cosmetic surgery without consent. And more than that we say: No lying, no shame. We say help the parents and the patients and help them by telling the truth. No lying" (Cheryl Chase quoted in Bloom, *Normal*, 123).

TWO

From Delight to Destruction:
The Double-Faced Power of Sex
Parashat Noach (Genesis 6:9–11:32)

STEVEN GREENBERG

The book of Genesis offers two very distinct portrayals of sex. The first is glorious and creative, and the second is frightful and destructive. It is perhaps this double evaluation of sexuality—its ability to express profound love, union, and care and its simultaneous capacity for degradation of self and other—that marks the particular Jewish ethical stance on sex. Sex is fully wondrous in the first chapters of Genesis, but sadly, after its early spring awakening, its darker and more troubling sides appear.

Every step of the creation is followed by an affirmation of its goodness. When finally the human is created, in God's image, the work is finished, and "God saw what God had created and behold, it was very good" (Gen. 1:31). The project seems to be going very well until we discover in the second chapter of Genesis that something "not good" has appeared: "It is not good that the human is alone" (Gen. 2:18). Human loneliness is the first acknowledged flaw, the first fly in the ointment of creation. Exactly what brings the original earthling (literally the translation of "adam" from *adama,* earth) and God to this awareness is not clear. According to midrash, the original adam was an androgynous creature (*Gen. Rab.* 8:1), so perhaps the Godlike creature has no loneliness because it is already whole. Or perhaps the threat of death that appears in the verse immediately prior—the threat of punishment for eating of the tree of knowledge of good and evil—creates a sense of doom that God cannot share. Whatever the cause, the problem is recognized and solved by splitting the earthling into two separate gendered beings.

The discovery of otherness and its overcoming in union is rapturous: "This it is! Bone of my bone, flesh of my flesh" (Gen. 2:23). Sex has been discovered, and at the moment of sexual union, the newly minted couple, in joy and delight, are as close to the original whole adam creature, the perfect image of God, as they can become. This moment is the first depiction of sex—the means by which two souls searching for complementarity join in intense pleasure and union and are more like the whole, interrelated, creative, ecstatic, vitality of God than at any other moment of their lives.

Edenic bliss is, however, tragically short lived. From sexual intercourse as the epitome of connection, we are introduced first to the sexual disharmonies of the

post-Eden world and then, a few chapters later, to the full fruition of those disharmonies, to sexuality as a dissolver of boundaries and as a tool of brutal self-aggran-
dizement, power, and violence. These countertestimonies to the goodness of sexuality surround the flood story, appearing before the deluge and after it. Beyond the
seductions of the serpent, the mutual recriminations of the couple, and exile from
Eden, the luminous world of sexual desire and fulfillment begins to reveal itself as
dark and dangerous.

We are told that before the deluge all the earth had become ruined. "All flesh had
corrupted its way upon the earth" (Gen. 6:12). The way of flesh is immediately understood by the rabbis to mean copulation and its corruption as perversion. "Rabbi
Yochanan said: beasts copulated with animals, animals with beasts, and they all had
intercourse with human beings, and humans had intercourse with them" (BT *Sanhedrin* 108a). It appears that cross-species intercourse unleashes the waters above and
below. Rav Simlai adds that perverse fornication brings *andromousia*—a Greek word
literally meaning "forced seizure"—to the world, a destruction that does not discriminate between the guilty and the innocent.

This image of perversity on Earth—and the subsequent unleashing of the chaotic
waters—suggests that the creation is tentative and reversible. It is as if God has God's
finger in a dam, strenuously holding back the waters below and above by a creative
will that is dangerously undermined when creation does not do its part. This is the
much more fraught and vulnerable account of creation that the Biblical scholar Jon
Levinson discovers in the books of Psalms and Job. The world could indeed return
to its primordial chaos, to *tohu vabohu* (from Genesis 1:2, describing the inchoate
nature of existence prior to its adoption of form), if we do not support the order of
creation and forever guard its demarcated boundaries.

As Avivah Zornberg emphasizes, the sins that bring on the flood are a mix of the
twin dangers of sexuality: a chaotic, self-dissolving, indiscriminate sexuality that, like
idolatry, makes everything equally sacred and so ultimately profane and a rapacious
sexual egotism that exerts the self upon everything.[1]

Then the rain came. We are taught that during the months of deluge there was a
moratorium on reproduction. The survivors on the boat, with all life expiring around
them, were bid to refrain from sexual relations. How could they engage in the pleasures of constructive union when all around them life was painfully being dismantled, disassembled, and dissolved into chaos?

A full year later, Noah emerges from the ark to a new world and to a repetition of
the call to be fruitful, multiply, and fill the earth. The language takes us back to the
dawn of the creation itself. Perhaps the world will now be rebooted without the troubling bugs of the past: loneliness will be healed, and sex will sustain people in loving
union without the overreaching that dangerously threatened to dissolve the self, the
other, and finally all creation in its wake.

The new world dawned, crowned with a heavenly rainbow full of promise. The
earth emerges from the flood into a spring like none other, with the desolation slowly
giving way to the forces of life in the soil that could not be dissolved by the combined

force of the waters above and below. In this strange new land, Noah begins to husband the earth. He plants a vineyard, harvests grapes, and produces wine. Whether in celebration of the survival of his clan, in ecstatic collusion with the indestructible plant life, or perhaps in response to a horrific absence, the obliteration of a human community beyond his wife and children, he drinks his merlot and strips off his clothes. One might imagine Noah romping around in his tent, making loud animal noises like one of the wild beasts he cared for during his extended voyage on the rudderless ark. Or perhaps, in a very different image of posttraumatic crisis, Noah, the guilt-ridden survivor, huddles naked in a corner of his tent, sobbing. Whichever it is, in the midst of his drunken stupor, Noah's son Ham (who we are reminded is the father of Canaan) sees his father's nakedness and runs to tell his brothers of their father's condition.

> Now when the two older brothers heard this they took a cloth, placed against both their backs and, walking backward, they covered their father's nakedness; their faces were turned the other way, so that they did not see their father's nakedness. When Noah awoke from his wine and learned what his youngest son had done to him, he said, "Cursed be Canaan the lowest of slaves shall he be to his brothers." (Gen. 9:20–25)

From these verses, we only know that Ham saw Noah drunk and naked and that his brothers, learning of the situation, enter backward into the tent and cover their father's nakedness. Ham's crime is so vague that commentators have no choice but to interpolate. According to Nachmanides, the medieval Spanish commentator, the story is about honor and shame between fathers and sons. Ham's accidental glimpse into his father's tent is not the crime. Ham's crime is his taking pleasure at the sight of his father's breakdown, his humiliating collapse into drunken disgrace. He runs to bring his older brothers to the tent so they, too, can gawk at the pathetic old man. Perhaps Shem and Yafet better understand the pressures; perhaps, being older, they remember the world lost to their father; perhaps they understand the guilt he shoulders. In any case, they do not gawk but cover their father without further shaming him.

However, understanding this primal moment of seeing the father truly naked does not help to explain what comes next. Why does Noah become enraged at what his youngest son "did" to him? It does not appear superficially that anything was done to Noah by Ham. Moreover, why is Canaan, Ham's son, the one mentioned for punishment and not Ham himself? And lastly, why is the punishment a curse of enslavement? Here is how the rabbis of antiquity read this text:

> "And Ham saw": Rav and Shmuel (disagreed). One said he castrated him and the other said he raped him. The one who claims that he castrated him explains in this way; that Ham thus prevented Noah from having a fourth son, which is why Ham's fourth son, Canaan, is cursed. The other claims he raped him by a comparison of expressions. Here it is written, "And Ham, the father of Canaan saw the nakedness of his father" and there

(Genesis 34:2) "And Shechem, son of Hamor the Hivite, chief of the country, saw her (Dina) and took her and lay with her by force." (BT *Sanhedrin* 70a)

The mix of careful reading and imagination here produces a rather shocking result. Rashi (Rabbi Shlomo Yitzchaki), the medieval Jewish commentator par excellence, quotes these two horrifying suggestions of rape and castration in his interpretation. Students of Rashi know that he does not employ this sort of legendary material into his commentary unless he finds that it solves problems intrinsic to the understanding of the text. Rashi cannot accept that Ham simply happened to see his father drunk and naked, found the sight amusing, and told his brothers. Something central to the language of the narrative prevents Rashi from taking the text at face value.

When Noah awakens and describes Ham's rather passive "seeing" of his nakedness as what his young son "did" to him, we are led to feel that something happened in the tent that has been covered up. It is for this reason that Rashi finds the earlier rabbinic reading helpful. This "seeing" was more than meets the eye. It was the kind of seeing that is about violence and possession, about control and domination.

"Seeing nakedness" comes up again later in Genesis. As the viceroy of Egypt, Joseph accuses his brothers, who do not recognize him yet, of espionage, the kind of seeing that reveals the enemy's weaknesses, the sort of piercing stare that precedes attack. "And Joseph remembered the dreams he dreamt and said to them, 'You are spies! You have come to see the nakedness of the land!'" (Gen. 42:9). To see nakedness is to prepare to appropriate, to take by force, to enforce one's power.

Ham sees his father in a position of weakness, and this seeing becomes an opportunity to seize control, unmanning his father one way or another. Castration is one way to deprive a man of all male privilege and power. Male-male rape is another way to show brutally and graphically who is in charge. In the ancient world it was what conquering generals did to their defeated foes. Penetrative anal intercourse in highly patriarchal societies symbolically empowers the penetrator and humiliates the penetrated. It turns women into wives and men into objects of scorn.

This reading of the midrash also solves one of the puzzles that has confounded the Biblical commentators. Why is Canaan punished for Ham's crime, and why with servitude? Ham wished to seize the power of the father for himself. In replacing the father, he would be lord over his brothers. The horrific Oedipal crime brings in its wake the opposite. His children would serve the children of his brothers.

Sex is indeed a double-edged sword. It can be a resource for two to become one flesh in loving union, an image of God. Through it, we treat one another as profoundly unique, beloved, honored, and celebrated. It can also be a way to dissolve all boundaries in chaotic faceless pleasure, and so to lose all sense of self and other. And at its worst, in the form of rape, it can become a horrific tool of domination and degradation, control, possession, humiliation, and violence.

The parasha then is not about male-male sex per se. There is no punishment for queer sex here. Instead, the crime and punishment is about the different aims and contexts of sexual relationships, not about sexual objects. Polymorphous sex that obliterates all boundaries and violent sex that exerts the self upon everything else. . . .

these are the dark sides of sexuality. Sex that preserves the self and the other and joins them together in joy, mutual care, and loving union is sex that, in the words of Genesis, is very good.

NOTE

1. Avivah Gottlieb Zornberg, *The Beginning of Desire: Reflections on Genesis* (New York: Three Leaves/Doubleday, 1995), 51–55.

THREE

Going to and Becoming Ourselves
Transformation and Covenants in *Parashat Lech Lecha* (Genesis 12:1–17:27)

CARYN AVIV *and* KAREN ERLICHMAN

Throughout *Parashat Lech Lecha,* people's bodies, names, and relationships change profoundly to signal transformation and covenantal belonging. Even the name of the parasha, "Go to Yourself," implies change and risk, a simultaneous movement from one figurative place to another, as well as a metaphorical homecoming. These significant themes emerge several times throughout the multilayered text, offering a potentially resonant narrative for queer people to understand afresh the transformations in their own histories, identities, and covenantal relationships.

The text begins with the patriarch Abram's journey from the land of his birth into Egypt, where he risks everything to travel to an unfamiliar place. Abram's wife, Sarai, also puts herself at risk—to pass as Abram's sister—as a way to prevent potential violence against them during their sojourns in a new place. In the process, Sarai is "outed" as Abram's wife, and they are cast out of Egypt, prompting another journey back to Canaan. How many lesbian, gay, bisexual, and transgender (LGBT) people have left their homes for uncertain journeys, to set off in search of new selves and communities? How many have broken with their past or have experienced painful brokenness with their families of origin? When reading "Go to Yourself," queer people remember so many of their own "ancestors"—people such as Del Martin and Phyllis Lyon, Audre Lorde, James Baldwin, and Harry Hay. Like Abram and Sarai, these pioneers left behind aspects of their past and their homes and forged new, often uncertain, paths. They took enormous risk in order to fully "go to themselves" and create new ways of being at home in the world. As queer writer Paul Monette said, "Home is the place you get to, not the place you came from."[1]

Covenant in *Lech Lecha* is marked not just by physical and spiritual journeys but also by physical changes to the body. After the couple returns to Canaan, the barren Sarai creatively, if problematically, solves her infertility challenges by asking her servant, Hagar, to act as a surrogate. Only after much anguish, jealousy, and triangulated hardship with Hagar and Abram is Sarai able to have a child and create another generation.

The most obvious transformation in "Go to Yourself" comes at the end, with the Divine outlining the ritual of circumcision, a physical marking that literally inscribes a sign of the covenant on the bodies of Abram and his male descendants. And the most public covenant marked by a transformation takes place when the Divine changes people's names: Abram to Abraham and Sarai to Sarah. In these acts of renaming, the Divine culturally and linguistically calls out, creating a new covenantal relationship with two people now figuratively reborn into their new names and identities. The addition of an *h* (*hey* in Hebrew) to both Abram's and Sarai's names symbolizes an abbreviated version of the Divine name (the tetragrammaton, *Yud-Hey-Vov-Hey*) and binds them in sacred connection to God and to each other every time their names are uttered or recorded. Even the Divine changes names, transitioning from Adonai to El Shaddai (Gen. 17:1). Hebrew is a grammatically gendered language, and Jews often characterize and interpret *Adonai,* which registers with the word "Lord," as masculine. However, if we read this text through a queer and gendered lens, in the changing of names from Adonai to El Shaddai, the Divine is turned upside down and renamed as "the Sacred Breast" (the word *shad* means "breast"). Name changes, then, mark *both* parties of the covenant.

Changing names to mark spiritual and physical transformation is thus a deeply Jewish value and is also common among queers, especially transpeople. Transpeople often mark their own journeys by changing names, and like God changing her name to reflect the new covenant with Abraham and Sarah, people in covenantal relationships with transpeople often also change names. When a child transitions, "daughters" become "sons," and a new covenantal relationship takes place. It is not just queers but also converts to Judaism, immigrants, and others who take on new names to reflect profound, new relationships.

Within the context of queer and feminist discourse, these *ritual, linguistic, and embodied* (particularly with regard to reproduction and circumcision) manifestations of covenant hold many layers and meanings. Covenants imply power, a sign of one's loyalty to the Divine, to other individuals, and to specific tribes or peoples. They are also signifiers of commitment and are guidelines for our behavior, bodies, and relationships. We embark on a range of journeys to "go to" and find ourselves as queers and as Jews. But how might we find useful wisdom in this text to think about our own covenantal relationships, families, and communities? Can a ritual involving "marking" (symbolic or real) be a signifier of queer Jewish inclusion or exclusion? How do gender and power inform covenant, identity, changes in the physical body, and spiritual and emotional transformations?

The covenants in *Lech Lecha* (and throughout the Torah) are relationships between the Divine and the Israelites and among ordinary people themselves. Mutuality is inextricably embedded in a covenant, even when the balance of power between the contractors is not equal, as when the Presence instructs, directs, or outlines the covenantal promise and changes the names and bodies of those covenanting.

In our own lives, we might think of covenantal relationships as those that involve a sense of the sacred, a mutually agreed upon contract, which is often imbued with solemnity and endurance and always entails ongoing negotiation, change, and evolution. As in Torah, covenants today still imply power, loyalty, commitment, some explicit boundaries of what is acceptable and unacceptable to do, and allegiances to specific people or tribes or families. But unlike the covenantal relationships outlined in *Lech Lecha*, we like to think that the ideals of contemporary feminist and queer covenants are often characterized by true egalitarianism, partnership, and empathy, rather than by inherently unequal power dynamics underneath a veneer of mutuality. In an ideal world, we like to think of our society's most solemn covenant, marriage, as a bringing together of equals.[2]

For queer Jews, social change and ritual or spiritual practices are not mutually exclusive; nor do they exist in a political vacuum. So too was Abram and Sarai's covenant with God, which both changed society by launching monotheism and began a historical narrative that climaxed at Sinai and fostered new forms of spiritual and ritual practice. Although there are many Jewish political activists who consider themselves secular Jews, and religious Jews who may not be political activists, certainly *Lech Lecha* teaches that the spirit and social action are inextricably linked.

In this vein, Jewish feminists and queer people have begun to reinvent Jewish rituals to acknowledge new ways of creating covenantal relationships charged with political and social meaning. Most of these innovations involve the celebration of intimate relationships and family, as well as new language, liturgy, and ritual to "mark" what is sacred and meaningful in our lives, to create covenants with one another and with our families and communities. Many queer family constellations reflect models of chosen family that extend far beyond the traditional template; these models more closely resemble the rich and diverse family structures of our Biblical ancestors than they do any mainstream traditional nuclear family in contemporary Western societies.

Not surprisingly, queer rabbis, academics, and activists have offered new rituals that echo and draw on the covenantal elements outlined in *Lech Lecha*, particularly regarding the boundaries and obligations that characterize sacred relationships (between human beings and between humans and the Divine). These new rituals affirm the lives of women, queers, and others and sanctify the covenants of those who have too often been excluded or ignored in more traditional Jewish settings and theologies. In this vein, queer and allied writers have created blessings and rituals that sanctify coming out, queer weddings, insemination at a doctor's office, divorce texts for same-sex couples, and a prayer for transgender people who are transitioning into new selves and bodies.

For example, scholar Rachel Adler has created a non-gender-specific *Brit Ahuvim* (Lovers' Covenant), deeply grounded in Jewish textual traditions. She writes,

> The agreement into which [the partners] are entering is a holy covenant like the ancient covenants of our people, made in faithfulness and peace to stand forever. It is a covenant of protection and hope. . . . It is a covenant of distinction, like the covenant God made with Israel. . . . It is a covenant of devotion, joining hearts like the covenant David and Jonathan made. . . . It is a covenant of mutual lovingkindness like the wedding covenant between God and Zion.[3]

Adler's *Brit Ahuvim* is likely to resonate with queer Jews for a variety of reasons. First, it provides a radical alternative to the *ketubah* (marriage contract), a document whose roots and intentions, although granting women some legal protections in the case of divorce or death, were clearly patriarchal. Second, Adler reclaims the concept of covenant and imbues it with explicitly feminist underpinnings of egalitarian partnership and mutuality. The *Brit Ahuvim* reflects a growing body of contemporary Jewish ritual and liturgy with enormous relevance for queer Jews.

Another radically creative and moving new ritual is a trans/genderqueer Jewish wedding by Rabbi Elliot Kukla, the first ordained transgender rabbi in the Reform Movement. Rabbi Kukla has written a ceremony that incorporates flexibility and choice into the Hebrew blessings to maximize the recognition of each individual's gender identity before the entire *kahal* (community) that has assembled to witness a couple's covenant to each other. In explaining the rationale for his choice of different Hebrew and English options, Kukla writes, "It is possible to indicate gender subtly within the liturgical flow of the service. This is a spiritually significant moment for these lovers and they deserve to be seen and recognized as fully as possible."[4]

In *Lech Lecha*, when the Source instructs Abram to mark all the (male) members of the tribe through the covenant of circumcision, the ritual serves as an important transition to "set oneself apart" from others, to create transformation through exclusionary boundaries of belonging. In our world, Adler's "provisions of the covenant" highlight how covenants set couples apart for one another in sacred ways that enhance mutual reciprocity, companionship, an ethic of care, and a "commitment of a life of kindness and righteousness." But in contrast to this idea of setting apart, the new rituals available to feminist and queer people mark journeys through inclusion and envision wider and more welcoming circles of transformation. Likewise, Kukla's flexible Hebrew blessing formulations allow space for queer Jews to "read themselves" into traditional Jewish covenantal texts that honor the complexities of gender and sexual orientation. When queers read *Lech Lecha* or want to craft meaningful ways to celebrate and signify transformative changes and their deepest commitments and covenants, they no longer need to feel excluded or alienated either from traditional texts or from Jewish ritual. There are fruitful opportunities to find meaning and insight in both.

The characters in *Lech Lecha* embarked on risky journeys to cultivate their covenantal relationships and families. In this parasha, as in our own lives, people change, they take risks with enormous leaps of faith, and they exercise power, even if unskillfully sometimes. And unfortunately, we, just like the characters in *Lech Lecha*, also demonstrate the capacity for cruelty and the ability to inflict suffering on those closest to us. But like the extraordinary and larger-than-life characters in *Lech Lecha*, we also possess the capacity for empathy and hope, to create individual lives, intimate relationships, extended families, and queer communities that are covenanted, meaningful, and sacred.

In *Lech Lecha*, many things considered impossible happen when the Divine intervenes and promises a covenantal relationship. For queer and feminist Jews, participating in Jewish communal life through publicly celebrated covenantal rituals was once thought of as impossible. We know that this is no longer the case, not because of a Divine promise of covenant but because of years of hard work creating meaning,

ritual, and places for LGBT people in the community. We envision a day when feminist Jews in the Orthodox world, transgender Jews across all denominations, and the
relationships between queer folks everywhere will be recognized and embraced fully,
in Jewish communities and in civil society. As queer Jews, we love the translation
of *Lech Lecha* as "Go to Yourself," because our journey leads us to and reflects our
authentic expression of our fullest selves. Simultaneously, and equally important, "going to ourselves" reaffirms our place in Jewish history and continuity, just as Abram
and Sarai did when they embraced their covenant with the Divine. With a covenant
that embraces all aspects of our identities, we celebrate, witness, and "go forth" toward ourselves from this contemporary moment of Jewish cultural and political
transformation.

NOTES

1. Paul Monette, *Halfway Home* (New York: Crown, 1991), 262.

2. We wrote this essay soon after the state of California legally recognized marriages for
same-sex couples in 2008, and shortly after the death of lesbian activist Del Martin, who was
one of the first queer people to marry her partner, Phyllis Lyon, after fifty-five years of commitment. Consequently, the political significance of certain covenants seems particularly relevant to us at this historical moment.

3. Rachel Adler, "B'rit Avuhim—Lovers' Covenant," ritualwell.org, http://www.ritu-
alwell.org/lifecycles/intimacypartnering/Jewishweddingscommitmentceremonies/site-
folder.2005-06-07.7123390896/copy_of_16loverscovenant.xml.

4. Elliot Kukla, "Trans/Gender Queer Jewish Wedding Service, ritualwell.org, http://
www.ritualwell.org/lifecycles/intimacypartnering/Jewishweddingscommitmentceremonies/
sitefolder.2005-06-07.7123390896/primaryobject.2008-02-11.6051078310.

FOUR

Looking Back to Look Forward
Parashat Vayera (Genesis 18:1–22:24)

GWYNN KESSLER

The first word of Genesis 18:1, *vayera*, which connotes both seeing and appearing, alerts the reader to the importance of vision throughout Genesis 18–22. Indeed, *Parashat Vayera* as a whole presents a virtual feast for the eyes. Casting our gaze across the whole picture, we are first brought into the circle, or at least right outside the tent, of Abraham and Sarah. We then peer far beyond this location to the blinding plains of Sodom. And finally, toward the end of the parasha, we are perched on a mountaintop, called *YHWH Yireh* (God sees) in the land of *Moriah* (Seeing).

Although vision provides a powerful leitmotif running through the parasha, many people have continued to see the story about God's destruction of Sodom as recounted in Genesis 19 in near utter isolation—especially when dealing with what the Bible says about "homosexuality." Instead of treating Genesis 19 as if it stands alone, here I contextualize the story of Sodom as part of its larger literary unit. The Torah invites precisely such a contextualization since the first explicit mention of God's plan to destroy Sodom (and Gomorrah) appears in Genesis 18:20,[1] soon after God appears to Abraham by the oaks of Mamre (18:1) and promises the birth of Isaac to Abraham and Sarah (18:10–15); Jewish tradition, insofar as both chapters (and the three that follow) are read together in the annual synagogue lectionary, also encourages us to set these chapters in dialogue.

In what follows, I interpret *Parashat Vayera* through one of its own leitmotifs: vision. However, instead of following a heteronormative, homophobic, fixed gaze that places primary import on a purported condemnation of "homosexuality" in the story of Sodom—thus placing queer readers in the role of passive and silenced sacrificial victims—I read *Parashat Vayera* with a "queer eye," which is never fixed, at least for too long, on, and from, one place. I open up various readings, using different characters and points of view, in an attempt to forefront the multiplicity of available interpretations of almost any given text. For queer theory, a central point is not to find one static, inherent meaning in a text but to view a text from multiple angles—to borrow a well-known rabbinic dictum, "to turn it and turn it"—until, at least for the moment, one glimpses as much as can be seen, differently. This type of reading acknowledges that interpretation is an active, as well as an open, process, which invites LGBTQ readers to offer alternative readings that alter the standard of vision, the frame of reference of visibility, and to further illuminate what can be seen and known from this parasha.[2] In such readings, where *queer* functions as an active verb rather than a more or less fixed noun, queer interpretation describes a process, a fluid movement between reader, text, and world, "that reinscribes (or queers) each and the relations between them."[3] Instead of asking what "the Bible says about homosexuality," queer readings turn the tables and ask what can LGBTQ people and their allies say—and teach—about the Bible.[4]

In order to reflect more broadly on the process of (queer) interpretation, I begin by using one queer, and feminist, strategy, that of highlighting a character positioned on the margins, "low and outside" any given narrative frame.[5] My starting point is the unnamed character of Lot's wife, who toward the end of the Sodom story "looks back" at where she is from and what she is leaving behind: "And his wife looked back from behind him and she became a pillar of salt" (Gen. 19:26). Other writers have filled in the story of Lot's wife's looking back by drawing from and building on midrashic sources;[6] here, my purpose is to use this *peripheral* character's act of looking back to explore a *central* Jewish preoccupation, Biblical interpretation—the very process of looking back at texts.

Obviously, for a tradition and a people that reconceive their texts and themselves in large part through repeated acts of looking back, as Judaism and Jews do, Lot's wife, who pays dearly for her perhaps uncontrollable, albeit certainly understandable act, represents an anomaly. We can, of course, delineate the differences between an apparently compulsive act of willed disobedience (Lot and presumably his family were all enjoined, "Escape for your life; look not behind you, nor stay in the plain; escape to the mountain, lest you be consumed")[7] and a Jewish compulsion to "turn it [the Torah] and turn it because everything is in it" (*Pirke Avot.* 5:22), which I take to mean interpret the Torah, over and over again, because "It is not in heaven" (Deut. 32:12)[8] but ours to interpret as we see fit—repeatedly. We can point out that looking at a smoldering site of destruction and looking into the Torah, with which, according to midrashic tradition, God creates the world (*Gen. Rab.* 1:1), are categorically different.

Despite these not insignificant differences, I am struck by Lot's wife's act of looking back, which still calls to my mind the value, the centrality, of such an act in and for Judaism and for Jews. Perhaps the lesson in Lot's wife's death is that it reminds us of the risks, the dangers, involved in looking back. *Lives are at stake.* Perhaps what might be considered problematic in Lot's wife's looking back is neither the act of looking back itself nor that she does so ostensibly against divine command but the inability to see things differently. We need to see with better eyes. If we do not constantly come up with new interpretations, which require continual looking back *and* seeing anew, the text, and its readers, stand in danger of becoming pillars of salt, calcified remnants, memorials—whether enduring or fleeting—to a past long since gone. My point is not to attribute blame to Lot's wife or to minimize the only act with which the Bible enlivens her; to the contrary, I want to use her act of looking back, despite its fateful consequences, as a call for contemporary readers both to look back again and again and to be able to see things differently so that we might move forward.

Seeing things differently, in the context of *this* queer interpretation of *Parashat Vayera*, entails refusing to allow the Sodom story line to take center stage, eclipsing all else. However important, and correct, it is to point out that elsewhere in the Hebrew Bible and in rabbinic tradition, the sin of Sodom lay not in "homosexuality" but far more primarily in an utter lack of hospitality, this corrective reading still, more often than not, takes the story of Sodom out of its immediate textual context, seeing and setting it apart from most of the rest of *Parashat Vayera*. When I look back at *Parashat Vayera*, I can neither turn a blind eye to the negative costs that the Sodom narrative has exacted on LGBTQ people over the centuries nor remain so blinded by that one segment that I am left unable to see anything else of relevance, of deep significance in this parasha and subsequent rabbinic interpretations for further queer readings. Instead of "detoxifying Sodom" by contextualizing this story amid pertinent verses *elsewhere* in the Bible—for example, Ezekiel 16:49, "Behold, this was the iniquity of your sister Sodom: pride, surfeit of bread, and abundance of idleness was in her and in her daughters; and she did not strengthen the hand of the poor and needy"—the strategy pursued here is to keep the story of Sodom more in its immediate textual context and ultimately, in so doing, "to put it in its place."

The literary context of the story of the destruction of Sodom is the far larger, and for Judaism the much more formative and foundational, story about the relationship between God and Abraham. In fact, the story of Sodom is framed by Abraham and God. At its beginning we read, "And the Lord said, Shall I hide from Abraham that thing which I do?" (Gen. 18:17), and it ends not with Lot's wife looking back but with Abraham: "And Abraham went early in the morning to the place where he stood before the Lord; And he looked toward Sodom and Gomorrah, and toward all the land of the plain, and beheld, and, lo, the smoke of the country went up as the smoke of a furnace. And it came to pass, when God destroyed the cities of the plain, that God remembered Abraham" (Gen. 19:27–29). It is time to avert a singular focus on what in the end amounts to only one of its awesome God sightings, only one of the places where God makes God's presence known to humanity—in the brimstone and fire—and to shift our gaze onto other aspects of this parasha. We too need, as God did, to remember Abraham, and we need to lift up our eyes and see other manifestations of the divine in *Parashat Vayera*.

If, as mentioned earlier, one queer reading strategy takes a point of entry into a text from a marginal character's perspective, another strategy views the central figures of a text differently, or queerly. Shifting from the periphery to the center, in the remainder of this chapter I look again at the characters, and actions, of God and Abraham.

"God appeared to him [Abraham] by the terebinths of Mamre" (Gen. 18:1). In comparison to the other ways God makes Godself known throughout this parasha, for example, in brimstone and fire, as the force that opens a woman's eyes so that she can see water and life instead of the death of her child (Gen. 21:19), and perhaps most frighteningly of all, in a voice calling for the sacrifice of one's child (Gen. 22:1), the first verse of *Parashat Vayera* seems exceedingly understated. Certainly it lacks the luster of other divine manifestations in the Torah; this is no burning bush (Ex. 3:2), no pillar of cloud or fire (Ex. 13:20–21), and no smoking mountain (Ex. 20:15). Added to that, this apparition is silent and fleeting. Even before one can grasp it, we, like Abraham, have missed it. The Torah does not record what transpired when God appeared to Abraham; the text abruptly shifts: "He lifted up his eyes and saw: here, three men standing over against him" (Gen. 18:2).[9] I find it odd that a parasha that takes its name from the act of seeing forefronts a profound lack of vision in its very first two verses. A simple reading of these verses leads one to picture Abraham as unable to see God; God appears, and Abraham sees three men.[10] His lifting up his eyes to the three men suggests that here, in this parasha's opening, he has averted his eyes from the divine.

But if Abraham here seems to lack a certain kind of vision, Jewish tradition has shot him through with an abundance of foresight—even in his youth. Most readers already have a vision of Abraham before coming to Genesis 18, midway through the Torah's narrative about him. We know that in answer to God's earlier call, Abraham leaves his homeland and his father's house (Gen. 12:1). The rabbinic midrash about Abraham smashing the idols in his father's idol shop has struck such a deep chord within Jewish imagination and resonated so much with collective Jewish self-fashioning that I have watched countless students, be they in a 6th-grade Hebrew-school class, seekers in synagogue adult-education courses, or university students, search in vain to find it in their Bibles. But that tradition is found in *Genesis Rabbah,* a 5th-century midrashic compilation:

> Terah [Abraham's father] was an idol maker. Once upon a time he went somewhere and left Abraham selling idols in his stead. A man came to buy one and Abraham said: "How old are you?" He answered, "Fifty-something." Abraham retorted, "Woe to a fifty-year-old who would bow to a one-day-old!" The man left ashamed. One time a woman came carrying a platter of flour. She asked Abraham, "Can you offer this before them?" Abraham got up and took a club in his hand and smashed the idols. Then he put the club in the hand of the largest remaining idol. When his father came home he asked, "Who did this?" Abraham said, "Why hide it from you? A woman came carrying a platter of flour and asked me to offer it to them. One said, 'I'll eat first.' Another said, 'I'll eat first.' Then this big fellow picked up the club and smashed them!" Terah said, "Are you kidding me? Do these have intelligence!?" Abraham countered, "Cannot your ears hear what your mouth says?"[11]

This midrashic tale offers a biographical sketch of a youthful Abraham, which is utterly lacking in the Biblical story itself. It paints a portrait of a passionate, even zealous, Abraham, who appears to be able to see nothing but God and wants to make sure everyone else sees things the same way. Young Abraham is, in essence, and in a very literal sense of the word, an *iconoclast*—one who smashes idols—and this image of Abraham has captured our imaginations.

Far less known is another rabbinic tradition that imagines Abraham, along with Sarah—into their nineties—as *genderqueer*. A tradition in the *Babylonian Talmud* (*Yevamot* 64a–b) states, "R. Ammi said, 'Abraham and Sarah were *tumtumin* [of indeterminate sex/gender],' as scripture states, 'Look to the rock from where you have been cut and to the whole from where you have been dug' (Isaiah 51:1) and after it is written, 'Look to Abraham your father, and Sarah who bore you' (51:2)." When I look back, when I remember, Abraham, I cannot help but superimpose this less-known tradition onto the far more pervasive one. I imagine Abraham as a genderqueer kid in his father's little shop of horrors, smashing the idols, the false ideals, of heterosexism and gender normativity with as much fervor as he smashed the wood and stone images of false gods.

I cannot help but hope for coming generations to search their Bibles—to turn them and turn them inside out—looking back for where it says that Abraham and Sarah were genderqueer, this teaching having become so well known. And I look forward to the day when we embrace these ancestors not as models of blind faith but as iconoclasts—breaking the old paradigms and ushering in a whole new way of seeing. Perhaps then, when we look back at *Parashat Vayera,* we will be able to see, with better eyes, the awesome vision not of a God who destroys with brimstone and fire or asks for a parent's willingness to sacrifice a child but the God who appeared, and perhaps still waits, in the trees, quietly saying *Behold, Here I am. Know me.*

NOTES

1. See also Genesis 13:13.

2. See Rosemary Hennesy, "Queer Visibility in Commodity Culture," *Cultural Critique* 29 (Winter 1994–1995): 37.

3. Nikki Sullivan, *A Critical Introduction to Queer Theory* (Edinburgh: Edinburgh University Press, 2003), 192.

4. See also *Take Back the Word: A Queer Reading of the Bible*, ed. Robert E. Goss and Mona West (Cleveland: Pilgrim, 2000); *Queer Commentary and the Hebrew Bible,* ed. Ken Stone (Cleveland: Pilgrim, 2001); and *The Queer Bible Commentary,* ed. Deryn Guest, Robert E. Goss, Mona West, and Thomas Bohache (London: SCM Press, 2006).

5. See Virginia Mollenkott, "Reading the Bible from Low and Outside: Lesbitransgay People as God's Tricksters," in Goss and West, *Take Back the Word* (see note 4), 13–22.

6. Rebecca Goldstein, "Looking Back at Lot's Wife," in *Out of the Garden: Women Writers on the Bible,* ed. Christina Buchman and Celina Spiegel (New York: Ballantine, 1993), 3–12; Michael Carden, "Remembering Pelotit: A Queer Midrash on Calling Down Fire," in Stone, *Queer Commentary and the Hebrew Bible* (see note 4), 152–168; and "Genesis/Bereshit," in Guest et al., *Queer Bible Commentary* (see note 4), 38.

7. Genesis 19:17. The verse is, however, stated in the second person singular.

8. See *b. Baba Metzia* 59b.

9. Translated according to Everett Fox, *The Five Books of Moses: A New Translation* (New York: Schocken Books, 1995).

10. Of course, one of the rabbinic solutions to this apparent problem, which confirms at least that there is a textual problem, is to read the following verse as "My Lord [God], if it please you, do not go on past your servant" (*b. Shabbat* 127a) and thus to insist that Abraham saw God, imagining that Abraham has asked God to wait while he takes care of his guests.

11. *Genesis Rabbah* 38:13. Translation following Burton Visotzky, *Reading the Book: Making the Bible a Timeless Text* (New York: Schocken Books, 1991), 65–66.

FIVE

When Gender Varies: A Curious Case of *Kere* and *Ketiv*

Parashat Chayei Sarah (Genesis 23:1–25:18)

RACHEL BRODIE

"In the Bible, women are rarely born, they almost never die and when they give birth it is usually to a boy." With that caveat, Yair Zakovitch, legendary Bible professor at Hebrew University in Jerusalem, began a series of provocative lectures on women in the Bible that continues to influence my thinking about the subject more than ten years later.

Even though Rebekah, who is introduced in *Parashat Chayei Sarah*, is one of the Bible's most celebrated female figures, she seems to qualify under Zakovitch's rubric. Consider: When Abraham is sent an updated family tree from his brother Nahor's branch of the family (Gen. 22:20–24), Rebekah's name appears under that of Nahor's son, Betuel. As a character, she first shows up to accept a marriage proposal, then gives birth to two boys (at once!), and her ultimate demise goes unrecorded. However, in the interim, the scenes that make up her narrative distinguish her as one of the stronger Biblical characters and—for a 21st-century queer, feminist reader—one of the most compelling.

We first meet Rebekah in Genesis 24 after Abraham sends Eliezer, his servant, to "the land of [Abraham's] birth" to find a wife for Abraham's son, Isaac. Once Eliezer has arrived, he decides that the right woman will be she who shows great hospitality to him and his camels by offering them all water. Rebekah, a cousin of Isaac, does precisely as Eliezer had hoped. He showers her with gifts and speaks with her family to arrange to take her back to Isaac to be wed, to which they agree after conferring with Rebekah.

The Rebekah that emerges from a close reading of the narrative in this chapter of Genesis is a complex amalgam of traits. As seen from the perspective of Eliezer, Rebekah is physically very attractive (24:16). She is also strong and muscular, capable of drawing hundreds of gallons of water for all of Eliezer's camels in a short time (24:20), thus confirming Eliezer's hope that the right woman for Isaac will be she who shows great hospitality to him and his camels. She is socially capable of acting forwardly and independently (talking to Eliezer—a stranger—as he waits by the well; accepting the gifts he lavishes on her after confirming to himself that she will be Isaac's bride; and issuing an invitation to host him as a guest at her family home). In addition,

Eliezer's test—to see if she would water his camels in addition to serving him—seems designed to reveal certain character traits: Rebekah proves to be hospitable and sensitive to the needs of animals, but her behavior also indicates a willingness to be servile and to put the needs of others, even complete strangers, first.

From Eliezer's perspective, this is a miraculous combination, one only God could have created (24:27). Physically and socially, the person he has encountered at the well seems a perfect match for his master's son, Isaac. Almost sacrificed like an animal by his own father, and grieving the recent loss of his mother, Isaac could benefit from Rebekah's sensitivity and servility, as well as her physical strength and confidence.

Of course, Rebekah is not a typical woman of the Bible, partly because of her "masculine" traits (physical strength, stamina, bold social behavior, and independence). Through the eyes of Eliezer the servant, the Biblical text itself seems to approve of the blending of stereotypically masculine and feminine traits. Might the character of Rebekah afford a more nuanced view of gender—one that extends beyond biological and social conventions? Perhaps, though a far more radical view of Rebekah and gender emerges from a close reading of Genesis 24, not in the narrative per se but on the page itself.

Five times in this chapter, the text refers to Rebekah using a word made up of three Hebrew letters: *nun-ayin-reysh* (verses 14, 16, 28, 55, 57). *Na'ar* (the three-letter word formed by these letters) refers to a young *man*. In printed versions of the Hebrew Bible, that word is printed in a smaller font and without vowels. Next to it, in the margins, is a "correction"—those same three letters but with the letter *hay* appended at the end. The significance? Add a *hay*, to make it *na'ar'ah*, and you get a word that means young *woman*. In these particular verses, it would mean that the character—a young man? a young woman?—would be the following:

(v. 14) The one who would reply, "Drink, and I will also water your camels."
(v. 16) Very delightful to look upon, a virgin, not sexually intimate with a man.
(v. 28) Running, telling all that had occurred to those in mother's home.
(v. 55) Asked: "stay ten more days and then go."
(v. 57) Called and consulted about the decision to stay or go.

A point of background: From approximately the 7th to the 10th century CE a group of men who came to be known as the Masoretes engaged in a process of standardizing the Biblical text (from the different versions and oral traditions that were known to them). They added letters (primarily vowels) and systematic notes for vocalization to the otherwise vowelless, punctuationless text. In some cases they made marginal notes indicating either their discomfort with a scribal tradition or the existence of competing traditions. One type of marginal note is called the *kere u'ketiv* (literally, "read and written")—it is a note that means "the text says *A,* but when you read it aloud, read it as (substitute) *B.*"

This particular case of *kere u'ketiv* involves substituting the term for a young woman (*na'ar'ah*) for the word that is actually written in the text: *na'ar* (young man). The vast majority of people who have heard this story (from ancient times until the present) or read it (since few editions indicate the existence of textual variants) have never had occasion to wonder about the oddity of this particular *kere u'ketiv*. Besides, there are some perfectly reasonable explanations offered for its existence, such as that it is not so much a *kere u'ketiv* as a spelling convention, and no letter *hay* was required, since the context made it obvious that it was referring to a female.

Were the Masoretes correcting a scribal error? If so, why does it appear five times in a row, all in reference to Rebekah? Why were they so concerned, when the Biblical text itself seems not to be, that future readers be clear about Rebekah's place within a rigid gender divide? Before trying to make sense of the Masoretic tradition, we need to unpack what it means to be considered a *na'arah*. The term is used to refer to a girl who is pubescent, still living under her father's care but eligible for marriage. In this liminal state, she is especially vulnerable to unwanted sexual attention and should therefore remain close to home.

Given these norms, Rebekah's circumstances are ripe for tragedy: she is very attractive, out of bounds (away from home), and takes candy from strangers, and her difficult brother is left in charge of the household because her father is not around. Dina, the other character who is referred to with this exact same *kere u'ketiv* (see Genesis 34:3, 12), facing similar circumstances, is abducted and raped. But not Rebekah, Rebekah's un-*na'arah*-like behavior is actually rewarded. As a result of being out and about, taking risks, transgressing social conventions, and defying rigid gender identification, she is even treated in a manner—rare for a woman in the Bible— that befits a person with agency (she gets to decide when to leave her home to journey to meet Isaac; verses 57–59), and her future is blessed (verse 60).

Is that why she is referred to as *na'ar*, a young *man*? If it were only a question of pointing out her nonstereotypical female behavior, we would not have needed this additional proof. That much we had already gleaned from the narrative itself. What does the *na'ar/ah* correction add?

Perhaps the fact that the word is made into a *kere u'ketiv*, given the very good reasons for referring to Rebekah as a *na'ar* in the first place, reflects an ambiguity inherent in the word itself, an ambiguity that embodies a deeper truth about the emergence of gender identity. Could it be that a *nun-ayin-reish* (whether *na'ar* or *na'arah*) is a "youth"—recently pubescent, whose gender resists categorization and whose identity has yet to be forced into a rigid binary system? Like the small window that often exists even in the most gender-conventional social systems, when it might be possible for, let us say, a pubescent boy to play Juliet on stage. If so, then by preserving the Masoretic tradition have we unintentionally lost a significant insight preserved by the Bible itself?

There is also a long tradition of deriving additional meaning from a *kere u'ketiv*. The Malbim (19th-century Russian Bible scholar) understood the *kere* to be the interpretation (*drash*) on the word and the *ketiv* as its literal meaning (*pshat*). Using the *na'ar/ah* example, this might mean that an individual's physiology (the literal/*pshat*) might point to one end of the gender continuum, but that person's lived experience (the interpretive/*drash*) is elsewhere on it. The assertion (only radical when applied to gender?) that the way people appear and the way they are inside might not be aligned is directly reflected in Rav Soloveitchik's (20th-century American Orthodox Talmudist) understanding of *kere u'ketiv*. He associates the *kere* with a person's exterior, public self, whereas the *ketiv* is more the interior, emotional life.

Combining these two perspectives, Rebekah may have been physiologically and emotionally more of a *na'ar*, while presenting to the world the image of (making people "read" her as) a *na'ar'ah*. Indeed, that seems to be how the servant sees her and exactly what he is looking for in an ideal partner for Isaac: a human manifestation of the divine gift of gender that is given to each of us in full spectrum.

SIX

Esau's Gender Crossing
Parashat Toldot (Genesis 25:19–28:9)

SARRA LEV

The story of Jacob and Esau, Rebekah's twin sons, is filled with deception and vulnerability, power and betrayal. The story opens with the twins' birth, the first—large and hairy—"emerged entirely red like a cape of hair and they named him Esau" (Gen. 25:25).[1] The second, we discover later, is "a smooth-skinned" man (27:11). But the story quickly reveals that the depiction of the firstborn, Esau, as stereotypically more masculine is only half the story, for the hairy hunter is also characterized as a stereotypically feminine character: emotional, kindly, and subservient. This feminine Esau continually approaches life with innocence, only to be shoved aside in favor of his more savvy, cool, and street-smart little brother.[2] The younger Jacob, though depicted in physical terms as the tent-dwelling smooth-skinned effeminate character, ultimately belies his femininity—with the help of his mother, no less—and lands himself smack in the role of patriarch of the family and, ultimately, of the nation (for another perspective on the gender roles of the brothers, see Yoel Kahn's essay on *Parashat Vayetzei*).

Both the Biblical text itself and rabbinic midrash on the story contain gender inversions in which Esau rejects his overtly male description and legacy in favor of what in contemporary terms we might think of as more "classically female" choices.[3] Our story opens as the text describes the relationships between the four characters in the family. The father, Isaac, and the mother, Rebekah, have each chosen a favorite son: "and Isaac loved Esau because the hunt was in his mouth, but Rebekah loved Jacob" (25:28). Although Isaac prefers Esau, his love is described as being contingent on his son's role as the hunter. In contrast, Rebekah's favorite is Jacob, whom she loves unconditionally. It is unclear, however, whose mouth the text refers to in this verse. Isaac loved Esau because the hunt was in whose mouth? Is it Esau's mouth that desires the hunt? Is he the stereotypically masculine figure who longs to go out into the field and kill? Or is it his father, Isaac, whose taste for venison drives Esau into the fields to act the role of "the man of the house."

And even if it is Esau whom the narrator portrays as hungry for the kill, how are we to understand the role of this narrator? Is this an objective narrator who describes Esau as loving the hunt, or is the narrator merely describing Isaac's own impression of his son? Can we not read the verse "Isaac loved Esau because [*he felt that*] the hunt was in his mouth" (25:28). Is this, in fact, a description of a parent's own image and expectations of his firstborn son for gender conformity?

Esau's unease with his role as hunter is hinted at just one verse later, when the text tells us that Jacob prepares a lentil stew, and Esau comes home from the field tired (25:29). The early sages believed that the Torah was perfectly concise, containing no unnecessary information. Verse 29, however, employs seemingly unnecessary information: "And Jacob made a [lentil] stew, and Esau came in from the field, *and he was tired.*" The text could more easily have given us all this information by saying, ". . . and Esau came in tired from the field." Furthermore, the verse that follows 25:29 again supplies the same information, making it twice redundant. The tradition of the Rabbis encourages us to find meaning behind the fact that the text sets off the phrase "and he was tired." Tired of what? A queer reader might say he was tired of hunting, tired of performing his role as a male.

Jacob tells Esau that he will not give him stew but will sell it to him for his birthright. Esau answers, "I am going to die anyway, for what do I need a birthright?" (25:32). Traditionally, Esau is ridiculed for his short-sighted response to Jacob—"if you do not feed me stew, I will die of hunger"—but this verse is actually quite profound. Recognizing that his birthright demands of him to be "the man," placing him in the hierarchical position of head of a patriarchal family, Esau understands that with this birthright he is saddled with a weariness close to death. His answer to Jacob is a comment not on his physical hunger but on an emotional hunger that runs much deeper. "If I keep this birthright, I am going to die anyway, so why should I have this birthright?"

Following this verse, the text tells us, "And Jacob gave Esau bread and lentil stew and he ate and drank and he got up and went, and he despised the birthright" (25:34). Again, traditionally we are taught to look down at Esau's behavior, to read this as sour grapes, and to feel proud that the *right* person inherited the birthright—not someone who would despise it. But if we again step into Esau's shoes, this is the moment when he has finally managed to walk away from the expectations placed on him as the firstborn son, and he disdains those expectations.

Of course, although selling his birthright is a move that ultimately frees him from the story of this dysfunctional family, and from his role as firstborn, a birthright is not easy to relinquish. Later, Esau's ambivalence about his choice does appear when Jacob has stolen not only his birthright but the blessing that goes along with it as well.[4] In this part of the tale, Rebekah overhears Isaac tell Esau to go hunt him something and to prepare it so that he can bless Esau with the blessing of the firstborn. Rebekah quickly makes arrangements to have Jacob supplant Esau by dressing him up to appear like Esau to the blind Isaac and by preparing Isaac's favorite dish from a lamb of their flock to seem like the hunt that Esau brought home (27:5–17). When Esau hears that his blessing has been given to Jacob, he cries, "'is it not so that he is called Jacob and he deceived me these two times! He took my birthright, and now he took my blessing!' And [then Esau] said [to his father], 'have you not spared me a blessing?'" (27:36). Although Esau willingly relinquished his birthright, even despising it later, this text expresses all the emotions of this gender-displaced firstborn son. Esau's anguish at losing both the birthright and the blessing comes through in multiple ways, first in his condemnation of his brother for having deceived him twice (including a pun on Jacob's Hebrew name—*ya'akov*—and the word *ya'akveni*, "deceived"). Esau does not stop there, however, but twice more expresses his pain—first at his loss ("He took my birthright and now he took my blessing!") and then by pleading with his father for the shreds of a blessing, which might be left over. Although Esau's selling his birthright allows him to walk away from the role he does not want, he must also abandon the privilege that came with this untenable situation—the love of his father (although conditional), his status as firstborn, and his very identity until this moment. In this verse lies all the pain involved in making that move, the betrayal of his brother, the loss of his status, and finally, the blessing of his father, who has supplanted him so easily for Rebekah and Jacob's well-prepared lamb chops.

Esau's emotional character comes out strongly in the short episode that describes his reaction to having been tricked. The text describes the moment when he first hears of the betrayal:

> And Isaac trembled very greatly and said "who is it then who hunted meat and brought it to me and I ate of it all before you came and I blessed him (and may he also be blessed)?" When Esau heard the words of his father he *cried such* a *great* and *bitter cry* and he said to his father: "bless me, me too, my father." (27:33–34)

The pained but nonaggressive response comes out in full force in this passage and continues through the remainder of the chapter. The cry that Esau cries is described with five different words—he *cried such* a *great* and *bitter cry*. It is a response of inward pain, rather than of outward rage. Esau's is not the macho response of Biblical men who experience an injustice and respond with rage and revenge.[5] Rather, it matches word for word the anguished cry of a Biblical woman—Hagar—as she puts Ishmael down in the desert and walks away so as not to watch him die ("she *lifted up her voice and cried*"; 21:16).[6] When Isaac explains that he has given everything away, Esau asks for the third (and fourth) time in six verses: "do you only have a single blessing? Bless me, me too, my father. And Esau *lifted up his voice and cried*" (27:38).

As the ultimate irony, Isaac responds to Esau's refusal of his role as patriarch by giving him a blessing that forces him back into the stereotypical role of male: "you shall live by the sword" (27:40). Through this blessing Isaac tries to compel Esau back into the masculine box out of which he is breaking. But even here, he is subverted, for although Esau may seem to follow this blessing with a macho expression of revenge, that, too, ultimately resolves into a less-than-convincing act of masculine power. Following his father's blessing, Esau's thoughts of revenge are turned inward (made in his heart) and are balanced by his care for his father's emotions even in this moment of betrayal: "And Esau said *in his heart, let the days of mourning for my father be over*, and I will kill Jacob my brother" (27:41). Esau does not even articulate the thought aloud, never mind carrying it out, and his first concern is his father. Unlike the responses of other males in the Torah (including the very vengeful male God), Esau's response is all words and no action. Never do we hear that Esau tries to carry out this internalized threat, even when his chance does arrive some two decades later (in

Parashat Vayishlach) when Jacob seeks to pass through Esau's land. While Jacob me-
ticulously and nervously calculates each moment of the reunion, Esau is purely emo-
tive: "And Jacob looked up and there was Esau coming, and with him—four hundred
men. . . . And Esau ran towards him and hugged him and fell on his neck and kissed
him and they cried" (33:1–17). Although both of them do shed tears in the end, all the
emotionally charged actions are attributed to the great hairy male Esau—he runs, he
hugs, he falls on the neck, and he kisses, and only after all this has happened does he
elicit tears (or perhaps a single tear?) from his brother.

The resonance of Esau's gender crossing can be also be found in a midrash that
explains the phrase "a man of the field" (25:27):

> R. Hiya bar Abba said: [Esau] declared himself [sexually] available like a field. Israel
> said before the Holy Blessed One: "Master of the Universe, is it not enough that we have
> been enslaved to the seventy nations, [must we be enslaved] even to this one who is
> penetrated like a woman?!" The Holy Blessed one answered them: "thus I shall punish
> him with that very language! Thus it is written: 'on that day the heart of the mighty of
> Edom will be like the heart of a woman in labor.'"[7]

The Biblical Esau is said to be the progenitor of the Edomites, whom the rabbis equate
with Rome. The Romans were known for allowing anal sex between men,[8] but sex in
the ancient world was not an act of equals. It was constructed of a ("true male") penetrator and a ("less than male") penetrated. In this midrash, the Israelites complain to
God that they are subject to the rule of Esau/Rome, who permits males to be in the
sexual role of females. God responds that their very complaint will be his ultimate
punishment—for having allowed "himself" to gender-cross, God will force upon him
the labor pains that his "chosen gender" endure.

In both the Biblical and rabbinic traditions, Esau's gender-crossing comes to bite
him in the back in the end. In the Biblical text, Esau cannot both act the role of the
male (the patriarch in the family) and despise the trappings that come with that role.
So too, in the rabbinic text, Esau cannot both be the dominant (male) nation and
also act the role of the (female) penetrated. Something must give—and in the end he
will be punished.

But whereas Rome did fall, the Esau of the Biblical text prevailed. Until the very
end he lived his life as he wished it, choosing reconciliation with his brother over
revenge, passion over detachment, and a life without blessing or birthright for a life
with integrity. After Esau, now the leader of the Edomites, hugs and kisses his brother
in what is the final episode between them, he says to Jacob, now the father of his own
nation, "let us go together and [start to] walk, and I will walk with you." Esau offers
Jacob the gift of true reconciliation—the opportunity to walk together, the opportunity for Jacob also to shed the skins that he wore to fool the world and take on a role.
But although Esau extends a hand to Jacob to move forward, Jacob again cannot shed
those old skins. Once again he proves that he has not learned emotion or connection.
Offering excuses to Esau about how his camp moves slowly, he tells him to start off
without them, that he will meet him up ahead. Instead, however, he again turns away

from the path of his brother, heading in the opposite direction, toward the city of Sukkot, east of the Jordan River.

But even in this great split all hope is not lost. Against the powerful blessing of his father, against the fate of being firstborn, and against a world waiting for him to act the role of the male and to live by the sword, Esau proves that there is another way, a way in which a more feminine ethos in a patriarchal world can still find its power. And in the end, many years later, when Isaac is 180 years old, the two brothers come together again to bury him—hopes of a new life begun.

NOTES

1. All references are from Genesis unless otherwise noted.

2. In no way do I mean to essentialize these roles as inherently male or female. My desire here is to show the ways in which the characters defy their own gender roles by subverting some of the rigid gender definitions of their own culture, and of our current culture.

3. To be clear, this essay intentionally conflates role definition in Biblical texts, rabbinic texts, and contemporary culture. In fact, the Biblical, rabbinic, and contemporary depictions of gender roles vary greatly. This commentary ignores those divisions in order to paint a queer picture for a contemporary world.

4. The blessing in these texts is understood as having a power of its own, sanctioned by God. The blessing of the firstborn son generally accompanies the birthright itself (the physical inheritance and position of "head of the family"). The understanding is that whatever blessing is conferred will actually come to be. There is only one blessing of the firstborn, and once it is given it cannot be revoked.

5. See, for example, Genesis 34:7, 13–26; Judges 19–20.

6. Interestingly, Jacob's first kiss of Rachel is also followed by this language (29:11). This story is replete with allusions that show karmic interconnections—Jacob's cry seems to be an echo of this very cry of Esau, which he himself caused. The only other place in Torah where these words are used occur when the Israelites hear the spies' frightening report of what can be found in the land Israel. At this point the Israelites lift up their voices and cry. One could make the claim that here, too, the Israelites are being depicted as "women"—crying and complaining over the false report of the spies.

7. *Bereshit Rabbah*, 63.

8. For the Romans one of the "men" had to be of lesser status, making him not quite a man. However, the rabbis did not make these distinctions between males of different status for the purpose of laws regarding anal sex between men; they prohibited all such sex.

SEVEN

And Jacob Came Out
Parashat Vayetzei (Genesis 28:10–32:3)

YOEL KAHN

> There are 600,000 interpretations of the written Torah for each and every verse. . . . For each and every soul amongst the 600,000 souls of Israel has a particular path in the entire Torah according to the underlying nature of its soul-root (*bechinat shoresh metziut nishmato*).
> —Rabbi Chaim Vital (b. 1543, lived in Safed)[1]

Sometimes, we find meaning or significance in Torah by striving to understand its "big ideas": all humans are created "in the Divine Image," or "know the heart of the other, because you were others in Egypt." Often, we consider Torah at the scale of a weekly Torah portion, whether looking at the story as a whole or even at an individual verse. But our tradition teaches that every aspect of Torah is a potential source of meaning, from the accent marks to the shapes of the letters or even the layout of the columns of the scroll (as Rachel Brodie demonstrates in her essay on *Parashat Chayei Sarah* in this volume). The Torah's truth can be disclosed in many ways. Each weekly portion is given a name, derived from the first significant word in the first verse of the portion. Often, the name also hints at or relates to the content that follows. The story of the patriarch Jacob is told over the course of three portions: first, *Toldot*, the story of the birth and youth of Jacob and his competing twin, Esau, then *Vayetzei*, in which Jacob sets out on his personal quest, and finally, *Vayishlach*, in which Jacob and Esau are reconciled.

The secret of Jacob's biography—and the closeted message of the Torah—is disclosed in the name of this portion, *Vayetzei*. The portion begins, "*va-yetzei Ya'akov*," customarily rendered as "Jacob left" or "Jacob departed," but the root of the Hebrew verb *y-tz-a* is the same as in the "*Motzi*" blessing for bread ("brings forth") and "*Yetzi'at mitzrayim*," the Exodus from Egypt. The true meaning of this phrase, as the narrative bears out, is "*Va-yetzei Ya'akov*: And Jacob came out."

Jacob and his older twin, Esau, are opposites. Seen as Jungian archetypes, they mythically embody the conflict and the triumph of the settled agriculturalist over the hunter-gatherer. Jacob, "a dweller in tents," defeats Esau, the "man of the (open) fields" (Gen. 25:27). For the modern reader, Jacob and Esau present the characteristics and behaviors of classic male typologies. Esau is the macho older brother, who goes for extreme sports and adventure travel. He is the silent, butch, NASCAR guy who lives from paycheck to paycheck, short on words and quick to act. Esau is ev-erything that his passive, nearsighted, unadventurous father, Isaac, is not—and the boys' father favors Esau (25:28). A mama's boy, Jacob stays close to home. In contrast to Esau's worldliness, he is a naïf, "*ish tam*," who lives in awe of his brother and father and subscribes to *Gourmet* magazine. Esau is butch; Jacob is femme (for a differ-ent perspective on the gender dynamics of Jacob and Esau, see Sarra Lev's essay on *Parashat Toldot*).

Closer reading reveals that Jacob is indeed a classic queer character. Like the trick-ster in folklore, Jacob is the marginal figure who lives on wits and subterfuge to con-trol his stronger brother. One day, Esau comes home from the hunt and says to Jacob, "Let me gulp some of that red stuff you are cooking!" Is it a coincidence that Jacob is stirring a pot of Esau's favorite food? Has he been cooking up this superprotein meal with the goal in mind of bribing his brother? Or did he intend this menu for himself, one more vain attempt to transform himself into someone he is not? Seizing the op-portunity, Jacob asks Esau to sell his birthright, the privileges that are the exclusive claim of the firstborn son. Esau, ever impulsive and lacking a 401(k), does not plan ahead; his future inheritance is trumped by the demands of the hour: "Look, I am about to die (from hunger). What use is a birthright to me?" (25:32). Having long anticipated such a moment, crafty Jacob has the legal papers already drawn up and waiting; he does not allow Esau to eat until he has sworn an oath.

Despite a regimen of Esau-inspired diets and self-improvement, as well as pur-chasing the rights to Esau's inheritance, Jacob realizes that he still has not earned his father's love or acceptance. With his mother's help, he once again uses his trickster and domestic skills and arrives at his father's deathbed in Esau-drag, having cooked up the one simple dish that Esau knows how to make, the one that their father can-not resist. Jacob hides his shameful body beneath smelly animal skins and only then asks for Isaac's blessing. Much as he now yearns to become like Esau—cooking and eating Esau's food, dressing in Esau's clothes—he still cannot pass. Isaac discerns Ja-cob's otherness, declaring, in a nonstandard translation of the verse, "The hands are the hands of Esau but the voice! The voice is of Jacob" (27:22).

Jacob runs from his family home, having secured the formal blessing reserved for Esau but more alienated and distant from his father than ever. He sets out on a jour-ney, heading toward Be'er Sheva, the ancestral home of his grandfather, Abraham. He flees without food or clothing and is wandering in the wilderness when he is over-come by a sudden darkness. He throws himself down in the middle of "nowhere"—as he has already discovered that his life is nowhere, without a sense of self (*Bereshit Rabbah* 68:10, cited by Rashi in his commentary to 28:16). His efforts to become more like the brother he is not, and thereby to secure his place in the family, have utterly failed him.

It is in the unknown place, the wild place, apart from civilization and expectation, that Jacob has a dream vision. God appears to him, standing by a ladder "set on the ground and whose top ascended to heaven" (Gen. 28:12). Jacob is invited to ascend the ladder, to imagine himself anew, in an entirely different way from the language and images he has known until now. He wakes up with a new consciousness and declares, "Surely God was in this place (*ha-Makom*), and I did not know!" (28:16). But where was the place where he encountered the presence of God? It was nowhere, the wild, unknown place; in Hebrew, *ha-Makom* not only means "the (physical) place" but is also a name for God. Thus, he did not arrive at "the (unnamed) place" but rather had a transformative encounter with the Unnameable Ground of All. What, therefore, can Jacob mean when he says, "God was in this place but I did not know?" The place to which he refers is himself; Jacob now understands that he himself, as he is, reflects the Divine Image that was his birthright all along. *Vayetzei Yaʾakov*: Jacob came out as his authentic self.

Renewed, invigorated, and newly emboldened, Jacob sets out to establish his new life, and makes three requests (Gen. 28:20–21). Having cast off the Esau-drag as he ascended the ladder, he asks for clothing of his own to wear on his journey. Jacob next asks for food, for he realizes that he can no longer eat the red meat and red lentil diet of Esau that he had become so expert at preparing. Finally, he asks for what he truly wants, and the fulfillment of this prayer will demonstrate whether God is truly with him (18:21). Jacob asks to "return to [his] father's house with integrity." Having come out and embraced his authentic self, Jacob's deepest yearning is to return home and find acceptance as he is, to find his place in the household of Israel.

Jacob's life unfolds happily. Years pass; he is an adult and the head of a family. Yet he has never reconciled with his brother, Esau. Just as he struggled with Esau in the womb before he was born, now once again, as he is about to encounter Esau alone, he engages in a tremendous struggle. A mysterious figure, not a human, wrestles with Jacob all through the night at the edge of the River Jabbok. The medieval commentator Rashi flatly declared, "It was the angel of Esau" (32:25). What representation of Esau still had such power over Jacob? It was not a human messenger whom Jacob had to defeat in order to transform himself, crossing the Jabbok/Jakob River and assuming a new identity. What Jacob had never defeated until now, despite all his accomplishments, was his internalized Esau; he had not yet taken full ownership of his identity and uniqueness. Only when he could finally subdue the belief that he still had to somehow become Esau could he complete his journey of reconciliation. So it was his own inner Esau that he wrestled with and ultimately defeated, though this defeat left him permanently wounded (32:33). Out of this struggle, blessing emerged, including the new name, Yisrael, "for you have wrestled with beings divine and human and have prevailed" (32:29).

The story of Jacob lends itself to being read as a classic coming-out narrative; but even were we to retell it stripped of its campy details, the story remains appealing because of its truth and resonance with so much of human experience: the yearning to uncover and realize the authentic self; the need to find food and sustenance as one lives out the journey; the heartfelt desire to integrate the whole self with "the ancestral house" of family, community, and culture; and the lifelong tasks of acceptance, integration, and connection.

NOTE

1. Quoted from a manuscript by Rabbi Moshe Chaim Luzzatto (Italy, late 18th century); in turn quoted by Isaiah Tishby, "'Kudsha Berich hu oraita ve yisrael kula chad'—Makor haamrah befeirush 'adrah rabah' le'Ramchel," *Kiryat Sefer* 50 (1975): 490n. 58.

EIGHT

Biblical Sex
Parashat Vayishlach (Genesis 32:4–36:43)

DAVID BRODSKY

People in premodern societies understood the world in fundamentally different ways from those of us living in contemporary Western cultures. As philosopher Michel Foucault and others have shown, these variations in worldview are often rooted in changes in the meaning of language or in the very lack of a word or concept in the premodern world. Language is not just the mode by which we express ourselves to others; it is also the way we formulate our thoughts to ourselves. A language's lack of a term for a concept, therefore, may be indicative of more than just the difficulty in expressing the concept; it may be indicative of the lack of the concept in general. For example, as scholars have shown, the lack of any term for homosexuality in the premodern world suggests that such cultures lacked the binary homo-/heterosexuality in which contemporary Western cultures operate.[1]

In *Parashat Vayishlach*, we encounter a similar cultural gap between our contemporary understanding and the worldview of the premodern societies in which the Biblical narratives are embedded. *Vayishlach* describes what has become known as the rape of Dinah (Genesis 34), but the text offers us no precise term for rape, a linguistic anomaly indicative of a gap between modern and ancient Biblical and rabbinic understandings of rape. In Genesis 34, Dinah, the daughter of Jacob and Leah, "went out to see the daughters of the land." She went to meet other women of the area in which her family had recently settled. In the process, a man of a neighboring community, named Shechem, "lay with her and oppressed her" (*va-yishkav 'otah va-ye'annehah*). Shechem then came to desire Dinah, so his father, the prince of the region, negotiated with Jacob and Dinah's brothers for Shechem to marry her. The brothers were scandalized by what had happened, a disgrace (*nevalah*) that "ought not be done in Israel," though precisely what this scandal was is never defined. Readers generally assume that Dinah's brothers found her rape to be the disgrace, but I argue that the real scandal was Shechem's having sex with Dinah without her *father's* permission.

In either case, the brothers then tricked Shechem and his people into circumcising themselves and joining the Israelite community, only to swoop down on them while they were recovering from the circumcision and slaughter them all. The story leaves the reader with many questions, not least of which is whether Dinah was raped.

In the context of "he lay with her," of course, one would be naive to assume that the "oppression" was not a reference to rape. And yet the Hebrew root '-n-h (in *va-*

ye'annehah), even in the grammatical stem in which it is found here, can be simply a generic term that can mean "to humble" or "to degrade" someone. Although this "humbling" is connected by the text to the sexual interaction, the sex itself could have been consensual. Nevertheless, we assume that the author of the story intended to state that Dinah was raped.

The question of whether Dinah was raped points to a larger problem for modern readers of this ancient story: Biblical Hebrew lacks a word that is specifically or even primarily devoted to expressing the concept of rape. Thus, even if the author wished to tell us that Dinah was raped, he or she lacked the language to do so in a clear and succinct way. The task for us will be to determine if and how these linguistic differences (between Biblical Hebrew and modern English) represent differences in understanding of the notion of rape. In addition, although the rabbis of the Talmudic Period used a different root ('-n-s) to express the concept of rape, they, too, lacked a term that was explicitly or even primarily devoted to this concept. Although Biblical and rabbinic sources lacked a term that was exclusive for rape (their terms for rape were generic for force or degradation), this difference from modern parlance does not imply that the authors of these texts had no notion of rape. Rather, their understanding of rape differed from that of the modern English-speaking reader.

In both Biblical and rabbinic literature it is quite clear that the victim of rape is precisely that, a victim, and he or she is, therefore, completely innocent of any wrongdoing and not deserving of any punishment. This point is made explicitly in Deuteronomy 22:23–27, which directly compares the victim of rape with a murder victim, intimating that although the rape victim is a "party" to the sexual sin that occurred, the rape victim is no more culpable for that act than a victim of murder. Rabbinic literature also exculpated the victim completely.[2] This understanding that the rape victim had the sexual sin acted upon her or him may have motivated the shift in the word used to express this action from Biblical Hebrew to the Rabbinic Hebrew of the Talmudic Period, a millennium later. Rather than use the Biblical root '-n-h, which connotes humbling and degrading, the rabbis used the root '-n-s, connoting force. The rabbinic terminology expresses the victim's powerlessness.

In fact, the root '-n-s is used not just regarding forced sex but also any situation in which a person is forced to commit a sin and is, therefore, innocent of the wrong he or she committed. For example, the Mishnah (edited ca. 220 CE) states that if a man vowed to dine with his friend and then fell ill or was prevented from meeting his friend because the bridge was out, he is "forced" ('-n-s) and innocent of the sin of breaking his vow (Nedarim 3:3). In the Babylonian Talmud's commentary on this mishnah, Rava, a Babylonian rabbi who lived a few generations after the redaction of the Mishnah, explicitly connects the innocence of the victim in this situation of "force" to the innocence of the woman who is "forced" into sex.

Nevertheless, although both Biblical and rabbinic sources seem to have a notion of the innocence of the rape victim, they do not seem to have a notion of rape as a crime in and of itself. "Force," in general, need not be a crime, and both the Bible and the rabbis fail to criminalize forced sex on its own. Although the rapist in Deuteronomy 22:23–27 is given the death penalty for his crime, the crime for which he is punished is not rape but adultery. Deuteronomy 22:28–29 makes this explicit when it describes the penalty for the rape of an unmarried, unbetrothed virgin girl: fifty silver pieces to be paid to the *father*. In the Genesis story of the rape of Dinah, Dinah was presumably single and a virgin, corresponding to Deuteronomy 22:28–29. Accordingly, the brothers *should* have exacted a fine (fifty silver pieces) and consented to the marriage. They certainly should not have killed Shechem merely for raping a single (unmarried and unbetrothed) virgin girl, even if she was their sister. What caused this very different reaction between Genesis 34 and Deuteronomy 22? The answer lies in a deeper understanding of Deuteronomy 22.

In rabbinic terms, the difference between the capital punishment that the rapist of the betrothed girl receives and the monetary punishment that the rapist of the single girl receives indicates that one act is a criminal case (*dinei nefashot*) and the other is merely a civil suit (*dinei mamonot*). In other words, rape in cases in which consensual sex would not be prohibited (such as with a single girl who is not a close blood relation of the rapist) is not a crime, although it is open to a civil suit.

But because rape is not actually prohibited anywhere in the Bible, the capital punishment is not for the rape itself but for the adultery that the rapist has committed. Rape of a single girl merely carries a fine (to make restitution to the father for his monetary loss, as we shall see later), but it is not actually prohibited.

To put the issue in rabbinic terms, rape of a single girl or woman is not a Torah prohibition, a violation of God's law, but merely a case of monetary damage, which results in a civil suit by one man to reclaim his loss against the responsible party. That this claim is merely civil (and that the rape of a single girl itself is not criminal) can be seen from the fact that even in the absence of rape (that is, a man who has had *consensual* sex with a single, virgin girl), the man must make monetary restitution to the girl's father (Ex. 22:15–16). Thus, it is not the rape for which he must make monetary restitution. Rather, the monetary compensation is for some other monetary damage, one that the case of rape of a virgin has in common with the case of consensual sex. Since Dinah was not married, from a rabbinic perspective, no crime was committed.

What claim does the father have against the man who has sex with his daughter? It would seem that in ancient Israelite culture, the daughter's sexuality was seen as the possession of her father, to be sold to the husband when he married her off.[3] In this light, the monetary restitution of both the rapist and the consensual seducer makes a certain sense: by taking away the daughter's virginity, both the seducer and the rapist have stolen the bride-price that the father would have received when he married her off. In Israelite culture, the father would have received some money for his virgin daughter. Once she had been raped, he would no longer receive that amount. Exodus and Deuteronomy 22 rectify the situation by having the rapist/seducer pay the civil damages he inflicted on the father. In fact, from this perspective, even the fact that Deuteronomy 22:29 has the rape victim marry her rapist (and does not permit the rapist to divorce her) begins to make a certain "sense." Not only does the rape cause the father to lose out on the bride-price that he would have received when he married her off, but he is also saddled with another mouth to feed, now that it will be much more difficult for him to marry off his nonvirginal daughter. Deuteronomy

22:28–29 "solves" this problem by having the rapist marry the daughter, taking on the obligation to feed and clothe her that that relationship entails.[4]

It is only once we understand that the father owns the rights to his daughter's sexuality that we can understand another famous Biblical rape: Amnon's rape of his half sister, Tamar, in 2 Samuel 13. In that story, King David's son, Amnon, is smitten by his half sister, Tamar (King David's daughter by a different mother). He contrives an elaborate scheme in which he pretends to be sick and gets Tamar to care for him alone, at which point he reveals his true intentions and rapes her. From a modern idea of traditional sexual ethics, we understand this incident to contain two transgressions: incest and rape. Yet the author of the story seems to have neither of these sensibilities.[5] Tamar implores Amnon, "Don't, brother. Don't oppress me [*'al te-'anneini*]. For such should not be done in Israel. Don't do this disgraceful thing [*nevalah*]. . . . And now, please speak to the king [our father], *for he will not withhold me from you*" (2 Sam. 13:12–13; emphasis added). As the author states through Tamar, the violation is having sex with her without first getting the permission of her father, not incest or the fact that she is an unwilling partner.

This explanation might be related to why, in *Parashat Vayishlach*, in Genesis 34:7, Dinah's brothers use the same term Tamar used, *nevalah*, to describe the outrage committed "in Israel." It may also help us understand why Shechem's willingness to marry Dinah, which according to the pattern set in Deuteronomy 22:29 should have righted the wrong, was not able to rectify the matter. Verses 12–13 in 2 Samuel 13 proclaim that sex with Tamar without her *father's* consent is *nevalah*. Likewise, the author of Genesis 34 explains that the brothers are depressed upon hearing the news of the rape of their sister "because a disgrace [*nevalah*] was done in Israel to lie with a daughter of Jacob, and thus should not be done" (Gen. 34:7). This double reference to Israel/Jacob ("Israel" being Jacob's God-given name), the clear reference to Dinah as the *daughter* of Jacob, and the statements both that this is *why* they were upset and that *this* is what should not be done, all seem best understood in the context of Tamar's explanation in 2 Samuel 13 that sex with her without her father's permission is *nevalah*.

In the story of Dinah as well, then, it would seem that it is the fact that Shechem had sex with Dinah without her father's consent—and not that it was against *her* will—that is the *nevalah*, the violation. Nonetheless, why use the word *nevalah*? *Nevalah* literally means "corpse," something that both is impure and imparts impurity. This wrong/impurity against the father threatens to render impure those with whom it comes into contact: Dinah and, ultimately, the whole family. Moreover, in Genesis 34:31, the brothers are upset that Shechem has made their sister "like a whore." I argue that sex with the daughter without the father's permission is akin to adultery (for which the punishment is death) for the author of this passage. It is a violation of the father's exclusive rights to the daughter's sexuality, which is akin to (although somewhat different from) a husband's exclusive rights to his wife's sexuality. Thus, as with adultery, the violation cannot be rectified after the fact, even if monetary restitution can be made. Although the crime was against Dinah's father, her brothers are also directly affected by the crime, especially since the father seems to be spiritually if not physically absent in the story: Jacob "deafens" himself at the beginning of the story (Gen. 34:5), and he refuses to act. The brothers become proxies for the absent father.

This understanding of rape and of the father as owning the rights to his daughter's sexuality may also help to explain the story of Sodom and Gomorrah in *Parashat Vayera*. Contrary to popular modern readings of the story, Biblical and most rabbinic sources fail to mention male same-sex intercourse as central to the crimes of the Sodomites. Instead, when the prophet Ezekiel reflects back on this episode, he names their refraining from helping the poor and the needy as among the chief sins for which they were destroyed (Ez. 16:49). The rabbis, likewise, blame the Sodomites' demise primarily on their lack of hospitality.[6] Although the rabbis do mention sexual sins among the sins that the Sodomites committed, male same-sex intercourse often fails to make the list (e.g., Babylonian Talmud *Sanhedrin* 109a–b), whereas inhospitality to strangers and to the poor can be seen as at the core of most of the stories listed therein.

Ezekiel and the rabbis are picking up on something inherent to the story itself: that the attempted rape (or, to use Biblical language, sexual "oppression") of the strangers is probably mentioned not to describe the wicked homosexual ways of the townsfolk but to demonstrate their extreme inhospitality. In a society that lacked hotels and other forms of lodging, home hospitality was a very important part of the culture, and the code of how to treat the wayfarer in one's home was a central ethic (as it is among Bedouin to this day). Not only do none of the people of Sodom offer to lodge the strangers, but they even attempt to impede the one person in their town who does offer them refuge. And what is more of an affront to the ethic of offering hospitality and safe refuge to wayfarers than raping and murdering them upon arrival? In fact, in the parallel to the story of Sodom in Judges 19, the Gibeonites also refuse to offer lodging and refuge to a wayfarer (and his concubine) and also try to force the one man who offers the traveler refuge to send the traveler out so they may rape him. This time, not only is rape attempted (and perpetrated, though not to the man), but the victim is even murdered: inhospitality can get no worse than that! Lot, then, it would seem, offers to give up his daughters to the townspeople in place of the men, not necessarily because homosexuality is considered a grave sin in the story but because the men are under his protection. As legal possessor of the rights to his daughters' sexuality, he has the right (and, he believes, the obligation to his guests) to offer them in the men's stead.

Returning to the question with which we began, although the Bible and the rabbis share with modern readers the notion that victims of rape are innocent, they fail to see rape as a crime unto itself, although they do see it as an extreme affront to the code of hospitality. The differences between Biblical (and rabbinic) sexual ethics vis-à-vis rape and modern sexual ethics are a good example of the fact that the "religious right" is selective when it attempts to enforce the Bible's so-called ban on homosexuality and when it claims to be upholding Biblical sexual ethics. The change in understandings of rape from the Biblical period to today should dispel the common myth that today's so-called traditional sexual ethics directly correspond to that found in the Bible. No one today, not even the so-called traditionalists, would argue that we should enforce Deuteronomy 22:29's mandate that the rape victim be married off to her rapist (with little or no possibility of divorce). And as I show in my essay on *Parashat Kedoshim*, Rabbinic Judaism forbade very little when it comes to same-sex sexual and sensual interactions. We should not make the mistake to think that the topic of homosexuality is the only way in which modern sexual ethics (be they "left" or "right") differs from Biblical and rabbinic sexual ethics.

NOTES

1. For citations on this topic, see my essay on *Parashat Kedoshim*.

2. See inter alia, Babylonian Talmud *Ketubbot* 51b and *Sanhedrin* 73a ff.

3. It would seem that this possession was understood to exist until the father handed his daughter's sexuality over to her husband, although this is not entirely clear. The rabbis later limited fathers' possession of their daughters' sexuality to daughters under twelve years old.

4. That the husband has such obligations is the implication of Exodus 21:10, especially as understood through rabbinic eyes (see Babylonian Talmud *Ketubbot* 47b).

5. Thus, it seems that the Deuteronomic Historian does not include siblings (or at least half siblings) under the category of incest as the Holiness code in Leviticus does. In this way, we see that even within short periods of time and place and between closely related yet slightly different groups within ancient society we find changes in "traditional" sexual ethics, let alone over such large expanses of time as from their time to our own.

6. See, inter alia, Avot 5:10; Avot de-R. Nathan, Version B, 30; and Babylonian Talmud *Sanhedrin* 109a. In fact, the Babylonian Talmud consistently uses the phrase "the attribute of Sodom" to refer to a situation in which one person has nothing to lose by helping yet refuses to help his fellow (see *Eruvin* 49a; *Ketubbot* 103a; and *Bava Batra* 12b, 59a, 168a). Neverthe-less, Ezekiel's statement (in chapter 16) that the Sodomites have done "abomination" (*to'evah*) before him may be a veiled reference to male same-sex anal intercourse, although *to'evah* has such a wide range of applications that this need not be the application intended. Likewise, *Genesis Rabbah* 50 can be read as connecting the sins of the Sodomites with male same-sex intercourse (although, even here, the sin could be the sexual violation of the stranger who has sought refuge among them), and Pirqei R. Eliezer (25), a medieval rabbinic text, connects the sin of the Sodomites directly to *mishkav zakhur*, male-male anal intercourse. I thank Gwynn Kessler for reminding me of the importance of these last two sources for this inquiry.

NINE

Joseph's Fabulous Technicolor Dreamcoat
Parashat Vayeshev (Genesis 37:1–40:23)

GREGG DRINKWATER

The story of Joseph, the longest continuous narrative in the book of Genesis, offers one of the richest and most detailed portraits of a single character in the entire Hebrew Bible. The Bible offers such an emotionally complex narrative about Joseph's life that both ancient and modern commentators feel drawn to analyzing and interpreting his every move and identifying with his many trials and triumphs. The Nobel Prize–winning German writer Thomas Mann even wrote a novel in four parts based on the life of Joseph called *Joseph and His Brothers*. Scholars, rabbis, and LGBT activists looking for "queer" openings in the Torah often focus on Joseph. The ups and downs and emotional drama of his life are pregnant with queer subtexts, making Joseph the figure many LGBT readers would vote the "most likely to be gay" of any character in the Torah.

The great rabbinic and medieval commentators make the modern task of "queering" Joseph even easier, with all of them having noted that Joseph had a certain "sensibility." Rashi, for example, wrote that Joseph "dressed his hair" and "touched up his eyes so that he should appear goodlooking." As we shall see, Rashi's insights echoed those of earlier midrashic commentary, suggesting that there is indeed "something special" about Joseph that has intrigued Torah scholars throughout the ages.

Although Torah scholars would not argue that Joseph was gay, with all the modern-day assumptions we ascribe to that word—a concept that did not even exist for the ancients—there is enough evidence to suggest that Joseph was in some sense "queer"—an outsider dwelling on the inside, a figure apart from his family, and someone who did not quite fit in. Let us explore the evidence of Joseph's "queerness" step by step.

Joseph the Na'ar

The initial description of Joseph in the opening lines of *Vayeshev* has perplexed commentators for two thousand years. These lines describe Joseph as a seventeen-year-old who tends the flocks with his brothers, but in this same passage the Torah also tells us that he was a "*na'ar*"—a "youth" or "lad." In Biblical times, a seventeen-year-old would certainly be an adult, so why is Joseph described as a *na'ar*? And regardless, why comment at all after having clearly listed his age?

In the midrash, the sages suggest that although Joseph was indeed seventeen, he "behaved like a boy, penciling his eyes, curling his hair, and lifting his heel" (*Genesis Rabbah* 84:7). Today, would not the more obvious interpretation of a man who wears makeup, does up his hair, and prances about be that he was effeminate or, to follow contemporary cultural stereotypes even further, that he was gay (as problematic as such stereotypes may be)? Although this interpretation might seem obvious from our modern perspective, in ancient cultures, particularly Greek and Roman culture, the line between a boy (as opposed to a man) and a woman was blurrier than it is today. Calling Joseph a boy is a way of feminizing him while questioning his emotional and social maturity. Calling him a *na'ar* also contrasts him starkly with his brothers, who are clearly understood as adults, and suggests that Joseph possessed a certain innocence—a concept often used in the Bible to imply a closer link to God.

Other commentators, also trying to understand the use of the term *na'ar*, note that the complete line says, "*V'hu na'ar et-bnai Bilhah v'et-bnai Zilpah*" (And he was a *na'ar* with the sons of Bilhah and the sons of Zilpah; Gen. 37:2). They suggest that what is really being implied is that Joseph was a helper to some of his brothers (the sons of Bilhah and the sons of Zilpah—Dan, Naftali, Gad, and Asher)[1] or perhaps even a servant.[2]

Whatever the intent of the term *na'ar*, its use in reference to Joseph certainly supports the idea of his being a "queer" figure in the sense of being apart from the rest of his family and possibly being feminized by his brothers.

A Special Coat for a Special Son

Joseph's father, Jacob, put Joseph on a pedestal. Right after the "*na'ar*" verse, the Torah tells us that Jacob "loved Joseph more than all his children, because he was the son of his old age; and he made him a coat with long sleeves" (37:3). This coat, or *ketonet passim* in Hebrew, is often described as a "coat of many colors" or, in our own times, as Joseph's "amazing Technicolor dreamcoat." Once again, it sets Joseph apart from his brothers: "When his brothers saw that their father loved him more than all his brothers, they hated him, and could not speak peaceably to him" (37:4).

That the coat visually symbolizes Jacob's preference for Joseph is highlighted by the use of the verb "saw" in this sentence. The text does not say the brothers "saw" the coat or "understood" or "felt" the lack of their father's love, it says that when confronted with the coat, they immediately "saw" that their father loved Joseph best. The coat itself is a profound visual signifier of the new hierarchy Jacob chooses to establish among his sons. Joseph is not the oldest son, and as Jacob himself knows from his experience with his brother, Esau, the birthright goes to the oldest son, in this case Reuben.[3] But as with Esau, a special garment once again plays a significant role in subverting the familial order.

In what other ways is the coat symbolic? Does it express a deeper, hidden reality that Jacob sees in Joseph, or is it a way to mask Joseph's immaturity, his "*na'ar*-ishness"? Biblical Hebrew has several different terms for clothing, including *beged* and *levush*. *Begedim* are clothes that impart an image or give significance to the wearer, making it clear that this person's actions and role are important. *Levush* is used to hide something or to cover up and make someone look like more than he or she really is. So what of Joseph's coat? Most Torah scholars would argue that Joseph's *ketonet passim* clearly falls in the *beged* category, honoring Joseph as someone who grows to become a *tzaddik*, or righteous person. Joseph's brothers, however, clearly read the coat as *levush*—as both an attempt by Joseph to put on airs and as material evidence of their father's failure to see Joseph for what he really is, or at least what they perceive him to be. The coat threatens Joseph's brothers because it marks Joseph as unique, setting him apart and perhaps above the others. The root of Joseph's name can also be used to create the word *hosafa*, or "excess." As scholar Avivah Zornberg notes, the brothers are threatened by "that which is additional, unique about Joseph"—his excess, that which makes him superlative and individual.[4]

What about Joseph himself? Does the coat help him cover up his own insecurity, the pain he feels growing up without a mother? Rachel, his mother, died when he was young—indeed, one midrash suggests that the coat itself was made from the remnants of Rachel's wedding dress. Does the coat allow him to act with an authority that he is not quite up to? Does he use his flashy "queer eye" coat as a crutch to project a false public image of confidence? Certainly, the emotional maturity that Joseph shows later in the story, when he finally seems to deserve the "chosen-ness" placed on him by his father and the coat, is nowhere to be found in these early verses.

The Dreamer

Central to the introduction of the Joseph story in *Vayeshev* is the recounting of two dreams that Joseph relates to his brothers, compounding their anger and hatred. In the first, he dreams that he and his brothers were all "binding sheaves in the middle of the field": "when behold!—my sheaf arose and also remained standing; then behold!—your sheaves gathered around and bowed down to my sheaf" (37:7). Joseph's brothers immediately respond by asking, "would you then reign over us? Would you then dominate us?" (37:8), and they hate him even more.

The classic commentators note the obvious visionary reference to the future, when Joseph's brothers will indeed come and bow down before him in search of grain, and also the sense in which Joseph's "sheaf" or power arose without the help of the brothers. What they do not explore is the seeming phallic and sexual imagery in the dream, with Joseph's "sheaf" remaining "standing" firm and erect, while the brothers' sheaves fall flaccid before Joseph's phallic power. Should it come as any surprise that Joseph's brothers would be angered and threatened by the sexual challenge implied by Joseph's dream? The triumph over the brothers is here envisioned in a manner that makes explicit reference to fertility (the grain being gathered into sheaves suggests the countless progeny of Joseph's seed), implying that it is Joseph through whom the covenant of Abraham will be carried. Joseph will be the link that brings the gift of ethical monotheism to future generations, not his older brothers. Once again, a birthright is usurped and hierarchies upturned. What more obvious response for the brothers than to attempt to emasculate their brother, to strike down and figuratively castrate the usurper, the "queer"?

The brothers journey off to pasture their father's flock in Shechem, a site that resonates with sexually charged imagery as the place where their sister, Dinah, was raped and which saw the brothers' extreme and violent response of killing every male of the town as they lay in bed recovering from a process of ritual circumcision. The men guilty of penetrating Dinah are symbolically castrated through circumcision so that they can be killed in a moment of sexual and masculine lack, marking a definitive triumph of the sons of Jacob over them.[5]

The brothers, now in Shechem, conspire to kill Joseph, and when they see him coming, they say to each other, "Look! Here comes the dreamer!" They do not call him by his name or reference him as their brother; rather, they distance themselves from him, calling him out as the dreamer, the "queer," as the Other who they now disown and refuse to empathize or even speak with.

How this moment resonates as a gay bashing! The brothers here become a gang of sexually insecure men, threatened by Joseph's challenge to their procreative authority, calling out "hey dreamer/queer" before violently reestablishing control over the perceived sociosexual threat. For what is gay bashing among men but the violently graphic enactment of a psychosexual drama obsessed with phallic power, an attempt to deny the capacity of the "queer" to threaten or challenge the heteronormative paradigm, a structure in which hierarchy and patriarchy must be preserved? Is this not the very challenge that Joseph represents?

Continuing the psychosexual theatrics, the brothers throw Joseph into a pit, a space that can be understood as the feminine antiphallus, that which in a patriarchal worldview represents the symbolic opposite of the erect sheath of Joseph's dream. That vision of sexual power, fertility, and triumph is here answered by casting the dreamer/queer into the earth, deep, dark, and womblike. The brothers' attempt at a definitive emasculation of Joseph, though, fails. Instead, the pit becomes a space of (re)birth, from which Joseph emerges and continues a journey independent of his brothers, taking on a new life and a new direction. Indeed, the pit is explicitly described as having no water, reflecting the moment in childbirth when a womb ceases to nurture and becomes a space from which new life must emerge—and quickly—if it is to survive.

Although after Joseph emerges from the pit his downward spiral is nowhere near complete (he will be yet sold as a slave and later put in prison, before rising again from rock bottom), from this point forward he stands apart from his family and takes on a new identity. Having been thrown in a pit and left for dead by his brothers is the ultimate familial rupture, creating a new dividing point in Joseph's life: before this moment and after. Such a narrative of rupture and transition clearly resonates with LGBT individuals who create new identities and new families of choice when rejected by their families of origin. As is clear later in the story, Joseph, like similarly rejected LGBT people, remains scarred by the event and must undergo a personal and familial trial before reconciliation is even possible. In the end, his dream-inspired vision of triumph over his brothers does indeed come to pass. But as he sits in the pit, alone, hungry, and bereft of fraternal compassion, he must understand himself as the ultimate outsider, the ultimate Other, aggressively struck down by men so threatened by his difference that they are unable even to speak to him.

Potiphar's Purchase

With Joseph's entry into Egypt the narrative continues, once again, with sociosexual drama. This time, Joseph, no longer a *na'ar*, becomes an object of sexual intrigue and power, eliciting a frank and explicit response from the Sages.

After Joseph's brothers make a last-minute decision to pull him from the pit and sell him as a slave, Joseph makes it to Egypt, where "Potiphar, an officer of Pharaoh, captain of the guard, an Egyptian, bought him from the hands of the Ishmaelites" (39:1). Throughout the Joseph narrative we are continually reminded of just how beautiful he is. After Joseph arrives in Egypt, we are told once again that he is "well built and handsome" (39:6), just before Potiphar's wife makes a pass at him.

All these references to Joseph's good looks led the sages of the Talmud to come to a surprising conclusion about why Potiphar bought Joseph. As we are told in *Tractate Sotah* 13b, "[Potiphar] bought [Joseph] for himself; but Gabriel came and castrated [Potiphar], and then Gabriel came and mutilated him for originally his name is written Potiphar but afterwards Potiphera." Let us unpack this sentence. When the rabbis write that Potiphar bought Joseph "for himself," they are suggesting, quite explicitly, that he bought him to use sexually. Potiphar is an official of the royal court—in Hebrew the term is *saris* (*sarisim* in plural). The same term is often used in the Tanakh to refer to castrated men, or eunuchs, some of whom served as officials in royal courts. In *Tractate Sotah*, the rabbis, motivated in part by the use of this term, are arguing that the angel Gabriel castrated Potiphar to prevent him from using Joseph as a sexual object.[6]

Sexual Advances

As the Joseph saga continues, we have yet one more piece of "queer" evidence that modern readers use to promote the idea of Joseph as the "gayest" character in the Torah. Shortly after joining Potiphar's household, Potiphar's wife makes an aggressive pass at Joseph—a pass that he refuses. And this is not the only time he refuses such an advance. As the midrash says, "when Joseph went forth to rule over Egypt, daughters of kings used to look at him through the lattices and throw bracelets, necklets, ear-rings, and finger-rings to him, so that he might lift up his eyes and look at them; yet he did not look at them" (*Gen. Rab.* 98:18). Although Joseph has a wife and children, he is portrayed as sexually chaste, or at least as a man with minimal interest in women. Certainly, a man who refuses the casual advances of women in Egypt's court should not automatically be labeled gay. There are plenty of other, perfectly obvious and admittedly honorable reasons why he may refuse. Joseph gives one such reason himself, telling Potiphar's wife, "How could I do this most wicked thing, and sin before God?" thus establishing himself as an exemplar of male modesty in the Jewish tradition.[7] Still, his sexual restraint does stand out when compared to so many other stories in the Torah, even that of his own brother, Reuben, whose challenge to his father's sexual authority seems the reason for his loss of the birthright of the firstborn.

Ultimately, the psychological and sexual evidence for Joseph as a gay figure remains indirect and vague. But do we really need explicit reports of sexual behavior or ambiguous gender identity to look at Joseph in a new light? Attempts to claim Joseph as a Biblical gay forefather might be a stretch, but we *can* understand him as being in some way "queer" because Joseph shares something in common with many LGBT people. He is, in every moment of his life, a man apart—an outsider dwelling on the inside—a man chosen by his father and by God for great things.[8]

NOTES

1. Bilhah and Zilpah were both Jacob's concubines (servants or "handmaids" of Rachel and Leah, respectively) and therefore secondary in stature to his other wives, Rachel and Leah. Although Bilhah and Zilpah were the mothers of several of the twelve tribes of Israel, they are not referenced among Judaism's matriarchs (Sarah, Rebecca, Leah, and Rachel). Being associated with the sons of Bilhah and Zilpah implies a link between Joseph and those within our communities who are marginalized. The siddur of Congregation Beth Simchat Torah, New York City's LGBT-outreach synagogue, draws attention to this marginalization by inserting Bilhah and Zilpah among Judaism's matriarchs in the Amidah prayer (the addition of even the standard four matriarchs, or *imahot,* in the Amidah remains controversial among many traditional Jews).

2. The term *na'ar* is used to mean "servant" earlier in Genesis (18:7) in reference to a household servant of Abraham who helps prepare the feast for the three angels that visit Abraham and Sarah in the opening lines of *Parashat Vayera* and, later, in Exodus in reference to Joshua, Moses's "servant" (33:11). The term resurfaces later in the Joseph narrative, when Joseph becomes known as an interpreter of dreams while in prison in Egypt. Then, he is referenced as a "*na'ar ivri,*" a Jewish boy/lad (41:12), which Rashi notes as a negative term akin to "fool."

3. But Reuben has already upset the sociosexual familial hierarchy by violating Bilhah, Jacob's concubine. As it says in *Parashat Vayishlach,* "Reuben went and lay with Bilhah, his father's concubine, and Israel [Jacob] heard" (Gen. 35:22). Commentators differ in their interpretation of just what Reuben did, with some charging rape and others limiting the crime to subverting his father's authority by having attempted to move Jacob's bed from the tent of Bilhah—where Jacob had begun to sleep after the death of his beloved Rachel—to the tent of Leah (Reuben's own mother). Whatever the case, Reuben has created some rupture with his father that does not go unpunished. Reuben, of course, later attempts to remedy the situation, hoping to reestablish the bonds of love with his father. But Jacob has made his choice, and there is no turning back.

4. Avivah Gottlieb Zornberg, *The Beginning of Desire: Reflections on Genesis* (New York: Three Leaves/Doubleday, 1995), 267.

5. Although circumcision marks the covenant between God and the Israelites and can therefore be understood as an embodied and positive link to the Divine, here circumcision is used as a form of physical violence and emasculation similar to the narrative we find in 1 Samuel 18.

6. This understanding is reinforced by Joseph's seemingly boastful comment, made after Potiphar has established Joseph as master of Potiphar's household. Confronted by Potiphar's wife, Joseph replies, "there is no one greater in this house than I" (39:9), seemingly confirming that only he, and not Potiphar, maintains masculine power and authority in the household.

7. Another interpretation cited by scholar Ra'anan Abusch, related to the discussion earlier of Potiphar as a eunuch, is offered by Philo of Alexandria. In his *Legum Allegoria,* Philo suggests that Joseph himself is a sort of symbolic eunuch, given his particular career trajectory in Egypt and his sexual self-control. Philo writes, "according to another account it would be noblest to become a eunuch, if [in this way] our soul should be able to escape wickedness and unlearn passion. So Joseph too, the self controlling character when pleasure says to him 'Sleep with me and, being human, indulge in human passions and enjoy the delights that come in life's course,' refuses to comply with her." Ra'anan Abusch, "Eunuchs and Gender Transformation: Philo's Exegesis of the Joseph Narratives," in *Eunuchs in Antiquity and Beyond,* ed. Shaun Tougher (London: Duckworth, 2002), 110–111.

8. A special thank you to Tovah Leah Nachmani and my fellow students in her inspiring Chumash class at the Pardes Institute of Jewish Studies, Jerusalem, summer 2006.

TEN

Yusuf Come Home
Parashat Miketz (Genesis 41:1–44:17)

DAWN ROSE

Miketz is part two of the continuing story of the boy who was different. As Gregg Drinkwater demonstrates in his essay on *Parashat Vayeshev*, Joseph is a child with a decidedly queer set of sensibilities. He dreams of things bowing over for him and wears Technicolor robes. Not fitting into the rough-and-tumble sphere of his many brothers, he instead arouses their jealousy and their ire. Like many boys who are different, he is treated brutally by his own siblings and cast out from his home and his family. Alone in the world, he becomes a slave, is pursued for sex, and ends up in jail for no good reason.

That is where our parasha, *Miketz*, begins. Joseph is in prison, guilty of nothing but his own desirableness. But his freedom is near. Pharaoh is plagued by dreams, and Joseph is the only one who can interpret them. As reward for his unique insights, he is made vizier, Pharaoh's right-hand man. He becomes suddenly and urgently the new savior *precisely* because of who he is and what he understands from his differing perspective. The entire nation will owe its survival to the boy who was different.

Yet Joseph's transcendence is unconsummated and incomplete. Still needed is the reconciliation with brothers and father. In the flow of the Torah narrative, this re-union is necessary to explain the presence of Jacob's family (and later the Israelites) in Egypt. It is also essential for the emotional and psychological closure of the story overall. The reconciliation of family members is often akin to accepting and embracing parts of one's self and one's own history. This notion of familial reconciliation as metaphor or even allegory of an individual's full acceptance of his or her composite self becomes all the more clear if we shift our lens just slightly, from the Joseph narrative of the Torah to its parallel story of Yusuf as told in the Koran.

In the Arab Muslim tradition, as in the Torah, Yusuf is the favorite son of Yakob and the object of his brothers' bitterness. Again he is left in a pit, found, sold into slavery, and carried away into Egypt. Whereas in the Torah, it is the wife of Potiphar who desires Joseph and tries to seduce him, in the Koran she is the wife of the vizier of Egypt. Legend identifies this woman as Zulaikha, a woman who obsesses over the exquisitely beautiful Joseph all her life. Yusuf's beauty and Zulaikha's love for him have been immortalized through the centuries in Arabic poetry and visual arts.[1]

According to an important epic love poem in Arabic and in contrast to the Torah, princess Zulaikha in a faraway land first sees Yusuf in *her* dreams when she is yet a child, and she falls madly in love. In this prescient vision, Yusuf tells her he is vizier of Egypt, but he does not reveal his name. When an offer of marriage comes to her from a distant Egyptian vizier, she accepts. She discovers, too late, that the vizier she marries is not the man of her dreams. Though surrounded by servants and riches, she becomes desperately unhappy.

When Yusuf finally appears as a slave for sale in the marketplace, she recognizes the man of her dreams and pays an astronomical price to have him. Her attraction for Yusuf becomes a scandal among all the courtly women. Zulaikha plots an unusual revenge against her detractors. Inviting all the women to her courtyard, she offers them sweet oranges and provides knives with which to peel the succulent fruit. Then she has Yusuf enter. Every woman is so taken by his beauty that they forget what they are doing and cut themselves. Yusuf goes to jail, not for the sin of seduction but perhaps to protect the women from their own lust for him.

By the time Yusuf is released from prison the vizier has died and Zulaikha's fortunes have taken a radical turn. Even as Yusuf becomes ascendant as the new vizier, she is now impoverished, living in a hovel by the side of a road. She has lost her health, her looks, her hair, and her sight. Her heart is at winter. She waits each day for one thing, the passing of Yusuf with his royal retinue. At last, one day, she realizes what she must do. She throws away an idol, which she has kept from the previous vizier's household, and comes to Yusuf, repentant. They are reconciled, and she becomes his wife. Her youth, beauty, hair, and vision are restored.

In Islamic mysticism, Zulaikha represents the soul of the Sufi, the Muslim mystic longing for Allah, embodied here as the beautiful and visionary Yusuf. According to Sufism, without Allah, man's soul is like a woman without her primary love object. Thus bereft, s/he loses everything, physically, spiritually, and materially. It is only with the reunification and consummation of the seeker with her/his Beloved that all these good things return to her/him.

In this identification of the male's soul as female yearning for the male God, Islam becomes the third of the Middle Eastern and Western triumvirate—Judaism, Christianity, and Islam—to incorporate imagery involving female passion as both descriptive and prescriptive of a (male's) path to intimacy with a (basically male) God.

For example, mystical Judaism teaches that man should have desire for God and "cleave" to him in mystical and ecstatic union. This state of human-Divine union is often called *yihud*, which is also the name in the Jewish tradition of the first quiet and secluded moments a newly married couple spends together (historically the time of consummation). Even in nonmystical Judaism, the daily ritual of tefillin or phylacteries is performed while reciting the Hebrew liturgical formula for betrothal.

Similarly, in Christianity, the Catholic Church is commonly referred to as the "bride of Christ." Among evangelicals, seeking intimacy with Jesus is often called "waiting in His Bedchamber." Recently, a prominent evangelical named his umbrella organization "Bride of Christ Ministries."[2]

Given the patriarchal, homophobic, and more-than-occasional misogynistic nature of these three world religions, it behooves us to inquire why imagery of female passion has been so widely incorporated into their theologies, mythologies, and mysticisms, especially as it involves the predominantly male religious path and experience.

There are numerous possibilities, all offering helpful perspectives. One way to explain this phenomenon is as an outcome of human epistemology, which, in this approach, is necessarily bifurcated. This means that our human knowledge cannot break out of the categories in which we think we know it. If the world appears divided by male/female to the (heterosexual) majority, then knowledge—even esoteric insights into mysticism—might also categorize itself thusly.

Second, it might also be explained as a function of language, meaning we have no words to describe certain experiences except the conventional formulations of "male and female."

A third solution presents itself that is perhaps more salient to our discussion of the Joseph, or Yusuf, narrative. Whatever we call them or however we know them, each person has many parts of themselves that, however contradictorily they *appear*, work in concert to form a whole. LGBT people often are far more conversant and comfortable with these composite parts than so-called mainstream heterosexuals. It is a matter of where and how we live and the fact that we have had to develop both new knowledges and vocabularies to describe those places. For example, consider a lesbian of the "old gay" designation *soft butch*. She is a woman who sometimes likes to look butch (masculine) but does not always want to behave that way. Sometimes in romance or sexuality, a soft butch might want to experience behaving more passively (more—traditionally speaking—female) than aggressively. For a soft butch comfortable with her own look and sexuality, that mix or balance can be a perfectly agreeable stand in the world and may filter out into other parts of her life in various ways.

The presence and prominence of female passion imagery in dominantly male religions and expressions suggests—from a place of LGBT special experience, knowledge, and language—that the soft butch is not alone. Others also want to appear "masculine" while at the same time wanting, in other arenas of their lives, also to experience a more passive or "female" role. Just as a soft butch might seek to express and experience the fullness of "masculine" and "feminine" in her intimate relations, so also do a *whole lot* of other people apparently, particularly in their relationship with God. Considering that God is altogether Something Else, Wholly Other, and Entirely Ineffable, the notion of widening the experiential and relational possibilities makes human sense. We can only reach out—at least in the beginning—in the modes we have in our human repertory. And we can only comprehend that reaching out in the human categories we possess, describe it with the words we know, and image it in the narratives we inherit. Thus, we inherit and develop notions and narratives of "cleaving" and *yihud*, "brides of Christ," and Zulaikha's unending passion for Yusef in our religious traditions.

Having said all this, I think we can return to the Torah portion at hand, *Miketz*, in which Joseph is released from prison, ascends to the highest possible position in Egypt, becomes the savior of the known world, and still awaits reconciliation with his brothers and father.

My question at this point is, For whom is the reconciliation between Joseph and his family most necessary? We can say that it is Joseph. Perhaps he secretly pines for his lost family. However, it is still true that he is a ruler of Egypt, rich, powerful, already well married, blessed by God, needed and loved by all.

On the other hand, perhaps, in and outside the narrative, it is Joseph's family that is literally starving. They had a child with special sight in their midst and they cast him out. In so doing, they brutalized their own possibilities and excised a necessary part of themselves. Now they are starving, not so much because they sinned and thus deserve to starve but, rather, in the way of "what happens" after you surgically remove an integral part of yourself.

But in the light of three religious traditions, all of which have "cast out Joseph" and yet retained a part of him to bring out in relationship with God, the questions cannot stop there.

What does it mean that those individuals and communities within Judaism, Islam, and Christianity who excise and excoriate LGBT persons and tendencies yet, as men, utilize, embrace, and experience the modes and images of female passion in their own relationship to God?

Is not there a part of them left starving as well?

Do they believe men are only allowed to be female in relationship with God?

Are they themselves allowed to be "female" only certain times and places and situations?

Does all that "femaleness" that comes up from within them during those sublime moments return quietly to oblivion the remainder of the day?

If not, how do they regard it and treat it when it lingers? How do they regard and treat others for whom it cannot be confined to the intimate moments with God, Jesus, or Allah?

Is it at all possible that their spiritual/mystical relationship with God is not somehow perverted by this hypocritical inconsistency?

Can the evidence and experience—dare I say the example—of LGBT lives help lead "heterosexual" coreligionists to a more fully integrated place in their relationship with God, with others, and with LGBT people?

Finally, can Joseph's—and Yusuf's—brothers finally and fully embrace Joseph—or Yusuf—and thereby fully embrace all the parts of themselves and ready themselves for a more authentic religious fulfillment?

We are still waiting to see how this story unfolds.

NOTES

1. See Na'ama Brosh and Rachel Milstein, *Biblical Stories in Islamic Painting* (Jerusalem: Israel Museum, 1991), for both the Yusuf narrative and its integration into Arabic culture, art, and mysticism.

2. See the organization's website, www.brideofchrist.com.

ELEVEN

Forgiveness as a Queer Response

Parashat Vayigash (Genesis 44:18–47:27)

DENISE L. EGER

Parashat Vayigash is the pinnacle of the Joseph cycle of stories in the book of Genesis. Joseph, sold into slavery by his brothers, has risen to a position of power and prestige in Egypt second only to the Pharaoh himself. During a famine, Joseph's brothers make their way to Egypt to seek food. Joseph engineers for them to meet. They do not recognize their brother because many years have passed, but Joseph recognizes them. Joseph has assumed a new name—an Egyptian name—and wears Egyptian clothes. He has transformed himself from beloved child of his father, Jacob, who once dressed him in a flamboyant coat of many colors, and from Hebrew slave into the architect of the Egyptian plan for sustenance during seven years of famine.[1]

Now in *Parashat Vayigash* he is face to face with his brothers, who were so cruel to him when he was a young boy. In truth, Joseph was a bit of a bratty kid. His father favored him above the other children, and he was sent to tattle on them and check up on them as they herded the sheep far from home. But the brothers went far beyond taunting a younger brother. Not only did they plan to kill him, only to sell him into slavery instead, but they told their father that he had been killed by a beast. Now many years later, Joseph in his position of power might have arrested his brothers and either had them killed or imprisoned for their poor treatment of him. Joseph might have treated them as cruelly as they had once treated him.

But instead Joseph puts them to the test. He longs to know if his father, Jacob, and his younger, full brother, Benjamin, are alive, and he tries to see if there have been any changes in the brothers as there have no doubt been changes in his own life. He speaks harshly to them the first time he encounters them in *Parashat Miketz*, perhaps due to feelings he built up after so many years. He puts the brothers through quite an ordeal so that he can see his youngest brother, Benjamin, and orders them to bring Benjamin to Egypt as part of an alleged test to prove that they are not spies.

Yet, when they do bring Benjamin to Egypt, Joseph is so overwhelmed with emotion that he must leave their presence. So many feelings at once leave Joseph out of control, and he must regain his regal composure. Joseph, alone in Egypt all these years, now has Benjamin near him. Reconciliation with his family, which once seemed impossible, is now within his grasp. Tears of relief, joy, and sorrow, perhaps combined with the layers of anger and hurt and the grief that come from lost time, combine in Joseph as he is confronted with the presence of his family and the knowledge that his older brothers have complied. He hopes that his brothers have changed as he has changed in the intervening years.

But Joseph still needs proof, and he sets up another test of his older brothers by planting a goblet in Benjamin's bag. When the brothers try to return to Canaan to bring their father down to Egypt, Benjamin is arrested by Joseph's servants. The brothers are aghast. It is clear that in the years since they sent Joseph to Egypt they have had regrets about their behavior. They have their own families now and have matured in their relationship to one another. The brothers are distraught and upset about having to try to explain to their father, Jacob, that now the youngest son, Benjamin, will be a slave to Pharaoh's vizier in Egypt and that both of the children of Jacob's beloved Rachel are gone.

This is where our parasha begins. Joseph's brother Judah pleads for the life of Benjamin to the unknown Joseph. He tells Joseph that it will kill his father, Jacob, to have lost both sons of his beloved wife Rachel.[2] Judah's eloquence and passion and willingness to change places with Benjamin and become the slave trigger deep emotions in Joseph. It was Judah so long ago that urged the brothers not to kill Joseph but to sell him into slavery, and now Judah is willing to become a slave himself to protect the life of Benjamin. Judah's voice engenders a moment of transformation for Judah as well. Once so long ago he was willing to sell Joseph. Now he himself protects a brother from servitude. In that moment Judah's words atone for the past; clearly this is a moment of *teshuvah*, repentance for the previous actions toward Joseph.

Joseph realizes the significance of the moment as well. At that moment he can no longer keep toying with his brothers. Joseph realizes that the past must remain the past but that only through revealing his true identity can he make his family whole again. He sees that there has been change among the brothers and also that his own actions could cause harm to his father. He understands that forgiveness can lead to reconciliation with his family, and he is able to see that his brothers too are ready to accept their role in the events of the past. Joseph can recognize that family is family, no matter how estranged they may have become. And now it is within his grasp to rebuild the family tie.

Joseph can no longer keep up the masquerade. "Joseph could no longer restrain himself before all who were standing in attendance on him" (Gen. 45:1). "I am Joseph," he says (Gen. 45:3). And in his revelation and his brothers' astonishment is a moment of true reconciliation. Joseph throws off his Egyptian royal identity and reclaims his connection with his family. And they, now matured and parents themselves, perhaps could stand in their own father's place, understanding what it might mean to rediscover a child.

With these words, "I am Joseph," Joseph reveals his true self, his true identity. Joseph reconnects with his past not only by his brothers' presence but inside himself to claim his place in the family. His revelation is met with astonishment and fear, weeping and ultimately reunion. The reunion is with his brothers, but it is also so much more. It represents reconciliation of self, of true identity. Joseph had hid his familial ties as a Hebrew perhaps because it was too painful to feel the rejection of his brothers or perhaps because a Hebrew slave had no real place in Egyptian society. But now Joseph can finally speak freely in Egypt about his God and his family. He connects with his roots, bringing them into his present. Joseph has his own journey of maturity in this parasha, and Pharaoh is so pleased to see him at peace and happy with himself that he grants to Joseph and his family a choice area of Egypt in which to dwell.

Joseph had been tormented by his family and banished because of who he was. Yet Joseph did not let his family paralyze him. His faith in his God and his willingness to utilize his own resources and talents helped him manage his differences in Egypt. Joseph utilized his God-given skill as a dream interpreter to create a different reality from that of a mere slave. He persevered despite his differences in faith and language from the Egyptians by using his talents to make a new life for himself. But Joseph also is able to keep open the idea of hope, that one day he might find a place in his family again.

Joseph, like many of us when confronted with the past, at first wants to repay in kind the hurt that was done to him. This kind of revenge is human nature. But Joseph overcomes this tendency. He lets his compassion and faith uphold him so that he stops short of replaying a terrible cycle of revenge. He allows himself to feel the love of his family even though they hurt him deeply. He can open his eyes up beyond his own disappointment and anger to see that the brothers who appear before him in Egypt are different from the brothers who sold him into slavery so many years before, acknowledging their changes along with his own. Joseph becomes self-aware and does not let the trauma of the past keep him reacting with childish habits.

In many ways Joseph's ability to learn this lesson trumps his father, who, though reunited briefly with his brother Esau, did not live among his brother and his people after their encounter.

Joseph's ability to forgive the wrongs done to him allows him to be all of himself— a Hebrew who lives as an Egyptian prince while revealed to his family. He tells his brothers as a sign of his forgiveness, "Do not be distressed or reproach yourselves because you sold me hither; it was to save life that God sent me ahead of you" (Gen. 45:4). Joseph is able to call on his faith as a way to frame his forgiveness.

In their moment of reconciliation, Joseph and his brothers begin a new kind of understanding. Joseph is able to resettle the entire family in Egypt. Through the act of forgiveness, Joseph's alienation from his family is alleviated, and the brothers who so cruelly treated him can find a new life in Egypt for themselves and for their own children. This message should not escape us. Forgiveness of family members has implications not just for those involved but for future generations. If we can find a way to forgive and to overcome the pains of the past rather than be stopped by them, perhaps our own lives will be lived with a new kind of fullness. Certainly this was true for Joseph, who overcame his past, refusing to allow his own anger and hurt to keep him down. Perhaps Joseph's story is a model for how LGBT Jews might grow into our own adulthoods, accepting ourselves and demanding our own place in our families.

But as LGBT Jews demand a place in family, Joseph's story also invites them to utilize forgiveness, reconciliation, and faith in the name of repairing the soul.

NOTES

1. In the rabbinic and midrashic tradition Joseph still clings quietly to the faith of his own ancestors while living an assumed lifestyle as an Egyptian.

2. Jacob had four wives, Leah, Rachel, Zilpah, and Bilhah.

TWELVE

Uncovering Joseph's Bones
Parashat Vayechi (Genesis 47:28–50:26)

JILL HAMMER

The beginning of Genesis promises us a story. It begins with the birth of the world and the blessings that the Holy One bestows on creation. The end of Genesis is about the memory of the story. *Parashat Vayechi*, the final parasha of Genesis, focuses on Jacob's deathbed blessings and the burial of Joseph. As the Israelites prepare for their long stay in Egypt, the tribe is sustained by the memories and teachings of the elders as they leave from the world of the living. The "beginning of all things" has become a steady progression of generations, and as one generation departs, it offers wisdom to the new generation that arises. The story continues because those who hear the story remember.

How will queer Jews remember? Only a few Biblical tales and rabbinic texts even hint at a queer Jewish story. Queer lives and memories are only beginning to be part of the Jewish landscape. Where are elders to be found? How are queer stories, values, ideas to be passed from one generation to the next? What can stories of tribal legacy mean to those whose spiritual, romantic, and family unions were shut out of Jewish life and even obliterated from history? *Parashat Vayechi* holds some answers to these questions, as it relates the story of blessings—and of bones.

The parasha signals its concern with memory from the outset. As the story opens, the aged Jacob, living in Egypt amid a large family, senses that he will soon die. Remembering his homeland, Jacob asks Joseph to bury him in the land of Israel, in the cave of Machpelah: "When I lie down with my fathers, carry me from Egypt and bury me in their grave" (Gen. 47:30). Through this request, Jacob shows his desire to connect with those who are part of his tribal story: his grandfather, Abraham; his parents, Rebekah and Isaac; and his wife, Leah.

Then, Jacob takes steps to ensure that his beloved Rachel's memory will never be forgotten, by adopting Joseph's two sons (Jacob and Rachel's grandchildren) as his own sons. He conducts a ceremony with Joseph's sons Ephraim and Manasseh, formally making them his heirs instead of Joseph, so that they will both inherit alongside his biological sons. This means that Rachel will be the mother of three tribes: Ephraim, Manasseh, and Benjamin. Jacob honors Rachel by making sure that a larger number of tribes remembers Rachel as a foremother.

Then Jacob proceeds to bless all his (male) progeny. Some—such as Judah and Joseph—he blesses with prosperity and leadership ability. Others—such as Asher,

Issachar, and Zebulun—he blesses with close connection to the land. Still others, such as Benjamin and Dan, will be warriors. Jacob reserves his angry comments for Reuben, Simeon, and Levi, the first-, second-, and third-born of Jacob and Leah. Reuben has had sex with Bilhah, Jacob's concubine. Simeon and Levi massacred the townsfolk of Shechem to avenge their sister Dinah's rape. In blessing the tribes, Jacob makes sure that the truth is not covered over. Rather, he chooses to remember honestly.

Memory is at the center of *Parashat Vayechi*. The stakes are high, for if the people do not remember, they will blend into Egyptian life, and the unique blessings of the descendants of Abraham and Sarah will be lost. Because of this danger, Jacob does his best to remember—though he is not the one who ensures the memory and continuity of the tribe. Jacob has given his children his good wishes, his blessing, even his anger, but it is Joseph—the queerest of all Genesis characters—who gives the newborn tribe the gift of memory.

We learn early on about Joseph that he is as beautiful as his mother, Rachel, and that he owns a multicolored coat. The only other Biblical personality who wears such a coat is a woman—Tamar, princess of the house of David. Midrash paints Joseph as a potentially gender-queer person: he "penciled his eyes, curled his hair, and lifted his heel" (*Gen. Rab.* 84:7). He's also one of the only Biblical men known for *not* sleeping with a woman (the wife of Potiphar). But even more to the point, Joseph is a "queer" Jew. His identity is mixed. He has an Egyptian name (*Tzafnat-paaneach*), speaks Egyptian, and wears Egyptian clothes. He marries Asnat, the daughter of an Egyptian priest.

Just look at Joseph's death scene as compared to Jacob's. Jacob's family bears him in pomp and circumstance to the land of Israel, where he is interred in the family tomb: "His children carried him to the land of Canaan, and buried him in the cave in the field of Machpelah, which Abraham had bought" (Gen. 50:13). The wailing for Jacob lasts seven days, and the Egyptian officers and Canaanite onlookers who attend the funeral are impressed. Jacob achieves what every patriarch hopes for: a grand tomb and offspring who remember him.

Joseph, on the other hand, has a very queer burial. He lives to see his great-grand-children, yet on his deathbed he does not bless his descendants. Instead, he summons his brothers. He says to them, "'I am dying, yet the Eternal will surely remember you and bring you up from this land to the land the Eternal promised to Abraham, Isaac, and Jacob.' So Joseph made the children of Israel swear: 'When God has remembered you, you shall raise up my bones from this place'" (Gen. 50:25). Then Joseph dies. The very last words of Genesis state, "Joseph died at the age of one hundred and ten years and was embalmed and placed in a coffin in Egypt" (Gen. 50:26).

This "end" of Genesis is the largest ellipsis in Biblical literature. Joseph is the one who rises and descends and rises again. We observe this cycle in his life story. As a young man, he is elevated above his brothers. Then, in their jealousy, his brothers throw him into a pit and sell him into slavery. Joseph is made head slave of an official's household, then thrown into prison because his master's wife falsely accuses him of rape—another tale of ascent and descent. Then, suddenly, he becomes viceroy over Egypt. His "last" descent is his death. Though he is buried, his burial is not final. The Hebrew people will carry his bones out of Egypt as they are redeemed. The burial and raising of Joseph's bones is one more reminder that Joseph is a symbol for the circle of life and death, victory and defeat, despair and redemption. Like the grain he stores to feed the hungry, Joseph is cut down and replanted again and again. But why does he need to do it one last time? Why does he want his bones disturbed?

The political truth is that Joseph cannot be buried in the land of Israel. He is an Egyptian potentate, and it would be impolitic for him to ask to be buried in Jacob's tomb. But there is a spiritual truth to this burial as well. Joseph knows that it takes more than a blessing to keep a people's identity alive in a foreign land for four hundred years, under the harsh conditions of slave labor. By insisting that he be buried in the land of Israel, not immediately but generations later, Joseph forces his descendants to remember that they made a promise; thus, the people will remember who they are and that they will one day be free.

Joseph reminds his people, through the presence of his bones, of how many times he descended and how many times he ascended, becoming ever more powerful. Joseph's descent and ascent show us that we too can grow and change.

More powerfully, Joseph asks the people to remember that *God will remember*. Joseph asks not only that his family remember him but that they remember that memory is a Divine attribute. Just as they remember the promise they made to take up Joseph's bones and bear them to the land of Israel, the Shekhinah will remember her promise to raise up the people and bring them out of Egypt to the land of their ancestors.

Yet the people do forget Joseph. When Moses comes from the land of Midian to redeem the Hebrews, the people are in despair. Only an old woman, Serach, the daughter of Asher, remembers that Joseph once said, "The Divine will surely remember you," and she tells the Israelites to trust in the freedom that Moses offers:

> What made them believe? The sign of [God's] redemption that had been told to them. They had this sign as a tradition from Jacob, Jacob having handed down the secret to Joseph, and Joseph to his brothers, while Asher, the son of Jacob, had handed down the secret to his daughter Serach, who was still alive. This is what he told her: "Any redeemer that will come and say to my children: pakod yifkod ("will surely remember") shall be regarded as a true deliverer." (*Ex. Rab.* 5:13)

This woman Serach is the rememberer of the tribe. She has lived to be so old, legend says, because it was she who told her grandfather Jacob that Joseph was alive—and Jacob rewarded her with eternal life. Serach brings the repressed truth to light. She tells the story everyone else has forgotten.

When the Hebrews are preparing to leave Egypt, it is Serach who remembers the bones of Joseph. A midrash tells how she guides Moses to the Nile, where the Egyptians have sunk Joseph's coffin. The Egyptians of Joseph's generation put the coffin in the Nile, so the Israelites will never be able to find it and, thus, will never be able to leave. But Serach foils their plan.

How did Moses know where Joseph's grave was to be found? They say that only Serach daughter of Asher had survived from that generation, and that she revealed to Moses where Joseph's grave was located. The Egyptians had made a metal coffin for him and then sunk it into the Nile. Moses went to the bank of the Nile . . . and called out, "Joseph, Joseph, the time has come for the Holy One to redeem his children. The Shekhinah and Israel and the clouds of glory await you. If you will reveal yourself, good, but if not, we shall be free of your vow that we should carry your bones with us to Canaan." Then Joseph's coffin floated to the surface. (*Midrash Tanchuma Yelammedenu*, Ex. 4:2)

It is as if Moses reminds Joseph that for memory to be valuable, it has to be able to move forward into the future. Memory cannot be a heavy burden on the people, like a lead coffin. It has to be light and portable, so that it can be carried into a new generation and a new reality. Joseph's coffin rises, showing that the memory of the past can be part of a reborn people.

As we read the "end" of *Parashat Vayechi*—"Joseph died at the age of one hundred and ten years and was embalmed and placed in a coffin in Egypt"—we see that it is not an end at all. Hundreds of years after his death, Joseph will summon his people to remember their ancestors, their past, their story. His coffin will be borne in honor alongside the Ark that bears the presence of the Shekhinah. He will be buried in the land of Israel, in the city of Shechem—the city where, long ago, he began his search for his brothers.

Joseph teaches us that remembering is as important as physical survival in establishing identity. Jewish memory encodes itself in text, in liturgy, in folktales and music and dance, in every way that humans express themselves. Queer folk too must find the gift of memory, even when memory has been repressed. We must search for the bones of our queer ancestors wherever they are hidden. We cannot leave Egypt without them, for when memories are lost or blotted out, a part of the tribal truth is obscured. Joseph is a messenger to LGBT Jews not (only) because the sages imagined that he curled his hair but because his bones waited hundreds of years for his people to find them. We now have the opportunity to be modern-day Serachs and show others where the bones of our ancestors may be found.

Memory is critical to creating positive LGBT identity, just as it is to a positive Jewish identity. A general reading list in LGBT spiritual history should include the Greek female poet Sappho, who loved women and poetry in ancient Greece; John Boswell's *Same-Sex Unions in Pre-Modern Europe*, which documents how same-sex marriage ceremonies occurred all over Christian Europe until the 15th century; and books about how Native American tribes made space for "two-spirited people" and those with a transgendered identity. Ritual and spirituality can be and have been applied to LGBT people, many times over. It is not true, as some people assert, that homosexuality is an ultramodern, ultraliberal 20th-century invention.

What is true of the larger world is also true of Jewish society. Talmudic tales of Rabbi Yochanan and Reish Lakish have homoerotic tropes. The poetry of male Jewish scholars of Muslim Spain expressed love and admiration for young men. In the 11th century, Yishaq ben Mar-Shaul wrote of one object of his admiration: "Lovely of eyes like David / he has slain me like Uriah."[1] Jews were writing what might be called queer literature hundreds of years ago, using the same midrashic images that have characterized Jewish imagination for millennia. Meanwhile, Maimonides notes the existence of lesbian-living women in Cairo in the 10th century, warning men to keep their wives away from such women, lest they be seduced! "A man should be strict with his wife in this matter, and should prevent women who are known to engage in this practice from visiting her."[2] Even this stern admonition shows that LGBT Jews have a presence in history. The bones of our queer Jewish ancestors lie waiting to be found.

Queer Jewish history is not yet part of a normative Jewish education. Like Joseph, these pieces of our history lie beneath the river of time, waiting for us to call out to them and say, "The Shekhinah and Israel and the clouds of glory await you." May all our ancestors one day reveal to us their bones.

NOTES

1. Norman Roth, "'Deal Gently with the Young Man': Love of Boys in Medieval Hebrew Poetry of Spain," *Speculum* 57:1 (1982): 31.
2. Maimonides, Mishneh Torah, *Issurei Biah* 21:8.

PART II

SHEMOT

The Book of Exodus

THIRTEEN

Making Noise for Social Change
Parashat Shemot (Exodus 1:1–6:1)

ELLIOT KUKLA

I was raised in a culturally Jewish family that practiced Buddhism. When I was a small child we lived in Hawaii, and my family was involved with a Tibetan Buddhist temple housed in a beautiful wooden building painted orange, red, gold, and green. It was located in the midst of a lush rain forest, ringed by a rolling lawn that had been carved out of the trees. Inside the temple there was a dimly lit, barefooted, hushed atmosphere. An altar was filled with photographs of Tibetan monks, bowls of fragrant fruit offerings, and curling tendrils of incense.

In the middle of the green lawn hung a large brass gong that was periodically rung to signal the beginning of feasts and celebrations. When I was five years old, I developed a bad habit. While the adults were inside in silent meditation, I used to sneak into the middle of the lawn and ring the gong. This happened often enough that the problem came to the attention of the Rimpoche, the spiritual leader, of the temple. He asked to speak to the small, chubby gong-ringer, and I was summoned to his room for a private chat.

I was terrified. My parents dropped me off at the doorway of his chamber, and I entered trembling. I was braced to be humiliated by this religious authority figure. But when Rimpoche began speaking, he told me that gong-ringing per se was not a bad thing. He told me that he could see that I had a lot of energy, a lot of anger that could be used to change the world. The key in growing up, he told me, would be to figure out the right moments to ring the gong and when I needed to respect the silence.

Even after years of rabbinical school and advanced Jewish study, this simple teaching remains one of the most influential religious lessons that I have ever received. As an adult, what I gleaned from his message is that there are times for each of us to sit in silent meditation. And then there are moments when we are called to make as much noise as possible, in order to call attention to exactly who we are and how we want our world to be. Ringing a gong at the wrong moment (like I did) is a mistake, but so is failing to sound one when the situation calls for it.

Although I learned this lesson from a Buddhist teacher, Judaism has its own form of gong-ringing. We find an example in *Parashat Shemot*, which tells the story of the people's crying out for liberation and change. The first verses of the portion open the second book of the Bible with a terse and action-packed account of both the beginning of the Israelites' oppression as slaves in Egypt and the seeds of their liberation. In just a few opening verses, the Israelites grow into a flourishing nation, threaten the Egyptian oligarchy, and become enslaved. This passage (Exodus 1:1–14) tells a primal tale of subjugation that has been repeated in various forms throughout history. At first the Hebrew people become a powerful minority group within the nation: "The Israelites were fertile and prolific; they multiplied and increased more and more, so that the land was filled with them" (Ex. 1:7). According to many of the medieval commentators on this text, including the pivotal medieval commentators Ibn Ezra and Rashbam, the nearly synonymous verbs used in this verse for fertility ("were fertile and prolific" and "they multiplied and increased") indicate the ample abundance and hardiness of the growing Hebrew nation. The language of this verse echoes the narrative of the creation of the world in Genesis (Gen. 1:20, 28) and suggests abundant fertility—the rapid creation of a Jewish world within the world of the Egyptians.

In the next verse, we learn that a new Pharaoh who does not "know" Joseph arose over Egypt. The Hebrew word *yada*, "to know," is central to the Exodus narrative, and it appears more than twenty times in the following fourteen chapters. The implication here is that the new leader of Egypt does not have a personal relationship with the Hebrews and sees them as a faceless mob to be controlled. Fearing an uprising within the growing group, he begins to repress the people and keep them weak with harsh labor.

The first step out of this classic story of repression does not come from God, or from a charismatic leader, but from the people themselves, who decide that it is a moment to "ring the gong" and cry out in protest. In the next chapter we read, "The Israelites, *they were groaning* from their bondage and *they shouted* out and *their wail* for help from the oppression went up to God. And God heard *their moaning*" (Ex. 2:24–25; emphasis added). Four different nearly synonymous verbs are used in these verses for crying out. Although each of these verbs is unique, they all appear in the plural form: *they* groaned, *they* shouted, *their* wail, *their* moaning. In my reading, the unusual language of this verse implies that while the Hebrew people were crying out collectively, many different types of voices were lifted up to God. The image that this passage offers is of a diverse chorus—tenors, altos, sopranos, and baritones; groaners, shouters, wailers, and moaners—who all came together to send a harmonized message to the Divine to say that it was time for change.

This message is received, and the very next verse reads, "God looked upon the Israelites and God *knew* them [*Va'yar Elohim et b'nei yisrael v'yada Elohim*]" (Ex. 2:25). In this context, the verb *yada* suggests that God knows and understands the suffering of the Israelites. God takes notice of each unique voice in pain and is moved to action. In the following chapter, God speaks to Moses out of a burning bush and sets into motion the events of the Exodus.

As has so often been the case at various points in history, the seeds of oppression began with an effacement of individuality. The Pharaoh enslaved the Israelites because he did not "know" them (Ex. 1:8). Their redemption begins with a wild, uncontainable assertion of individuality of voice when the people cry out in a harmony (or perhaps cacophony?) of unique voices (Ex. 2:24). Unlike the Pharaoh, God responds to these cries by "knowing" the Israelites, hearing their distinctive voices and understanding the particularities of their pain.

This message is relevant for the story of Jewish oppression and redemption, as well as for the history of LGBT liberation. LGBT liberation also includes moments of uncontainable crying out of dissimilar voices. Sylvia Rivera, a transgender woman and early gay-rights activist who was at the Stonewall Inn in New York City the night of the riot in 1969 that sparked the modern LGBT liberation movement, said in an interview with LGBT activist Leslie Feinberg, "We were not taking any more of this shit. . . . It was time. It was street gay people from the Village out front—homeless people who lived in the park in Sheridan Square outside the bar—and then drag queens behind them and everybody behind us" (*Workers World,* July 2, 1998). The moment that Rivera is describing mirrors the Israelites' calling out in *Parashat Shemot*: a group of varied and highly marginalized individuals coming together to cry out for change.

Oppression, both literally and metaphorically, has silenced queer voices throughout history. Gay essayist David Sedaris writes about being pulled out of class in order to take part in speech-therapy lessons for his lisping voice. After a few months of torturous enforced lessons Sedaris notices that there was a distinct pattern in which students were tapped for speech therapy and suggests that the sign on the door ought to read "Future Homosexuals of America."

> None of the therapy students were girls. They were all boys like me who kept movie star scrapbooks and made their own curtains. . . . At the beginning of the school year, while we were congratulating ourselves on successfully passing for normal, Agent Samson [the speech therapist] was taking names as our assembled teachers raised their hands, saying, "I've got one in my homeroom," and, "There are two in my fourth period math class." . . . Did they hope that by eliminating our lisps, they might set us on a different path, or were they trying to prepare us for future stage and choral careers? (Sedaris, "Go Carolina," in *Me Talk Pretty One Day* [New York: Back Bay, 2001], 12)

Sedaris's story illustrates the pressure to "pass" that many queer folks experience throughout our lives. The term *passing* is used by different social groups to express the pressure to appear as something we are not (or not simply): being seen as gentile when we are Jewish, passing as middle class when we are poor, and being related to as straight when we are queer. In the transgender community, *passing* refers to being seen as one's preferred male or female gender as opposed to either being recognized as trans or being identified with the gender we were assigned at birth. Although all these experiences are unique, what they have in common is the opportunity to move through the world being seen as someone who has a different (and usually more privileged) set of experiences.

Queer folks, Jews, and queer Jews are particularly used to passing. Both queer and Jewish identities are not necessarily (or not always) visible. Although some of us might not have a choice about being seen as queer and/or Jewish in all places and at all times, others have the mixed blessing of passing when we choose to. As a child I remember my grandmother, who was a Holocaust survivor, complimenting me over and over on the fact that I "didn't look Jewish." The stories of Matthew Shepard, Brandon Teena, and countless other LGBT people who have been murdered because of their identities tragically illustrate that many people need to pass in order to survive. However, sometimes we keep passing out of habit, because we have internalized all the messages telling us to conform.

For queer people in the 21st century there are many ways to pass. In a world of increasing legislative and social advances, passing may not be about appearing straight but about appearing "just like everybody else." In general, I think the capacity to pass within the mainstream signifies positive advances—everyone should be able to marry their partner if they choose to, and certainly no one should have to fear for their lives. Passing is often the only (or the best) option available to us. My grandmother's anxiety around "looking Jewish" was one that I have never really lived with, and I thank God for having been born in a different era. However, there have been moments that I have feared for my life because of "looking trans." In those moments (at international borders, on deserted streets, in public bathrooms) I pray for the capacity to pass as someone who is not transgender.

And yet Jewish tradition teaches that there is spiritual value in the refusal to pass, in the insistence in looking and sounding different. The second book of the Torah is known as Exodus in English, referring to the external action in the text—the story of leaving Egypt and travelling through the desert to the Promised Land. But in Hebrew it is known as *Shemot*, "names," a reference to its deeper, internal meaning. In Judaism, names signify individuality, the uniqueness of each person. In the world of *Parashat Shemot*, the story of leaving Egypt begins with the lifting of diverse voices and the persistent claim to be seen and "known" by name in the fullest sense of the word.

Last year at Kol Nidre I delivered a sermon on the power of diversity. Afterward, in the swirling crowd, I felt someone tug at my jacket. I turned around to find a nine-year-old boy in lavender, shiny Powerpuff Girls sneakers. "I really liked your sermon," he whispered before disappearing into the crowd. During Sukkot his mom told me that he had been hassled about his shoes at school all week, but after hearing my sermon he had decided to keep wearing them. I do not really think it was my words that affected him but the visual power of a gender-nonconforming rabbi on the bimah. It took years of struggle by LGBT activists refusing to look or sound like everybody else that allowed me to be standing there that night.

Wearing lavender sneakers may seem like a small, quiet statement. But I do not think it is so in the fourth grade. It is this type of insistence on being fully ourselves and lifting our quirky, distinctive voices and instincts, in the face of vast social pressures, on which the story of the Exodus is built. It is a moment of gong-ringing that (unlike my five-year-old rebellion) was perfectly timed.

I learned as a chubby young gong-ringer that sometimes we need to be silent. There are moments when queer folks need to learn how not to see ourselves as outsiders on the lawn but to sit quietly inside the sanctuary with other people. There are times when it is more important to connect with others across lines of difference and diversity than loudly to proclaim who we are. The Israelites spent hundreds of peaceful years within Egypt before a new king arose and oppressed them. In those years they did not need constantly to announce their minority status, as they lived peaceably within the empire, building deep ties of empathy and relationship with the Egyptian ruling class.

However, there are also times, such as this week's parasha, for gong-ringing, moments when we need to shout out in all our purple-sneaker glory who we are and how we want our world to see us. Resisting social pressure in the fourth grade is one of those moments of gong-ringing world change. I imagine this small boy striding to school in his Powerpuff Girls sneakers standing on the shoulders of previous generations: David Sedaris and his persistently lisping voice, Sylvia Rivera fighting back at Stonewall, and the Israelite people calling out—each with a distinctive voice, to demand an immediate end to slavery and an immediate, expansive liberation.

FOURTEEN

Uncircumcized Lips
Parashat Vaeira (Exodus 6:2–9:35)

JHOS SINGER

Behold the children of Israel have not listened to me, so how
will Pharaoh listen to me??? And I have uncircumcised lips!!
—Exodus 6:12

What a provocative image—uncircumcised lips. What could it possibly mean? To my imagination, this verse both sexualizes and constrains Moses. He is poised to speak, to deliver a message that could change the world, and he falters. He is either going to remain silent, be misunderstood, or have to slice away the foreskin of his mouth. I imagine him holding still, unspeaking, keeping his truth inside, eyes darting, heart racing, breath shallow. I imagine him mumbling, straining to be heard, but met with furrowed and confused brows. I imagine him with a ruby wound around his freed lips, speaking in agony, his beard streaked crimson. I can feel his frustration, desperation, and anger at having been chosen to deliver God's message of liberation. After all, it is not so unlike having to come out, again and again and again. . . .

Parashat Vaeira details the early days of Moses's leadership and the dramatic beginning stage of the liberation of the Israelite slaves from bondage in Egypt. The opening dialogue begins after Moses's initial (and unsuccessful) attempts at liberating the Israelites. God is giving him a reassuring pep talk.[1] But Moses snaps back, "Behold the children of Israel have not listened to me, so how will Pharaoh listen to me??? And I have uncircumcised lips!!" (Ex. 6:12).

The phrase Moses uses is "*Ani aral s'fataim*," which literally translates as "I am [of] uncircumcised lips." *Aral* means "foreskinned" or "uncircumcised," though it can also mean "blocked," "sealed," or "impeded."[2] This same word occurs in other places in the Torah to mean: unyielding (Lev. 26:41), restricting (Ex. 19:23), or a foreskin itself (Gen. 17:10–11). *Aral* is alternately defined as restrict power/lose control.[3] *S'fataim* literally means "lips," though it can also mean "speech" or "edge."[4] Blocked speech, sealed lips, unyielding edge, restricted power, lose control . . . As a queer person, I find these images altogether too familiar. How many times have I found myself in an awkward social situation or encountered a homophobic joke or listened to a sexist remark only to feel myself go silent, feel my power drain out of me, or lose my voice? How is it that I can know myself so well, be so firmly at home in my gender freakiness, and yet find myself back in the closet in the blink of an eye?

I have officiated in some very high-end, blingy, glitzy, expensive weddings. It is always a bit odd for me, having grown up poor; I am often torn at fashionable events. One part of me loves being in the midst of such luxury, marveling at the myriad ways an orchid can dress up a plate, sipping fine wine, indulging in exquisite cuisine, and dancing the night away. The sheer extravagance and delicacy of it is truly thrilling and totally beyond my own means. Unfortunately, I never quite feel I belong. There is always some twitchy part of me thinking, "Hmmm, wonder when someone is gonna notice I'm a queer street rat and throw me outta here?" Like Moses, I have found myself in circumstances in which my sociological roots clash wildly with my good fortune. I usually look for some other outlier to chat with just to play it safe.

During the reception at one such wedding, I engaged in a conversation with the born-in-Poland-in-1928, escaped-to-Argentina-in-1938, emigrated-to-Israel-in-1950, and retired-in-the-United-States-in-1980 grandmother of the well-heeled, Prince Charming–esque groom. It was a storybook wedding, dazzling with gems and beautiful people, the Pacific Ocean stretched out below us, the temperature made perfect by a balmy midsummer zephyr. Dreamy. Grandmama was very happy with the wedding, and she took my elbow while saying, "Rabbi, rabbi . . . Ach, in all my days, zis vas zeh most beautiful vedding ceremony, so, rabbi, tell me about yourself."

Of course I was charmed. I told her how I had come to perform her grandson's wedding, where I studied, where I lived, how many goats I tended. . . . "Ach, you are a vonder, such a beautiful ceremony. I am zo grateful." She sipped her martini and regaled me with tales about her life. I was enthralled and captivated by her sass and strength. I felt the enormity of her life story, saw the miracle of every perfectly coiffed gray hair and the agony of every wrinkle. In that moment she represented the most resilient, proud, and beautiful aspects of Judaism: femininity, age, and family. She radiated Divine presence, and for a second, my guard was down.

She began to speak about her children, telling an anecdote about her second pregnancy that was remarkably similar to my pregnancy tale of woe, and I felt an intense connection. In that moment we were one, and I completely forgot that I am a transgendered man who has experienced pregnancy and is no longer a woman in polite company. Unfettered and unselfconsciously, I blurted out, "I know what you mean—when I was pregnant, that happened to me too!"

She looked at me with eyes that had seen everything but this and shot back, "Tzeh! And since when does a man get pregnant!?" The spell snapped, the connection cracked, my face flushed, and suddenly I had uncircumcised lips. I laughed dully, and stupidly stuttered, "Oh, uh, you know, I mean, when my, uh, wife, yeah my WIFE, was, uh, pregnant. . . ." She looked at me suspiciously. The conversation ended abruptly. I wandered off, with my spirit retreating into a dark and musty closet packed full of cackling Pharaohs and groaning Israelites. And, of course, God. Good old God rattling around my closet, saying, "Now you get back out there and tell them I sent YOU to tackle homophobia and all its variations. Scat! Get! Go on, now! Don't worry, I'll be with you, just get your tranny tuchas back out there and tell the Truth!" My reply? *Ani? Ani aral s'fataim!*

Coming out is a lifelong process. Most of us have to come out about something—whether or not it is connected to our gender, affectional nature, or sexuality. Some of us converted to Judaism, are former Chassidim, or have placed children for adoption; others have been incarcerated, have track marks, or have any number of former identities hanging up in our old closets. Telling our story, being honest about who and what we have been, we blow minds and stereotypes. "You're a lesbian?!? But you are so, well, pretty." "Dad, did mommy know that Richard used to be your boyfriend?" "You could have knocked me over with a feather when I found out he was born a woman!" Every time we come out or show up as our true self, we are carrying out an act of social revolution, challenging the status quo, taking on Pharaoh. And like Moses, most of us are ill prepared for the task.

Upending the Egyptian power structure in 1250 BCE would have been a daunting task for a proven leader whose skills had been tried, tested, and honed; yet the task is given to Moses, who had spent years hiding out in Midian, tending goats. His life up to that point had been a strange combination of poverty[5] and privilege,[6] passion[7] and pastoralism (Ex. 3:1), random acts of kindness[8] and senseless moments of brutality.[9] It does not seem that he was groomed or trained in politics or social reform. So I have to wonder: how did Moses end up as the head of this endeavor?

Perhaps it was as simple as this: he has a moment of epiphany. Out in the desert, Moses "turns aside" from the well-beaten path of his life and turns his attention to a mysterious blaze (God, brilliantly disguised as a burning bush). A voice calls him, "Moses, Moses." He answers, "*Hineini* [Behold me, here I am]" (Ex. 3:1–4). For one fragile moment, Moses is illuminated. Fully present and bathed in light, Moses "comes in."[10] And perhaps Moses, for one crystalline instant, fully integrates the disparate parts of his life. For a moment, he seems to be in the dominion of wholeness and truth, fully present, ready to serve. But then God starts talking, making demands, and Moses hides his face. The reverie is broken.

As it happens, this Divine call is not for Moses's benefit alone—far from it. God says, in essence, "Son, you and I are going to change the world!" (Ex. 3:6–10). God has chosen Moses, not for personal spiritual enlightenment but rather to lead a socioeconomic-cultural revolution. Moses balks: "Who am I that I should go to Pharaoh and free the Israelites from Egypt?" (Ex. 3:11).

God does not answer that question but simply assures Moses that he will have Divine support (Ex. 3:12). Later, more backup arrives; Moses's brother Aaron is signed up to be the spokesman of the movement (Ex. 4:14–17). Moses is poised to launch: Divine revelation? Check. Heavenly host? Check. Ground support? Check. Roll it out, we are off to topple the dominant paradigm.

Many of us in the queer community are very much like Moses at this stage in his life. We are sexualized and constrained the minute our nature is known, and the only way to become less exotic is through radical social change. Flawed and undertrained for the job of ridding the world from the scourge of homophobia, sexism, and intolerance; nevertheless, if you are queer, you have been appointed to do just that. Being queer often starts with a flash of self-realization. At some point, we experience a moment of personal clarity about who we are, which forever changes the way we interact with the world. We fall in love, we begin to live our truth, and just like that, we have turned and stepped off the established path of gender and affection norms forever. Our "coming in" instantly impels us to "come out"—to tell our story, to challenge Pharaoh to free our people. Some of us, like Aaron, will immediately blaze forward and become full-time professional queers, and thank God for that! But the bulk of us will stumble, bumble along, wondering how anything as personal as whom we love or how we feel in our own skins is anybody's business. Who would not want to bask in the glow of wholeness and never have to come out, ever? Most of us would like to just stay in Midian, minding our own business, as if nothing had happened. But we have to leave, and we have to go back to Egypt. Like Moses, we will question God when God tells us we are the right person for the job, and balking quietly we will head out for Egypt.

We go back to Egypt every time we show up at a PTA meeting as a queer family, every time we introduce our partner, every time we push for unisex bathrooms, every time we reveal our truth. Each time we come out, we are taking on the daunting task of reshaping the hearts and minds of everyone we touch. When we come out and our parents and our children love us anyway, and our friends and colleagues do not blink an eye, when the birth certificate has both dads' names on it, when we get the job anyway, then we know that Pharaoh is weakening. It can be exhausting and overwhelming, and certainly there will be days that we will feel unable even to open our mouths to speak. It is then that we turn to our forebear Moses, who despite his *aral s'fataim* was able to access his Divine revelation of "coming in" to strengthen his "coming out" in the world. Like Moses, let us not be stopped despite the impediments we encounter. Let us growl or mumble or cut away anything that would prevent our message from being spoken. And soon, when our works and words have brought about a time of freedom, may our mouths be oceans of song, our tongues alive with exultation like the water's waves, our lips filled full of praises like heaven's dome,[11] with nary a foreskin in sight.

NOTES

1. "I am Adonai. . . . I have heard the groan of the Children of Israel whom Egypt enslaves and I have remembered my covenant. Therefore say to the Children of Israel, 'I am Hashem, and I shall take you out from under the burdens of Egypt; I shall rescue you from their service; I shall redeem you with an outstretched arm and with great judgments. I shall take you to me to be my people and I shall be God to you'" (Ex. 6:2–7).

2. F. Brown, S. Driver, and C. Briggs, *Brown-Driver-Briggs Hebrew and English Lexicon* (Peabody, MA: Hendrickson, 1996), 790.

3. From Matityahu Clark, *The Etymological Dictionary of Biblical Hebrew* (Jerusalem: Feldheim, 2000), based on the commentaries of Samuel Raphael Hirsch.

4. *Brown-Driver-Briggs Hebrew and English Lexicon*, 973.

5. Moses was born a Hebrew slave (Ex. 2:1).

6. He is rescued and admitted into the Egyptian royal house to be raised as a son, by one of Pharaoh's daughters (Ex. 2:10).

7. He yields to a murderous rage, resulting in the murder of an Egyptian slave driver (Ex. 12:2).

8. He defends the safety and honor of a group of shepherdesses in the desert (Ex. 2:16–17).

9. He commits murder and then runs (Ex. 2:13–15).

10. Many thanks to Joshua Lesser for the insight of "coming in."

11. *Shabbat Siddur—Kol Haneshamah,* Nishmat prayer (Wyncote, PA: Reconstructionist Press, 1996), 236.

FIFTEEN

The Ritual of Storytelling
Parashat Bo (Exodus 10:1–13:16)

JASON GARY KLEIN

"When did you come out?" This is a common question among queer-identified people who are getting to know one another. For queer Jews, the answer may begin with
Parashat Bo, which opens with the final three plagues and continues through the beginning of the physical exodus from Egypt. *Parashat Bo* not only tells of a one-time
liberation in Jewish mythic history; it is also a tale of the future, setting the stage for a
ritualized storytelling in every generation. This ritualized story has particular significance for queer Jews.

Three times in this portion God commands the Israelites to tell their children the
story of the Exodus. Although the physical preparation for leaving Egypt was a one-
time Biblical event, telling the story as if we had been there—a telling concretized by
symbolic foods and rituals—becomes the central part of the observance of Passover
throughout time.

Exodus 12:1–20 is a section of the text called *Parashat HaChodesh* (portion of the
month). Not only is this section read during the regular cycle of Torah reading, but it
is repeated on the immediate Shabbat before the month of Nissan, some two or three
weeks before Passover. The text itself sets the calendar with which the Jewish people
count time to this day: "The Lord said to Moses and Aaron in the land of Egypt:
'This month shall mark for you the beginning of the months; it shall be the first of
the months of the year for you'" (12:2). This is the proclamation of freedom par excellence: the Israelites will no longer be controlled by a Pharaoh but will instead have
control over their own time. The paradox of the passage is that the Israelites are about
to celebrate their first festival of freedom in the land in which they are still enslaved.
Parashat HaChodesh continues as God instructs the Israelites how to prepare for the
night of the tenth plague and the physical journey out of Egypt that will take place
two weeks later. Paschal lambs, blood on doorposts, and girded loins usher in the
first festival of freedom that shall be celebrated "as an institution for all time" (12:14),
with unleavened bread as one of its central symbols.

Although the special reading ends there, chapter 12 continues by explaining details
of this first Passover ritual:

> And when your children ask you, "What do you mean by this rite?" You shall say, "It is
> the Passover sacrifice to the Lord because He passed over the houses of the Israelites in

Egypt when He smote the Egyptians but saved our houses." The people then bowed low in homage. And the Israelites went and did so; just as the Lord had commanded Moses and Aaron, so they did. (Ex. 12:26–28)

Not only does the commandment include a specific ritual of preparation, but it also includes instructions for what to tell your children when they ask, "What do you mean by this rite?" The end of verse 28 reveals that the Israelites already "did so"; not only had they agreed to perform the ritual of the Paschal lamb to prepare for the Exodus, but the children were already beginning to ask questions, and the elders were already beginning to tell the story to their children. Rashi asks how the Israelites "did" so when it was only the beginning of the month: how could they have *done so* already? He answers his own question by stating that, from the moment the Israelites agreed to the ritual of the Paschal lamb to prepare for the Exodus, they were rewarded for their actions. Nachmanides, a 13th-century Torah scholar from Catalan, points out that "so they did" is an expression that occurs many times throughout the Torah and implies that the Israelites did not omit a single detail. Rashi's commentary continues with an even more vibrant image than that of Nachmanides. He explains, "They did not drop a word from every command of Moses and Aaron," as if the Israelites went back to their homes carefully bearing baskets filled with words and preventing any word from dropping.

Twice in the sixteen verses at the conclusion of *Parashat Bo* (13:1–16) the text speaks of telling the story to our children. Verse 8 reads, "And you shall explain to your son on that day, 'It is because of what the Lord did for me when I went free from Egypt.'" Verse 14 is similar but includes a question as well: "And when, in time to come, your son asks you, saying 'What does this mean?' you shall say to him, 'It was with a mighty hand that the Lord brought us out from Egypt, the house of bondage.'"

As the Haggadah, the book used to tell the story of Passover, developed, the idea of telling the Passover story four different ways to four sons emerged in the Mechilta, a halachic midrash on the book of Exodus. The Mechilta drew together the two passages in *Parashat Bo* about telling one's children plus additional verses in *Parashat Vaetchanan* (Deut. 6:20ff). There are many ways of telling the story.

Passover may be only a once-a-year holiday on the Jewish calendar, but the remembrance of the story of Passover is a perpetual imperative. Weekly observance of Shabbat is linked both to creation and to the Exodus;[1] the day of rest is at once a reminder of a perfect world at the beginning of time and of the potential for a broken world to be redeemed; the injunction to "remember the coming out of Egypt all the days of your life" (Deut. 16:3) is taken seriously by the framers of the Jewish prayer book, who quote from the Song at the Sea in the Exodus story (15:11) in both evening and morning prayers daily.

Not only are there many ways of telling the story, but the story never gets old.

The Exodus is a foundational story of the Jewish people with which LBGT people can empathize. It is a coming-out story, a story that begins with strangers in a strange land and continues through struggle and liberation. Like the Jewish community remembering its story day after day, reenacting it year after year, the connections woven among members of the queer community also usually begin with stories, particularly those of "coming out," their own kind of exodus. The telling of one's own coming-out story as lesbian, bisexual, gay, or transgender is likely to be even more personal than retelling the story of the Israelites leaving Egypt. These stories are the quintessential points of connection for queer people everywhere: they are stories of internal struggle, often stories of hurt and persecution, and stories of self-realization and more public pride. For queer Jews, telling coming-out stories is a primary way we might understand the injunction that in every generation each person is required to imagine that he or she personally left Egypt.

Gay-pride celebrations typically are scheduled during the month of June, when in 1969 the Stonewall Rebellion in New York City occurred. Many people describe these riots protesting police repression and legal discrimination as the foundational moment of the contemporary LBGT movement. Although pride marches are generally seen as moments of celebration, the coming together of the queer community and the proclamation of our presence is a ritual reenactment of Stonewall. Like the Passover seder in which Jews typically pour some wine out of their glasses for each of the ten plagues in order to remember the suffering of the Egyptians, gay-pride celebrations often include moments of silence and memorials that honor those—this time from *within* our community—whom we have lost to suicide, to hatred, to gay bashing.

The ritual storytelling that *Parashat Bo* commands becomes formally established in the Passover seder and is particularly significant since Passover overshadows the rest of the year. This echoes with the yearly ritual of pride parades: both communities' stories of struggle and triumph are our central shared experiences that transcend one observance a year. The very act of storytelling is not only liberating unto itself but also an act of community building. When people share their stories and listen to the stories of others, they become part of a collective narrative that is stronger than the sum of its parts. Some of our personal stories may be filled with pain, but we may be filled with hope by hearing someone else's more uplifting story. Our personal stories may be full of pride and optimism, but challenges become shared and empathy is developed when we listen to others' stories of pain.

Judaism suggests that the Exodus is not merely a physical journey from one place to another. The Hebrew word for the book of the Torah that contains this story is *Shemot*, which means "names of." So the story is also framed with the concept of making a name for oneself, of being empowered to tell one's story and of naming one's people. For queer people, pride is an assertion of difference and a way of naming a group of people. In addition, our ancestors' celebration of the first Passover within Egypt, the place of oppression, implies that there is always liberation to celebrate, and yet there is always more work of liberation to be done.

Contemporary Passover Haggadot often weave aspects of the evolving story of the Jewish people into other stories of liberation. As Michael Walzer explains in *Exodus and Revolution*, "Wherever you live, it is probably Egypt; there is a better place, a world more attractive, a promised land. . . . There is no way to get from here to there except by joining together and marching."[2] Jewish experience can inspire queer experience by revealing that the telling of a story, particularly a coming-out story, is in itself a sacred act and that, in the words of the Haggadah, whoever expands the telling of the coming out of Egypt is worthy of praise.[3] Perhaps the more we talk about our various coming-out experiences, even those of us who are already well seasoned at telling our stories, the closer we will get to a world in which all will be free.

There is another simple point that is shared by both communities. By telling our stories we are aware of how the previous generations helped create the privilege that many people experience as both LGBT and as Jewish. This practice brings a humility and a gratitude that challenges notions that "we liberated ourselves," which contemporary Jews and queer people often have. Indeed, we stand on the shoulders of those who have come before us. *L'dor va'dor nagid godlecha*; from generation to generation we will tell these great holy stories.

NOTES

1. The Ten Commandments in *Parashat Yitro* in the book of Exodus refer to Shabbat in relation to the six days of creation (20:10). The Ten Commandments in *Parashat Vaetchanan* in the book of Deuteronomy refer to Shabbat in relation to the Exodus (4:14).

2. Michael Walzer, *Exodus and Revolution* (New York: Basic Books, 1985), 149.

3. Rabbi Yeshiah of Torini the Elder cites B.T. *Pesachim* 116a in *Hagadah Shel Pesach* (Jerusalem: Mosad Harav Kook, 1998).

꒐ꑱ ꒐ꑱ

SIXTEEN

Into Life: The Humanism of the Exodus
Parashat Beshalach (Exodus 13:17–17:16)

JAY MICHAELSON

1. An Exodus from Death into Life

The exodus from Egypt, told in part in *Parashat Beshalach*, has symbolized the movement from servitude to freedom for generations. Whether for African American slaves or for gay, lesbian, bisexual, and transgender elders, the story resonates far beyond its Israelite particularity to any struggle for liberation. Witness the "Stonewall Seder," commemorated in some LGBT-outreach congregations every June, or the long tradition of Negro spirituals in which "Let My People Go" took on poignant, immediate meaning.

Yet there is another, deeper aspect to *yetziat mitzraim* (the exodus from Egypt) beyond the move from bondage to freedom. As many Jewish scholars have noted, freedom is the beginning of the Israelite quest, not the end of it. The parting of the Red Sea in *Parashat Beshalach* is a cinematic moment, but it is not the climactic one: that comes at Mount Sinai. Egypt is the womb, and the Red Sea is the birth canal—but it is at Sinai where the Israelites come of age and begin their forty-year adolescence. Only upon finally entering the Promised Land can the Israelites be said to have attained adulthood.

So if freedom is only the beginning, what comes next? The traditional Jewish answer usually has something to do with responsibility, covenant, and the monotheistic imperative to ethical and religious life. These are, of course, borne out by the content of the Torah's texts, which soon shifts attention from history to law, and by the Jewish calendar, which moves from the Exodus-focused Passover to the Torah-focused Shavuot.

But I suggest an alternative reading. Recall that Egypt, too, had its laws. The Egyptians also had a sense of responsibility to, and covenant with, their Creators, along with a code of ethics and ritual behavior, even if it was quite different from that of the Jews. They even had their own *toevot*—their own taboos—some of which are recorded in the Torah. Ultimately, what differentiates ancient Egypt from ancient Israel, and what makes the Exodus not just a liberation story but an affirmation of love and life, is not law but the way law relates to the value of life.

Egypt, both in its literary construction and, to a great extent, in historical fact, was a death-obsessed culture; its lasting monuments are not palaces but tombs. As all those who have visited the Valley of the Dead, or even the Metropolitan Museum of Art in New York, know, Egypt created beautiful, lavish coffins, mummified their dead pharaohs and nobles, and regarded this life as merely an entryway to the next one (to use a Talmudic image). They even buried their noble dead with supplies needed to make the transition. I think it is fair to characterize ancient Egyptian culture as at least equally weighting the life of this world and the next one—if not privileging the latter outright.

Not so the incipient Israelite faith. Today, what happens after we die is one of the basic questions that many people assume religion is supposed to answer. But Judaism does not really do that. When I used to teach high school students—and even now, as I teach adults—it is always a bit embarrassing to reveal that Judaism does not have clear answers about death and the afterlife at all. The Torah is entirely silent on it; the Bible speaks contradictorily and in metaphor. Later, some texts say there is a heaven and a hell, but other texts seem to deny them. Some rabbis think there is transmigration of souls; some think there is not. There is a diversity of opinion on the subject, because our core texts do not even address it. Judaism is a religion of life, not death.

This is not to say that death is unimportant. The Torah is concerned with tombs as a marker of ancestry and land; it records in detail Abraham's bargaining for the Cave of Machpelah and describes in the portion preceding *Beshalach, Bo*, how Moses went out of his way to bring Joseph's bones out of Egypt. But it never mentions an afterlife or whether there is reward and punishment in the "next world" or how we should govern our lives in anticipation of what comes afterward. It never implies that this world is but a prelude to the next one. Nothing.

On the other hand, the Torah does go into great detail about tort law, the minutiae of tabernacle design, the performance of ritual sacrifice, and a myriad of other details about the life of this world. The Israelites are told to "choose life." They are promised a long and fruitful life if they abide by God's commandments. And it is assumed that the normative life (with only marginal exceptions, such as the *nazirites*—Jews who took ascetic vows) is lived in the world, with family, economic activity, and the sorts of daily intercourse with humanity that, in renunciatory or monastic traditions, is a sign of perdition, not salvation.

In other words, the exodus from Egypt is one from death into life—from a culture that denies this world to one that embraces it.

2. *"Choosing Life" Today*

Today, the way this dynamic plays out has shifted radically. Today, it is Western religious fundamentalists who denigrate the life of this world in favor of the next one—including, in their way, Jewish fundamentalists. And it is the "humanists" who embrace it.

Gay liberation, as Gloria Steinem said of feminism, is really humanism. If we look closely at the basis of liberated sexuality, at its core is a value of life as opposed to death: expression over repression, love over fear, the flowering of human potential over the trampling of it in the name of something else. Obviously, this is not an un-mitigated hedonism; the acceptance of one's sexuality does not imply the indulgence in all of one's passing lusts or whims. But it is a fundamental affirmation of the good-ness of human life and a rejection of the claim that the basic human impetus to love, and to express that love in an embodied way, is to be subjugated to something else.

After all, it is *possible* for a lesbian or gay man to live a heterosexual lifestyle; our ancestors have done it for generations. It just requires repression, deception, double lives, and unethical sexual behavior done "on the side" or "on the sly." A religious fundamentalist would say that this is exactly what God demands—though of course they would phrase it differently: perhaps as "wrestling with my own private demon" or "struggling to serve God" or "making sacrifices in the name of holiness."

This is the rhetoric of death. It is the way of expressing the belief that there is something unworthy about the fundamental structure of this-worldly existence. The heart is wrong. Sexuality is unreliable or evil. And there are more important values than living out one's fundamental truth. In other words, it is the rhetoric of Egypt—transformed and translated into a Jewish or Christian idiom, but Egypt nonetheless.

This rhetoric has become even more prevalent in the past few years, as the scien-tific evidence of sexuality's innateness has mounted. Only a decade ago, most Ameri-cans still believed sexuality to be a choice and homosexuality to be a "lifestyle." Now, thanks to reams of data on neurology, genetics, homosexuality in other species, and the like, the preponderance of the evidence has shifted, and public opinion has as well. A 2001 Gallup poll showed that 56 percent of Americans believed that homo-sexuality was "something one was born with"—up from 13 percent in 1977. This shift has political consequences: fully 79 percent of those who believe homosexuality to be innate also support same-sex marriage or civil unions. Faced with this shift in scien-tific and public opinion, many in the antigay camp have shifted their message, from "choice and change" to "cope and repress." After all, they now say, pleasure is not always good, and religion demands sacrifice.

It is important to note that the value of life as I have articulated it is, indeed, a se-rious challenge for many religious people; we in the gay-rights community are delud-ing ourselves if we think it is really no big deal. In essence, it demands that human experience be taken seriously as we read our sacred texts. Of course, the halacha has long accepted that "new information," such as what we now know about homosexual-ity, properly colors legal decision-making. But, taken seriously, the value of "choosing life" says more: that to live life fully matters. That God does not want the trampling of the heart. That although control is often a Jewish value, repression of one's basic orientation to love is not. This is what it means to move from death into life, deferral to embrace, today.

These principles have far-reaching consequences. By now it is well known that there are plenty of interpretations of the Levitical prohibitions on male-male sexual-ity (Lev. 18:22 and 20:13), several of which are contained in this volume.[1] It is within the scope of Jewish hermeneutical tradition to read the verses as prohibiting all gay and lesbian sex or just male sex or coercive sex or anal sex or cultic sex or perhaps just sex outside a relationship or maybe bisexual sex or sex that constitutes adultery. Who knows—and how do we decide?

In difficult cases, we decide by turning to fundamental values and core principles. And if those core principles include an affirmation of life, then that value must influence how we interpret the text. Now we ask whether a God who loves life would ask God's LGBT children to throw it away. And from that answer, the textual interpretation follows—not in its specificity but in its general orientation, in its refusal to accept "cope and repress" as consistent with core values of *yiddishkeit*.

In part, the principle of "life" comes from experience, not revelation—and that is a challenge to authority-based revealed religion. But in the case of Judaism, that revelation is necessarily preceded by the liberation from bondage recorded in *Parashat Beshalach*: the movement from death into life is the condition for revelation to take place. Even before the theophany of Sinai, Israel is told that life, not death, is the way of God and that the Torah is a "Tree of Life" to those who uphold it. And these general principles have legal consequences. The principle that the Torah's ways are all pleasant, for example, is carried through even to the most minute of legal issues, such as whether a thorny plant can be used for the ritual of the *lulav*. And the injunction to "choose life" becomes one of the Biblical sources for the Jewish rules about *pikuach nefesh*, saving lives even at the expense of fulfilling commandments.

Yes, let us be honest: there are contrary voices as well—ascetic ones that demand more repression than expression and rabbinic ones that describe this world as precisely an antechamber (*prozdor*) to the next one. Some of these voices can be dismissed as later historical accretions or the rabbinic outlook as opposed to the Biblical one, but some may not. Certainly, "choosing life" is a matter of degree and interpretation: the Torah has plenty of rules and restrictions, which do indeed restrict one's enjoyment of life, but ostensibly in the service of a holy and ethical existence. The question is still alive and well today.

But in leaving the tombs of Egypt to plant the Tree of Life in Israel, the sweep of the Israelite narrative is unmistakable: out of the abstract and into the concrete; out of afterlife and into reality; out of death and, as Franz Rosenzweig ended his philosophical masterpiece, *The Star of Redemption*, Into Life.

NOTE

1. In this volume, see the essays by David Brodsky (*Kedoshim*), Elliot Dorff, David Ellenson, and David Greenstein and my own essay on *Parashat Metzora*.

ꚙꚙ ꚙꚙ

SEVENTEEN

The Necessity of Windows
Parashat Yitro (Exodus 18:1–20:26)

MENACHEM CREDITOR

Most mornings, in order to help me decide what to wear, I look out the window, thus engaging with the world as it is, grounding my decision in the context of the outside world.

I remember learning during a midrash class at the Jewish Theological Seminary that, if I were a "real" rabbi, I would not have looked out the window to help me make a crucial decision. Instead of drawing on the world around me, I would have taken a volume of Jewish text from the shelf and poured over its pages in order to know truly what was going on in the outside world. In the view of many traditional Jews, Judaism's sacred texts contain all wisdom and all knowledge, offering up a world so complete and so complex that the texts alone can answer all human questions. The text, my teacher ironically explained, would have sufficed in helping me make my decision as a "real" rabbi.

And so this is the tension we face as we build our structures of ethics, logic, and tradition. We must continually decide how often we will utilize "windows," looking to and learning from the outside world for understanding, versus the energy we devote to looking inward, making decisions based on truths found entirely within our tradition and our sacred texts. Do we most readily encounter wisdom by turning inside ourselves or by looking beyond? Can we find holiness when we engage with ideas and truths found outside our tradition, or is our only path to God paved by the light of inherited Torah?

Moses's encounter with his father-in-law, Jethro (*Yitro* in Hebrew) in *Parashat Yitro* suggests an adaptive leadership practice of interfacing with wisdom beyond self-contained tradition in order to answer responsibly and to understand fresh challenges. The day after Jethro joined the Israelites in their journey,

> Moses sat as judge among the people, while the people stood about Moses from morning until evening. But when Moses' father-in-law saw how much he had to do for the people, he said, "What is this thing that you are doing to the people? Why do you act alone, while all the people stand about you from morning until evening?" Moses replied to his father-in-law, "It is because the people come to me to inquire of God. When they have a dispute, it comes before me, and I decide between one person and another, and I make known the laws and teachings of God." But Moses' father-in-law said to him, "The

thing you are doing is not right; you will surely wear yourself out, and these people as well. For the task is too heavy for you; you cannot do it alone." . . . Moses heeded his father-in-law and followed his recommendation. (Ex. 18:13–18, 24)

We have much to learn from this interaction. Jethro's open offer of criticism, and Moses's easy acceptance of this unsolicited advice, offers us a model of open communication. Few people show each other such mutual respect and acceptance as Moses and Jethro. But the most significant lesson of this conversation between Moses and Jethro only becomes readily apparent when we remember that Jethro was not an Israelite. Although his daughter, Zipporah, married Moses and played a crucial role in the birth of the Jewish nation, Jethro was a Midianite priest, someone completely external to Israelite culture—a true outsider. And yet it is Jethro's "outsider" perspective and wisdom that saves the day, inspiring Moses to set up the system of judges that became a hallmark of Jewish notions of justice and community. Moses does not look within for his solution. Instead he relies on the "window" of Jethro to help him see that which he might otherwise have missed entirely.

Let us now consider this example of a healthy mutual relationship—an interaction in which Moses looked outside his tradition for wisdom—within the context of a teaching in the Talmud brought by Rabbi Chiya bar Abba in the name of Rabbi Yochanan: "A person may only pray in a room which has windows, since it says, 'Now his windows were open in his upper chamber towards Jerusalem (Daniel 6:11)'" (Talmud *Bavli Brachot* 34b). We are allowed to pray only in a space with windows. Rooms without the ability to see beyond their interiors are unacceptable environments for sacred communication. Similarly forbidden is the practice of praying while facing a mirror. Furthermore, the quotation from Daniel indicates that the windows were in the "upper chamber," indicating to commentators that the purpose was not only the beauty of the outside world but communion with God, who is usually imagined "in the Heavens." King Solomon, when he built the Jerusalem Temple, followed this holy architectural rule, making "windows for the Temple, recessed and latticed" (1 Kings 6:4).

This lattice adds a mystical dimension to the concept of sacred windows, perhaps connected to the dialogue found in the Song of Songs, a Biblical erotic love poem, in which we read of the hiddenness and longing of two lovers whose mutual yearning is amplified through a window. In Jewish tradition, the groom is taken to refer to God, and the bride is interpreted to refer to the Jewish people, hungry to join with God. We read of the bride's vision of the groom:

> My beloved is like a gazelle or a young stag. There he stands behind the wall, gazing through the window, peering through the lattice. . . . My dove, in the crack of the rocks, hidden by the cliff, let me see your face, let me hear your voice; For your voice is sweet and your appearance is beautiful. (Song of Songs 2:9, 14)

God, the groom, is hidden behind the latticework. And perhaps Solomon, the reputed author of the Song of Songs, meant to connect this love affair with God and the creation of sacred permeable space. How, Solomon might ask, is it possible to seek Ultimate Truths through prayer if your environment is a closed one?

Our tradition offers us some answers. Moses's willingness to allow wisdom to come from without, Daniel's architectural design, and Solomon's mystical longing for Divine Love beyond the latticed window teach us that we can and must make decisions within our holy communities without closing out the outside world and without closing our "windows" to the Divine. Our tradition also teaches us about the power of studying with others—that we will not uncover truth alone. The traditional yeshiva student works always in *hevruta,* with a study partner, and the concept of the minyan teaches us that for some prayers, it is possible to access the power of the divine only when we worship as a community. We cannot do it alone.

Rabbi Haym Soloveitchik, a prominent Modern Orthodox scholar, in his controversial paper "Rupture and Reconstruction: The Transformation of Contemporary Orthodoxy," considers exactly this problem. More and more Orthodox Jews, when faced with new questions, look to books, he tells us. If the text says it is correct, then it is the Truth. But he also points out how disconnected this new trend is from its traditional heritage. In the "Old Country," when you had a question about something, you did not look it up; you asked your *bubbie.* Rabbi Soloveitchik brings powerful examples that illustrate what is happening within the new paradigm of Orthodox decision-making: if the texts contradict the practices of *bubbie* (and her generation), then the practices are wrong, and the book is right. This "closed-system" approach removes the window, and its value of sacred-openness, from Jewish decision-making. Rabbi Soloveitchik writes,

> Zealous to continue traditional Judaism unimpaired, religious Jews seek to ground their new emerging spirituality less on a now unattainable intimacy with [God], than on an intimacy with [God's] Will, avidly eliciting Its intricate demands and saturating their daily lives with Its exactions. Having lost the touch of [God's] Presence, they seek now solace in the pressure of [God's] Yoke. (*Tradition* 28, no. 4 [Summer 1994]: 76)

I am a Conservative rabbi. I feel torn at times between desiring God's Presence in the latticework of my sacred community and God's Yoke embodied in the written word of generations past. How am I called to act, if I am to be a "real" rabbi?

Paulo Coelho, the author of *The Alchemist,* weaves a well-known Hasidic parable into his recent *Warrior of the Light*:

> A young man went to a rabbi to consult him about what to do in life. The latter led him over to the window and asked:
> —What do you see through the glass?
> —I see people coming and going, and a blind man begging in the street.
>
> Then the Rabbi showed him a great mirror and again asked the man:
> —Look into this mirror and now tell me what you see.
> —I see myself.

—And now you no longer see others! See how the window and the mirror are both made of the same material, glass; but because there is a thin layer of silver on the glass, you see nothing but your own figure. You must compare yourself to these two types of glass. With a window, you saw others and had compassion for them. Covered with a thin layer of silver all you see is yourself. You shall only be worth something when you have the courage to tear off the silver coating over your eyes, so that you can see and love others once again. ([New York: HarperCollins, 2004], 111)

As Melanie Aron, a Reform rabbi based in California, has taught, "When you pray you are not meant to be thinking only of yourself. You must pray in a room with windows, so that even in your prayer, even in your personal spiritual quest, you remain aware of the world around you. Windows allow, even require, us to look out. They insist that we take note of the community in which we live, its needs, its concerns" ("Learning from Everyday Objects," sermon on August 12, 2001).

It is my conviction that a "pure" process, untainted by the outside world, is not holy. In order to be a holy decision, a process needs the touch of God, the intimate mixing of the known and the unknown, the inside and the outside, Moses and Jethro. Otherwise, as Thomas Jefferson wrote, "we might as well require a man to wear still the coat which fitted him when a boy" (letter to Samuel Kercheval, June 12, 1816; inscribed on the wall of the Jefferson Memorial). The fabric of our tradition must grow as we do, be it a question of liturgy, human relationship, or ritual practice. Ours is a holistic and nonsystemic structure with the strength to define that which is holy by more than what is already known.

When confronted with the question of LGBT inclusion, the responses of traditional Jewish networks range from mirrorlike (self-enclosed and unchanging) to transparent, from defensive to expansive. Thin layers of silver are difficult to dispel, but the windows of Jewish prayer environments demand nothing less. We look out and God looks in through those portals. And without those windows, we are radically alone, invisible to a hidden God. But with the windows, now that is the restoration of God's living Presence.

"The Lady of Shalott," a poem by Alfred Lord Tennyson, written around 1843, tells of a weaver in a tower who lives under a curse that she may not look at the world through her own eyes but must only see it reflected in a suspended mirror. When she finally does look out the window, there is consequence: her loom shatters, and her life as a "real" artist ends. We face a similar challenge and must consider the consequence of retaining a window to God while resisting the temptation to board it up for the sake of our own maintenance. We must struggle to use our windows and to bring God into our decision-making. But we must be equally cognizant of the impacts of relying not only on established answers.

May we, with God's help, redefine ourselves, become more expansive, and not become any less real in the process.

The Lady of Shalott, Part II

There she weaves by night and day
A magic web with colours gay.
She has heard a whisper say,
A curse is on her if she stay
To look down to Camelot.
She knows not what the curse may be,
And so she weaveth steadily,
And little other care hath she,
The Lady of Shalott.

And moving thro' a mirror clear
That hangs before her all the year,
Shadows of the world appear.
There she sees the highway near
Winding down to Camelot:

But in her web she still delights
To weave the mirror's magic sights,
For often thro' the silent nights
A funeral, with plumes and lights
And music, went to Camelot:

Or when the moon was overhead,
Came two young lovers lately wed:
"I am half sick of shadows," said
The Lady of Shalott.

(Alfred Tennyson, "The Lady of Shalott," in *Alfred, Lord Tennyson* [New York: Oxford University Press, 1990], 33)

EIGHTEEN

Laws and Judgments as a "Bridge to a Better World"

Parashat Mishpatim (Exodus 21:1–24:18)

DAVID ELLENSON

In Judaism, as in every religion, teachings collide with one another. Yet it would seem that the Jewish attitude toward homosexuality, on the basis of two passages found in Leviticus as well as later Jewish exegesis on these passages, is unequivocally negative. The first passage, Leviticus 18:22, states, "Do not lie with a male as one lies with a woman—it is an abomination," and the second, contained in Leviticus 20:13, asserts, "If a man lies with a male as one lies with a woman, the two of them have done an abhorrent thing. They shall be put to death."

The simple meaning of these texts appears quite clear. Rabbi Tzvi Weinreb, executive vice president of the Orthodox Union, built on these Levitical statements in an op-ed, "Orthodox Response to Same-Sex Marriage," in the *New York Jewish Week* (March 26, 2004), and has summarized the position of traditional Judaism on homosexual behavior as "clear and unambiguous, terse and absolute. Homosexual behavior between males or between females is absolutely forbidden by Jewish law, beginning with the biblical imperative, alluded to numerous times in the Talmud and codified in the Shulchan Aruch." Indeed, such behavior, "an act characterized as an 'abomination,' is prima facie disgusting," maintains Rabbi Norman Lamm, former president of Yeshiva University, in his article "Judaism and the Modern Attitude to Homosexuality," in the 1974 *Encyclopaedia Judaica Yearbook*.

As the famed legal philosopher Ronald Dworkin explains in his *Philosophy of Law*, in a chapter entitled "Is Law a System of Rules?" "Rules are applicable in an 'all or nothing' fashion. If the facts a rule stipulates are given, then the rule is valid, in which case the answer it supplies must be accepted." The Biblical "rules" expressed in these Levitical passages that prohibit male-male sexual relations seem clear cut and negative and the consequences attached to the rules so seemingly absolutely condemnatory of homosexual relations that the positions advanced by Rabbi Weinraub and Rabbi Lamm appear incontrovertible.

Nevertheless, "the plain meaning" of such Biblical statutes and the attitudes that flow from them have not gone unchallenged on either religious or moral grounds. One way in which such challenges have taken place is through engagement in reinterpretation of these passages. For example, scholars such as Rabbi Steve Greenberg and Rabbi Bradley Artson have provided alternative readings of these texts. Rabbi Greenberg, an Orthodox rabbi, in his *Wrestling with God and Men: Homosexuality in the Jewish Tradition*, contends that Leviticus 18:22, "Do not lie with a male as one lies with a woman—it is an abomination," should be understood as "And [either a female or] a male you shall not sexually penetrate to humiliate—it is abhorrent." As Rabbi Greenberg reads Leviticus, the verses in question are not about anatomy. Rather, they prohibit exploitative sexual relations and demand that sexual partners treat one another with respect.

In another effort to reinterpret these texts, Rabbi Artson, director of the Conservative Movement's Ziegler School of Rabbinic Studies, in a responsum he authored, contextualizes the Levitical prohibitions. He argues that they must be viewed against an ancient Near Eastern background in which same-sex male relations were part of the idolatrous practices of pagan religious cults. The proscriptions in Leviticus are primarily part of a fundamental Biblical polemic against idolatry, not homosexual acts per se. Both these readings—and others not cited—possess the virtue of approaching the Levitical texts in such a way that they can no longer be viewed as blanket condemnations of all homosexual relations. These efforts at reinterpretation can be applauded because they seek new meanings in these ancient texts, meanings that empty these passages of a contemporary justification for discrimination and violence directed against homosexuals.

Yet, as laudatory as these attempts are, such examples of reinterpretation may not be sufficiently satisfactory. Although Rabbi Greenberg and Rabbi Artson object to the consequences that flow from Leviticus 18:22 and Leviticus 20:13 and therefore offer alternative readings so that new outcomes can flow from the texts, the harsh precision and the overt homophobia of the Levitical text seems so palpable that it is difficult to feel sanguine about reinterpretation as a method to obviate the traditional understandings and implications of these texts.

Catholic scholar Elizabeth Schussler-Fiorenza has suggested a more methodologically radical theological solution in her powerful book *In Memory of Her*. In that work, Schussler-Fiorenza argues that reinterpretation does not always constitute an adequate means for dealing with ethically troublesome texts. Instead, she boldly states that an axiom that guides her own work is that the divinity and authority of any passage in Scripture that diminishes the humanity of another ought to be questioned altogether. In short, her book suggests that the process of reinterpretation is sometimes unduly limiting and that another scheme must be discovered for rectifying morally problematic passages in Holy Scripture, a scheme that requires looking elsewhere in Scripture at alternative texts that can provide for a principled correction of morally repugnant passages.

Two passages in *Parashat Mishpatim* embody overarching principles of judgment that provide correctives to the Levitical texts cited earlier, and they offer a way of providing for the emergence of a more just and different Jewish teaching regarding homosexuality. Exodus 22:20 states, "You shall not wrong a stranger or oppress him, for you were strangers in the land of Egypt," and in Exodus 23:9, the Torah proclaims, "You shall not oppress a stranger, for you know the feelings of a stranger, having yourselves been strangers in the land of Egypt."

The attitudes contained in these passages indicate that the experience of oppression demands sensitivity and response on the part of Jews to the needs of others.

They reveal a wide-ranging philosophy that lies at the heart of Judaism and embody a crucial teaching that is instructive and determinative for the formulation of Jewish actions and deeds. They indicate that the Torah itself provides overarching attitudes and principles that can and should surmount these specifically vile rules that diminish the humanity of LGBT people. As the medieval Spanish rabbi Ibn Ezra states, *"T'kar kol ha-mitzvot l'yasher ha-lev*—the essential purpose of all the commandments is to make the heart upright" (Ibn Ezra, Commentary on Deuteronomy 5:18). In short, the overarching principles contained in these passages can trump the rules contained in Leviticus and provide for repair and improvement of the text and the world.

Modern writings in the philosophy of law clarify and underscore this point, indicating how legal systems achieve this constructive task by distinguishing between the weight attached to conflicting rules on the one hand and principles on the other that are both found within the same legal system—as the aforementioned passages in Leviticus and Deuteronomy are. As Dworkin himself has argued, "principles," in contrast to "rules," are general notions—often moral ones—embedded in a legal system that possess a gravitas that a rule alone simply does not. Although the weight assigned a principle cannot always be determined exactly, principles are generally decisive in rendering judgment.

This understanding that Dworkin provides regarding the role that "principles" in contrast to "rules" occupy in the legal system is expanded on and clarified in the work of the late professor Robert Cover of Yale. In his insightful article "Nomos and Narrative," Cover argued that law itself functions in two modes, one "imperialistic" and the other "jurisgenerative." The imperialistic approach is marked by an emphasis on authority and the application and enforcement of rules. This is undoubtedly the manner in which virtually all devotees of Jewish law—even liberal ones—have understood halakhah. Indeed, this is what has led exegetes such as Rabbi Greenberg and Rabbi Artson to wrestle with the "rules" in Leviticus as they have.

However, the latter mode of jurisgenesis that Cover has adumbrated seems more promising for our enterprise. In this mode, law is viewed as embodying a *paidea*—the highest educational ideal of the community—that is embedded in a master narrative of the community, and the ongoing rendering of judgments attempts to give this *paidea*—this ideal—ever more exact and just application over time. So perceived, law constitutes a "bridge to a better world."

In this way, Cover provides for a theoretical approach to the issues of Jewish law—including judgments regarding homosexuality—that reinterpretation does not. For law "is not merely a system of rules," nor is Torah—the Teaching, as Franz Rosenzweig once labeled it, that guides the life of the Jewish people. Instead, Torah and the normative guidance the Teaching contained in Torah provides must be situated in a larger context of narrative discourse and meaning. This approach "privileges" principles over rules, and in this instance, it means that Torah must be viewed in an expansive manner. From this perspective, there is no doubt that the broad ethical principles contained in Exodus should by necessity take legitimate religious-legal precedence over the narrow proscriptions provided in Leviticus.

For Jews, the primary orienting narrative of "discourse and meaning" that the Bible provides tells of how an enslaved Jewish people went beyond the "narrow straits" in which the Egyptians had confined them as they celebrated a journey "from degradation to freedom." The Exodus passages cited from *Parashat Mishpatim* indicate that rejoicing in that freedom for themselves alone was not enough. Instead, the principles that animate that narrative—as *Parashat Mishpatim* suggests—provide a different religious imperative. Jews, precisely because their narrative reminds them over and over again that they "were strangers in the land of Egypt" and therefore know "the feelings of a stranger," must have empathy for others and alleviate the venomous impacts that accompany acts and attitudes of discrimination and oppression against others. A messianic goal—the creation of a more just world—lies at the heart of the Jewish story, and the responsibility imposed on each generation of Jews is to allow that goal to be more fully approximated even if that means that we must change traditional beliefs and understandings of Jewish law.

Parashat Mishpatim teaches that a "more inclusive and tolerant Judaism" must be forged, a Judaism in which the *paidea* of justice and redemption for the oppressed will be achieved. The principles expressed in Exodus 22:20 and 23:10 demand that Jews and others not discriminate against LGBT persons or tolerate readings of the Torah that would legitimate such discrimination. Instead, these principles demand a reading of Jewish tradition that requires that the LGBT community receive the same privileges and entitlements that heterosexuals enjoy. This position is surely the most religiously compelling one for Jews to adopt in regard to the LGBT community in our day, as Jews seek to realize the moral obligations that the narrative and principles of our Torah impose on our community.

NINETEEN

Building an Inclusive Social Space
Parashat Terumah (Exodus 25:1–27:19)

MARK GEORGE

Parashat Terumah provides the initial instructions for building the *mishkan*, Israel's wilderness Tabernacle, the portable sanctuary in which the Israelites carried the Ark of the Covenant during their journey through the desert. The Tabernacle's sacred space created a meeting point between the Israelites and God, but it also helped define the boundedness of the people Israel.

Parashat Terumah is characterized by an institutional rhetoric, focusing on structure, design, and ritual more than the social space the Tabernacle would provide. The parasha is filled with descriptions of furnishings and structures, along with details about dimensions and materials. There are promises of further divine pronouncements concerning the people, as well as actions and provisions that must be performed in perpetuity. These institutional concerns are told to Moses as he stands on the top of Mount Sinai, in the presence of the deity. They are the pattern, *tabnit*, of the Tabernacle that he and the people are to follow closely in order to maintain their connection to God (Ex. 25:40).

For all the attention that *Parashat Terumah* devotes to the details of the Tabernacle, it is not a blueprint. The descriptions of the size and materials of the ark, or the framework of the Tabernacle, are insufficient actually to construct them. For example, the thickness of the ark's walls is not specified, and neither are the directions in which its poles should run, whether along the ark's length or width. How the Tabernacle's framework was to be assembled remains a matter of much scholarly debate. The narrative leaves many aspects of the Tabernacle's design unclear, suggesting that the actual *construction* of this space was not the primary concern of *Parashat Terumah*.

If the narrative of *Parashat Terumah* was not intended to help in the construction of the Tabernacle, why so much detail? The text itself suggests one answer: God wants to dwell among the people (Ex. 25:8), and this divine desire necessitated the Tabernacle's construction. The God of Israel is holy and commands Israel to be holy (Lev. 11:44), a sentiment echoed at the beginning of the Sinai section of the text when God states that, while the entire earth is God's, Israel shall be "a kingdom of priests and a holy nation" (Ex. 19:6). Holiness requires attention to detail in order to protect and preserve the divine. Because the Tabernacle is a divine dwelling, special care must be given to its construction.

A second explanation for such a lavish sacred dwelling is that Israel entered into a formal relationship with its God at Mount Sinai (Ex. 24). That relationship required an appropriate space within which to practice the cult, that is, the rituals and worship of God. Such worship could not occur just anywhere. On the contrary, it required a suitably sacred space, which in time would be the Jerusalem Temple. But with the Israelites not yet in the Promised Land, much less able to use the Temple, the Tabernacle filled the gap.

Both these explanations assume that the reason for the Tabernacle is a concern about God. In the first answer, God needs a place to dwell among the people and therefore commands the building of the Tabernacle. In the second, the people need a place to worship God, so they must build the Tabernacle. But these answers place too much focus on God and God's needs. The Priestly writers of these narratives are as interested in the people, Israel, as they are in God. These writers understood Israel to have a unique position in the divine economy. As the people of HaShem, they serve a special role in creation, because *as a people*, Israel acts as priest vis-à-vis the rest of the peoples of the world. This role is not restricted to the priests alone. Rather, it includes all of Israel, male and female alike. And this "democratic" understanding of Israel's role in the world is realized in the very structuring of the Tabernacle.

Menahem Haran, writing about the Tabernacle, argues that there is a logic and system to this space.[1] This system was predicated on a series of "zones of holiness," which had their reference point at the center of the Tabernacle, the "most holy space." "Most holy space" was surrounded by "holy space," and then "court space," in a hierarchical structure. Moving outward from the most holy space, and thus away from the presence of HaShem, the degree of holiness in space decreased. The way in which objects were made, in both materials and workmanship, mirrored the decreasing holiness of Tabernacle space, as did determinations of who could enter each zone.

Although this basic insight to the logic of Tabernacle space makes sense, it stays within the thought-world of the writers and the text. The organizing principle of holiness is internal to the logic of the Tabernacle narratives, the focus of which is God. It also assumes that space is a given, a neutral medium within which the Tabernacle is built. But geographers and sociologists argue that space is not a given; rather, it is something that societies produce and that, in turn, reproduces the social structures and hierarchies of those societies.[2] Space is, in fact, social space, and how such space is created, organized, and given meaning is determined by the people and societies that use it. Therefore, we need to read the Tabernacle as a reflection of Israel, which produced this space, as much as being concerned about God.

Given the importance of family and lineage to the priests' identity, one might expect this space to reflect their social values, including ideas of gender roles and family. Surprisingly, the organization of the Tabernacle shows that the Priestly writers of *Terumah* had a broad, inclusive understanding of Israel in the world. Within the Tabernacle, there are three social zones that correspond to its spatial divisions. First, and most broad, is the zone defined by the assembly (*'edah*); second is the zone defined by genealogy; and third, the most restrictive space, is the zone defined by hereditary succession. If a person is a member of the "assembly of Israel," whether male or female, that person may enter the first zone, court space (assuming ritual purity requirements are met; cf. Lev 12:4). If a person is both a member of the assembly and of the proper genealogical line and gender, an Aaronide (descendant of Aaron) and male, he may enter the second zone, holy space. If a person is of the assembly, a male Aaronide, and the eldest son, who inherits the position of high priest, then he may enter the third zone, most holy space.

The social structure and hierarchy organizing Tabernacle space is expansive and inclusive, reflecting the Priestly writers' "democratic" understanding of Israel's role in the world. The determination of one's status in the assembly of Israel is *not* established by biology or genealogy, at least not exclusively. What qualifies someone to be a member of the assembly is being one of the people who entered into a covenant relationship with HaShem at Mount Sinai (Ex. 19–24). Permission to enter the court space also means, for males, being circumcised, as a sign of participation in the covenant. This is an expansive, nonbiological, even queer idea of community. It does not matter whether that male is a descendant of Jacob or a sojourner, *ger*, in Israel's midst. As Exodus 12:48 shows, circumcision renders a *ger* "as a citizen of the country." In the Tabernacle's spatial logic, a person's social status as an Israelite, rather than that individual's practices, is what marks that person as an insider. Thus, thinking expansively, the ancient queer Israelite was in the community, whereas the straight non-Israelite would have been out. Some scholars are skeptical about the expansiveness of such statements, but such statements are important ways of showing how the narratives are liberative, portraying an understanding of "Israel" that is open, affirming, and inclusive of the entire community, in all its diversity.

The other implication of this organizational logic is that the rest of the peoples of the world are integral to Israel's self-understanding and identity. Entry into Tabernacle court space depends on a person's being a member of the Israelite assembly. But for this logical distinction to have any meaning or validity, there must be people who do not meet it. Even an open, affirming, and inclusive community has boundaries. Without them there is no community. Non-Israelites, that is, those who are not members of the assembly, are required for Israel's identity as that which the community is not. Israel is related to them, even as it is distinct from them. The genealogies of Genesis (especially chapters 5 and 10) locate Israel's ancestors within the larger economy of peoples of the world. Israel's ability to differentiate itself from those peoples is necessary for the functioning of Tabernacle space.

Parashat Terumah narrates God's desire (to dwell among the Israelites) and God's plan for how that should be accomplished (through the Tabernacle). It does so by assuming God's perspective, narrating what God might see as God looks out of the Tabernacle, toward the east, from the most holy space where God meets with Moses from above the cover, between the cherubim (Ex. 25:22). Yet reading Tabernacle space from the perspective of the people, it becomes apparent that the Tabernacle is a space with social concerns squarely in its sights. The priests articulate a broad understanding of who is part of the assembly that could enter Tabernacle court space, including all those who had covenanted with the divine—women, men, queers, and sojourners alike. But the very building of inclusive community is nonetheless predicated on a boundary past which others may not enter. For the Priestly writers, all the peoples of the world are related, and Israel, figured inclusively, plays a particular role among the nations. That role involves its special relationship with HaShem, which was established in the covenant at Mount Sinai. That role is analogous to the priests' role in Israel, those who can enter into Tabernacle holy space. Like the Israelite priests, who are singled out from among all the assembly of Israel for a particular social role, so, too, is Israel singled out from all the peoples of the world for a particular social role. Unlike the biological and genealogical ways in which priestly identity is determined, Israel's identity as the assembly is not so narrowly defined. Rather, the assembly, Israel's definition of family and community, is open and affirming of all those who choose to participate in the rituals and observances for Israel's God.

NOTES

1. Menahem Haran, *Temples and Temple-Service in Ancient Israel: An Inquiry into Biblical Cult Phenomena and the Historical Setting of the Priestly School* (Winona Lake, Ind.: Eisenbrauns, 1985).

2. Émile Durkheim, *The Elementary Forms of the Religious Life,* trans. Joseph Ward Swain (New York: Macmillan, 1915); Henri Lefebvre, *The Production of Space,* trans. Donald Nicholson-Smith (Oxford, U.K.: Blackwell, 1991); Edward W. Soja, *Postmodern Geographies: The Reassertion of Space in Critical Social Theory* (London and New York: Verso, 1989).

TWENTY

When the Fabulous Is Holy
Parashat Tetzaveh (Exodus 27:20–30:10)

MARLA BRETTSCHNEIDER

How many times have I heard queers sneer some version of "those texts just don't speak to me" or "there is nothing recognizable" or "there isn't anything in the Bible that relates to the world as I know it." Yet *Parashat Tetzaveh*, in its exquisite attention to detail and ritualizing of the beautiful, is a queer text that speaks to *me*. One might say that its resonance to queer life for me is based on stereotype, given the text's flamboyance. Yet the flamboyant is a slice of queer life that is real to me, and much beloved. Though *flamboyance* is commonly associated with excess and negatively valenced, in *Tetzaveh* we find an alternative framing of flamboyance as the site that brings G-d near to us as (a) people.

Earlier in Exodus, in *Parashat Terumah*, the *Mishkan,* or *Ohel Moed,* has been constructed. It is a ritualistic meeting place, sometimes referred to in English as "the tent of meeting" between the Israelites and G-d. The *Ohel Moed,* the tent of meeting, is the only place where sacrifices can be made. *Parashat Tetzaveh* follows, offering a robust mix of extreme moments. In the parasha's opening lines instructions are given for lighting the eternal flame, signifying the constancy of G-d's presence. Moses's brother, Aaron, and Aaron's sons are named as the ones to attend to this task and to keep the flame alight through the ages. In a flash, Aaron and his sons are anointed and ordained to G-d as priests. Without much ado, the fanfare thus begins.

The text instructs in the creation of sacred adornments: a breastpiece, an *ephod* (an elaborate embroidered garment), a robe, a headdress—all lavish and lush. There are robes with pomegranates and tiny golden bells so that when the wearer walks they make a tinkling sound. The *ephod* is to be made of gold, blue, purple, and crimson yarns and fine twisted linens worked into designs. Lazuli stones are attached, bordered in frames of gold, to remember the tribes of Israel. These vestments are a remembrance before the Lord. There is a breastpiece deemed an "instrument of decision" far more awesome than powdered wigs and the flowing robes of Supreme Court justices. It is mounted in elaborate design with sapphire, turquoise, amethyst, emerald, and other richly colored precious stones. There is a fringed tunic and a sash of embroidered work.

Yes, these sumptuous clothes are to be worn. Yet they are worn, admired, and created as devotion, highlighting the religious principle of *hiddur mitzvah,* or "beautification of the mitzvah," the idea that it glorifies G-d and elevates any commandment or ritual if it is done in an aesthetically pleasing way. Preparing stunning attire is therefore a prayer. Wearing a magnificent frock is an aspect of one's love of G-d. A pleasing sight is a divine offering. These clothes and fabulous accoutrements are ordered for no other reason than "dignity and adornment" (28:40). Yves St. Laurent would be proud. Any boy in the Castro, West Hollywood, or Chelsea knows the rules. The femme, the butch, and the dyke take up such ablutions religiously.

As *Tetzaveh* continues, there are bulls and rams, splashing blood, and the laying on of hands. This is the stuff of great queer rituals. The text describes sumptuous food to be eaten and fired as a fragrance. Luscious portions are to be consumed, some forbidden. Two yearling lambs are offered daily, in the morning and at twilight. Wild libations for the lambs are concocted, made of wine, oils, and flour. There is blood dabbed with the finger on the right ear, the thumbs of the right hands, and on the big toes of the right feet. Blood gets dabbed here, poured there, sprinkled on that, and dashed against every side of the altar round about. These offerings from Aaron and his descendants, not following the bloodline of Moses, are what will stand the test of continuity, as G-d wants it offered this way throughout the generations (29:9, 29:28, 30:8, 10).

Is it fair to offer this contemporary queer reading of the text, delighting in such showy demonstrations? Contemporary queer theory puts much emphasis on the concept of performativity, which challenges the notion that identity is "inherent" in a person or group. Characteristics and actions that we commonly assume to be "natural" are exposed as constituted through "performative" acts, challenging commonsense notions of what is "true" or "real" while simultaneously forging new meanings. We actively create who and what we are—consciously or not—through our performances, including speech acts, within historical and extant shifting contexts of consciousness. These performative gestures come to be seen by ourselves and others as our "natural" identities. Such acts are then named as effects of what is taken to be the inherent identity, the process flipped on its head. Through the repetition of the acts they come to be seen as normal in the first place.

Tetzaveh does not disappoint us children of contemporary queer theory. It is Aaron and "some" descendants who are consecrated.[1] The ancient rabbis and many others through the years have puzzled over the questions of why Aaron was chosen and not Moses and why some descendants were chosen and not others or all of them. Historically, scholars have looked for preordained "reasons" that actually only they have the power to invent and legitimate since the text does not offer us any explanation. Rather than seek some "natural" cause or some special trait inherent in Aaron and his particular descendants, queer theory encourages us to understand that it is through the utterances, speech acts, and other performative gestures in this moment that the priesthood as a structure *then* associated with Aaron and some of his descendants is created and the Tent of Meeting conjured and authorized as a holy place. These elaborate instructions for the layers of clothing are essential to the birth of the priesthood. Wild rituals are ordered, and through their performance, things and spaces are made the holiest of holy. Preparing certain foods, eating, and not eating are central to the process. These acts are foundational aspects of what we take to be core and given hierarchies of Jewish communal existence, namely, that some Jews are *Cohanim* (descendants of Aaron through this priestly line) and that *Cohanim* are at the top of the Jewish hierarchy.

Ordinary people in the "world" of the Biblical text did not wear such finery. Designs for the lavishness of apparel and its wear for most people were not set down in sacred texts. The rituals of consecrating both altar and human were not everyday activities. The food cited in this parasha is rich, fatty, opulent. Why were the events and people in this textual moment so flamboyant, and how does this flamboyance connect to queerness—in a contemporary sensibility—and the public presentation of self? It is often in the extreme incarnations of the everyday that we are most conscious of navigating between the human and divine. Often it is through clothes and related components of affect that we push boundaries, given the disciplinary injunctions and effects of such in historical and cultural context. Frequently it is through pushing boundaries that we connect to the present and the holiness of what is before us and how we are situated. Daring to go beyond the now helps clarify the structures within which we function, often enabling a renewed embodied presentness that many have associated with the holy (including the philosopher Martin Buber). It is often in the extreme that we encounter ecstasy, bits of the divine. Consecrating Aaron and his descendants as priests requires nothing less. A queer reading can lay claim to those bits of divinity expressed in the flamboyance of queer culture. We reclaim the power of the dramas we effect in our acts and relations.

The extravagant clothes, rituals, meals, sacrifices, and anointings are central to the creation of the priesthood. Reading *Tetzaveh* from within a contemporary culture that associates queers with flamboyance and flamboyance with ruin, the parasha offers up a sigh of relief and a moment of validation. By providing a glimpse into a world that creates flamboyance and then marks it as holy, *Tetzaveh* opens up an opportunity to appreciate the fabulousness of contemporary queer culture. In the text, this space of excess is named not as some hedonistic den but as the Tent of Meeting—the dwelling place of the divine. Queers have heard endless rants about the godlessness of our most prized sites and practices of pleasure, meaning, and relationship. As a counterpoint, in *Tetzaveh* it is here—in this place of lavish beauty—that G-d will meet with the Israelites, speak to us, and abide among us.

NOTES

1. Exodus 28:1 cites Aaron's four sons by name (Nadav, Avihu, Elazar, and Ithamar). The Ramban understood this passage to suggest that any children born to these four sons after this point would automatically be part of the priestly class, but the grandsons of Aaron already alive when the priesthood was established were not automatically included.

TWENTY-ONE

Mounting Sinai
Parashat Ki Tisa (Exodus 30:11–34:35)

AMICHAI LAU-LAVIE

I

Friday night on a Tel Aviv dance floor: I am surrounded by hundreds of shirtless men, a pulsing mass of dancers, the air thick with sweat, lust, and—for me, eighteen years old, my first time out at a gay club—excitement mixed with a heavy dose of guilt. The club is only twenty minutes away from the Israeli Orthodox neighborhood where I grew up, but also thousands of light years away from childhood. I close my eyes, and for a moment I am reminded of dancing at the Yeshiva, surrounded by young men in white shirts, faces glistening with sweat, rocking wildly in tight circles around the Torah scrolls.

Eventually I too take my shirt off, fear replaced, temporarily, by a newfound freedom. My eyes meet those of a handsome man dancing close by. He is checking me out, and I like it, but then the guilt kicks in—a medley of voices invades my mind— every rabbi who ever taught me: "Abomination. Sin. Modesty. What of desecrating the Sabbath or disrespecting your parents who would be mortified to know you are here?" I stumble off the dance floor, heading outside for some fresh air, and as soon as I am alone I burst into tears. How can something that feels so right also feel so wrong? How do I reconcile my religious and gay selves? What of my old life do I keep as I embrace this new and confusing reality?

Torn between passion and prohibition, body and Bible, I found myself that night yearning for clarity, for a healthy balance, a yearning that will chart my journey and continues to underscore my personal and professional life.

Almost twenty years and many dance parties later, the yearning for clarity lingers, but a healthy balance has been steadily built, thanks to great teachers, wise lovers, and unexpected encounters with the sacred, providing me with possible models of fusion between my sexual and spiritual identities. One such fusion was revealed, surprisingly, at a Bible class, several years ago—transporting me back to another dance party: an event of mythic proportions containing both the fragments of separation and the seeds of reconciliation itself. I opened the book and found myself at the foot of Mount Sinai, surrounded by a gyrating mass of ecstatic dancers, circling a shining sculpture—the golden calf. I was always taught to judge these sinners harshly, but now, as I imagined myself dancing with them, I discovered another angle—an untold story, the other side of the coin. Through a careful rereading, this terrible tale reveals a subversive message that offers a compelling fusion of sex and spirit, body and soul.

II

Chapter 32 in *Parashat Ki Tisa* in the book of Exodus opens with an absence and with a yearning: "And the people saw that Moses was delayed in descending the mountain" (Ex. 32:1). Moses had been gone for forty days and by this time was presumed missing by the people who had grown to depend on him for security and direction. They demanded reliable leadership and a tangible proof of security and turned to Aaron, high priest in training and interim leader, who led them in the first successful fundraising campaign in Jewish history. They collected gold, molded a recognizable icon from their Egyptian days, and were comforted. When Moses finally returned on the following day, bearing the Ten Commandments, he discovered a wild party, centered on the golden calf—his unlikely replacement. The frenzy was interrupted by the literal shattering of the sacred words, as the physical depiction of divinity clashed with the metaphysical. It ended badly, with the first religious conflict within the Israelite ranks leading to three thousand casualties.

Although the "official" moral of this Biblical text focuses clearly on the rift between monotheism and the worship of idols, I want to read it as a pivotal metamyth that can be seen allegorically as a coded description of the perennial, all-too-human conflict between spirit and matter.

It is an incident that exacerbates the divide between our base instincts and our highest consciousness—symbolically happening simultaneously at the bottom and on the top of the mountain that represents the vertical connection between humanity and divinity. Seen from this angle, the Golden Calf story is more than a stark warning against worshiping matter. It is a reminder of a skeleton in our collective closet—an unresolved memory of a great psychic wound. But, like all wounds, it can also present an opportunity for *Tikkun*—for deeper healing—and, in particular, for sexual healing, a significant but overlooked element of this story.

III

There is no direct implication that the worship at the foot of Mount Sinai involved sexual misconduct, but it has been often interpreted that way. The basis for this reading is a single incriminating word that has caught the eye of most classical interpreters of Scripture. Exodus 32:6 describes a scene in which the people "rose up to make merry," an odd expression that is translated elsewhere as "got up to play," "pursued pleasure," or "frolic."

The Hebrew word in this verse is *l'tzachek*, a word that usually means "laughter" and is responsible, for instance, for the naming of Isaac (Gen. 17:17), for the act that led to the exile of his brother Ishmael (Gen. 21:9), and for the public indiscretion of Isaac and his wife Rebecca (Gen. 26:11). This act of laughter is sometimes associated with deviant forms of idolatry or violence, but it is most often linked to sexual behavior. One midrash on this verse in Exodus elaborates,

"*L'tzachek*—the people committed adultery and even spilled blood" (*Midrash Tanchuma*, Ki Tisa, 20).

The Biblical author chooses very few words to tell us what led to the creation of the golden calf—thus, the emphasis on the people's "laughter" seems to be significant, suggesting various modes of excessive behavior—including sex. Feeling abandoned—and driven by the human urge to touch, see, smell, and taste life—the builders of the calf yearned for a tangible and accessible deity. Like children who are comforted by a doll or adults who find solace in substances or distractions, the "children" of Israel needed a fix—a security blanket for the senses. "This is your God, Israel!" (Ex. 32:4), they exclaim as they surround the image, expressing what reads like an authentic religious sentiment, enabling them to experience union with one another and with the mystery of life, as represented by a familiar Near Eastern symbol of fertility.

But the party does not last. The excess of laughter is met with excessive violence; the law prevails as both sexual and idolatrous impulses are harshly repressed. The Judaism that will eventually evolve from Sinai will be the Judaism of the law—offering the world a courageous iconoclastic reality but also a culture deeply suspicious of the physical and intolerant of any "deviant" sexual behavior. This moment in Exodus, I find, is our "original scene"—our psychic wound—a collective memory of passion gone wrong, of the death of desire. What comes right after the laughter and the punishment is the establishment of the Mosaic law—forever forging a strict and unforgiving moral code on Judeo-Christian consciousness.

Read allegorically, as I did during that eye-opening Bible class, this Biblical text manifested itself as a split-screen snapshot of the parallel drives for connection with a force greater than oneself: a cosmic, timeless, and psychological battle—words versus image, law versus lust, mind versus body.

The human yearns for the tactile object; whereas the divine is but an elusive concept. The people Israel represent here the demands of the body, and Moses—literally lost in a fog—represents abstract thought, the disembodied letter of the law. Then, as now, this myth is the story of our human struggle with urges and desires, as we try to sublimate or integrate values, morals, and laws of a "higher" sense of appropriate social conduct. But can these powerful forces coexist harmoniously? Is there another solution to this conflict that does not end in a brutal denial of the sensual?

Perhaps possible solutions are found not in the story itself—written, after all, by the winner in this religious war between pagans and monotheists—but, rather, between the lines. Reading Exodus 32 as a metaphor freed me to listen to, and comprehend, the motives of the people, identify with their yearning, and honor their experience as a legitimate religious expression, complete with drums, laughter, and eros. Had I been there, I would have danced too.

IV

It took me years and one eye-opening Bible class to realize that I actually did dance around the golden calf—and did not die. That one fateful Friday night on a dance floor in Tel Aviv, I experienced my own private shattering of the law, reenacting, un-consciously, the central mythic battle of my inherited legacy. My sexual urges crashed against the voices of the law—and something did die inside of me: an old fear of dis-obedience. After I was done crying, I went back inside and kept on dancing. A voice, clear inside my head, was saying, "You are made in the image of God—and this too is sacred." The rabbis were still murmuring dissent, but their voices were fading as the beat and the bass reverberated in my dancing body.

As a product of strict Orthodox upbringing, I was programmed to accept that law, defer doubts, and repress my sexual urges. I was taught to regard my body as a vessel, a necessary tool inferior to my mind. At some point in my midteens, realizing my desires and coming out to myself, I understood that an inevitable gap was widening between the world I had been born into and the world I was drawn toward. My role models, parents and teachers, represented a sacred tradition that I loved and cared for, but they failed to address my yearning for intimacy and love—on my terms. My sexuality became a repressed secret, a source of fear, pain, and shame.

And then, that night on the dance floor, everything crashed, and everything started. I did not know it at the time, but that night represented a new way of inter-preting that ancient battle at Sinai, deprogramming, one dance move at a time, my own fears and, perhaps, centuries of internalized sexual repression and homophobia coursing through my veins.

Dancing with my shirt off, I had a revelation—suddenly knowing, deeply, that my body was holy and my sexuality sacred—owning it, for the very first time. Only years later, as I delved into this intensely personal reading of Exodus 32, did the pieces fit together and that night of yearning and tears was fully understood: my own private Sinai, a personal milestone of hope.

V

"The wounded deer leaps highest," wrote Emily Dickinson, reminding us that healing happens when we are ready to deal with our pain and leap on ahead, dancing.

In my search for a model that will honor both my sexuality and my faith, I found Exodus 32—focusing not on the ending and death for God but on the courageous act of dancing with God. Reading between the lines, I created my own midrash of pos-sibility. I chose to join the dance, to listen to the untold story of the dancers, to laugh passionately with these forgotten ancestors, who, like me and like so many others, like you perhaps, had to sublimate their laughter and accept the yoke of a silencing law. As a religious Jew and a proud gay man striving to balance Bible and body—law and laughter—this radical rereading of revelation provided, finally, a possible model, a blessing to live by, an eternal dance.

TWENTY-TWO

Listening to Heart-Wisdom
Parashat Vayakhel (Exodus 35:1–38:20)

JILL HAMMER

There are two modes of revelation in the Torah. One mode is that of Sinai; revelation comes from a mountaintop, in the form of laws and principles. The law treats everyone equally. It is a transcendent law, Divine in origin, and descends to touch every member of the covenant with its truths. The other mode is that of the *mishkan*, the Tabernacle or Sanctuary. As the Israelite people build the *mishkan*, the shrine they will carry through the wilderness, they rely on their inner wisdom and individual gifts. Although the pattern of the *mishkan* comes from the Eternal, the gifts that make the sanctuary what it is come from the depths of the human heart. The *mishkan* is replete with images of love and relationship: images we can use to transform our experience of what Torah is.

Both of these models appear at the beginning of *Parashat Vayakhel*. Moses assembles the community and reminds them of Shabbat: "Six days you shall work, and the seventh day shall be for you a holy Sabbath. Whoever does work on it shall die" (Ex. 35:2). Moses is communicating in the mode of Sinai, in which law is paramount. Yet Moses then moves into the second mode, that of the *mishkan*. He says, "These are the things God has commanded: Take from among you a gift for the Eternal. All those whose hearts are willing shall bring a gift for the Eternal" (Ex. 35:5). The Tabernacle cannot be built only according to law. It must be built by those whose hearts are willing.

The people immediately respond to this plea. "Everyone whose heart lifted him up, and everyone who was moved by a spirit of generosity, came bringing the gift of the Eternal for the work of the Tent of Meeting, for its service, and for the sacred vestments: men and women, all who were generous of heart" (Ex. 35:21–22). Notice that the genders, so carefully separated by Torah law, come together to create the sacred shrine. There is no division between man and woman. All desire to be part of the building of the Tabernacle.

The Israelites respond, not out of obedience, as they did at Sinai, but because their hearts speak to them. (In the Biblical conception, *lev*, "heart," refers to the thoughts of the mind as well as the emotions.)[1] In fact, their hearts respond to them with very specific wisdom: the men who work the metal and gold are called *chacham lev*, "wise-hearted," and the women who spin the wool are named as *nasa liban otana bechochmah*: "those whose hearts lifted them up in wisdom." An inner sacred truth is coming out of the people through acts of creation. As the Tabernacle grows in beauty, every single Israelite becomes part of the process of putting it together.

There is a spiritual model that teaches us to distrust the heart, mind, and body and trust only the wisdom of sacred text. This spiritual model sees the perceptions of the self as deceptive and encourages the believer to ignore inner thoughts, emotions, and sensations, accepting only those truths that come from an outside, transcendent source. People with this kind of spiritual model often see LGBT people as deluded, because they claim that LGBT people are listening only to their inner sense of identity and not to Scripture. A true believer, these people imply, would not pay attention to "false" notions that come from the self.

Yet the Torah tells us that the Tabernacle cannot be built without the wisdom of the heart. The yarn cannot be spun, the jewels cannot be set, the sockets cannot be fit together without the inner knowing of individual people. The beauty of the *mishkan* comes from the beauty of the generous-spirited hearts that design and build it. So, too, we can only build sacred community when the wisdom of the individual heart has a recognized place alongside the sacred text.

The Talmud makes this very point in a midrash about the chief artist of the *mishkan*. The Bible describes this artist, Betzalel, as "endowed with a Divine spirit of wisdom, understanding, and knowledge" (Ex. 31:2). The Talmud relates,

> Betzalel's name reflected his wisdom. God said to Moses, "Tell Betzalel to make the Tabernacle, the Ark, and the vessels." Yet when Moses relayed the message to Betzalel, Moses changed the order: first the ark, then the vessels, and finally the Tabernacle. Betzalel turned to Moses and said: "Moses, our teacher, normally one first builds the house, and then places the furniture inside. Yet you said to make the vessels and then the Tabernacle. These vessels that I will make—where shall I put them [if the Tabernacle is not ready]? Didn't God tell you, 'tabernacle, ark and vessels'?" Moses replied in amazement, "You must have been in God's shadow [*betzel el*] and overheard!" (*Berachot* 55a)

In this midrash, Moses gives instructions for the building of the *mishkan* that are different from what God instructed. Betzalel intuits that something is wrong and asks for clarification. Should he not build the structure before the furniture and not the other way around? An astonished Moses makes a pun on Betzalel's name: Betzalel is the one who "stands in the shadow of God/*betzel el*." Through Betzalel's inner wisdom, he has intuited what God wants, and the midrash implies that God agrees with Betzalel rather than Moses. Moses, who is supposed to be a recorder of God's voice and a channel for God's law, is less accurate than Betzalel, who is responding to his own inner sense of right and wrong. This fact seems to imply that the understanding of the heart can be just as revelatory, or more so, than obedience to text.[2]

Although it is true that the heart cannot always be trusted, sometimes our inner knowing tells us that a religious leader does not, cannot, have it quite right. Divine wisdom has to work within the context of the body. Knowing one's inner nature, yet being told that one should ignore this inner nature in favor of an imposed heterosexual identity, has caused many queer people to give up on religion. So, too, women have often fled religious institutions that persist in dictating what the roles of women will be, rather than paying attention to the needs and gifts of individuals. Others, too, feel shut out when they speak their truth. Betzalel teaches us not to give up: we must inquire of our religious leaders, using our sense of heart-wisdom, and tell them what we believe to be spiritually true. Perhaps, if we speak wisely and live wisely, they will hear the echo of the Divine in our words and deeds.

Midrash Tanhuma tells of a group of women who bring their bronze mirrors as a donation to the Tabernacle.[3] Moses sees these gifts as abominable. He believes that mirrors represent the vanity and sexuality of women and rejects them violently: "Take sticks and break the legs of those who brought them. What use are such mirrors?"[4] The medieval commentator Rashi is even clearer, adding, "Moses rejected the mirrors because they were made to serve the evil inclination."[5]

Moses believes that the gift of the mirrors, a gift that honors the body, sexuality, and beauty, insults the Tabernacle. Yet the Holy One corrects Moses, saying, "Moses! You have contempt for them? It was these mirrors that raised up all these hosts in Egypt! Take the mirrors and make out of them the washbasin and its stand for the priests, so that they can purify themselves."[6].

In this same midrash, the Holy One tells Moses the story of how, when their husbands were despondent because of slave labor, the women would beautify themselves using the mirrors and would take food where their husbands were sleeping. They would bring the mirrors and initiate sex games with their husbands, saying, "I am more beautiful than you!"—to which the husbands would answer, "No, I am more beautiful than you!" In this way the couples would become aroused and would make love, conceiving the next generation of Israel and reviving their despairing spirits. The objects Moses has despised are sexual, but they are not vain. By inspiring love and arousal, they kept the people's hope alive, allowed them to form families, and ensured that there would be another generation. Therefore, the mirrors are made into the washbasin of the priests, so that the priests will "see themselves" as they enter the Tabernacle. Through the washing ritual, the priests will find heart-wisdom *and perhaps not disconnect their sexuality* from themselves as they prepare to do Divine service.

These mirrors, which Moses at first rejects as unsuitable for service because of their "illicit" erotic content, are placed at the entrance to the Tabernacle to show that everyone is made in the Divine image. The story of the mirrors teaches us that the wisdom of the heart is also the wisdom of sexuality and the body and the wisdom of love.

At the heart of the Tabernacle is a further sign that heart-wisdom is welcome in holy places. *Parashat Vayakhel* tells of the making of the cherubim: the two mysterious winged creatures that spread their wings over the Ark of the Covenant, providing a throne for the Shekhinah, the Divine Presence. Jewish tradition conceives of the cherubim as human beings with wings, facing each other across the Holy Ark. Their gazes look toward each other but do not quite meet. Instead, the two gazes intersect at a point above the Ark. Dr. Aviva Zornberg has suggested that "God is at the place where the two gazes intersect."[7]

The Talmud conceives the cherubim as two beings locked in sexual embrace. Relying on an old tradition, the Talmud claims that on Shavuot, the anniversary of the day Torah was given to Israel, the people would gather in Jerusalem and the priests would open the Holy of Holies and reveal to them the two cherubim in sexual embrace: "When Israel used to make the pilgrimage, they would roll up for them the veil and show them the cherubim which were entwined with one another, and say to them: behold, the love of God for you is like the love of male and female" (*Yoma* 54a). According to this midrash, God rests not only in heart-wisdom but in the embrace of two bodies. There, too, the Shekhinah reveals Herself. And lest we think that holiness can reside only in the union of a man and a woman, we should note that although some midrashim imagine one cherub as male and one as female, most midrashim do not. In fact, the Torah text itself seems to ordain that both cherubim be made the same.[8] The embrace of the cherubim is less about gender than it is about intimacy and love. At the core of holiness is the wisdom of love.

The heart-wisdom of the Tabernacle is a counterpart to the legal wisdom of Sinai. It does not negate that wisdom but, rather, tempers it with compassion for the individual and respect for the truths of the body and the emotions. The two wisdoms can benefit from each other. Perhaps the deepest sign of this reciprocity is the menorah that is described in *Parashat Vayakhel*: a seven-branched candelabrum, with seven bowls for flame, each one shaped like an almond blossom. The menorah is a stylized tree: it represents the Tree of Life. Like a tree, the Torah must grow in response to the wisdom of the heart.

NOTES

1. See Proverbs 17, 18, and 19, in which *lev* always refers to thought processes.
2. A Chasidic commentator, Mordechai Yosef of Ishbitz (the *Mei haShiloach*), adds that Betzalel's wisdom is not just in the content of what he says and does but also in his way of being: "If you compare the curtain Betzalel made to one made by another, you will see that the one made by Betzalel has more grace and balance than any other, even if the two curtains are fashioned in the same manner." (Mordechai Yosef of Ishbitz, *Mei haShiloach*, on Ex. 36:30).
3. Exodus 38:8.
4. *Midrash Tanhuma Pekudei* 9.
5. Rashi on Ex. 38:8.
6. *Midrash Tanhuma Pekudei* 9.
7. Aviva Zornberg, lecture on *Parashat Vayakhel—Pekudei,* Jerusalem, March 1998.
8. Exodus 37:8.

TWENTY-THREE

A Knack for Design

Parashat Pekudei (Exodus 38:21–40:38)

LISA EDWARDS *and* LAURENCE EDWARDS

Parashat Pekudei seems a gay man's paradise. It concludes the book of Exodus with a detailed account not only of the fabrication—piece by intricate piece, including the *fabulous!* fabrics, furnishings, and window treatments—of the *mishkan* (Tabernacle) in the wilderness but also of the design and creation of the garments worn by the high priests who were to tend the altar of the *mishkan*. It also reminds us that God appointed two lead designers, Betzalel and "with him" Oholiab, "carver and designer, and embroiderer in blue, purple, and crimson yarns and in fine linen" (Ex. 38:23).[1] They are not straight, are they?

From where comes our tradition's attention to detail, this passion for design and construction, for building a suitable dwelling for God, and for the proper attire to tend the altar of worship?

In *The Women's Torah Commentary*, Rabbi Elana Zaiman notes that the root of *Pekudei*, p-k-d, often occurs in the Bible in connection with birth: Sarah giving birth to Isaac (Gen. 21:1), Hannah to Samuel (1 Sam. 2:21). On the basis of this connection, Zaiman suggests that birth imagery is also active here, in the "birth" of the *Mishkan*/Tabernacle.[2] Birth, specifically childbirth, is one tangible and essential means of transmitting culture, of sustaining identity over generations, and the root *p-k-d* reminds us of this fact.

Here, however, the root has another meaning at the level of *peshat*, the simplest, contextual understanding. *Pekudei* refers to the accounting, the records, the inventory of all the materials donated and used, as well as the labor involved, in the construction of the wilderness sanctuary—"These are the records of the Tabernacle [*Pekudei hamishkan*], the Tabernacle of the Pact, which were drawn up at Moses' bidding" (Ex. 38:21). This parasha accounts, recounts, and summarizes the conclusion of that work.

P-k-d thus relates to another means of cultural preservation and transmission. If birth is one essential aspect of sustaining identity, equally crucial is the concern for careful record-keeping and the creation and preservation of the material artifacts that bear testimony to civilization.

In a fascinating study entitled *A Passion to Preserve: Gay Men as Keepers of Culture,* researcher and writer Will Fellows argues, mainly through oral histories, that we ought to be exploring our community's stereotypes more than we have.[3] He chooses to spend less time on the argument that gay people are just like everyone else and more time on what else, besides our choice of sex partners, makes us different. In the book, he looks particularly at the prevalence of gay men interested in historic preservation, by which he means "not only the saving [and restoration] of buildings but also the saving of smaller objects and documents, as well as the compilation of family and community history."[4]

Fellows, on the basis of both his own experience and extensive interviews, describes five qualities that he sees as characteristic of "preservation-minded gay men":

- gender atypicality: "the boy who is not like other boys"
- domophilia (a word invented by Fellows): "I was always fascinated with houses and what happens inside them"
- romanticism (with a small *r*): "the exceptionally imaginative and emotional ways in which many gay men relate to the past"
- aestheticism: "*Artistic* once served as a code word for gay and rightly so"
- connection- and continuity-mindedness: as in E. M. Forster's brief command, "Only connect"; includes appreciation of elders, oral histories, saving old objects

Although Fellows's work is concerned only with gay men, his study helps confirm that there are many connections between Jewish sensibilities and LGBT sensibilities on this topic of preservation, for he also connects the gay passion for preservation to a gay passion for religion. He points out the marvelous similarities based on the etymologies of the English words: *preservation* is from the Latin, meaning "to observe beforehand, to protect, to guard"; *restoration* is from Latin derivations, meaning "to make stand again";[5] and *religion* also comes from Latin, meaning "to bind together again, to put back together again."[6]

We want to expand on what Fellows does, though, because we think that many people know the yearnings that Fellows describes, know what it means to be drawn to preserving records of the past, to restoring a sense of the past. We think it is part of why LGBT people are drawn to Judaism in what seems like disproportionate numbers. For the basics of this passion to preserve are also what living a Jewish life demands: being connected to a past, building on a past—a communal past, a communal history, and our own individual pasts. Fellows takes note, for example, of the large number of gay men who got into their passion to preserve through their grandmothers. How many LGBT Jews came to Judaism through a grandparent? Like the gay men whom Fellows interviews, most of those who do this preserving of LGBT culture and history do so not in order to live in the past but, rather to let the past live in and touch us. There is a "longing for connectedness."

There are yet other passions we have in our community for restoring, rebuilding, preserving. Take, for example, the ever-growing interest in Yiddish language and culture. In this movement, too, LGBT people seem to be represented in disproportionate numbers.[7] And elsewhere in the Jewish world, as well, consider the many queer rabbis and cantors out and about in the world today or the number of thoughtful Jews evidenced by the call for a Torah commentary such as this one.

Queer Jews also fit Fellows's restoration category, building connections to the past—with continuous improvements and embellishments. Could there be a more contemporary example of this phenomenon than the expansion in understanding of what, and who, constitutes families—not only same-sex marriage, of course, but also what Marla Brettschneider calls "the family flamboyant"?[8] How ironic that the very people accused of being boundary crossers and tradition smashers are in the forefront of preserving, reclaiming, and reworking traditions.

Part way through *Pekudei*, the Israelites deliver all the completed parts of the Tabernacle of the Tent of Meeting, including "the service vestments." Though some assembly is required, the text tells us that "when Moses saw that they had performed all the tasks—as the Eternal had commanded, so they had done—Moses blessed them" (39:43). Clearly this massive project, involving all the people, had been completed dutifully and most beautifully down to the last detail. With what words did Moses bless them? asks the midrash, noticing the absence of said blessing in the Torah, and it answers that Moses said, "May it be God's will that the divine Presence rest upon the work of your hands."[9] How much of the queer participation in Jewish life today— the energetic commitment to the religion and culture pouring in from the fringes— comes with a *longing* for a blessing such as this one? Would that more queer participants could offer their talents and service, arising from natural inclination, with the *expectation* or, better yet, *certainty* of such a blessing.

If the book of Exodus, concluding with the completion of the Tabernacle in *Pekudei*, "births" the Jewish interest in creating sacred space—in building the perfect building in which God would choose to dwell and in designing the ritual role and ritual garb of the priests who tend the sacred place—it also births a passion handed down generation to generation (*l'dor vador*) to preserve, repair, and reconstruct that which has been handed down, to keep sacred space and sacred passions a living, breathing way of life.

NOTES

1. All translations from the Jewish Publication Society edition, 1999, revised 2005–6 by David Stein.

2. Elana Zaiman, "Pekudei (38:21–40:38): The Birthing of the *Mishkan* (Tabernacle)," in *The Women's Torah Commentary*, ed. Elyse Goldstein, 179–84 (Woodstock, VT: Jewish Lights, 2000).

3. Will Fellows, *A Passion to Preserve: Gay Men as Keepers of Culture* (Madison: University of Wisconsin Press, 2004).

4. From Fellows's letter of inquiry to participants, in *A Passion to Preserve*, p. 15.

5. *American Heritage Dictionary*, including appendix 1.

6. Fellows, *A Passion to Preserve*, 244.

7. Jeffrey Shandler, "Queer Yiddishkayt: Practice and Theory," *Shofar* 25, no. 1 (2006): 90–113.

8. Marla Brettschneider, *The Family Flamboyant: Race Politics, Queer Families, Jewish Lives* (Albany: SUNY Press, 2006).

9. Rashi's commentary on the Torah: "He [Moses] said to them: 'May it be God's will that the Shekhinah abide in the work of your hands. And let the graciousness of Adonai Eloheinu be upon us, establish You upon us the work of our hands, establish the work of our hands' [Psalm 90:17]."

PART III

VAYIKRA

The Book of Leviticus

TWENTY-FOUR

Bodily Perfection in the Sanctuary

Parashat Vayikra (Leviticus 1:1–5:26)

CHARLOTTE ELISHEVA FONROBERT

The concluding chapters of the book of Exodus focus on the construction of the Tent of Meeting, also known as the Tabernacle, or *mishkan*. *Parashat Vayikra* opens the book of Leviticus with a survey of the sacrifices to be conducted in that sanctuary. With the exception of Leviticus 2, which deals with the grain offering—the *minhah*, consisting of fine flour, oil, and frankincense—the sacrifices listed and expounded on in this parasha consist of animal sacrifices: the burnt offering of either bull, ram, male goat, or birds (Lev. 1:3–17); the sacrifice of the "well-being" offering (often translated as "peace" offering, *shelamim*),[1] constituted by cattle, sheep, or goats (Lev. 3:1–16); the sin offering of a bull or, depending on who the offending party is, a goat or sheep and, depending on the economic ability of the person who brings the offering, birds or meal offering (Lev. 4:1–5:13); and finally the guilt offering (Lev. 5:14–26). The parasha therefore details the sacrificial service as a means to maintain and nurture the relationship of the community with the divinity.[2]

Framed as a speech of instructions given by God to Moses from the Tent of Meeting, the parasha presents a carefully structured choreography of ritual practice, involving priests and laypeople of various social standings and economic abilities. The envisioned stage is the Tent of Meeting, and the parasha devotes detailed attention to this spatial framing. That is, the sacrificial script instructs people to move from wherever they bring their offerings to the proscenium of the stage—the door of the Tent of the Meeting (Lev. 1:3; 4:4) or "before the Tent of Meeting" (Lev. 3:8.13), where the priests, the sons of Aaron, take over. The priests move between the altar in the courtyard in front of the Tent and the door, where the person bringing the offering remains. Again and again, the laypeople, members of the people of Israel, are instructed to bring the animal to the door where the actual slaughter of the animal is to take place. The priests then continue with the processing of the carcass in order to turn it into a proper offering on the altar.

In the midst of all this, the foregrounding and therefore emphasis of gender in the parasha is palpable,[3] as in almost every case the gender of the animals to be sacrificed is not only implied (as in bull, ram) but emphasized: "If his offering be a burnt sacrifice of the herd, let him offer *a male without blemish [zakhar tamim]*" (Lev. 1:3; compare 1:11, 4:3, 4:22, 5:18, and 5:25). In other cases, the parasha specifically mentions that the animal can be either male or female, as is the case with the peace offering (Lev.

3:1 and 3:6). Finally, in some cases the animal should be "a female without blemish [*neqevah temimah*]" (Lev. 4:28 and 4:32). Clearly, the gender of the animal matters to the priestly writers, and it seems to play an important role in the symbolic work that sacrifices are to play in the design of the relationship between God and the people of Israel. Insofar as a queer reading entails being suspicious of any insistence on unequivocal markers of gendered identities, I focus attention on this priestly insistence on gendered "unblemishedness."

Let us therefore briefly examine the phrases *zakhar tamim* and *neqevah temimah*. There are perhaps two ways of reading them, either as "male/female, unblemished"—that is, the animal should be male/female *and* unblemished—or alternatively as "unblemished as a male/female animal." The first reading is perhaps somewhat less interesting, since the gender of the animal is merely one additional required characteristic, whereas in the second reading the animal to be sacrificed is not just a generic animal without blemish but is to be without blemish *as* a gendered animal. These two readings do not necessarily contradict each other, and they are ultimately not that different from each other, but they provide different emphases.

As to the first reading of male/female *and* unblemished, an early and quite interesting, albeit problematic, Jewish reading of the gender symbolism involved in the sacrificial script of this parasha is provided by Philo, the prolific 1st-century Alexandrian interpreter of Biblical literature for the Greek-speaking world. As a scholar who was well trained in Hellenistic methods of interpreting ancient texts, Philo generally applies an allegorical approach to the Biblical texts, as we will see in this context as well. The allegorical method entails moving from the specific to the general, from text to meaning and from the physical world to the world of the intellect, which in turn has profound consequences for how someone reads gender. At the very least, Philo recognizes the importance of gender in these opening verses of Leviticus. However, he provides an example of a reading that translates the duality of the Biblical text into an essentialized and essentializing gender dualism, arguably foreclosing any queering of the text. He writes, "In the first place the whole burnt offering is a male, because the male is both more complete and more dominant than the female, and closer akin to causal activity, for the female is incomplete and in subjection and belongs to the category of the passive rather than the active."[4] Here Philo provides a reading that not only essentializes the gender duality of the Biblical text, by ascribing generic qualities to male and female, but ascribes a clear hierarchy to the two. Ultimately, for Philo's allegorical approach the gender symbolism of the parasha has little to do with the sacrificial context per se but, rather, with the general principle of "being": "So too with the two ingredients which constitute our life-principle, the rational and the irrational: the rational which belongs to mind and reason is of the male gender, the irrational, the province of the sense, is of the female. Mind belongs to a genus wholly superior to sense, as man is to woman."[5] The overall dualism that juxtaposes mind with sense, the rational with the irrational, serves as Philo's hermeneutic key and is mapped onto the gender duality in the Biblical parasha. The Biblical emphasis on requiring a male sacrificial animal has symbolic significance. That is, a male animal is required for approaching the divinity because to Philo it connotes completion and dominance. As female is associated with the physical—sense and the body—it lands at the bottom of the hierarchy, a pattern Philo readily adopts from his Greek and Platonic education.

Let us consider the second reading. That is, *tamim* (unblemished) qualifies the adjective *zakhar* (male), as does *temimah* for *nekevah* (female). In that regard, these expressions in our parasha point forward to the detailed description of what constitutes the "unblemishedness" of a burnt offering further on in Leviticus, namely, in *Parashat Emor*: "You shall offer, that you may be accepted, a male without blemish [*tamim zakhar*], of the oxen, of the sheep, or of the goats . . . : blind, or broken, or maimed, or having a growth, or scurvy, or scabbed, you shall not offer these to the Lord, nor make an offering by fire of them upon the altar to the Lord. . . . You shall not offer to the Lord *that which has its testicles bruised or crushed, or broken, or cut*" (Lev. 22:19–24; emphasis added).[6] *Tamim zakhar*, or unblemished as a male, therefore, is at least partially constituted by the integrity of the animal's testicles. As pointed out by Jacob Milgrom, the term *tamim* derives from the verb *tamam*, "to be complete."[7] A better translation of the adjective therefore might be "complete," or the animal that is "completely male," whole in its genitalia also. Early rabbinic law with regard to the firstborn adds further imaginative descriptions of the potentially blemished male genitalia: "If it has no testicle or only one. Rabbi Ishmael says: If it has two sacs it has two testicles; if it has only one sac it has only one testicle. Rabbi Akiva says: It should be set on its buttocks and squeezed: if there is a testicle there, it will in the end come forth" (*mBekhorot* 6:6). Perhaps the detailed attention to and imagination of the testicles have to do with notions of fertility and concerns about whether an animal damaged in its genitalia would be fertile, rather than with notions of masculinity per se, if that notion can be applied to animals at all.[8] Still, the Biblical (and later the Mishnaic) texts have a clear notion of an ideal set of "complete" or "unblemished" genitalia to establish the male identity that would allow the animal to be served up on the altar. Rather than moving away from the realm of the physical and the body, as Philo does, we might argue that the rabbis delve more deeply into that realm.

Notably, there is no equivalent for the female case, for *nekevah temimah*. The Torah nowhere spells out further what that term might mean. Even though the first part of Leviticus 22:19–22 ("blind, or broken, or maimed," etc.) clearly applies to this animal as well, we are left to wonder how *temimah* in its femaleness is to be imagined. Might that mean that the Torah has a notion of male "wholeness" or "unblemishedness" but not female? Early rabbinic law has perhaps something interesting to offer in this regard. The Mishnah provides an entire detailed list of "blemishes" that invalidate a sacrificial animal (*mBekhorot* 6).[9] Granted, that list is placed in the context of discussing the firstborn animal, but as the Mishnah reflects on the blemishes having to do with the gender identity of the firstborn (after all, the firstborn is supposed to be a male animal), and on blemishedness in a sacrificial animal in general, these reflections are not irrelevant in this context:

> By reason of the following blemishes firstborn animals may not be slaughtered either in the Temple or in the provinces:[10] if it has white specks or rheum in the eye that are not lasting . . . or if it is a *tumtum* or an *androginos*; such may not be slaughtered either

in the Temple or in the provinces. Rabbi Ishmael[11] says: *No blemish is greater than this.* But the Sages say: It does not count as a firstborn animal but may be shorn and used for labor. (*mBekhorot* 6:12)

The detailed rules of the firstborn animals are not of interest to this discussion. But the requirement for the firstborn to be male, supposedly unambiguously so, provides the Mishnah with one of the many occasions to introduce the notion of the dually sexed (the *androginos*) or the nonsexed (or not-yet-sexed) animal (*tumtum*). If that firstborn animal is not readable as an animal with a clearly recognizable gender identity, it is not a valid male firstborn. That is, the Mishnah introduces the third (and for that matter, fourth) category, to challenge the model of dual-sexedness of animals and humans that it inherits from the Torah and that it cultivates further. As with all such challenges, the question that arises is, of course, whether this challenge reinscribes and therefore reinforces the gender duality or whether it transcends it and thus provides a model for thinking in queer or transgender terms.

As to the immediate question about the lack of a specification of femaleness in the Torah, Rabbi Ishmael's comment is of interest. His statement evidently refers to the *androginos*. There is no blemish greater than a firstborn *androginos* animal, a suggestion that allows for two differently nuanced readings: either Rabbi Ishmael wants us to consider the dual-sexedness of the animal as the blemish (in comparison with which there is no greater), or the presence of a vaginal opening in addition to the penis is considered the blemish. Certainly, the vaginal opening is not considered to have a positive presence of its own. That is, the vaginal opening itself is the blemish. As far as the Mishnah is concerned, I do not believe the issue can be resolved, and Talmudic literature explores both options. Either way, the "blemish" of dual-sexedness operates only as damage to the "maleness" of the animal, especially when maleness is required in order to establish its status as sanctified and therefore as a sacrificial animal. Sanctity in this case does not allow for ambiguity.

I conclude with the argument that the rabbis provide us with the tools for a queer reading vis-à-vis the role of gender in the sacrificial script of our parasha, a reading that is worth considering in comparison to Philo's reading discussed earlier. Although few contemporary readers would presumably agree with Philo's misogynist dualism, my reading does in some way follow him by considering the gender symbolism at work in the parasha, that is, by moving away from the physicality of the sacrificial script laid out here, from the profusion of blood and killing at the Tent of Meeting in the desert or later the Temple in Jerusalem. Rabbinic tradition itself favors what may be called a replacement theory or a spiritualization of sacrifice, in which study of Torah,[12] acts of loving kindness or charity,[13] and prayer[14] come to replace sacrifice as the form of maintaining the relationship between human and divine and to function as modes of worship. In that respect, Philo and the rabbis share a common interest. However, they arrive at this conclusion in different ways, Philo by way of allegory and the rabbis by way of analogy. Both of these modes of reading have radically different implications. Philo's allegorizing seeks to transcend the embarrassment of the physicality of the Biblical text, in this case its sacrificial script. In the rabbinic case, the study of Torah (as well as acts of charity and prayer) do not come to "spiritualize" the sacrificial mode of worship, by favoring the cognitive or spiritual over and against the body, but they are understood to be analogous to it. That is, the preference of these modes of relation to the divine does not derive from a sense of embarrassment at the physicality of sacrifice enshrined in our parasha. It is because the rabbis take the corporeality of the text seriously that the rabbinic tradition moves to analogy (the prayer service mirrors the sacrificial service, etc.). The Biblical concern with the body and the testicles of the animal (and the priest, for that matter) is further developed, and that focus allows the sages to introduce genital ambiguity, to introduce the categories of *androginos* and *tumtum*. Now it may be objected that the sages do so by declaring these to be blemishes with respect to the sacrificial stage, a fact that hardly endorses queer bodies. True, but here we are not bound by *halakhic concerns,* and we can read the rabbinic texts against their own grain. As much as the Mishnah seeks to project an ideal embodiment of animal and priest, the overabundance of blemishes in its catalogues suggests that the idealized and perhaps even utopian unblemished body on the sacrificial stage is, perhaps, an impossibility and can always only be approximated. In that respect, all of us who are offstage are queer.

NOTES

1. See also Baruch A. Levine, who suggests "a sacred gift of greeting" in his *JPS Torah Commentary to Leviticus* (Philadelphia: Jewish Publication Society, 1989), 15.

2. Jonathan Klawans writes, "The purpose of the daily burnt offering—and perhaps some other sacrifices as well—is to provide regular and constant pleasing odors to the Lord, so that the divine presence will continually remain in the sanctuary." Jonathan Klawans, *Purity, Sacrifice and the Temple: Symbolism and Supersessionism in the Study of Ancient Judaism* (Oxford: Oxford University Press, 2006), 72.

3. Both Levine and Klawans gloss over these gender issues.

4. The translation is based on the classic translation by F. H. Colson, in the Loeb Classical Library, *Philo,* vol. 7, *The Special Laws* I (Cambridge, MA: Harvard University Press, 1938), 215. Jacob Milgrom rejects Philo's insistence on a symbolic reading of the text and offers a pragmatic reading, according to which "the male is economically the more expendable, the female being the one to supply milk and offspring." Jacob Milgrom, *Leviticus 1–16: A New Translation with Introduction and Commentary* (New York: Doubleday/Anchor Bible), 147.

5. Ibid., 215.

6. Biblical scholars usually attribute this text to the Holiness Code. But for our purposes, I am not concerned about the distinction between the priestly writing and the Holiness Code.

7. See Milgrom, *Leviticus 1–16,* 147.

8. The notion of blemish in the testicles applies to the priest himself as well, however, since the list of blemishes in animals is mirrored by the list of blemishes for the priest in Leviticus 21:16–24.

9. That chapter is followed by another one with an extended list of blemishes, this time of the priest, blemishes that would disqualify him from the sacrificial service (*mBekhorot 7*). I do not have the space here to elaborate further on this wildly interesting text, which depicts the idealized body of the priest.

10. That is, neither can the animal be used for sacrifice ("slaughtered in the Temple") nor is it demoted to a regular animal that can be consumed as regular food ("slaughtered in the provinces").

11. Some manuscripts have Rabbi Simeon.

12. For example, *bMenahot* 110a; *bMegillah* 3b.

13. *bSukkah* 49b.

14. For example, *bBerakhot* 32b; *bTaanit* 27b. The purpose of Klawans's entire book, cited in note 2, is to argue against this replacement theory, which he rejects as a form of supersessionism. However, he often goes too far in his dismissiveness with respect to inner-Jewish distancing from sacrifice as a mode of worship, especially in the rabbinic case, which leads him to forced readings of some of his sources.

TWENTY-FIVE

HaNer Tamid, dos Pintele Yid v'ha Zohar Muzar: The Eternal Flame, the Jewish Spark, and the Flaming Queer

Parashat Tsav (Leviticus 6:1–8:36)

NOACH DZMURA

Symbols transform over time. Their life span consists of a birth, a coming-of-age, and then a long slow fade into obsolescence during which we repeat the symbol endlessly with little or no comprehension of its original meaning. Throughout this process, symbols are adorned with new meaning, while retaining some vestige of the old, layer upon layer. Because the shifting meanings instilled in symbols broadcast cultural identities, we can begin to understand how cultures change—and how people themselves change—by tracing a culture's most powerful symbols as they transform through the telling and retelling of stories. Like most religions, Judaism is rich with symbols, and its key text, the Torah, remains a repository of many of the foundational symbols that, despite thousands of years of transitioning, still help define Jews as a people. One such symbol within the Jewish tradition, the eternal flame, or *ner tamid*, which we can trace back to *Parashat Tsav,* could today function as a source of hope, especially for queer Jews, for whom the term *flaming* has generally been considered pejorative. Examining the transitions of this "eternal flame" might help us unearth a new symbol of queer Jewish pride through which the "flamers" among us might ground themselves within the ever-shifting landscape of Jewish culture.

The symbol of the eternal flame tells a story about Jews' relationship to God, first and foremost. But the story of this symbol also provides insight into Jews' relationships with neighboring cultures. By tracing the eternal flame back to its earliest moments in the text, we learn something about stewardship—about the resources a culture values and those it can afford to expend. The eternal flame can help Jews understand their role in manifesting and maintaining God's presence in their lives. It can give new insight into the meaning of the word *eternal* that we might not otherwise have surmised. This brief survey of the *ner tamid* shows that *eternal* might have less to do with notions of "unchanging" or "the status quo" and more to do with "a well-tended relationship that changes and grows." Most important for LGBT people, the story of the *ner tamid* tells how a God outside of human beings became a God who becomes visible in human hearts through human action in the world.

Tracing the Eternal Flame through Time

One of the first instructions a reader encounters in *Parashat Tsav* (a section of Leviticus devoted to the minutiae of sacrificial offerings) is to tend a fire on the altar of the Lord: Leviticus 6:5 says, "And the fire upon the altar shall be kept burning thereby, it shall not go out" (*Ve-ha-aish al ha-mizbe'ach tukad bo, lo tichbe*), a commandment repeated nearly verbatim in the next verse, Leviticus 6:6, which differs only in its reference to the fire as an "*aish tamid*," a continual fire. The instruction is addressed to the priests, Aaron and his sons, who are to kindle this light on the altar before the *Mishkan,* where sacrifices are brought on behalf of the Israelites. Clearly, the double reference to not extinguishing the flame suggests that this "*aish tamid*" is of central importance to the human relationship with God. Indeed, the Rambam, citing the Sifra, a Midrashic rabbinic text, suggests that the first mention applies to the priests, but the second applies to everyone else. In this reading, it is incumbent on all Jews to preserve this literal fire, not because it is a part of the ritual of sacrifice, or because it serves any practical purpose, but solely because it is a symbol of the presence of the Divine.

Who would have guessed that the electric light or gas flame that we see in synagogues today over the Ark of the Covenant, the one we call *ner tamid,* eternal flame, has its root in that priestly flame? Who might have guessed that such a symbol of the Divine would have moved from a huge outdoor bonfire to the inside of our bodies to *dos pintele Yid*, the Yiddish term for the spark of Jewishness that mystics say all Jews possess? Since that little flame burns eternally in the heart of each Jew anyway, perhaps queer Jews may be justified in calling themselves "flamers" as an ecstatic affirmative!

There is an earlier reference in the Torah to the eternal flame, in *Parashat Tetzaveh,* which is typically cited as the source of the commandment still observed today to kindle such a light:

> Ve-atah tetsaveh et bnei yisrael va-yikhu elecha shemen zayit zakh katit la-ma'or leha'a lot ner tamid / And thou shalt command the children of Israel, that they bring unto thee pure olive oil beaten for the light, to cause a lamp to burn continually. (Ex. 27:20)

Is this eternal flame in *Parashat Tetzaveh* the same as the one in *Parashat Tsav* that "must not go out"? Both lights are commanded by God, they are both to burn all the time, and they are both kindled in the same place on the altar of the *Mishkan,* and later in the altar of the Temple. They sound the same so far. However, the language used to refer to the lights is different: one kindled light is an oil lamp that must burn continuously (*ner tamid*), and the other is a wood-burning flame (*aish tamid*) that must be kept burning and not go out (*tukad-bo, lo tichbeh*). Can both these fires be the eternal flame that was commanded and that we still remember to this day? Even in Torah, symbols transform.

The similarities in the two lamps at least symbolically outweigh the differences and teach us that the external appearance of a thing does not always reveal its true nature.

A lamp and a bonfire kindled for the sole purpose of obeying God's command has the same symbolic meaning, no matter its external form. Each light is kindled following an imperative command to do so, and each has been used by commentators as the "source" of the commandment to perpetuate an eternal flame, even after the destruction of the Temple and the end of priestly sacrifices.[1] From this fact we can infer that although these lights are physically different, they are symbolically identical. They are meant to call to each other through time and space as a representation of the relationship between the Eternal and the people.

Since the destruction of the Second Temple, there has been no altar and no flame. What can we learn about Jewish culture and about being queer from an "eternal flame" that was not eternal and no longer flames?

Rekindling an Old Flame

When I see the light above the *Aron haKodesh* (Ark of the Holy, the container that holds the Torah) in synagogues today, to me it seems a bit forlorn. I do not feel the momentous power of the present-day incarnation of this symbol in the way that the ancient Israelites must have felt the power of an eternally burning fire. The priest's *ner tamid* would have been visible in the daytime as a pillar of cloudy smoke and at night as a column of bright light, a visible connection between earth and heaven, between humans and the Divine. In the time of the Temple, this eternal flame on the priests' altar was meant to hark back to the days of wandering in the desert, when God traveled with the Children of Israel as a pillar of fire and a column of smoke,[2] and even earlier to objects that symbolize the connection between earth and heaven from Sumer and other Middle Eastern cultures, including the phallus, pillars, columns, or trees.[3] Has the contemporary transformation from open flame to electricity robbed this symbol of some of its power? My sense of awe and dread is not kindled by the light above the Ark. Instead, I feel a vague sense of concern about the power source in the event of a summer brownout. Will the auxiliary generator kick in? Is it solar powered?

The service leader never draws our attention to the light. The cantor does not extol its virtues in song. We do not stand before it in awe with always-renewing layers of meaning as we do before the Torah scroll. We do not hear it or smell it like we would a wood fire. We scarcely notice it. The little light above the Ark appears to have lost something in translation as it moved from literal fire, which both sustains life and can become the bearer of death, and which demonstrated God's physical presence and power, to a rigidly contained movement of electrons inside a glass bulb that reminds us vaguely of the Divine, like a tape recording of a thunderstorm. It seems a quiet, mild-mannered, unassuming little light. It does not seem to want to draw much attention to itself, just glowing there benignly in the Friday-evening twilight.

The original *ner tamid* was an open flame, a visible pillar of fire, casting heat and light, the engine of combustion generating noise and smoke. The *ner tamid* in our synagogues today is distant from that sensory experience. It is a symbol of a symbol.

Do we simply suffer from the remoteness of our connection to the Divine, or is there another way to think about this transformation of symbols? What am I missing? How did this light bulb replace the bonfire?

Two Flamers

Answering those questions requires looking at the symbol of the eternal flame beyond the priests' *ner tamid*, as it manifests itself at two other points in the narrative history of the Jewish people: the Exodus from Egypt and the Maccabean Revolt. Though they take different form, each iteration of an eternal flame in Jewish tradition symbolizes not only the connection between God and Israel but also the covenant, *brit*, that defines that relationship.

The Pillar of Fire

An eternal flame was important to Jews even before the Israelites were formally recognized as Jews. During the flight from Egypt, God went before the Children of Israel as a pillar of fire by night and a column of cloud (might this have been white smoke?) by day. The Bible tells us this fire is the presence of God, what we might imagine is a "miraculous fire," and never mentions a fire created and fed by humans.

> And the LORD went before them by day in a pillar of cloud, to lead them the way; and by night in a pillar of fire, to give them light; that they might go by day and by night: the pillar of cloud by day, and the pillar of fire by night, departed not from before the people. (Ex. 13:21–22)

I think the miracle of the pillar of fire and the column of smoke is that it might represent a real fire and the first eternal flame that the Israelites carried. Aside from being a portentous symbol of the power and eternal presence of God, a wonder to see and a comfort of light to a people wandering in a profound metaphysical darkness, a pillar of fire and a column of cloud generate in one's neighbors and enemies a recognition of a tribe's singularity (no other people carries fire before them day and night) and of their might. (Who can afford such a waste of combustibles in the desert? How many people and baggage-laden animals does this tribe contain?) On seeing this wonder, the neighbors would certainly suppose that this new people heralded by light and cloud and wandering through the desert are wealthy and numerous. Wealth and numbers would tend to garner respect and a lack of willingness to attack these strangers for plunder. The eternally burning fire is a symbol to outsiders, as well as to straying members of the tribes, of the link between the power of God and the fortunes of the Children of Israel.

The Menorah

When Jerusalem was overrun and the Maccabees reclaimed the Temple from the Seleucid dynasty (approximately 164 BCE), their first action was to rekindle the flame in the Temple's menorah, which miraculously burned for eight days on only one tank of oil. At this point, the symbol of the eternal flame required visible assistance from humans. It had gone out and needed to be relit. The new emphasis that the symbol of the eternal flame acquired was on the active role of the Children of Israel in maintaining the relationship with the Divine.

But the Hasmonean dynasty, founded roughly twenty years after the Maccabean Revolt, was short lived, lasting for only a hundred years. Eventually the Temple was destroyed, sacrifices and huge bonfires were a thing of the past, and self-governance of a Jewish state was lost for close to two thousand years. The people were scattered to the four winds, and over hundreds of years, the single Temple was transformed by the work of the Rabbis and Sages into the form of the present-day synagogue. Sacrifice was no longer possible, and prayer replaced sacrifice as the means through which an eternal relationship with the Deity was tended.

The Eternal Flamer

The eternal flame transformed again. This time, it went in two directions, to meet the needs of the different kinds of Jewish lives. Both aspects of the eternal flame "went stealth," blending in with their surroundings. One aspect of the symbol took up residence above the *Aron haKodesh* in the Synagogue, in the form of an oil lamp, and later a light bulb, that remained lit at all times. Although it retains little of its original character, it is still called the *Ner Tamid*, the Eternal Flame. Instead of sacrifices burnt on an altar, we offer prayers to feed its transformed flames and nurture our relationship with the Divine.

The other aspect of the Eternal Flame moved into the realm of mysticism and became visible only to those with eyes to see beneath the surface. *Dos pintele Yid* is the Yiddish expression, and *Nitzotz HaYehudi* is the Hebrew, for "The Jewish Spark," a clever way of expressing a turn from an external God to whom we owe our allegiance to an internal God that forms the core of one's Jewishness. *Dos pintele Yid* clearly refers to a flame that will never go out that resides in every Jew.

How can queer Jews fan the flame of eternity that resides within? One way might be to recognize that "flaming queen" is not a pejorative but an indicator of one's spiritual health. Queer people do not often speak of their "pintele queer" (perhaps a modern Hebrew rendering, *zohar muzar,* or "flaming queer," might work, especially since the Zohar is one of the preeminent mystical texts), yet all queer Jews, no doubt, feel that they have an inner flame that animates them not only as Jews but as queers.

Through this series of transformations, some light is shed on the notion of *Eternal* that might help in conceptualizing the Deity. We come to understand that *eternal* does not mean "changeless" or even "deathless." In modern Hebrew, *tamid* is translated as "always," but in Biblical Hebrew it also has the meaning of "an activity regularly performed" or perpetual maintenance.[4] So rather than a flame that burns without ceasing, we come to understand the *ner tamid* as a flame that must be tended regularly, incessantly. *Eternal* means "well tended"; it contains an element of memory and human action. Eternity—that which is timeless because it encompasses all time—is based on relationships that occur in time. The Israelites wandering in the desert fed the pillar of fire with wood, the priests tended the fire with wood and fed it with the fruits of a harvest, and the Maccabees provided oil (and perhaps a very conservation-minded wick). Today we fan the electric flames of the *Ner Tamid* in synagogue with our prayers, and we stoke the "*zohar muzar,*" our inner flamer, with our flamboyant support of one another and ourselves. Inspired by this theme, Rabbi J. B. Sacks, one of the first openly gay Conservative rabbis, wrote, "it becomes a holy task to be as flaming as G-d compels us to be, to weave this new flame into our greater identity as a people, and so to live with greater integrity and honor." Rabbi Sacks noted that Ralph Waldo Emerson wrote that "every great achievement is the victory of a flaming heart," and then Rabbi Sacks continued by saying, "may we continue to stoke our inner flame, so that we might attain the greatest achievement of all: to live not merely with ourselves but as ourselves, before God and with humanity."[5]

NOTES

1. In *Commentary on the Torah* (San Francisco: HarperSanFrancisco, 2001), Richard Elliot Friedman uses the verse in *Parashat Tsav* to introduce the commandment of the eternal flame, rather than the verse in *Parashat Tetzaveh,* which is more commonly seen as its source.

2. "And the LORD went before them by day in a pillar of cloud, to lead them the way; and by night in a pillar of fire, to give them light; that they might go by day and by night" (Ex. 13:21–22).

3. "The pillar is often an emblem of the phallus, while two pillars symbolize the Yoni or entrance to the world. The sun in Egypt is shown as a phallic pillar rising from the Eastern horizon, and the pillar of fire which preceded the Israelites is apparently the celestial phallus . . . associated with the midday sun." James Edwin Thorold Rogers, *Bible Folklore: A Study in Comparative Mythology* (London: Kegan Paul, Trench and Co., 1884), 345.

4. F. Brown, S. Driver, and C. Briggs, *Brown-Driver-Briggs Hebrew and English Lexicon* (Peabody, MA: Hendrickson, 1996), 556a [Hebrew], s.v. "tamid," definition 2.

5. Personal communication between Rabbi J. B. Sacks and Gregg Drinkwater, a coeditor of this volume. I am grateful to Rabbi Sacks for his insights connecting the "*aish tamid*" of *Parashat Tsav* with the *pintele Yid* and the idea of flaming in the queer community, and I thank Gregg Drinkwater for sharing those ideas with me.

TWENTY-SIX

Nadav and Avihu and Dietary Laws: A Case of Action and Reaction

Parashat Shemini (Leviticus 9:1–11:47)

TAMAR KAMIONKOWSKI

Parashat Shemini embraces and rejects the human impulse to recognize homoerotic passion as a holy act.[1] The story of Nadav and Avihu offers a glimpse into the human impulse to break through a range of restrictions that societies place on individuals regarding gender-defined emotions and behavior. The rest of the Torah portion, which details the dietary laws, may be understood as an attempt to redirect human activity from fluid and passion-driven to regulated and staid. As we progress through the parasha, human behavior becomes increasingly regulated by the content of the text.

Thus, although on the surface it may seem that these two sections of the Torah portion (the story of Nadav and Avihu and the laws of *kashrut*) are independent of each other, a queer reading of the text actually emphasizes the points of connection between the acts of Nadav and Avihu and the series of food-related prescriptions.

Shemini begins with a section that is often overlooked by general readers of the text, but it lays important groundwork for a queer reading of the Torah portion. The portion begins, "on the eighth day." For a full week, Nadav and Avihu had been sequestered with other new male initiates of the family of Aaron in the rather tight quarters of the Tent of Meeting in the midst of the desert. For seven days, they have been eating and drinking in the presence of God's fiery and smoky manifestations. Finally, on the eighth day, the same ritual day as a traditional circumcision, it is time for the new priests, who have had a rare and almost unprecedented intimacy with God, to take their place within the community. Nadav and Avihu, along with other initiates of the family, perform their priestly duties for the first time for the community of Israel. Probably inundated by the experiences of the past week (close proximity to other men, an abundance of food and drink, sleeping in a sacred space infused with divinely associated smells and sights), they must now perform a series of very carefully prescribed ritual actions. As in a drag show, the individual performer and the audience experience a transformation through the specific sights and sounds, the elaborate costumes and every move of the performer. In the Torah narrative, the performance ends with an extraordinary climax: YHWH reveals himself to the entire community in a blaze of fire. According to the priestly perspective that is represented in this Torah portion, God reveals himself to the community only this one time—at the consecration of the

Sanctuary/Tent of Meeting and the ordination of the priests. As the community witnesses this extraordinary event, they shout out and fall to the ground.

It is against this backdrop that the famous story of Nadav and Avihu is set. On
this eighth symbolic day, a new beginning and a new level of intimacy with God is
marked. As readers, we have only one verse in which to understand what acts Nadav
and Avihu perform. The verse gives us no information about their state of mind or
their intention. Instead, the text specifies a series of actions. Each man takes his fire
pan, puts coals on the pan, places incense on the coals, and then offers God that
which they have just prepared. This may seem like rather innocuous behavior; however, in a highly prescribed ritual world, Nadav and Avihu may have broken a host of
rules through these few actions. Did they use the right coals? Did they use the appropriate incense? If so, were they offering this incense in the correct geographic space
within the Tabernacle? Were they dressed correctly? The only comment that we have
for guidance is the narrator's description of the final product that they had created
together as a strange fire, *aish zarah,* which Moses had not commanded.

Immediately, a fire emerges "from before YHWH and consumes them and they
die before YHWH" (Lev. 10:2). Twice in this verse, the text says "before YHWH," a
rather uncommon occurrence. Some readers imagine that this fire of God emerges
from the heavens and descends down upon the two men. However, it is more likely
that the fire emerged from the Holy of Holies, the most holy inner sanctum of the
Tabernacle, just feet away from the outer court by the entrance where they were most
likely standing. Why does the text not end with "and they died"? Perhaps the emphasis on the fact that they died in the presence of God illuminates what they were seeking in the first place—a more intimate experience of the Divine Presence. They were
in fact taken into the private divine sanctum and thus experienced what no other
men had experienced—a level of impassioned intimate connection with their God. I
will return to this point later.

The history of interpretation on this passage has informed the way many readers engage with this text today. The most common reading is that Nadav and Avihu
committed a willful sin, an offense against God, and that they were punished by God.
This dominant reading—that they transgressed God's commandments, God's wishes,
and that they were killed by God—reinforces the sin-and-punishment motif that is
undoubtedly a central motif in Biblical texts. However, not every commentator has
agreed with this reading.[2] Philo reads the actions of Nadav and Avihu and God's response as altogether positive. According to Philo, Nadav and Avihu consciously chose
to sacrifice or shed their physical bodies in order to ascend to a more divine realm. In
De Somniis 2:67, Philo writes, "They were not seized by a savage, evil beast, but were
taken up by a rush of fire unquenchable, since in sincerity they cast aside sloth and
delay, and consecrated their zeal, hot and fiery, flesh-consuming and swiftly moving,
to piety, a zeal which was alien to creation, but akin to God. They did not mount
by steps to the altar . . . but wafted by a favoring breeze and carried even to the re-
volving heavens were they like the complete and perfect burnt offerings resolved into
ethereal rays of light" (473).[3] Philo further argues that Nadav and Avihu had stripped
themselves of all their garments and stood naked before God.[4] Philo's reading can be

expanded through a queer reading lens. These men, having been in close proximity to other men for a week, and in the presence of the male figure that elicits trembling, passion, and is seemingly unattainable, choose to risk all the cultural norms and legal prescriptions of their generation in order to merge with this ultimate male figure. In a world with highly prescribed rules regarding every aspect of their behavior, rules that are infused with strict boundaries regarding what it is to be male and female, what it means to be religious leaders, they break through all the boundaries for the sake of love and the desire for an ultimate merging. The singing duo Indigo Girls express this desire poetically in their song "Strange Fire": "I come to you with strange fire / I make an offering of love / The incense of my soul is burned / By the fire in my blood."[5] God accepts the men and takes them into his innermost sanctum, and he consumes them in an act of burning passion. There is no indication that God is angry with them; in fact, one could argue the opposite. God's verbal response is, "I am made holy through those that come close to me" (Lev. 10:3). Thus, God's holiness is supported and even enhanced by the acts of Nadav and Avihu. This text offers an example of homoerotic attraction between human males and the male God of the Bible. Each desires to come closer to the other. Nadav and Avihu strip themselves literally and figuratively—they strip themselves of their clothing, of societal expectations, of confining rules—and they come forward. God meets them in a passion of fire, taking them in completely.

But in a fashion that we would expect both from the Biblical text and most societies, there is a response to the transgression of boundaries and to acts of passion. The response contains both a benefit and a loss. The loss is an erasure of the story of passion, and the benefit is the establishment of necessary boundaries. The Torah text and its commentators reconstruct a story of unbridled love and longing into one of willful sin and divine punishment. The dominant narrative that emerges from rabbinic and medieval commentators is that Nadav and Avihu erred by making a decision on their own that had not been commanded by Moses (in other words, they acted with arrogance and challenged Moses's authority regarding matters of law), that they were not worthy to make such offerings because they were not married (again, a connection to a desire for normative living and maintaining boundaries), or that they were drunk with wine and acted irresponsibly.[6] Within these rabbinic debates, a desire for intimacy with the divine and the merging of the human and divine male figures is completely erased.

In addition to the tradition's having effectively expunged this story of love and merging, from a pragmatic perspective, there are some dangers in raising up the actions of Nadav and Avihu. Had the entire community rushed to become one with God, there would be no Israel. For as much as there is an element of beauty to the bonding, it results in the loss of life. Nadav and Avihu do not live to experience other moments of passion, to experiment with boundary crossings, to stretch past the prescriptions of their assigned roles as priests—their potential contribution to their society is lost. So it is Eleazar and Ithamar, the more conservative sons of Aaron, who establish and maintain the priestly line and the interpretation of these roles. It is then that God commands, "Drink no wine or other intoxicant, you or your sons, when you enter the Tent of Meeting, that you may not die. This is a law for all time throughout the ages, for you must distinguish between the sacred and the profane, and between the unclean and the clean" (Lev. 10:9–10). The role of the priests will be to maintain and be accountable for the maintenance of clear-cut boundaries.

In a seemingly abrupt change of tone and content, the rest of the parasha enumerates the dietary laws. In great detail, we are given lists and categories of forbidden and permissible animals for Israelite consumption. There are many different theories regarding the reason for these dietary laws. For our purposes, the work of Mary Douglas is most informative.[7] Douglas has shown that the laws of *kashrut* serve to function as boundary markers. Animals that fall outside of what fits into the "natural" structure of the universe are forbidden. A common example might be animals such as lobsters and crabs: as sea animals they belong in the water, yet they transgress their place in nature by walking on land as well. As the parasha proceeds in great detail with lists and categories, with prohibition after prohibition, the acts of passion by Nadav and Avihu are lost, and the importance of maintaining clear boundaries with regard to flesh emerges victorious.

A queer reading, one that engages the text by focusing on culturally imposed boundaries and categories and the advantages and disadvantages of transgressing those boundaries, helps us to see that it is not happenstance that the dietary laws follow the story of Nadav and Avihu. Like the swing of a pendulum, the dietary laws are the response, the text's way of imposing further restrictions and categories in a world in which people believed that chaos and death could ensue if there were not rigid classifications.

Parashat Shemini is one of many Torah texts that contain homoerotic themes set within a religious context, and one purpose of this commentary has been to bring that theme to the surface. Additionally, this parasha offers a valuable lesson regarding the human impulse to break through boundaries and to defy the role and identities imposed on individuals by a society. The text suggests that the problem with this human impulse lies not within the moral realm but within the pragmatic realm: passion at the cost of death. The rabbinic and medieval commentators may have chosen to emphasize a negative reading of the Nadav and Avihu story in order to downplay the ecstatic and potentially destructive elements within Judaism. Although it is important to maintain boundaries, order, and structure to prevent ecstatic, potentially destructive relations with the Divine from rupturing the community, something is lost in that suppression: passion. It is a cost that the rabbinic and medieval commentators thought worthy of paying for a Judaism that did not become death obsessed. Perhaps it is time that we revisit that cost. How might we reclaim passion as a means of strengthening, not rupturing, community?

NOTES

1. My commentary assumes that the God portrayed here was conceived by its writers and early audiences to be a male God. Furthermore, the narratives focus on the male element of

the community of Israel, the priests (women were excluded from participation). As I read this text, I imagine males in relationship with other males and with a male God. In the few places where the text mentions the "people," *'am*, for my purposes in this reading, it is irrelevant whether women are included in those passing references.

2. Opinions expressed in the Sifra, the *Pesikta de-Rab Kahana,* and *Leviticus Rabbah* point to a line of interpretation arguing that Nadav and Avihu suffered the death penalty through accidental transgressions and that God was saddened by the death of the two men.

3. Translation taken from *Philo,* trans. F. H. Colson and G. H. Whitaker, Loeb Classical Library (Cambridge, MA: Harvard University Press, 1929–1930). Although the early rabbis did not move in Philo's direction, the Kabbalists, centuries later, did consider the idea of Nadav and Avihu's merging with the divine as both worthy of honor and as dangerous.

4. *Legum Allegoriarum* 2:57–58, pp. 259–61. Leviticus 10:5 indicates that the bodies of Nadav and Avihu were carried out of the Tabernacle by their tunics, which has raised the question of why their garments were not burnt up in the fire. It may be that just as the skin of sacrificial animals are not offered up to God, the tunics are the symbolic equivalent of animal skin, and so the garments would not have been consumed by the fire of God.

5. Indigo Girls, "Strange Fire," from their 1987 album *Strange Fire.*

6. These interpretational lines can be found in sources such as Sifra, *Pesikta de-Rab Kahana,* and *Leviticus Rabbah.* For a solid presentation of post-Biblical exegesis on this passage with a focus on Philo, see Robert Kirschner, "The Rabbinic and Philonic Exegesis of the Nadab and Abihu Incident (Lev. 10:1–6)," *Jewish Quarterly Review* 73 (1984): 375–93.

7. Mary Douglas, *Purity and Danger: An Analysis of Pollution and Taboo* (London: Routledge and Kegan Paul, 1966), and later, Mary Douglas, "The Forbidden Animals in Leviticus," *Journal for the Study of the Old Testament* 59 (1993): 3–23.

TWENTY-SEVEN

Nagu'a: Touched by the Divine
Parashat Tazri'a (Leviticus 12:1–13:59)

AYALA SHA'ASHOUA MIRON

If this film is touching on a social or politically oriented issue, let him be a soldier. Let him come from a development town, let him serve on a destroyer; let him be a war widow. Let him be a *ba'al teshuvah*.[1] But if he must be homo[sexual]—then let him suffer. At least don't let him enjoy it. The country is on fire, there's no time for self searching, a war is going on, the audience will not consent. There are dead relatives, why would they identify with me?

These are the opening words of an unusual monologue at the beginning of Amos Gutman's *Nagu'a*,[2] a daring film made in Israel in 1983. The actor playing the main character gazes at the spectator straight in the eye, not allowing him or her to look away. This is probably the first time the word *homo* (as a slang word for homosexual) is uttered in an Israeli film with full meaning and not just as a careless curse. This is the first feature film made in Israel whose main character, as well as its director, relates to his sexual orientation openly.

Israel in the early 1980s was once more in a state of war, the Lebanon War. But for the first time since the country's establishment, the war was seen as a choice and not as a forced or defensive war. As the penetration into Lebanon deepened, the voices questioning the necessity of the war became louder, and the protests in the main square of Tel Aviv became increasingly massive. These protests foreshadowed a new era both for Israeli society and Israeli cinema. They raised new challenges and doubts. They allowed a public discussion of questions concerning other choices that Israeli society had made through the years of constant existential struggle, such as the repression of the traditions and history of Sephardic Jews, identifying them as "Arab." They created an atmosphere that made it eventually possible to deal openly with those who were pushed to the margins of society, people and groups that Israeli society chose to disregard. They cleared the stage for dealing with the infected, with the inflicted, with the forgotten, and with the oppressed. The 1980s in Israeli cinema were, according to a cultural study by NYU Middle Eastern studies scholar Ella Shohat, the time for "The Foregrounding of Marginality."[3]

"Where am I in all of this?" asks Robby, the main character in the film, created in Amos Gutman's image, in his opening monologue, which concludes with a series of challenging, daunting questions: "What will make you pay? . . . What will make you cry? I live my homosexuality. The film is all that's left. All that's left is the call, the necessity, to make the film."

Nagu'a was Amos Gutman's first feature film, following a short film by the same title (later known as "the short *Nagu'a*"). *Nagu'a* in Hebrew means "infected, afflicted, diseased," but if taken literally, it could simply describe the state of being touched. The question the film raises very pointedly for us, looking at it today, from the perspective of more than twenty years, is: Can we identify the potential to turn what was considered two decades ago as a forbidden and afflicted contact, an irrational fear of infection from an inexplicable "disease," into a purifying and redeeming touch?

I believe this is also the question underlying the seemingly dry and technical descriptions of *Parashat Tazri'a*.

Tazri'a is probably one of the most marginal, disregarded, and thus challenging Torah portions. Its usual coupling with *Metzora* ("leprous") naturally did not help raise its appeal or popularity with synagogue goers, Torah readers, and commentators. The treatment this pair of parshiyot, *Tazri'a-Metzora*, unofficially suffers might be a reflection of the treatment we are challenged to reexamine toward people suffering from the skin diseases and bleeding detailed in these Torah portions: exclusion and alienation.

When a woman at childbirth bears a male . . .[4] (Lev. 12:2)

When a person has on the skin of his body a swelling, a rash, or a discoloration . . . (Lev. 13:2)

When a person has a scaly affliction . . . (Lev. 13:9)

These are a few of the main titles or topic areas covered in *Tazri'a*, followed by a series of skin diseases described with repulsive and minute details, including the size, depth, shape, and spectrum of colors and shades that the mark itself or the hair growing on it go through. The narrative does not spare the reader from any of the details, until our reservation turns into mere disgust. If we are not ready simply to skip these details and go on to the next parasha (which is not an easy challenge in itself, since it deals, as mentioned before, with leprosy), we are likely to ask, Why do we need these descriptions of disease in the midst of our Torah (incidentally, *Tazri'a* is precisely in the middle, as the twenty-seventh parasha out of fifty-four)? What would be the point of going over these details year after year? And why is the childbearing woman included in the list of skin diseases, actually giving the portion its title?

I suggest that *Tazri'a* does not only offer us a simple test of patience and endurance; *Tazri'a* offers us a substantial test case to examine our real social potential for tolerance and inclusion, the potential to turn a touch from a moment of fear into one of redemption. *Tazri'a* pushes us to ask ourselves how tolerant we really are of variations from our picture of an "ideal" human body. How willing are we to examine, look into, consider, and understand these differences carefully before throwing them into one generalizing basket of rejection? We can expand this challenge and ask ourselves how comfortable we are with divergence, diversity, and deviation from the "norm" in general, both in others and in ourselves.

The word *tazria* comes from the phrase *Isha Ki Tazria,* which literally means "when a woman brings forth seed." It is a unique Biblical expression that most commentators have interpreted as "a woman conceiving a child." The word *zera* (on which the word *tazria* is based) means both "seed" and "sperm" in Biblical and modern Hebrew, and it usually relates to men or to a seed planted in the earth. The use of the word in this parasha, therefore, associates the woman with the earth, bringing forth the fruit that was planted in her. Ibn Ezra, who is known for his language sensitivity, thus concludes, "The meaning of *Tazria*—gives forth a seed, since she is like the earth."[5]

This interpretation unexpectedly links *Parashat Tazria,* a story of disease, to the creation story. The third day of creation describes the earth's potential for re-creating and regenerating itself through the seed. The creation story in *Bereshit* (Genesis) presents us with pure primary potential, when the world is still in perfect order, when everything still goes according to God's grandly organized plan. Reading *Bereshit,* we can almost see or hear the flapping of the wings of angels and other heavenly creatures, which, according to midrash, were created on the second day.[6] It is much harder to hear this flutter while reading *Parashat Tazria.* What do snowy white angels have to do with greenish-reddish-yellowish skin abnormalities or the heavy blood discharges that follow childbirth?

The thread connecting the "seeding" and childbearing woman with the flourishing seeding earth is very thin, and it goes through the Hebrew verb for seeding, *tazria.* At first the growth and fertility cycle happens within "normal" boundaries, within the normal growth span. But then, the parasha asks, what do we do, how do we relate, or what do the angels sing, when the growth goes out of hand, when the normal reveals its unexpected faces and asymmetrical expressions and turns "abnormal"?

Tazria invites us to explore a different realm of perfection, which has to do not with the heavenly powers of creation but with the power of a human gesture. The *cohen,* the priest, representing society, is the one who defines the *Nega,* the affliction. He offers the necessary steps to redeem the infection and invites the infected back into society, through his touch of grace. The priest is called to visit the infected, to examine their conditions, to measure the marks on their skin and pay careful attention to the differences that they show over time. The priest is called to frame and reframe the *Nega,* the "touched" area. His willingness to look and get in touch with the infected body, his closeness, and his repeated attention are all part of a gesture that turns the site of "infection" into one of purity.

If we are willing to use the infection as a metaphor for other forms of difference in relation, we can appreciate the effort these regulations make to stretch the boundaries of the community to maintain itself, and everyone in it, as holy. If we go a step further, we can also learn that the marginalized and oppressed are not only a challenge to society but also an opportunity, an invitation to bring hidden treasures into light.

Rashi reminds us in his commentary to *Metzora* of an old midrash concerning *tzara'at* (an infection or affliction) in a house (expanding greenish or reddish spots on the walls):[7]

"and I will place a tzara'at affliction"—This is a good tiding to them, that the afflictions are to come upon them—because the Amorites hid treasures of gold in the walls of their houses all forty years that the Israelites were in the desert, and as a result of the affliction he breaks down the house and finds them.[8]

In this mysterious midrash, Rashi relates to the regulations concerning house leprosy: if the priest finds that the walls of a house are afflicted with leprosy (expressed as growing green or red spots on the walls), the house has to be torn down and rebuilt.

By reminding us of this midrash, Rashi offers us an unexpected perspective that helps us see beyond the greenish lichen nibbling at the walls of our houses. Rashi invites us to challenge ourselves by identifying the affliction as a sign, as a challenge, thus allowing it to turn into a hidden treasure. The opportunity that Rashi and this optimistic midrash present to us is the belief that the *Nega*, the affliction, when touched by a well-meaning, purifying hand, can turn into a blessing for us, for society. It can reveal hidden treasures that were kept in the walls, waiting for redemption. These hidden treasures are, first and foremost, the human touch, human grace, the human ability to see beyond the physical.

Amos Gutman, who was a promising young film director, sounding a very personal and unyielding voice, succumbed to AIDS. The last film he made before he died at the young age of thirty-nine deals, like the majority of his films, with life as a gay man in a tight and unified society that leaves little room for people who challenge accepted norms. However, in this swan song, Gutman turns away from the pessimism of *Nagu'a*. Unlike his former films, in which sexual relations are exposed in generous doses, giving the grounds to critics to accuse Gutman of creating pornography, not much sexual contact happens in this film. Here, Gutman's hero, Thomas, touched by the deadly disease, chooses to avoid physical relationship with his lover, Jonathan, in order to protect him from being infected by the virus. The film's title, *Amazing Grace*, reflects a slight opening of a new realm of thought and feeling for Gutman.[9]

Although the film portrays a somber reality, following the life of a dying young man on a farewell visit to the small family he has left behind, Gutman still allows himself to go a small step beyond his typical decadent style. For a few very delicate moments, people allow themselves to expose their deep longings and hopes. These are the moments when the shadow of the afflicted touch reveals the potential of human grace.

NOTES

1. *Ba'al teshuvah* (*teshuvah* = repentance): a person deciding to change his or her life style and live according to the Jewish religious laws.

2. *Nagua* (Israel, 1983), directed by Amos Gutman, screenplay by Amos Gutman and Edna Mazia.

3. Ella Shohat, *Israeli Cinema: East/West and the Politics of Representation* (Austin: University of Texas Press, 1989), 209, 214–215.

4. The Hebrew *Tazri'a* literally means "brings forth seed."

5. Ibn Ezra on Leviticus, 12:2.

6. According to *Bereshit Raba,* portion 3, sign 8.

7. According to *Baba Metzi'a* 25, page 2.

8. Rashi on Leviticus 14:34.

9. *Amazing Grace* (Israel, 1992), directed by Amos Gutman, screenplay by Amos Gutman, produced by Dagan Price.

TWENTY-EIGHT

It's the Purity, Stupid: Reading Leviticus in Context
Parashat Metzora (Leviticus 14:1–15:33)

JAY MICHAELSON

For gay and lesbian Jews and their allies, *Parashat Acharei Mot* contains some of the most infamous passages of the Torah, condemning as they do at least some forms of male homosexual behavior. Often these verses are read completely without context, and sometimes they are read only in the context of the other sexual prohibitions of Leviticus 18 and 20. Yet the wider context of the Levitical prohibitions within the Holiness Code and related portions of Biblical text is essential to understanding their meaning and significance. In fact, although today one hears all sorts of "explanations" of why "homosexuality" is prohibited in Leviticus 18, a review of the chapters around it reveals an agenda entirely different from those usually proffered today.

The two portions preceding *Acharei Mot*, *Tazri'a* and *Metzora* (usually read together as a "double portion") contain some of the most obscure, and seemingly alien, laws of the Torah. In these portions, we learn about the laws of leprosy (actually *tzaraat*, a skin disease similar to leprosy but different in various ways), seminal emissions, and menstruation; here we are told the detailed method of the sacrificial sin-offerings and wave-offerings and the methods of purity and contamination. In fact, the extended *sugya* (topical section) to which *Tazri'a* and *Metzora* belong begins in the previous parasha, *Shemini*, which describes how Aaron's sons Nadav and Avihu brought "strange fire" (*eish zarah*, which can also be translated as "foreign fire") into the Tabernacle and were destroyed. The Hebrew text, in the first verses of Leviticus 10, is actually a bit ambiguous as to exactly what happens; it is not clear whether God sends out a fire to destroy the young priests or whether they are consumed by their own creation (see Tamar Kamionkowski's essay on *Parashat Shemini* for an alternative reading). But the response is clear: a "team meeting" between Moses, Aaron, and Aaron's remaining sons, in which new rules are set forth for regulating priestly behavior and maintaining the purity of the Israelite nation.

The "minutes" of this meeting are quite lengthy. Their essence, both textually and in the context of what archeologists tell us regarding the cultic practices of ancient Canaan, which were varied, syncretic, and often ecstatic in nature, is contained in Leviticus 10:9–11: "Do not drink wine or strong drink, you and your sons, when you come into the tabernacle, so you don't die. This will be an eternal law for your generations, so you can discern between holy and secular, and between impure and pure, and so you can teach the children of Israel the laws that God speaks to them through

Moses." The injunction—to discern and distinguish, separate and sanctify—is the essence of Biblical Judaism. Indeed, it is a double distinction, both internal (this is a worship of discernment) and external (it separates Israelites from Canaanites); Israel is distinguished by its distinguishing. Nadav and Avihu invented their own ritual and imported "foreign" cultic practice—a double sin. Israelite worship is not to be an ecstatic bacchanal in which distinctions are erased and the god(s) known in wild abandon. It is to be precise, mindful of distinctions, and separated from anything "unclean" or foreign.

This general rule is explicated, in great and often gory detail, in the eight chapters that follow. Chapter 10 discusses clean and unclean, pure and impure, permitted and forbidden. Chapter 11 spends forty-seven verses on which animals may be eaten and which are "abominations" (here the Hebrew word is *sheketz*, whose exact meaning, like that of Leviticus 18's *toevah*, is unknown), before repeating the injunction "to discern between impure and pure." Chapter 12, the first of *Parashat Tazri'a*, describes the laws of separation of the "impure" mother following childbirth; chapter 13, the specific diagnosis for *tzaraat* (fifty-nine verses); and chapter 14 (the beginning of *Parashat Metzora*), its spiritual-physical remedy, which involves quarantine (i.e., separation to contain the contaminating agent) and special offerings and whose fifty-seven verses are closed again by the injunction "to teach when something is impure, and when it is pure." Finally, and ending *Parashat Metzora*, are fifty-seven more verses, this time of chapter 15, describing how seminal and menstrual emissions render a person *tameh* ("impure") and how *tahara* ("purity") is to be regained after them. The parasha concludes, "thus shall you separate the children of Israel from their impurity, and they shall not die from it by defiling my tabernacle which is among them" (Lev. 15:31).

All this distinguishing and separating acts as a prelude to the Levitical material known as the "Holiness Code," which begins in chapter 17 and is so named because of its repeated injunctions to the Israelites to be *kadosh*, "holy." Although all this material is assumed by Biblical scholars to be of the same priestly origin ("P" in the nomenclature of Biblical criticism), it is the Holiness Code and the material surrounding it that is perhaps at the heart of the Levitical purity agenda.

The general theme of this material is quite clear. This part of the Torah is not about what is "natural" or what is ethical or unethical. It is about what is pure and what contaminates, what is proper for Israelites, and what is to be left to other nations. Indeed, Leviticus 18 itself is quite clear on this point. After reciting the prohibitions on incest, male homosexual behavior, bestiality, and sex with a menstruating woman— all of which seem to be equivalent in gravity—an explicit rationale is provided: "Do not impurify yourself with all these things, because with all these things the nations, who I am sending away before you, impurified themselves, and impurified the land." ("Impurified" is a bit clumsy, but it is meant to translate *titamu*, the same word as *tameh*; words such as *defiled* fail to make the connection.)

As anthropologist Mary Douglas describes, however, these concerns are not limited to this portion of the priestly code; they undergird the way the Bible describes the creation of the world (order from disorder), how it orders the social realm, and how, in general, the ordered cultic worship of YHWH defined itself in opposition to contemporaneous spiritual practices. This text is about ancient cultic purity and the prohibition of foreign actions and mixtures that contaminated it. It is not about "homosexuality," a concept invented in the 19th century, nor is it about the family, nature, or morality. After all, what do menstruation, vultures, leprosy, and male-male anal sex have in common? Ethics? Hardly.

It is also worth observing how much more weight is given today to one verse in Leviticus 18 than the forty-seven verses of chapter 11, fifty-nine of chapter 12, and fifty-seven of chapter 15. Both religious bigots and antireligious activists sometimes act as if the Bible is all about homosexuality, but a lot more of it is about leprosy—about 220 verses more, to be precise. And why? Because both contaminate the cultic purity of the Israelite nation and blur the distinctions between Israel and other. Now, such subjects may not suit anyone's political or religious agenda—"God hates shrimp" does not quite have the punch of "God hates fags"—but it is what is in the text.

Ironically, much of the struggle with texts such as Leviticus 18 is attributable to a well-intentioned but ultimately misguided hermeneutic of making Torah texts "relevant" to our own day. Because skin diseases do not play a significant role in most contemporary spirituality, and menstruation is rarely a hot-button political issue, the texts of *Metzora* are generally accorded far less import than those of *Acharei Mot*—and yet this prioritization is a contemporary import into the text of the Torah, which contains no such order. Of course, homiletical and political uses of the Torah succeed precisely when they do address contemporary concerns. Yet when we clumsily attempt to make the Torah "relevant" to our times, we often import our own biases and agendas into a text that, like it or not, is about ancient cultic purity and the prohibition of foreign actions and mixtures that contaminated it.

If this world of purity and danger seems distant from our own, well, perhaps it is. Perhaps the Biblical obsessions with cleanliness and separation from other nations do not speak to us as they did to their original audience. I find, however, that discarding the criterion of "relevance" opens, rather than closes, the text. When we release our own religious/spiritual agendas about what sacred texts are *supposed* to say, we are taken on a journey of discovery into what they actually *do* say.

For example, we know from the archeological record that these sexual practices were forbidden because people were doing them, expressing their religiosity in unorthodox, hybrid, and "foreign" ways that were abhorrent to the priestly elite in Jerusalem. What was Israelite religion really like? Can we imagine a religio-cultic world at war between the "purifiers" and the "mixers," those who sought separation and those who blessed the blending? For that matter, can we really conceive of a religion in which the body, not the soul, was the site of holiness and sin? And what must it have been like to live in a world without technology, to yearn so deeply for the forces of order that they were deified—and to fear chaos so intensely as to demonize it?

This is not to say that when Leviticus 18 is viewed in the context of boundary patrol, the "problem" of male-male sexuality disappears. Indeed, it may intensify. Of the many iterations of religious queer identity proposed in recent years, some of the most interesting connect homosexuality with liminality and an upsetting of categories of sexual binarism and dimorphism. Curiously, in both contemporary queer theory and contemporary gay spirituality—two discourses that almost never interact with each other—binaries are the problem and queer sexuality is the remedy. In queer theory, gender and sexual dimorphisms are social constructions that invariably efface difference, administer power to the powerful, and subject the weak/disfavored to the rule of the strong/favored.[1] Dyads such as them/us, black/white, and female/male are inexact, indeed incorrect, simplifications of actual experience, and they invariably subordinate one side to the other. Many contemporary philosophers have argued that even the basic dualisms of self/other and presence/absence contain within them the seed of oppression, marginalization, and subjugation;[2] as soon as we divide, we begin to conquer. In this regard, homosexuality, like other forms of sexual and gender variance, can serve as "a potentially privileged site for the criticism and analysis of cultural discourses"[3] by eluding the heteronormative expectations of gender and sexual roles.

Likewise, the leading writers of the half-anthropological, half-fantastical literature of "gay spirituality"[4] regard gender hierarchy as, if not oppressive, at least constricting and reductive. From this perspective, the ancient spiritual roles of "those who walk between," including shamans, healers, and other intercessors with the infinite, undermine gender and sexual categories and hierarchies. These writers draw on diverse traditions, from the gender-variant Galli of the Mediterranean[5] to, most importantly, shamanic and "primitive" traditions around the world.[6] Over 150 Native American traditions,[7] for example, believed that people we would now label as gay or lesbian possessed two spirits, one masculine and one feminine, and accorded them special significance in society. Some were medicine men (or women or neither men nor women), some assumed gender roles different from their anatomical sex, some were shamans and warriors. None was "virtually normal." Of course, our understanding of these cultures is still greatly attenuated, but we do know that "third-gendered" and "two-spirited" people are emissaries of the sacred in numerous religious traditions. Symbolically, ordinary life is the place of distinctions; therefore, those who transcend distinctions likewise transcend ordinary life. As such, in their defiance of conventional boundaries, the gender-variant shamans of the Plains Indians (including Omaha, Sioux, Iban, and Hidatsa people) and Siberia (including the Chukchi, Yakut, and Koryak tribes), the *basir* of Borneo, and the male *isangoma* of the Zulu were seen to be in closer contact with the "other dimension"—that of the spiritual.

Yet if Leviticus 18 is about order and chaos—indeed, if Judaism sets itself up against a (real or imagined) "other" that sacralizes the liminal—then liberated sexuality, and *a fortiori* transgressive sexuality, may be transgressive of the basic ordering norms of Biblical Judaism itself, which extend beyond the Holiness Code to dietary laws that divide water creatures from air creatures and air creatures from earth creatures and that abhor any transgression of these boundaries.[8] Even the basic structure of Genesis is implicated: God saw that it was good—because now it was ordered, whereas before it was not. Or, taking another cue from Douglas (this time from *Leviticus as Literature*), we can see the precision of the sacrificial offerings as mirroring the precision of the design of the Tabernacle, and even the structure of the Biblical text itself.[9] Indeed the prohibitions, and the symbolism, extend even down to garments: *shatnez*, the Biblically proscribed blending of wool and linen, was prohibited precisely because it was sacred to the Egyptians (possibly like forbidden sexual unions) and, according to many symbolic interpretations, because it is an improper blending of what should be kept separate. Some traditional Jewish commentators see the Levitical ban on male anal sex in the same way.[10] The very Hebrew word for holiness, *kadosh* (etymologically related to *kedeshah*) carries the meaning of "separate."

The Levitical understanding of liminality is squarely opposed, perhaps even deliberately, to the sacralization of boundary crossing found in certain shamanic cultures, hypothesized in the ancient Near East, and celebrated by latter-day spiritual thinkers, many of whom are themselves constructing their views in deliberate opposition to "Judeo-Christian" religious thought.

So it is not that the textual problems disappear when one engages with the text on its own terms, but at least they are then the "problems" of the Bible rather than of those who seek to manipulate Biblical text for their own contemporary purposes. And, of course, it is by no means clear that the categories posited by the Bible should be taken as given—queer Biblical commentator Ken Stone has argued that "the binary opposition between 'Israelite' and 'Canaanite' turns out, in large part, to be an effect of particular biblical discourses"[11] and that the entire sexual distinction between the two groups was invented by Biblical authors seeking to demarcate pseudoethnic, rather than ethical-sexual, boundaries.[12] Nor should we take the categories as desirable; demonizing chaos, for example, has long gone hand in hand with demonizing women.

But at least now we are making theological headway, investigating the peculiar religion of the ancient Israelites, with its multiple anxieties and boundaries, rather than contemporary homophobia. Personally, for all my reservations regarding these ancient texts, I find that they can take on a cast of wonderment, as long as I do not try to make them "relevant" or reduce their foreignness to domesticity. When I let them be what they are—ancient, cultic, and strange—I find that, in a contemporary world devoid of magic, these tribal taboos possess a power of enchantment.

NOTES

1. See David Halperin, *One Hundred Years of Homosexuality* (New York: Routledge, 1990), 43–48; Jonathan Ned Katz, *The Invention of Heterosexuality* (New York: Dutton, 1995); Eve Kosofsky Sedgwick, *Epistemology of the Closet* (Berkeley: University of California Press, 1990). For applications of queer theory to questions of Jewish identity, see Daniel Boyarin, Daniel Itzkovitz, and Ann Pellegrini, eds., *Queer Theory and the Jewish Question* (New York: Columbia University Press, 2003). On gender dimorphism specifically, see Gilbert Herdt, *Third Sex, Third Gender: Beyond Sexual Dimorphism in Culture and History* (New York: Zone, 1996).

2. See, e.g., Emmanuel Levinas, "Diachrony and Representation," in *Time and the Other and Additional Essays*, trans. Richard A. Cohen, 45–51 (Pittsburgh: Duquesne University Press, 1987); Jacques Derrida, "Like the Sound of the Sea Deep within a Shell: Paul De Man's War," *Critical Inquiry* 14, no. 3 (Spring 1988): 590–652.

3. David Halperin, *Saint Foucault: Toward a Gay Hagiography* (New York: Oxford University Press, 1995), 61.

4. Examples include Randy Conner, *Blossom of Bone: Reclaiming the Connections between Homoeroticism and the Sacred* (San Francisco: HarperSanFrancisco, 1993); Toby Johnson, *Gay Spirituality: The Role of Gay Identity in the Transformation of Human Consciousness* (Maple Shade, NJ: Lethe, 2004); Mark Thompson, *Gay Spirit: Myth and Meaning* (New York: St. Martin's, 1988).

5. See Conner, *Blossom of Bone*, 99–125; Will Roscoe, "Priests of the Goddess: Gender Transgression in Ancient Religion," *History of Religions* 35, no. 3 (1996): 295–330.

6. See Conner, *Blossom of Bone*, 19–61. On Native American religion and homoeroticism, see Will Roscoe, *Changing Ones: Third and Fourth Genders in Native North America* (New York: Palgrave, 2000); Walter Williams, *The Spirit and the Flesh: Sexual Diversity in American Indian Culture* (Boston: Beacon, 1986).

7. See Roscoe, *Changing Ones*, 222–47 (providing index of documented accounts of 157 Native American tribes with "third gender" traditions), 39–67 (discussing Navajo traditions), and 137–67 (Yuman traditions); Williams, *Spirit and the Flesh*, 17–109.

8. See Mary Douglas, *Purity and Danger: An Analysis of the Concepts of Pollution and Taboo* (New York: Routledge, 2002), 59–61; Ken Stone, *Practicing Safer Texts: Food, Sex, and Bible in Queer Perspective* (London: T. & T. Clark, 2006), 46–50. As Stone notes, Douglas did not greatly engage with sexual prohibitions in her early work. On Douglas's views on sexual taboos, see Stone, *Practicing Safer Texts*, 4–6; Jeffrey Stout, *Ethics after Babel: The Languages of Morals and Their Discontents* (Princeton, NJ: Princeton University Press, 2001), 156–61. But see Mary Douglas, *Leviticus as Literature* (Oxford: Oxford University Press, 1999), 20–25 (refuting much of her earlier book's theories).

9. Douglas, *Leviticus as Literature*, 19, 221–23.

10. See Steven Greenberg, *Wrestling with God and Men: Homosexuality in Jewish Tradition* (Madison: University of Wisconsin Press, 2005), 175 (citing Ibn Ezra).

11. Stone, *Practicing Safer Texts*, 59. See also Jonathan Tubb, *Canaanites* (Norman: University of Oklahoma Press, 1998); Israel Finkelstein and Neil Asher Silberman, *The Bible Unearthed: Archaeology's New Vision of Ancient Israel and the Origin of Its Sacred Texts* (New York: Free Press, 2001).

12. See Tikva Frymer-Kensky, *In the Wake of the Goddesses: Women, Culture, and the Biblical Transformation of Pagan Myth* (New York: Ballantine, 1993), 200–202; Stone, *Practicing Safer Texts*, 58–61.

TWENTY-NINE

How Flexible Can Jewish Law Be?
Parashat Acharei Mot (Leviticus 16:1–18:30)

ELLIOT N. DORFF

This section of the Torah stings more than any other. One verse in it has been the source of immense pain for gay men for literally thousands of years: "You shall not lie with a man as a man lies with a woman; it is an abomination" (Lev. 18:22). Although lesbians are not mentioned here or, for that matter, anywhere else in the Bible, the classical Rabbis on their own authority later forbade lesbian sex as well.[1]

What shall we make of this verse in our time? The Jewish tradition has interpreted and narrowed many other morally problematic verses in the Torah, making the death penalty virtually inoperative,[2] defining the "stubborn and rebellious son" who the Torah says is to be stoned (Deut. 21:18–21) so narrowly that such a person "never was and never will be,"[3] and changing "an eye for an eye" (Ex. 21:24) from retribution to monetary compensation.[4] On the other hand, the Rabbis expanded the many Torah verses that give us valuable moral norms to make our tradition truly a treasure trove of moral guidance on many, many other matters.[5]

The verse in question, though, has very little legislative history. The only thing that the Rabbis of the Talmud discuss about it is whether it forbids two unmarried men who are traveling on business to share a bed at an inn. Although Rabbi Judah and some later rabbis think that it does, the majority opinion through the ages is that it does not, because "Jews are not suspected for such things."[6] Even the leniency bites!

What this lack of legislative history means is that any contemporary treatment of this topic cannot rely on a long effort by rabbis of the past to modify the harshness of this law and its rabbinic extensions for gay men or lesbians. One must rather create new arguments. In doing that, how one understands the authority of Jewish law and the methods one uses to interpret and apply it take on crucial importance.

For contemporary Orthodoxy, the Torah's prohibition in Leviticus 18:22 and its rabbinic extensions are complete and unchangeable: neither male-male nor female-female sex acts of any sort are permitted. The most lenient position among Orthodox rabbis has been to distinguish the sin from the sinner, but many Orthodox rabbis would not make that distinction and would ban gay men from being honored in the synagogue by being called to the Torah or leading services. Until the movie *Trembling before G-d* appeared, some Orthodox Jews even maintained that there were no gay and lesbian Orthodox Jews, but that claim has now been thoroughly disproved.[7]

On the other end of the spectrum, Reform Judaism encourages Jews to deepen their ties to the Jewish tradition through education and action but does not see Jewish law as being authoritative and thus ultimately leaves it to individuals to express their Jewish identity as they choose. It is thus a bit surprising that it took as long as it did for Reform positions on these issues to congeal. In 1973, the Reform synagogue organization admitted its first member congregation that had specific outreach to the gay and lesbian community (Beth Chayim Chadashim in Los Angeles). It was not until 1990, though, that its seminary opened its doors to gays and lesbians, and it was not until 2000 that its rabbinic organization endorsed the actions of those Reform rabbis who perform commitment ceremonies for gay and lesbian couples—as well as those who refuse to do so.

It has thus been primarily within the Conservative movement that the debate about the status of homosexuals and homosexual sex has been carried on. In 1990 and 1991, both the synagogue and rabbinic organizations of the movement approved an identical resolution that narrowed the subjects of the debate by declaring that they "support full civil equality for gays and lesbians in our national life, and deplore the violence against gays and lesbians in our society, and reiterate that, as are all Jews, gay men and lesbians are welcome as members in our congregations, and call upon our synagogues and the arms of our movement to increase our awareness, understanding and concern for our fellow Jews who are gay and lesbian."[8] This statement clearly came out against civil discrimination in social issues such as jobs, housing, and healthcare. Moreover, many Conservative Jews who oppose *Jewish* ceremonies to unite gay couples favor *civil* marriages for gays and lesbians. So the issues narrowed down to two—Jewish commitment ceremonies or marriages for same-sex couples and ordination of gay and lesbian rabbis—both of which depend, in the eyes of many observers, on how one deals with Leviticus 18:22 and its subsequent rabbinic expansion.

After all, if homosexual sex is prohibited by Jewish law, one certainly would not want to create a public ceremony celebrating a union in which such prohibited acts would presumably take place. On the contrary, to do so would be to "put a stumbling block before the eyes of the blind" (Lev. 19:14), which the Rabbis understood to mean the morally as well as the physically blind,[9] for such a ceremony might mislead people into thinking that homosexual sex is both permitted and worthy of public celebration. Furthermore, to ordain homosexuals as rabbis would make no sense, for rabbis should be models of what it means to live as a serious Jew, and so ordaining homosexuals would make about as much sense as ordaining rabbis who intentionally and repeatedly violate the laws of Shabbat. Both of these conclusions, however, depend on retaining the ban on homosexual sex in the first place.

On December 6, 2006, the Conservative Movement's Committee on Jewish Law and Standards (CJLS), the committee charged with making official decisions in Jewish law for the Conservative Movement, approved two rabbinic rulings, one of which (by Rabbi Joel Roth) maintains the traditional ban on gay and lesbian sex and therefore also on celebrations of same-sex unions and ordination, and the other (by Rabbis Daniel Nevins, Avram Reisner, and me) permits Conservative rabbis to perform commitment ceremonies for gay and lesbian couples and allows Conservative seminaries to ordain gay men and lesbians. This latter ruling did so, though, by retaining the Torah's ban—as the Sages of the Talmud understood it—on gay anal sex. The CJLS also voted not to approve two other rulings that would have overturned the ban on gay sex altogether.[10]

As one of the authors of "the middle position" that passed, I will explain our rabbinic ruling from my perspective—which, I should note at the outset, is different to some extent from that of each of my partners in this effort. Because I specialize in medical ethics, I became familiar with many gay Jews after I was appointed in 1981 to an AIDS task force at UCLA Medical Center. I served as vice president of Nehama, Jewish AIDS Services, established by the Jewish Federation Council and Jewish Family Service of Los Angeles to help Jewish AIDS patients and their caregivers with food and social services. Furthermore, after the CJLS first dealt with homosexuality in 1991–1992, my daughter came out to my wife and me as a lesbian. As a result, I have had considerable personal involvement with the Jewish gay and lesbian community and wanted to overturn the ban altogether if I could find a way to do that, within my understanding of Jewish law.

From the beginning of this process, however, I suspected that the CJLS and the Conservative Movement as a whole were not ready for that bold a step, and I did not want the perfect to be the enemy of the good. Those concerns led me to contribute to the analysis I present here.

Leviticus 18:22 is itself ambiguous. Although men and women can have sexual intercourse vaginally, anally, or orally, by far the most common form is vaginally.[11] If vaginal sex is what is intended by the verse, though, then a man physically cannot have sex with another man as a man has sex with a woman, for the simple reason that a man does not have a vagina. Modern Biblical scholars have thus suggested a variety of meanings of the Biblical verse.

Whatever the verse originally meant, though, is legally irrelevant because the Jewish tradition is based on the way that the classical Rabbis of the Mishnah and the Talmud and then rabbis throughout the ages to our own time have interpreted the Torah (in contrast to how other Jews, Christians, Muslims, and modern Biblical scholars do). The classical Rabbis and their successors during the Middle Ages understood the verse to ban anal sex by men, as David Brodsky illustrates in his essay about *Parashat Kedoshim* in this volume. All other forms of homosexual sex acts the Talmudic Rabbis prohibited by rabbinic enactment.

As rabbis committed to uphold and foster Jewish law and tradition, Rabbis Nevins and Reisner and I certainly did not approach the prospect of overturning two thousand years of rabbinic precedent lightly. Two factors, though, prompted us to do so in this case. First, scientifically we now know about sexual orientation. We understand, as our ancestors did not, that homosexual acts are not rebellions against Jewish law by people who are all presumed to be heterosexual; that was clearly the Rabbis' presumption in ruling, as noted earlier, that men on a business trip may share a bed because Jews are not suspected of rebelling against Jewish law by engaging in homosexual sex acts. Science also has demonstrated that discrimination against gays and lesbians in our society has produced much higher rates of suicide, smoking, and depression, together with many other threats to the physical and psychological well-being of gays and lesbians.[12] Further, interventions to convert gays and lesbians into heterosexuals simply do not work and usually make matters worse, so we surely should not urge homosexuals to try such interventions.[13]

In addition to these scientific findings, Jewish values motivated us. Specifically, the Talmud declares that honor of our fellow human beings is so great a value for us Jews that it may supersede rabbinic legislation that undermines that honor.[14] It is clearly a dishonor to gays and lesbians to maintain that their sexual acts are an "abomination"; that view, in fact, has directly produced many of the assaults on the minds and bodies of LGBT people just enumerated. It is also both cruel and demeaning to rule that they may never engage in any sexual expression. Celibacy is a Catholic way of spirituality; it is not a Jewish one. Furthermore, the Torah and the Talmud are at one in declaring that "it is not good for a person to live alone," that we need intimate companions, including sexual ones.[15]

These two factors then—science and our concern for other human beings—led us in this case to overturn the rabbinic *extensions* of the Torah's ban. That we maintained the Torah's ban on male-male anal sex is clearly not ideal, for a majority of gay men enjoy it, but it is not a total legal fiction either, for research indicates that between 20 percent and 50 percent of gay men do not engage in it, most for fear of HIV/AIDS or because they simply do not like it.[16] We retained the Torah's ban both because we judged that as contemporary rabbis we have the authority to change what rabbis in the past had done but not what the Torah itself demands, except in emergency situations, and also because, frankly, we knew that the Conservative Movement was not ready to abandon this commandment of the Torah. In any case, our ruling requires that rabbis interviewing gay couples in preparation for their commitment ceremony, and admissions committees considering candidates for rabbinical school, respect the privacy of the people involved with regard to their sexual practices, just as they do with regard to heterosexuals.

This ruling, with its one important drawback, permits Conservative rabbis to perform public, Jewish commitment ceremonies for gays and lesbians, and it opens the doors to gays and lesbians to become rabbis. It also asks that Jewish gay men and lesbians seek to raise Jewish children, whether through alternative insemination, surrogacy, or adoption. We Jews are in deep demographic crisis, and we need all Jews to help us ensure the physical as well as the spiritual continuity and vibrancy of the Jewish tradition. Only by at once thinking expansively about the social needs of all Jews and reading the Levitical ban in *Acharei Mot* narrowly may we most successfully build our Jewish communities in the 21st century.

NOTES

Abbreviations:

J. = Jerusalem (Palestinian) Talmud (edited c. 400 CE)
M. = Mishnah (edited by Rabbi Judah ha-Nasi, c. 200 CE)
B. = Babylonian Talmud (edited by Ravina and Rav Ashi, c. 500 CE)
M.T. = Maimonides's *Mishneh Torah* (completed in 1177 CE)
S.A. = Joseph Karo's *Shulhan Arukh* (completed in 1563)

1. *Sifra*, Acharei Mot 9:8.

2. M. *Makkot* 1:10.

3. B. *Sanhedrin* 71a.

4. M. *Bava Metzia* 8:1 and the Talmud thereon.

5. For some examples of that expansion, see my books on Jewish ethics: *Matters of Life and Death: A Jewish Approach to Modern Medical Ethics* (Philadelphia: Jewish Publication Society, 1998); *To Do the Right and the Good: A Jewish Approach to Modern Social Ethics* (Philadelphia: Jewish Publication Society, 2002); *Love Your Neighbor and Yourself: A Jewish Approach to Modern Personal Ethics* (Philadelphia: Jewish Publication Society, 2003); *The Way into Tikkun Olam (Fixing the World)* (Woodstock, VT: Jewish Lights, 2005).

6. M. *Kiddushin* 4:14; B. *Kiddushin* 82a; M.T. Laws of Forbidden Intercourse 22:2; S.A. Even Ha-Ezer 24.

7. *Trembling before G-d,* a documentary movie directed by Sandi Simcha Dubowski that first aired in 2001, includes interviews with gay and lesbian Orthodox Jews in both the Modern Orthodox and the Ultra-Orthodox communities in North America and Israel. Some have left the Orthodox world of their upbringing, but many continue to affirm their Orthodox Jewish identity and belong to Orthodox synagogues and communities.

8. *1990 Rabbinical Assembly Proceedings* (New York: Rabbinical Assembly, 1990), 275.

9. B. *Pesahim* 22b; B. *Mo'ed Katan* 17a; B. *Kiddushin* 32a; B. *Bava Metzia* 75b.

10. Readers can find all four of those rulings in their entirety, as well as one-page summary statements written by their authors, at www.rabbinicalassembly.org under the link "Contemporary Halakhah." There was also a third opinion (by Rabbi Leonard Levy) that the committee approved, which is also available at that website, but it was approved by the smallest amount of votes possible for validation (six votes out of the twenty-five members), and it largely comes to the same conclusions as Rabbi Roth's does, although through different reasoning, and so I have not presented it here as a separate stance. To the consternation of many gays and lesbians; however, Rabbi Levy, unlike Rabbi Roth, argues that at least some gays and lesbians can convert into heterosexuals, and those that think they can should try to do so.

11. Robert T. Michael, John H. Gagnon, Edward O. Laumann, and Gina Kolata, *Sex in America: A Definitive Survey* (Boston: Little, Brown, 1994), chap. 7, esp. 135, 139–147.

12. On suicide, see R. I. Kitts, "Gay Adolescents and Suicide: Understanding the Association," *Adolescence* 40, no. 159 (Fall 2005): 621–628; G. Remafedi, S. French, M. Story, M. D. Resnick, and R. Blum, "The Relationship between Suicide Risk and Sexual Orientation: Results of a Population-Based Study," *American Journal of Public Health* 88, no. 1 (1998): 57–60; and Jay Paul et al., "Suicide Attempts among Gay and Bisexual Men: Lifetime Prevalence and Antecedents," *American Journal of Public Health* 92, no. 8 (2002): 1338–1345, the latter of which found that 12 percent of urban gay and bisexual men have attempted suicide in their lifetime, a rate three times higher than the overall rate for American adult males, and that

younger men were attempting suicide earlier in their lives, usually before age twenty-five. A search on www.pubmed.gov under "gay, suicide, teen" produces dozens of references.

On depression, see A. R. D'Augelli, "Developmental Implications of Victimization of Lesbian, Gay, and Bisexual Youths," in G. M. Herek (ed.), *Stigma and Sexual Orientation: Understanding Prejudice against Lesbians, Gay Men, and Bisexuals* (Thousand Oaks, CA: Sage, 1998), 187–210; K. Y. Ritter and A. I. Terndrup, *Handbook of Affirmative Psychotherapy with Lesbians and Gay Men* (New York: Guilford, 2003).

On smoking, see R. D. Stall, G. L. Greenwood, M. Acree, J. Paul, and T. J. Coates, "Cigarette Smoking among Gay and Bisexual Men," *American Journal of Public Health* 89 (1999): 1875–1878, according to which 48 percent of gay men smoke, compared to an overall rate of 27 percent among U.S. men.

13. For a bibliography of studies demonstrating these assertions, see the one compiled by Judith Glassgold that serves as the appendix to the Dorff, Nevins, and Reisner responsum on homosexuality at www.rabbinicalassembly.org, under the link "Contemporary Halakhah."

14. B. *Berakhot* 19b; B. *Shabbat* 81a–81b; 94b; B. *Eruvin* 41b; B. *Megillah* 3b; B. *Haggigah* 16b; J. *Nazir* 56a.

15. Genesis 2:18; B. *Yevamot* 118a; B. *Ketubbot* 75a; B. *Kiddushin* 7a, 41a; B. *Bava Kamma* 111a. Both the Torah and Resh Lakish in the Talmud were, of course, speaking of marriage between a man and a woman, but they indicate the need we all have for a stable, intimate, caring, and supportive relationship.

16. Two longitudinal studies conducted by researchers at the University of California, San Francisco, the Urban Men's Health Study (Catania et al.) and the Young Men's Study (Osmond and Catania), indicate that only 50 percent of the gay men surveyed engage in anal sex. Edward O. Laumann, in *The Social Organization of Sexuality: Sexual Practices in the United States* (Chicago: University of Chicago Press, 1994), found that 20 percent of gay men never practice it. A survey conducted from 1994 to 1997 in San Francisco by the Stop AIDS Project, though, indicated that over the course of the study the proportion of men who have sex with men engaging in anal sex increased from 57.6 percent to 61.2 percent, so the Laumann estimate is probably much too high. See Centers for Disease Control, "Increases in Unsafe Sex and Rectal Gonorrhea among Men Who Have Sex with Men—San Francisco, California, 1994–1997," *MMWR*, January 29, 1999, 45–48.

THIRTY

Sex in the Talmud: How to Understand Leviticus 18 and 20

Parashat Kedoshim (Leviticus 19:1–20:27)

DAVID BRODSKY

The Holiness Code, of which *Parashat Kedoshim* is a part, contains the only exhortation against same-sex intercourse in the Hebrew Bible.[1] Leviticus 18:22 states, "Do not lie with a man the 'lyings'[2] of women; it is an abhorrence (*to'evah*)." As with the other sexual prohibitions in Leviticus 18, the prohibition against same-sex intercourse is reiterated in Leviticus 20. Leviticus 20:13 states, "If a man lies with a male the 'lyings' of women, the two of them have done an abhorrent thing; they shall both be put to death—their bloodguilt is upon them."

This prohibition has often been mischaracterized as a prohibition against homosexuality. In a 1992 responsum on the subject, Joel Roth, a Conservative rabbi, states, "Lev. 20:13 clearly calls homosexuality a *to'evah*."[3] Yet the subject of this verse is not female homosexuality, and it probably is not even male "homosexuality." Instead, the subject of Leviticus 20:13 seems to be some specific form of male same-sex intercourse and not homosexuality as a category or identity. This is a subtle yet significant distinction that had a profound effect on the rabbinic evolution of the law. The late-twentieth-century French philosopher Michel Foucault and his student David Halperin have argued that our classification of people into homosexuals and heterosexuals is a recent development.[4] Classicists and historians have largely confirmed these findings, as have scholars of the Bible and rabbinics. These numerous studies have shown that reading our notions of identity into earlier texts that mention sexual acts is problematic and misleading. Neither the Hebrew Bible nor any of the texts of the Rabbinic Period (the first seven centuries of the Common Era) make any mention of sexual orientation or identity, although they mention opposite-sex and same-sex sexual activity.

No evidence exists that the rabbis (of the Rabbinic Period)[5] read the Torah as prohibiting any form of sexual or sensual interaction between men other than anal intercourse, nor is there any evidence that they chose to outlaw other forms of same-sex sexual or sensual interactions as a "fence" around this Torah prohibition. In addition to this lack of an explicit prohibition, a number of passages in rabbinic texts positively suggest that no such prohibition existed during the Rabbinic Period. That the rabbis prohibited only anal penetration between men corresponds with the cultural mores of the Rabbinic Period, which evince a strong reaction to male-male sexual *penetration* but little concern for other intimate contact between men. In fact, until Maimonides's innovation in the 12th century of distinguishing between sensual contact with and without desire, prohibiting same-sex contact would have been too impractical to implement or even to fathom prohibiting.

The Rabbinic View: The Ethical Problem

The rabbis of the Rabbinic Period felt extreme opprobrium for the act of anal intercourse between men and for those men who engaged in such acts.[6] Because men who engage in anal intercourse with other men willingly violate a law so serious that it carries the death penalty (Lev. 20:13), the rabbis assumed that they would also murder, commit idolatry, and any and every other immoral act.[7]

What lies behind the rabbis' opprobrium for male-male anal intercourse? In *Genesis Rabbah* (63:10), the Jewish people cry out before God, "Master of the Universe, it is not fair that we should be subjugated to the seventy nations [of the world], but certainly not to this one [Rome] which is penetrated like women."[8] In this passage, the male who is penetrated is equated to a woman and is viewed as inferior. The one who is penetrated is not fit to rule, and it is an added disgrace to be ruled by someone who has been so subjugated himself.[9] For the author, being penetrated by other men makes Roman men (and thereby Rome itself) "like women." If penetration is a form of "conquest" of the Other, then to be conquered by men who themselves have been "conquered" is like being conquered by a second-rate empire that itself is subjugated to others.

As rabbinic studies scholar Michael Satlow has noted, this rabbinic attitude toward penetration as an essentially demeaning act of domination over the penetrated party is closely related to the Roman attitude toward penetration. In Roman culture, it was deemed appropriate for adult male citizens to penetrate their social inferiors, women and male slaves, but penetrating their equals, or their superiors, was considered to be a disgrace to the one penetrated. This suggests that women in general occupied a position of subjugation. In the Roman world, penetration was inherently a debasing and conquering act, one appropriate for women and low-status men but abhorred among equals or with one's social superior.[10]

This understanding helps to explain the implication in the Babylonian Talmud (*Sanhedrin* 73a) that, from one perspective, for a male to be raped is worse than for a female, since it is "not his normal way."[11] Rashi explains that it is not a man's way to be penetrated, and therefore there is a great disgrace and embarrassment involved in having been penetrated.[12]

Now we are in a position to understand why the rabbis felt such a need to prohibit particularly anal intercourse between men. Although the rabbis may not have approved of two men being amorous with each other, if such activity did not include anal intercourse, it did not violate the rabbinic sensibility that an adult Jewish male[13] must never be sexually penetrated and thus conquered. In this way, then, to allow this sexually conquering act in a monogamous relationship does not ameliorate the situation at all. Indeed, to condone it through the giving of a *ketubbah* (a Jewish wedding contract) to two men is only to sanction the demeaning of one man by another.[14]

Inherent in rabbinic "homophobia" is a form of misogyny.[15] To leave this homophobia unchallenged is to leave this brand of misogyny firmly rooted in the Jewish tradition. Whether we are liberal American Jews, evangelical Christians, or ultra-Orthodox Israeli Jews, our sexual ethics have changed drastically from those of the Talmudic Period, and indeed most of us outright reject many of the rabbis' sexual ethics. For example, few Jews or Christians would accept that rape is not a crime[16] or that an unmarried girl should be married off to her rapist (Deut. 22:28–29). Those looking to the Bible for arguments in favor of the "sanctity of marriage" might be troubled by the rabbinic practice of "marriage for a day."[17] Whether liberal or traditional, modern sexual ethics diverge in many ways from Biblical (and rabbinic) standards. But for some reason, when it comes to the topic of "homosexuality," some people pretend as if our modern sexual values must be completely congruent with those of the Rabbis.

The Halakha

Mishnaic and Talmudic Law

The Levitical prohibition against "lying with a male as one lies with a woman" has been read by many modern rabbis as a ban on any and all sexual acts between two men and as a crime warranting the death penalty. Whatever the original intent of the Bible, the rabbis of the Rabbinic Period did not read the verse that broadly. The sexual ethic of their cultural milieu was concerned uniquely with anal intercourse between men and not with amorous interactions per se. The rabbis were also reluctant to mete out the death penalty, which led them to restrict the Biblical prohibition to its most narrow interpretation. Whenever the Torah called for the death penalty, the rabbis read the Torah (*de-oraita*)[18] prohibition in its most limited sense. Often they would then add a rabbinic prohibition (*de-rabbanan*)[19] to cover the broader sense of the law. Rabbinic prohibitions, however, were at most punishable by lashes.[20] The other option open to them was to use more minor prohibitions in the Torah (which did not result in the death penalty) to cover the broader scope of the prohibition.

As with all the other sexual transgressions listed in Leviticus 18 and 20 (i.e., the prohibitions against incest, adultery, and bestiality), the rabbis read Leviticus 18:22 and 20:13 (prohibiting male-male intercourse) as limited to the act of penetration itself.[21] Because they assumed that the Bible could only be prohibiting anal penetration, they were puzzled by the purpose of the additional phrase in the verses: "as one lies with a woman" (which, as noted earlier, can be translated more literally as "the lyings of women"). Once the Bible had already stated that it is forbidden for a man to lie with a man, it was obvious to the rabbis that the only form of penetration (which is how they understood the term "to lie") between men could be anal penetration. Therefore, the Bible had no need to add the extra phrase "the lyings of women." The rabbis interpreted the plural "lyings of women" to mean that when a man has sexual intercourse with a woman who is Biblically prohibited to him, both vaginal intercourse and anal intercourse are prohibited, and each carries the same penalty (death, or *karet*[22] and lashes, depending on the prohibition—of course, if the woman is not forbidden to him, then neither anal nor vaginal intercourse with her is prohibited).

Thus, the Babylonian Talmud (*Sanhedrin* 54a–b) states, "'The lyings of women'— the verse teaches you that there are two forms of sex with a woman [vaginal and anal]. R. Ishmael said, 'Behold this came to teach [about men] and it turned out to have already been taught.'"[23] The phrase "it came to teach [about X] but turned out to have already been taught" appears a number of times in rabbinic literature. In all those instances it means that the point the analogy has been brought to make has already been made or is intuitively obvious. Since the assumption is that the Bible would not make an analogy unnecessarily, if the analogy between heterosexual sexual acts and homosexual sexual acts sheds no light on the latter, then it must "actually" have been brought to shed light on the former. In other words, this hermeneutic reverses the direction of the teaching: instead of teaching from hetero- to homosexual sex acts, the hermeneutic claims the analogy was made to teach from homo- to heterosexual sex acts. Rashi explains,

> "It came to teach" about males, that they are guilty if they have anal sex [*she-lo' ke-darkah*]. "And it turned out to have already been taught"—The verse was not necessary for male-male intercourse, since it is obvious to us that *all male-male intercourse must be anal* [*she-lo ke-darko hu'*]. Rather, this phrase "the lyings of women" must have come to teach us that if someone penetrates a woman, whether vaginally [*ke-darkah*] or anally [*she-lo' ke-darkah*], he is guilty.[24]

Joel Roth argues that the phrase *she-lo' ke-darko/ah*, literally "not the normal way," is a reference to anal *and* oral sex. For Rashi, however, this phrase cannot mean oral sex as well, or it would not serve to explain why the plural "*lyings* of women" (*mishkevei ishah*) is not needed for male sex since there is only *one* form of sex with a man.

ONE HOLE OR TWO?

In case there was any further doubt about how many forms of penetrative sex are considered forbidden (at least from the Torah), the Talmud is quite explicit further on in the passage (*Sanhedrin* 54b–55a):

> (A) One who penetrates[25] a male nine years and one day old [or older] and (B) one who penetrates an animal whether the normal way [*ke-darkah* = vaginally] or not the normal way [*she-lo' ke-darkah* = anally] and (C) the woman who causes the animal to have sex with her whether the normal way [*ke-darkah* = vaginally] or not the normal way [*she-lo' ke-darkah* = anally] is guilty.

When it comes to women and animals (B and C), the author of this passage goes out of his way to specify that *both* ways/orifices constitute sex. In other words, the author states that whether a man has sex with an animal *ke-darkah* (vaginally) or *she-lo' ke-darkah* (anally), or if a woman is penetrated by an animal in either of the two ways that constitutes sex with her (anally or vaginally), it falls under the Torah prohibition against sex with an animal. This clearly establishes that women and animals have two orifices, which, if penetrated by a penis, constitute sex for legal purposes.[26] When it comes to penetrating males (A), however, the author feels no need to specify the multiple forms of that sexual encounter. Especially since penetration of the male (A) is stated before penetration of animals and women (B and C), the reason for this omission would seem to be that no clarification is needed regarding penetration of the male: there is only one possible form of penetration that would constitute sex (at least as defined under the Torah prohibition).

If this passage (*baraita*)[27] on its own were not clear enough on this point, the debate on it in the Talmud that follows is even more explicit. The Talmud brings two challenges against this *baraita*, ending with a very revealing defense. Rav Nahman bar Rav Hisda challenges the *baraita*, arguing that although the *baraita* is correct that women should be considered to have two orifices the penetration of which constitutes sex, animals should only be considered to have one. In contrast, Rav Papa is quoted as challenging the *baraita* by arguing that women should only be considered to have one orifice the penetration of which constitutes sex, whereas sex with animals should be forbidden by every orifice they contain (i.e., ears, nostrils, mouth, etc.). To conclude the debate, the Talmud repeats the *baraita* (which, by virtue of its early provenance, is the more authoritative passage) as disagreeing with and thereby overriding both of their positions. The *baraita* has the last word: women and female animals each have two orifices the penetration of which constitutes sex. This leaves the vagina and the anus as the obvious two orifices. Since men do not have vaginas, it leaves men having only one forbidden orifice, and thus the sole prohibition of anal penetration.

In recent years, a new position has appeared arguing that *she-lo' ke-darkah* should be read as all nonvaginal forms of penetration (that is, anal, oral, and perhaps even other nonvaginal forms of intercourse) and that, therefore, by analogy, men have more than one forbidden orifice as well. The Talmud is conclusive in the quoted passage, however, that *she-lo' ke-darko/ah* refers to a single orifice for a man (the anus). If *she-lo' ke-darko/ah* included other orifices as well, then Rav Papa's challenge would make no sense, since these other orifices would already have been covered by the *baraita* under the category *she-lo' ke-darko/ah*.

This new understanding redefining *she-lo' ke-darko/ah* in this broader way has been proposed by Joel Roth, who bases his argument on two main passages from the Babylonian Talmud. Upon closer examination, neither passage appears to support his case.[28] Roth's first source is *Yevamot* 83b, which addresses the status of the hermaphrodite (*androginos*) as a person who has the laws of both men and women apply to him/her. The Talmud is addressing Rabbi Eliezer's statement in the Mishnah (*Yevamot* 8:6) that "regarding a hermaphrodite, a man is stoned to death [in punishment for having had sex with the hermaphrodite] like a male." Rabbi Eliezer's statement begs the question: To what precisely does "like a male" refer? Does it mean that a man is stoned to death for having any kind of penetrative sex with a hermaphrodite (with the hermaphrodite's penis *and* with the hermaphrodite's vagina, i.e., whether the man was penetrated anally by the hermaphrodite's penis or the man penetrates the hermaphrodite's vagina) just as a man is stoned for having any kind of penetrative sex with a male (i.e., penile-anal intercourse)? Or, on the other hand, does it mean that a man is stoned for having sex with a hermaphrodite *in the manner* that one has sex with a male (i.e., with the hermaphrodite's penis but *not* with the hermaphrodite's vagina)?[29]

A statement is brought in the name of Rav that a man is punished for having sex with a hermaphrodite "from two places." In other words, Rav is reading the Mishnah the former way: as punishing any form of penetrative sex with a hermaphrodite, whether the hermaphrodite is the penetrator or is penetrated.[30]

The anonymous voice of the Talmud challenges Rav with the following tannaitic tradition:[31]

> Rabbi Eliezer[32] said, "Regarding a hermaphrodite, one is punishable with stoning like in the case of a male." To what does this refer? With his male organ [*zakhrut shelo*, = penis; i.e., if a man had penetrative intercourse with the hermaphrodite's penis— by the hermaphrodite penetrating the man's anus], but with his female organ [*nakvut shelo* = vagina; i.e., if the man penetrates the hermaphrodite's vagina], he is exempt [since, in this case, the man would be having "heterosexual" intercourse with the hermaphrodite].

The anonymous voice of the Talmud is hereby challenging Rav's position by questioning how he can read Rabbi Eliezer as punishing sex with both the hermaphrodite's penis and the hermaphrodite's vagina when the tannaitic tradition makes explicit that sex with the hermaphrodite's vagina is exempt.

In a 2006 responsum on homosexuality, Rabbis Elliot Dorff, Daniel Nevins, and Avram Reisner read the *zakhrut* as referring to the hermaphrodite's anus.[33] Roth correctly refutes this interpretation, demonstrating that the word *zakhrut* consistently refers to the penis, even when describing the hermaphrodite's genitalia, but he jumps from there to assuming that the *baraita* is referring to oral stimulation of the hermaphrodite's penis.[34] Having proven that the *zakhrut* is not a reference to the (hermaphrodite's) anus, he seems to think that he has demonstrated that this passage is not referring to anal intercourse, leaving oral intercourse with the hermaphrodite's penis as the only other obvious option. But proving that the *baraita* is not referring to penetration of the hermaphrodite's anus is not tantamount to proving that it is not referring to any type of anal intercourse, as the *man's* anus has not been eliminated. Moreover, no mention of mouths or oral sex occurs in this *baraita* or in the surrounding passage to suggest such a radical reading. The only new information this *baraita* offers on the subject is that when the hermaphrodite's penis is the genital the hermaphrodite uses to have sex with a man, that intercourse is forbidden the same as if they were both men. Rather than defining what is considered (forbidden) sex with the hermaphrodite's penis, it tells us to apply the definition from the case of (forbidden) sex between men to this case. Therefore, this passage leaves the definition wherever it was, which we have seen has consistently been anal intercourse (that is, intercourse in which a penis penetrates a man's anus). This passage, therefore, is not a basis for proposing that oral intercourse was considered sex or that oral sex between men (or between men and hermaphrodites) was forbidden by the rabbis.[35]

The second text Roth cites to support his argument for an expanded view of male-male sexual prohibitions is *Sanhedrin* 55a, in which Rav Ahdevoi bar Ammi asks Rav Sheshet what the law is regarding a man who penetrates himself. Rav Sheshet brushes him off as someone who is asking inane hypothetical questions that could never occur. Rav Ashi, who lived a few generations later, takes Rav Ahdevoi's question seriously and explains that Rav Sheshet is correct that the situation could never occur when it comes to an erect penis, but with a flaccid penis, it is possible for *some* people (with the correct anatomical dimensions). Although Roth attempts to read oral sex into this debate, the fact that Rav Ashi asserts that it is impossible with an erect penis but possible with a flaccid penis shows that Rav Ashi understood his predecessors to have been discussing anal and not oral auto-penetration. Rav Ashi's point is that the erect penis is not flexible enough and is pointing in the wrong direction to be able to be manipulated to penetrate a person's own anus. A flaccid penis, on the other hand, could easily be manipulated in that direction, and, as long as the man is well endowed when flaccid, his penis could be maneuvered to penetrate his own anus.[36] Were Rav Ashi referring to oral self-stimulation, as Roth proposes, then Rav Ashi's argument would be reversed. The erect penis reaches closer to the person's mouth and is easier for oral self-stimulation than the flaccid penis.[37]

A Rabbinic Fence around the Torah?

All of the foregoing discussion was by way of countering Roth's assertion that oral sex between men was considered a *Torah* prohibition. The general assumption by most people, however, is that although the rabbis did not consider it a Torah prohibition, they did make it a rabbinic one. The question then is, did the rabbis add a rabbinic extension to the prohibition against male-male anal intercourse to cover other forms of sexual/sensual interaction?[38] In addition to the lack of any mention of such an extension for male same-sex interactions, several passages exist that together seem to demonstrate that the Biblical prohibition was *not* extended for same-sex male interactions.

First, in the Babylonian Talmud (*Berakhot* 24a), Rabbi Isaac states that for a man to see merely "a handbreadth of a woman['s body] is *'ervah* [nakedness/sexual sin]," thus broadening the sexual prohibition in heterosexual interactions beyond the scope of the Torah prohibition.[39] The redactors of the Palestinian Talmud also understand looking at a woman's body as an extension of the prohibition against having intercourse. It states, "One who looks at the heel/rump[40] of a woman is like one who looks at her vagina, and one who looks at her vagina, is as if he has sex with her" (PT *Hallah* 58c). In contrast, when it comes to same-sex interactions, we find countless examples of rabbis going to and being naked in the bathhouse without any concern that the Torah prohibition against men having anal intercourse with other men may have been extended to include men looking at other men's bodies.[41]

In fact, numerous stories tell of rabbis kissing other rabbis, albeit in a purely platonic sense. The rabbis were so comfortable with the notion of two men having intimate contact that they read that the "thigh" under which Abraham had his slave put his hand to swear an oath to him was actually Abraham's penis. That is, according to one rabbinic reading of Genesis 24, Abraham had his slave hold Abraham's penis in his hand and swear by it (*Gen. Rab.* 59:8 on Gen. 24:2; see also Rashi on Gen. 24:2). Indeed, the rabbis may even be right: the Bible may have intended this reading. Whether it did or not, the rabbis make no effort to conceal this reading. Quite the contrary, they make explicit what otherwise was implicit. I am not claiming that the rabbis read anything sexual into this interaction. What I wish to point out is the contrast between their comfort with two men having physical contact even with each other's genitalia and their prohibition against men and women having any such contact.

This contrast demonstrates that the fence they extended around the heterosexual prohibition was explicitly and implicitly rejected for same-sex interactions. It reveals that the rabbis of the Rabbinic Period did not prohibit (Jewish) men from physical contact with one another, including genital contact.

The reason for their different treatment of same-sex and opposite-sex nonpenetrative physical interactions can be best understood from the Talmud's explanation for why the sages permitted men to be alone with one another. Whereas a man and a woman are forbidden from being in seclusion (*yihud*) with each other, the sages permit two men to be alone together (Mishnah *Kiddushin* 4:12). Commenting on this mishnah, the Babylonian Talmud (*Kiddushin* 82a) declares that Jewish men are not suspected of male-male anal intercourse, and with that statement it dispels any suspicions that it was going to extend the fence around the Torah to other male same-sex interactions. Since the rabbis of the Talmudic Period understood any extension of the prohibition as applying to all men or to no men, as applying at all times or at no time, they chose not to extend the prohibition.

I am not claiming that the rabbis failed to add any rabbinic prohibitions onto the Torah's proscription of male-male anal intercourse so that men could have nonanal sexual intercourse with one another. Their reason was far more practical: the rabbis could not afford to limit interaction between members of the same sex as they had between members of the opposite sex. If the rabbinic decree were extended for men with men as it had been for the opposite-sex sexual prohibitions, then men (all men) would lead particularly lonely and isolated lives. Essentially, until married, men could not have contact with just about anyone (if anyone at all), and once married, only with their wives. Society would have to be changed completely and drastically, and not for the better. Additionally, they would have to explain why it was that all previous sages and religious men had violated this rule, as rabbinic literature is replete with stories of men hugging and kissing other men and of being in the bathhouse with other men. Since the rabbis did not have the concept of homosexuality, they did not distinguish between homosexuals and heterosexuals, assuming that all Jews are equally disinclined to male-male anal intercourse. The Babylonian Talmud (*Kiddu-shin* 82a) concludes, therefore, that no rabbinic fence around the *de-oraita* decree was needed. This left no sexual or sensual interactions between men prohibited (*de-oraita* or *de-rabbanan*) except for anal intercourse.

Maimonides's Ruling

Once we come to Maimonides (1135–1204), however, the picture changes entirely. Maimonides's great innovation was distinguishing between engaging in nonpenetrative sexual/sensual activities (such as kissing and hugging) with and without desire.[42] For Maimonides, only engaging in such activity with desire is forbidden. Engaging in such activity in the absence of desire, though strongly discouraged, is not to be understood as technically forbidden. With this distinction, which is not found in the material from the Tannaitic and Amoraic Periods, Maimonides is now able to include men with men in the prohibition against kissing and hugging. Only when a man desires another man is he forbidden by law from hugging or kissing him. In this way, Maimonides could extend the prohibition without needing to condemn the numerous rabbis in the Rabbinic Period known to have kissed or hugged other rabbis as a way of expressing praise, nor need he change his society drastically by stopping all men from any and all interactions with all other men.[43]

Conclusion

The rabbis of the Rabbinic Period (the first seven centuries of the Common Era) understood the Torah prohibition of male-male sexual activity to be limited to anal intercourse. There is no evidence to suggest that they instituted a rabbinic decree to expand the prohibition beyond the Torah prohibition, while there is substantial evidence demonstrating that they explicitly chose *not* to add a rabbinic decree. It was not until Maimonides, many centuries later, that this ruling was changed.

The rabbis' reason for not adding a rabbinic prohibition onto the Biblical prohibition of *mishkav zakhur* ("intercourse with a man") is simple and practical. Until Maimonides, the prohibition against *mishkav zakhur* was understood to be a prohibition against any and all men having anal intercourse with any and all other men. If the rabbinic decree were extended for men with men as it had been for the opposite-sex sexual prohibitions, then men would lead particularly lonely and isolated lives.

NOTES

1. When the Deuteronomist compiled her or his list of sexual prohibitions (Deut. 27:20–23) no prohibition against same-sex intercourse was included. This conspicuous absence should encourage us to take seriously the fact that the author of the Holiness Code is the only voice within the Bible that expresses a prohibition against same-sex intercourse: other voices in the Bible may not be of the same opinion.

2. The Hebrew phrase *mishkevei ishah* is usually rendered in English as to "lie with a woman," but it literally translates as "the lyings of women." Rabbinic literature makes much of this plural construct.

3. Joel Roth, "Homosexuality," in *Responsa 1991–2000: The Committee on Jewish Law and Standards of the Conservative Movement*, ed. Kassel Abelson and David J. Fine (New York: Rabbinical Assembly, 2002), 615.

4. Michel Foucault, *The History of Sexuality*, 3 vols., translated by Robert Hurley (New York: Pantheon Books, 1985); David M. Halperin, *One Hundred Years of Homosexuality, and Other Essays on Greek Love* (New York: Routledge, 1990); idem., "Is There a History of Sexuality?" in *The Lesbian and Gay Studies Reader*, ed. Henry Abelove, Michele Aina Barale, and David M. Halperin (New York: Routledge, 1993); Eva Cantarella, *Bisexuality in the Ancient World*, translated by Cormac Ó Cuilleanáin (New Haven, CT: Yale University Press, 1992); Holt N. Parker, "The Teratogenic Grid," in *Roman Sexualities*, edited by Judith P. Hallett and Marilyn B. Skinner (Princeton, NJ: Princeton University Press, 1997), 47–65; Jonathan Walters, "Invading the Roman Body: Manliness and Impenetrability in Roman Thought," in Hallett and Skinner, *Roman Sexualities*, 29–43; and Amy Richlin, *Garden of Priapus: Sexuality and Aggression in Roman Humor*, rev. ed. (New York: Oxford University Press, 1992). On the Bible, see Saul M. Olyan, "'And with a Male You Shall Not Lie the Lying Down of a Woman': On the Meaning and Significance of Leviticus 18:22 and 20:13," *Journal of the History of Sexuality* 5 (1994): 179–206. On rabbinic literature, see Michael Satlow, *Tasting the Dish: Rabbinic Rhetorics of Sexuality* (Atlanta: Scholars Press, 1995); idem., "They Abused Him Like a Woman: Homoeroticism, Gender Blurring, and the Rabbis in Late Antiquity," *Journal of the History of Sexuality* 5 (1994): 1–25; and Daniel Boyarin, "Are There Any Jews in 'the History of Sexuality'?" *Journal of the History of Sexuality* 5 (1995): 333–55.

5. Throughout this chapter, I use the term *rabbis* to mean the rabbis of the Rabbinic Period. The Rabbinic Period is composed of two subperiods: the Mishnaic Period (roughly, the first two centuries CE) and the Talmudic Period (the mid-3rd through the 7th centuries), also referred to as the Tannaitic and Amoraic Periods, respectively.

6. For an analysis of the sources of the perspective, see Satlow, *Tasting the Dish*, 198–222. For further sources on the topic of homosexuality and Judaism, see the sources cited in Satlow, "They Abused Him Like a Woman," 3n. 7. In addition, see Boyarin, "Are There Any Jews?"; Chaim Rapoport, *Judaism and Homosexuality: An Authentic Orthodox View* (London: Mitchell Valentine, 2004); and Steven Greenberg, *Wrestling with God and Men: Homosexuality in the Jewish Tradition* (Madison: University of Wisconsin Press, 2004).

7. See PT *Sanhedrin* 23b–c (6:6). For more on the rabbinic tendency to associate murderers, idolaters, and sexual deviants with one another, see David Brodsky, *A Bride without a Blessing: A Study in the Redaction and Content of Massekhet Kallah and Its Gemara* (Tübingen: Mohr Siebeck, 2006), 153–59.

8. See Satlow, *Tasting the Dish*, 213.

9. For further evidence of the rabbis' equating the penetrated male with women, see PT *Qiddushin* 61a (1:7). See also Boyarin, "Are There Any Jews?" 345.

10. Cantarella, *Bisexuality in the Ancient World*, 98ff.; Parker, "Teratogenic Grid"; Walters, "Invading the Roman Body"; Richlin, *Garden of Priapus*; Greenberg, *Wrestling with God and Men*, 196–201.

11. The passage also acknowledges that in some ways it is worse for a female to be raped, but that is not the aspect of the passage that interests us here.

12. BT *Sanhedrin* 73a, s.v. *de-l'av 'orheih*.

13. The rabbinic analog to the Roman adult male citizen.

14. BT *Hullin* 92a–b.

15. See also Greenberg, *Wrestling with God and Men*, 201–3.

16. See my essay on *Parashat Vayishlach* in this volume.

17. BT *Yevamot* 37b.

18. The term *de-oraita* literally means "of the Torah." It is used to refer to the Torah prohibition, as distinguished from those decrees by the rabbis (called *de-rabbanan*, "of the rabbis") that extend the prohibition. The term *de-oraita* should not be confused with Biblical law itself. Many prohibitions deemed *de-oraita* by the rabbis are not to be found explicitly stated anywhere in the Bible. One of many examples of this is the thirty-nine categories of work on the Sabbath (e.g., sowing, threshing, winnowing, and the like), all of which are deemed to be *de-oraita* by the rabbis but are not explicitly stated anywhere in the Bible.

19. See note 18.

20. Technically, only a Torah prohibition can warrant lashes. The rabbis, however, read the Torah as granting them power to make decrees. People who violated these rabbinic decrees were thus violating the Torah. The punishment, therefore, was *makkat mardut*, "lashes of rebelliousness," for defying the rabbis (thus, for example, *Mishnah Nazir* 4:3, BT *Yevamot* 52a, and *Ketubbot* 45b).

21. Indeed, Satlow points out that PT *Qiddushin* 58c (1:1) explicitly states that the prohibition is specifically penile penetration (*Tasting the Dish*, 192–93). Boyarin ("Are There Any Jews?" 334–47) derives this same conclusion from BT *Niddah* 13b.

22. *Karet* is most commonly defined as "death by heaven," or at least as some penalty meted out by God rather than a human court (BT *Moed Qatan* 28b).

23. Cf. Sifra, Qedoshim, chapter 10, halakha 11. On this passage, see Satlow, *Tasting the Dish*, 194–97; Boyarin, "Are There Any Jews?" 346–47.

24. Rashi on BT *Sanhedrin* 54a, s.v. *harei zeh ba le-lamed* and s.v. *ve-nimtza lamed*.

25. Following the manuscripts. The printed edition has a significant scribal error.

26. Though unmentioned, we are intended to understand that the Talmud is referring only to a case in which the sexual union is prohibited by the Torah (such as incest or adultery). Otherwise, how could all sex between females and males over the age of nine be forbidden? That heterosexual intercourse *she-lo' ke-darkah* (between a man and a woman who were not forbidden to each other) was not deemed forbidden (at least not from the Torah) is stated outright in BT *Sanhedrin* 58b.

27. A *baraita* is a passage attributed to the Tannaitic Period (i.e., to the first half of the Rabbinic Period). See note 5.

28. See his responsum "Homosexuality Revisited," submitted to the Committee on Jewish Law and Standards of the Conservative Movement, December 2006.

29. Thus Saul Lieberman reads the Mishnah and the ensuing debate in both Talmuds and the Tosefta (Lieberman, *Tosefta Ki-feshuta* on *Yevamot*, 94–96).

30. Following the alternative reading discussed in note 35, Rav would be reading R. Eliezer as including the hermaphrodite's anus along with his/her penis as part of his/her masculine self. In either case, Roth's reading is unfounded.

31. In other words, it cites a tradition from the Tannaitic Period (ca. first two centuries CE).

32. I am here following Saul Lieberman (*Tosefta ki-feshuta* on *Yevamot*, 94–96), who in turn is following the printed edition and some manuscripts. Alternatively, other manuscripts follow the Tosefta (*Yevamot* 10:2) in recording this as a statement by R. Eleazar (ben

Shamua). If it is R. Eleazar, then he is quoting R. Eliezer's statement from the Mishnah and adding his own comment. These variants do not affect my central point that oral sex is not being discussed in this passage.

33. Elliot Dorff, Daniel Nevins, and Avram Reisner, "Homosexuality, Human Dignity and Halakhah: A Combined Responsum for the Committee on Jewish Law and Standards," 25n. 31; available online at http://www.rabbinicalassembly.org/teshuvot/docs/20052010/dorff_nevins_reisner_dignity.pdf.

34. Roth, "Homosexuality Revisited," 12, which can be found at http://www.rabbinicalassembly.org/teshuvot/docs/20052010/roth_revisited.pdf.

35. The Talmud seems not to mention a prohibition against a man penetrating the hermaphrodite's anus, probably because that would get into the impossible question of whether we categorize the hermaphrodite's anus as part of the hermaphrodite's male self or the hermaphrodite's female self. Since it is only prohibited *de-oraita* to have intercourse with the hermaphrodite's male self, the anus, it would seem, is left as not prohibited. Alternatively, both sides of the debate that ensues in the Talmud over this mishnah could be regarding R. Eliezer's position. Both could be attempting to define what he means when he says that it is forbidden to have sex with a hermaphrodite in the manner that one has sex with a male. When Rav says that it is forbidden for a man to have sex with a hermaphrodite from two places, he could mean the hermaphrodite's penis and anus (just as with men intercourse with either their penis or anus is forbidden). Even following this reading, at a minimum, the *baraita* brought by the anonymous voice of the Talmud to challenge Rav would mean that a man who is penetrated (anally) by a hermaphrodite's penis receives the death penalty for having male same-sex intercourse. It also would mean that a man who penetrates a hermaphrodite vaginally is not guilty of this crime. It leaves ambiguous, however, the case in which the man penetrates the hermaphrodite anally. Would that be considered "like a male" or not? Whereas the hermaphrodite's penis clearly pertains to the hermaphrodite's masculine half, and whereas the hermaphrodite's vagina clearly pertains to the hermaphrodite's feminine half, to which half does the hermaphrodite's anus pertain? This question is similar to the dispute (also involving Rav) between Rav and Samuel in BT *Sanhedrin* 54b in which they are debating whether a boy's anus is considered developed for sexual purposes (to count as sex if he is penetrated) when it reaches the age of maturation of a girl's vagina (three years old) or when it reaches the age of maturation of a boy's penis (nine years old). In other words, they are asking whether the boy's anus as penetrated object ought to be classified as feminine or masculine. Here, in BT *Yevamot* 83b, too, the dispute would be whether the hermaphrodite's anus counts as part of the hermaphrodite's feminine or masculine self. If it is part of the hermaphrodite's feminine self, then it is abnormal *but permitted* intercourse; if it is part of the hermaphrodite's masculine self, then it is *mishkav zakhur*, forbidden male-male intercourse. Although the passage can be read viably in a number of different ways, none of those ways brings oral sex into the picture. Oral sex is simply not being discussed in this passage.

36. That is, if it could reach far enough to meet the Rabbis' minimum definition of penetration. The Rabbis argue over whether the penis merely has to touch the inner ring of the anus or whether the head of the penis must be inserted into the anus. For this definition, see, among other sources, BT *Sanhedrin* 73b. The law, by the way, followed the latter definition.

37. Thus Dorff, Nevins, and Reisner also understand this passage. See their responsum "Homosexuality, Human Dignity, and Halakhah," 43n. 32.

38. It is often assumed that the rabbis included men with men in the extension to the

prohibition from the rabbis' reference at certain points to *kol ha-'arayot*, "all forbidden sexual transgressions" (see, most notably, Sifra, *Acharei Mot*, 13:15 on Lev. 18:6). This is Rapoport's assumption, for example (*Homosexuality*, 2). Yet the rabbis often use this phrase to refer to all of the sexual transgressions *except* men with men. One example of this is BT *Qiddushin* 81b, in which Samuel is quoted as saying that a person is forbidden to be alone with *any* of the *'arayot*, yet no subsequent amora or the stam of the Babylonian Talmud question how he could say this when the very next mishnah states that according to the majority opinion two men may sleep in the same bed together and even in the same cloak. In fact, none of the classic medieval commentaries on the Talmud (e.g., RoSh, Nachmanides, Tosafot, RiTVa', Tosafot RYD, RaShBa', Rashi, Meiri, RaN) notice this problem. RaN even referenced the subsequent mishnah to make a different point, without mentioning this potential conflict with Shmuel's statement.

The Shiltei ha-Giborim, a post-Maimonidean rabbinic authority, however, did notice this conflict, arguing that Samuel followed the minority position in the subsequent mishnah, that two men should not sleep in a room alone together (see his comments numbers 3 through 5 on p. 33a of the RiF). As I note later, Maimonides introduced the notion of differentiating between people who engage in sexual interactions with and without desire. This change allowed for an extension to the male same-sex prohibition with the application of that prohibition only to a minority of Jewish men, a radical departure from the earlier law.

39. The anonymous portion of the Talmud rejects the plain meaning of this statement because it understands this ruling as having already been derived from the Torah through the following midrash: "Why did the Torah [Num. 31:50] list the jewelry of the outer and the inner body together [i.e., bracelets and finger rings, which go on the outer body, and clitoris rings and the like, which go on the inner body]? To teach you that any man who looks at the little finger of a woman, it is as if he looks at her vagina" (BT *Berakhot* 24a). The rule itself is not questioned, however, only from which statement (R. Isaac or the midrash) it is to be derived.

40. The word *'ekev* means "heel." In context, however, the redactors of the Yerushalmi seem to be reading the passage as referring to the buttocks. Whatever the original meaning of the statement, and whichever understanding the redactors of the Yerushalmi had, we find the passage extending the prohibition beyond intercourse to include gazing at her body.

41. As just one example, see the Palestinian Talmud, *Avodah Zara* 42b (3:1). See also *Semahot* 12:12.

42. *Hilkhot Issurei Biah*, 21:1 and 21:6.

43. Maimonides goes so far as to make this prohibition against hugging and kissing with desire (whether male-male or between men and women who were forbidden to them) a Torah prohibition, for which Nachmanides (a 13th-century Spanish rabbi) strongly criticizes him (*Hilkhot Issurei Biah* 21:1, and *Minyan ha-Mitzvot*, Negative Commandment #353; Nachmanides, *ha-Sagot ha-Ramban le-Sefer ha-Mitzvot*, Negative Commandments, #353). Maimonides demonstrates his inclusion of male-male interactions in the Torah prohibition by positioning the prohibition against hugging or kissing "any of these [aforementioned] sexually prohibited persons" (Maimonides's Negative Commandment #353) after Negative Commandment numbers 350–52, which prohibit intercourse between men. That is, in his book in which he lists and explains the 613 commandments, Maimonides seems purposely to place the prohibition against men having sex with other men such that it becomes included in the prohibition against sensual interactions as well. Maimonides is too careful an author for this to have been by mistake.

THIRTY-ONE

Fear Factor: Lesbian Sex and Gay Men
Parashat Emor (Leviticus 21:1–24:23)

JOSHUA LESSER

There was an audible buzz of excitement in the room when I entered bearing home-made brownies. There were nearly a dozen of us in Kirsta's humble New Orleans apartment for the screening, and I was the only man allowed in. I knew some of these women from engaging in LGBT and AIDS activism together. Most of them were lesbians or bisexual women. As I passed my plate of brownies around, I checked to see if the women were comfortable with my presence as the sole male. Even Justin, Kirsta's boyfriend, had been banished, since absolutely no straight men were permit-ted. They agreed it was because they were comfortable with me, though one woman asked, "You're gay, and you're not grossed out?" "Not at all. I am curious." With the lights dark, we all began to watch an instructional video on female ejaculation.

The woman's assumption about gay men's "vaginophobia" highlights an all-too-common sexism among gay men. I never understood the discomfort, particularly from a community that is often at ease speaking about sex. My sexual orientation is not determined because I am repulsed by the opposite sex but, rather, because I am more attracted to my own. I think it is important to have knowledge about sexuality and human bodies in general. I remember one afternoon at summer camp when I sat around with a group of women who all shared about the trials and tribulations of their periods, especially the discoveries of their first one. They debated the pros and cons of tampons and pads and even described laughable mishaps. At fifteen, I felt honored and privileged to be let into a conversation that felt treasured and reserved for the rarest of men. Conversations like these have continued and have made me a better ally to women. When Eve Ensler's *Vagina Monologues* first came to the stage, I went to see it immediately—one of only three men in the whole theater—because I was interested in what vaginas and the women who have them have to say. As a queer Jew, I feel it is important for queers of all genders to understand Judaism's stance on lesbian sexuality, and that by extension dictates an openness to women's bodies and sexuality.

There is some irony that *Emor,* a portion so hyperfocused on the male body, with its description of the physical perfection needed to become a *cohen*, priest,[1] is also one of only two portions that has any *halachic* connection to lesbian women's sexu-ality. The connection in the portion is minor because lesbian sex raises a profound challenge. In the Torah all of women's sexuality is seen as an extension of men, which precludes lesbian sexuality. For instance, adultery is defined as a man sleeping with another man's wife. Since polygamy is clearly permitted, men could be married to women and still have sex with other women. Because sexuality is so male-oriented in the Torah, lesbian sexuality is not mentioned at all, causing many scholars to wonder if lesbian sex even existed in the minds of the authors of the Torah. Rabbi Steven Greenberg asserts that "only sexual acts that involve penile penetration were under legislative scrutiny in the Torah."[2] Thus, we find only later generations of rabbis reading lesbian sex and its prohibitions into the Torah—and it revolves around men.

Lesbian sex, due to this sexist privileging of male power, escapes the focus placed on male-male sex. The basis of prohibitions for lesbian sex is found in the Talmud's reading of verses from *Parashat Emor,* "They shall not marry a woman defiled by harlotry, nor shall they marry one divorced from her husband. For they are holy to God. . . . When the daughter of a priest defiles herself through harlotry, it is her father she defiles; she shall be put to the fire" (Lev. 21:7, 9). In the Talmud,[3] there is a connection drawn between the word "harlotry" (*liznot* or *zonah*) and the term *mesolelot,* which in contemporary translations is also rendered as "harlotry" or "sexual lewdness." Rashi, in his 12th-century commentary, more specifically defined *mesolelot* as women rubbing their vaginas together, based on his reading of the Talmud *Yebamot* 76a. This elucidation becomes legally significant, because there is rabbinic panic that two women playing with each other's genitals may cause one to lose her virginity and perhaps more specifically pierce the hymen. In this passage in *Yebamot,* Rav Huna and Rabbi Elazar argue whether engaging in *mesolelot* would make a woman ineligible to marry a priest. Rav Huna argues that it would, whereas Rav Elazar says it would not. The law follows Rav Elazar, suggesting that lesbian sexuality is seen as a "minor infraction," according to rabbi and scholar Rebecca Alpert.[4] In fact, scholars such as Jacob Milgrom in his commentary on Leviticus are in agreement that lesbian sexuality is not prohibited at all.[5] This interpretation makes sense since it seems like commentators are stretching when they expand the definition of "harlotry" in *Emor* to include lesbian sex. This implausibility reinforces the hypothesis that the idea of lesbian sexuality was foreign or inconsequential to the Biblical authors.

Another text in Leviticus, with some rabbinic acrobatics and sleight of hand gets interpreted as prohibiting lesbian sex is "You shall not copy the practices of the land of Egypt where you dwelt . . . nor shall you follow their customs" (Lev. 18:3). Clearly, neither text indicates anything about lesbian sexuality on the *p'shat* (the simplest, level of interpretation). Rather, these become the hooks on which the rabbis hang their condemnation of lesbian sexuality.

When the rabbis scripturally combat their spiritual nemesis Egypt, accusations of homosexuality, incest, and female polygamy are raised. When elaborating on the "customs" of Egypt, the rabbinic authors of *Sifra* and *Leviticus Rabah*[6] (on this portion) claim that in Egypt "a man would marry a man, or a woman a woman, or a man to a woman and her daughter or a woman would marry two men."[7] Perhaps the rabbis were also commenting about their contemporary situation. Rebecca Alpert surmises that the authors of these works were critiquing the encroaching and often despised Roman culture, in which same-sex unions were known, and without regard for accuracy the rabbis metaphorically exchanged Egypt for Rome.[8] Scholars of antiquity ssuch as Ruth Karras and Craig A. Williams remind us that in Biblical times, the threat of gay and lesbian sex was related not to the socially constructed sexual identities as we view them today but, rather, to a concern about who is penetrating and who is penetrated. They build on Michel Foucault's claim that sexual orientation and its connection to one's individual identity is a modern phenomenon created by bourgeois capitalism in which the object of one's desire defines a sexual identity, in contrast to the view in antiquity, which focused on one's sexual role (penetrator or penetrated), regardless of gender.[9] Steven Greenberg's recognition of the Torah's concern for penetrative sex is similar to Foucault's view in that penetration is considered the primary determinant and the object of one's penetration is secondary.

This interpretation opens up the possibility that the halachic prohibition against lesbian sex is deeply rooted in the sexist assumption that women are meant only to be passive sexually. Certainly, the imagination of the Torah could not evoke a woman with penetrative power except as a form of extreme violence used to debase the enemy, as in the case of Yael's hammering the tent peg into Sisera's brain (Judges 5:23–27). In a patriarchal society that privileges men and the ability to penetrate, a woman's penetrating a man is the most extreme form of debasement. The episode with Yael and Sisera seems to be a case in which a woman's gender is being used only to cause embarrassment to the enemy; otherwise women are meant to be passive.

In addition to discussions in *Emor*, other passages in the Torah and the word in the Talmud, lesbian sexuality is discussed in Rambam's 12th-century codification of Biblical laws called *Mishneh Torah*. He says that lesbian sex is prohibited, but since there is no Biblical citation, it does not prevent women who have engaged in sexual contact with other women from marrying priests, nor is it deserving of a severe punishment (i.e., it does not require flogging). He takes a leap, which is perhaps a recognition of lesbian sexuality in his time, and warns husbands to keep a watchful eye and to be strict with their wives and to be mindful of the female company they keep.[10]

Some people might argue that the difference between lesbianism being a minor infraction or no infraction and gay male sex being an abomination requiring the death penalty heightens a gulf between a Jewish gay male's and a Jewish lesbian's experience of Judaism. This argument does not take into account how gender historically created barriers to participation. All these Talmudic discussions highlight that historically Jewish sexuality is a heterosexual man's world.

The patriarchy of Biblical Judaism and its subsequent generations ultimately erected great barriers to the full inclusion and spiritual recognition of women, including lesbians. Despite the liberating reconstruction of contemporary Judaism that women envisioned at the end of the 20th century, it was not until the emergence of scholars such as Judith Plaskow and Rebecca Alpert that lesbians found a theological home within this new Judaism. It was this courageous, evolved Judaism, sparked by women and informed by feminist, queer, and universal values, that has, in turn, allowed men like me to claim leadership in this Jewish landscape.

It is at this nexus where lesbians and gay men can find common ground. We should also not forget that try as we might to argue that scripture treats gay men and lesbians differently, much of the bias that gays and lesbians experience today lumps homosexuality together regardless of gender. Male sexuality, gay or straight, is so dominant in our culture that women are confronted by it and almost without choice made familiar with it. We must be aware of lesbian sexuality and its admittedly limited presence in Jewish text so that we do not make the same mistake as our forefathers and add further insult by continuing to pretend that women's sexuality does not exist.

It behooves gay men to become better allies to lesbians. Doing so entails that gay men not fear women's bodies and sexuality, but rather be educated so that we can understand the distinctions and the commonalities and better support one another in addressing sexuality in Jewish tradition. Furthermore, such an understanding begins to raise interesting questions about how each community relates to terms such as "top" or "bottom," "femme" or "butch," so that we break out from the confining nature of roles and our assumptions about them. If we were able to share about sexual experiences from an embodied place free of fear, then we would discover an opportunity to break from our Jewish heteronormative patriarchal definition of sexuality as being centered around penetration. This could be a groundbreaking conversation if we can overcome our discomfort. Our entire community could benefit from reexamining our relationship to our sexual identities through each other's eyes and each other's genitals.

NOTES

1. Leviticus 21:16–23.

2. Steven Greenberg, *Wrestling with God and Men: Homosexuality in the Jewish Tradition* (Madison: University of Wisconsin Press, 2004), 86.

3. *Shabbat* 65a and *Yebamot* 76a.

4. Rebecca Alpert, *Like Bread on the Seder Plate* (New York: Columbia University Press, 1997), 30.

5. Jacob Milgrom, *Leviticus: A Book of Ritual and Ethics* (Minneapolis, MN: Fortress, 2004), 197.

6. Both are Midrashic commentaries on Leviticus.

7. Sifra, Acharei Mot 18:3 (also *Genesis Rabbah*).

8. Alpert, *Like Bread on the Seder Plate*, 29.

9. Michel Foucault, *The History of Sexuality, Vol.1,* trans. Robert Hurley (New York: Vintage, 1990).

10. *Mishneh Torah, Issurei Bi'ah* 21:8.

THIRTY-TWO

Neither Oppress nor Allow Others to Oppress You
Parashat Behar (Leviticus 25:1–26:2)

JACOB J. STAUB

> When Moses
> broke the sacred tablets on Sinai, the rich
> picked the pieces carved with:
> "adultery" and "kill" and "theft,"
> the poor got only "No" "No" "No."
> —Ilya Kaminsky, "American Tourist," *Dancing in Odessa*

The queer perspective questions all norms—not only norms of gender role and definition or sexual orientation but *all* norms. From a queer perspective, norms are human attempts to simplify, classify, and regulate the complexities of reality. Reality, however, is inevitably messier than the categories we impose. There are always exceptions that do not conform to our classifications. The establishment of norms of any kind, therefore, is a process that essentially and inevitably excludes and pushes difference to the periphery, forcing diversity to mold itself into preset categories and condemning that which does not fit in. It is inherently oppressive.

Among the most pervasive of normative assumptions that a queer perspective challenges is that hierarchy is natural and inevitable: economic hierarchy, social class distinctions, hierarchies of power. We are encouraged to assume that the state of inequity is built into reality. Some people are always wealthier than others; we can upend the current hierarchy, but when we do, the new order will itself be hierarchically ordered. *Parashat Behar* calls this assumption into question. It is a powerful text on which we can ground the queer perspective, because it subverts the legitimacy of class distinctions.

Leviticus 25, the first chapter of *Behar*, contains the only regulations in the Torah about land tenure and the rights of landowners to sell or mortgage their land.[1] The law of *Shemitah*, or the sabbatical year, requires that in the seventh year, the land is to have a Sabbath (Lev. 25:2–7). No sowing, reaping, or pruning is permitted.

The Torah, however, is not content to explain *Shemitah* once. It does so three times. The version of this practice described in Exodus 23:10–11 arises out of a concern for the poor, who are given exclusive access to the growth of the land in the sabbatical year. The version in Deuteronomy 15 emphasizes the remission of debts and the freeing of indentured servants.

By contrast, Leviticus 25 seems unconcerned with either of these rationales. Instead, it declares, "In the seventh year the land shall have a Sabbath of complete rest, a sabbath of the Lord." The text is focused on the sanctity of the land itself, and on God's ownership of the land. We are to let the land rest as a periodic reminder that it does not belong to us. Rather, it is ours temporarily, as an *ahuzah*, a long-term lease.[2]

There is significant evidence that the *Shemitah* year was observed in ancient Israel. There is little evidence, however, for the observance of the ritual of land tenure, the *Yovel*, the Jubilee year,[3] which is mentioned only in Leviticus 25. At the beginning of the fiftieth year, the shofar is sounded, and release (*dror*) is proclaimed to all the inhabitants of the land,[4] all of whom reclaim the right to their ancestral lands. That is, any sale of land is temporary; every fiftieth year (the Jubilee), ownership of the land reverts to its original owner—to the descendants of those who were originally allotted their tribal portions by Joshua at the time of the original conquest of the Land of Israel. "The land must not be sold beyond reclaim, for the land is Mine; you are but strangers resident with Me. Throughout the land that you hold, you must provide for the redemption of the land" (Lev. 25:23–24). If poverty has forced you to sell your land, or if you have hired yourself out as an indentured servant, in the Jubilee year, everything is equalized, all inequality rectified.

The practice of the *Shemitah* and *Yovel* years reflects an extraordinary concern of the Torah to attend to the needs of the poor and to prevent excessive class distinctions. These institutions represent an acknowledgment of economic inequity and a regularly set attempt to ameliorate its consequences. *Parashat Behar* is a central text in ongoing discussions about the political leanings of Jewish tradition.

Contemporary interpreters disagree about whether the consistent tendency of Jews in the modern world to be more liberal than their non-Jewish neighbors can be traced to ancient Jewish teachings and core Jewish values. Some argue that the centrality of the narrative of the Exodus from slavery in Jewish ritual and consciousness[5] helps to explain why American Jews, for example, were prominent among the leaders of the labor movement, were early supporters of the civil rights movement, and consistently vote to the left of their own economic interests.[6] They believe that Judaism stands with the oppressed and the powerless and that, ideally, Jews ought to work toward the elimination of class distinctions.

Other interpreters resist, citing the long historical experience of Jewish communities in the Diaspora, under both Muslim and Christian rule. They note that community *kehillot* were ahead of their time in caring for orphans, widows, released hostages, and all those community members in economic need but that the needy were assisted according to their class history—that the orphaned daughter of a wealthy family, for example, was matched, and her wedding feted, very differently than was a woman whose parents had been poor.[7] They acknowledge that Judaism mandates a social safety net that provides for the basic needs of the poor, but they do not agree that Jewish principles demand a commitment to radical egalitarianism.

Parashat Behar allows us to transcend the debate. The Jubilee text may describe an ideal that was never implemented, but its utopian character is precisely what gives it such breathtaking power. It questions all social and economic distinctions in the agrarian society of ancient Israel. It questions all *norms*, even as basic an economic practice as owning a piece of land that you have bought.

Acknowledging the existence of economic oppression, of foreclosures and slavery, it assails the existence of these de facto realities on the most radical of bases: the land belongs to God, so it is not yours to sell, no matter how dire your economic straits.[8] And since the Israelites are God's servants, they cannot sell themselves into permanent slavery.[9] This text itself serves to queer the economic and social status quo in ancient Israel.

Mishnah Avot 5:9 elevates the importance of the laws of *Behar*, attributing the Destruction of the Temple and the Exile to the violation of these particular laws. The medieval commentator Ramban understands the violation of the laws of *Shemitah and Yovel* as following from the Israelites' failure to acknowledge the work of creation.[10] In Ramban's understanding, if one acknowledges that the world is created, it follows directly and clearly that one would understand that God is the sole owner of the land and that human "ownership" is always temporary.

The sabbatical year ameliorates injustice, by reminding us that the earth belongs to God and must be cultivated accordingly. The Jubilee year eradicates injustice, or it would have if it had ever been instituted in a comprehensive way. If contemporary strict inheritance taxes attempt to limit inequalities across generations, the Jubilee year eliminates them entirely. It demands that we recall that we are *all* servants of God and that all hierarchies of distinction are false. It reminds us that the earth and its fullness belong to the Lord, so that our accumulated wealth is not ours. It queers conventional assumptions about the inevitability of social and economic hierarchy.

Pursuing the objective of queering all norms, we can learn from the rationales with which *Parashat Behar* seeks to subvert economic and social hierarchies. Inasmuch as we were all slaves in Egypt and were redeemed by God, we have no right to oppress others because they are different, or to allow ourselves to be oppressed. The Torah suggests that only God the Redeemer has that right, not the very human *poskim* (halakhic authorities) who read and misread texts in order to establish norms that regulate, exclude, and oppress. Inasmuch as everything we have ultimately is a gift from its true Owner, we are not permitted to utilize our God-given resources to degrade other human beings, or to allow ourselves to be degraded.[11]

Alas, our text can only be stretched so far, because it rests on another norm—the ancient division of the land of Israel into tribal holdings that it regards as permanent and divinely ordained. It presumes that all Israelites descend from those who settled the land after the conquest of Canaan, when the land of each of the tribes was neatly divided among members of the tribe. At the Jubilee, the original position to which everyone is to return is the land that is presumed to have belonged to one's clan since the original conquest of the land. The Jubilee offers nothing to those who do not fit into an accepted, ancient category: those without clear, unblemished Israelite lineage, those without children to inherit their land, those with same-sex partners, those who do not wish to be farmers.[12] Like all utopian visions, it rests on its own assumptions of what is ideal.

Here I turn to the fragment of Ilya Kaminsky's poem quoted in the epigraph. In wryly noting the difference in the way that the commandments are experienced by the rich and the poor, the poet implicitly suggests that before Moses smashed the tablets, the commandments would have been observed uniformly by rich and poor, or perhaps that there would have been no such class distinctions. Of course, much like the never-implemented Jubilee, there never was a moment of intact tablets, intact commandments. Moses smashed them before he had delivered them to the people. And of course, if there had been such a hypothetical, ideal moment, it would have been full to overflowing with norms: Sabbath observance, respect of parents, not speaking God's name, not coveting, and so on. From a queer perspective, would we prefer the intact tablets, the broken ones, or neither of them?

Surprisingly, the rabbinic answer to this question is both of them: "Rabbi Joseph taught: '. . . that you smashed, and you shall deposit them . . .'[13] teaches us that both the tablets and the fragments of the tablets were deposited in the ark."[14] This Talmudic passage imagines that both sets of tablets were placed in the Ark of the Covenant, carried around at the center of the Israelite camp in the wilderness for forty years, and then placed in the Holy Temple in Jerusalem. The broken and the whole were at the center of the Israelite cult, the one testifying against the other in a tandem of ineffability. Like the hypothetical Jubilee text that has stood through the ages as a perpetual critique of the imperfect, unjust state of our communities, so in the rabbinic imagination, at our spatial center rested a graphic, material acknowledgment that however we try to interpret and execute the divine will, we can never get it right, because God's will is beyond transcription. How very queer!

NOTES

1. For a full discussion, see Baruch A. Levine, *The JPS Torah Commentary: Leviticus* (Philadelphia: Jewish Publication Society, 1989), 168–169, 270–274.

2. See ibid., 172.

3. Jacob Milgrom, *Leviticus: A Book of Ritual and Ethics* (Minneapolis, MN: Fortress, 2004), 307.

4. This proclamation is the inscription on the Liberty Bell.

5. "In every generation," we recite in the Passover Haggadah, "We are required to view ourselves as if we ourselves [were slaves in Egypt] and were liberated." This theme is reinforced in every morning and evening service and is a central point in *Parashat Behar*.

6. See Michael Walzer, *Exodus and Revolution* (New York: Basic Books, 1985). Walzer makes an eloquent and persuasive case that the Exodus theme is a powerful and essential factor in the drive toward "this-worldly redemption, liberation, and revolution" (ix).

7. See Daniel Nussbaum, "Tzedakah, Social Justice and Human Rights," *Journal of Jewish Communal Service* 60:3 (1983): 228–238; Mark R. Cohen, *Poverty and Charity in the Jewish Community of Medieval Egypt* (Princeton, NJ: Princeton University Press, 2005); and S. D. Goitein, *A Mediterranean Society: The Jewish Communities of the Arab World as Portrayed in the Documents of the Cairo Geniza* (Berkeley: University of California Press, 1967).

8. See *Sifra Behar* 6:1, which has God saying, "My deed (of ownership of the land) has first priority."

9. The commentator Abraham Ibn Ezra on 25:42 explains that the redeemer becomes the new owner. See *The Commentary of Abraham Ibn Ezra on the Pentateuch, Volume 3: Leviticus*, translated by Jay Schachter (Hoboken, NJ: Ktav, 1986), 154. Obadiah Sforno elaborates: "Since he is My servant, it is not in his hand to sell himself as a total slave." See Sforno, *Commentary on the Torah, Volume 1,* translated by Raphael Pelcovitz (Brooklyn, NY: Mesorah, 1989), 27.

10. See Ramban's comment on 25:2, as translated by Charles Chavel: Ramban, *Commentaries on the Torah, Leviticus* (New York: Shilo, 1974), 416.

11. "You shall not rule over him ruthlessly; you shall fear your God" (Lev. 25:43).

12. In fact, the text explicitly excludes city dwellers from its regulations. Those who sell property within walled cities are not entitled to repossess it at the Jubilee (Lev. 25:29–30).

13. Deuteronomy 10:2.

14. Babylonian Talmud, *Baba Batra* 14b.

THIRTY-THREE

"Less Is More" and the Gift of Rain: The Value of Devaluation in *Behukotai* and Cixous's Desire-That-Gives
Parashat Behukotai (Leviticus 26:3–27:34)

SARAH PESSIN

> Speak unto the children of Israel, and say unto them: When a man shall clearly utter a vow of persons unto the LORD, according to thy valuation, then thy valuation shall be for the male from twenty years old even unto sixty years old, even thy valuation shall be *fifty* shekels of silver, after the shekel of the sanctuary. And if it be a female, then thy valuation shall be *thirty* shekels.
> —Leviticus 27:2–4

"God, if you do X for me, I will repay my debt to you with a donation in the amount equivalent to the value of . . . myself (or my daughter or my nephew or my wife)." It is this sort of divine-deal-making that *Parashat Behukotai* has in mind with its reference to the "vow of persons," and it is in the spirit of helping us properly play this odd version of "Let's Make a Deal" that we are given an actual "fee schedule"—a list of monetary worth of men (equals high value) and women (equals you guessed it . . .). For those of us who have the goal of keeping the Tanakh relevant to modern life, this sort of passage—one that overtly ranks men higher than women—seems to invite a throwing in of our respective towels.

In an effort to offset the distasteful implications of this passage, the Union for Reform Judaism's Torah commentary enthusiastically assures readers that this fee schedule refers to "the valuation—not the value!—of a person."[1]

To be sure, there are other commentaries that make this same point: women are worth less *money*—it is not that the Torah is saying that they are *worth less* (or worthless) in general! OK, but how much better off are we even with this reading? That women's "valuation" (not value!) would be significantly lower, in a Leviticus context, than the "valuation" of men points, we rightly fear, to the kind of patriarchal underpinnings at play in that society that might have led readers initially, even if wrongly, to read into these verses that "the Torah values women less than men." Lower market value arguably reflects some much deeper patriarchal forces at play, patriarchal forces of which the Tanakh reveals ample evidence throughout and which are in many cases consistent with what might seem to modern-day readers the devaluation of women in general.

In the spirit of grappling with the deeper issue, let us approach this Leviticus 27 "man more/woman less" fee schedule as an invitation to wrestle overtly with the problems of the broader patriarchal system against which this passage appears, a patriarchy in which women are not equal to men—or more broadly stated, a patriarchy in which "marginal" groups are not equal to white heterosexual men.

There are a few general ways that modern readers might choose to grapple with this patriarchy. One approach is to throw in that proverbial towel and give up on the Tanakh as a viable text for contemporary living. Another is to embrace an edited text of the Tanakh—one that abridges away this set of verses, as well as all unseemly devaluations of LGBT people, of women, and of other "marginal" groups. A further angle still is to work feverishly hard to translate away any apparent patriarchal overtones—one popular strategy (especially in liturgical contexts) is to change all the "he" talk to "they" or even "she" talk. In this context of Leviticus 27, of course, this last strategy would not yield much fruit, resulting, as it would, in an inexplicable chart that talks about a series of "she" or "they" valuations ranging (in the course of Leviticus 27:2–7) from ten to fifty shekels.

Is there a way, though, to keep the "man high/woman low" structure of this chart and read into it a complete upturning of patriarchal assumptions?

For the purposes of our reading, let us simply use the Leviticus 27 chart as a springboard for the following broader patriarchal/phallocentric sentiment:

White Heterosexual Men: Good; Other(ed) People: Not So Good

In this "other" group, let us envision any or all "othered" people—anyone pushed to the margins of the straight, white, male "norms" of the society in which we still live. This group can include any woman. This group can include any person of color. This group can include any member of the LGBT community.

One approach to the predicament of being Othered within society is to fight back against the very terms of the Otherness. In the history of feminism, we can find an example of this sort in Simone de Beauvoir's *The Second Sex*: "The women of today are in a fair way to dethrone the myth of femininity; they are beginning to affirm their independence in concrete ways; but they do not easily succeed in living completely the life of a human being."[2] Here, the goal is not only to fight one's way out of the Otherness but to "dethrone" the very terms of the Otherness—in this case society's constructed category of the feminine. Although this "I am woman, hear me roar" approach is powerful, notice how it seems to agree fully with our equation of "Otherness" with "Not So Good." As it relates to any marginalized group, we might say that this approach asks the Othered to rise above their societally imposed Otherness (accepting the premise of "Otherness = Not So Good") and to claim their role in "normal" society, "living completely the life of a human being," right alongside the men (accepting the premise of "White Heterosexual Man = Good"). Here, the goal is to overcome one's marginality. Here, the victory of the Othered is found in the eradication of Otherness.

However, there is a completely different way to theorize the victory of the Othered. What if Otherness itself was the entry into precisely the kind of full living that de Beauvoir associates with moving *away from* Otherness? In this way of thinking, the margin itself becomes the crucial vantage point from which to live most fully as human being. The idea is not to valorize the suffering that comes with this Otherness but to recognize nonetheless that it is only from this place of social devaluation that one enters the real.

Using the concept of "the feminine" as a broad marker for anyone—bi, gay, or hetero; male or female—who lives outside the norms of the "masculine economy," and speaking of the "feminine text" (or "feminine writing") as a unique outpouring of that "feminine" perspective, Hélène Cixous sees vital, life-giving, abundant life force precisely from the place of devaluation:

> A feminine text cannot fail to be more than subversive. It is volcanic; as it is written it brings about an upheaval of the old property crusts, carrier of masculine investments; there's no other way. There's no room for her if she's not a he. If she's a her-she, it's in order to smash everything, to shatter the framework of institutions, to blow up the law, to break up the "truth" with laughter.[3]

A Sephardic Jewish French feminist (who rejects the label "feminist" and theorizes herself the "Jewomen"),[4] Cixous theorizes the Othered voice as laughter!—the volcanic eruption marking the very rupture of the male economy. In this view, we are offered a refreshingly positive valuation to being Other.

Returning to our chart, we might mark this theoretical framework as a complete subversion of what we have seen thus far:

White Heterosexual Men: Not so Good; Other(ed) People: Good

The idea is not that it is good to be subordinated per se but, rather, that it is in the place of the subordinated and Othered that we find the fount of life, the unbounded flow of creative spirit to which the masculine system—or in Cixous's words "economy," echoing the Levitical notion of valuation—can never give rise.

With Cixous's message in hand, we are able to return to *Behukotai* with fresh possibilities for finding strength in our parasha's valuation of the male over the female and, with it, as we have suggested, the valuation of the white heterosexual male "norm" over the marginalized Other. For in Cixous's emphasis on the unbounded life force from the place of devaluation, we now find a message of pride and life precisely in *Behukotai*'s lower feminine valuation at Leviticus 27. With Cixous's message in sight, we can see why it is precisely the undervalued, marginalized space that holds the promise of laughter and the fullness of life itself. Here, "less" (the space of the undervalued) is "more." Here, Otherness is a mark of wonder, not a badge of shame.

We might add further that it is *only* in the devalued space of the socially deval-ued that Cixous locates "the-desire-that-gives." As we have already alluded to, Cixous speaks of two "economies." The first is a masculine economy (for our purposes read: "White Heterosexual Man," or anyone in the "norm" of society) rooted in dualities and oppositions, invested in the rigid conceptual confines of phallocentric structures. In contrast, we find the feminine economy (for our purposes read: all socially deval-ued individuals), a nondual space of fluid play, multiplicity, and abundance.

Although there are many ways to theorize the difference between these two econo-mies, Cixous draws our attention to "giving." For Cixous, one of the key outcomes of the masculine economy is that it marks the death of giving; for Cixous, all "givings" are erased in this masculine economy of "tit for tat" exchange. Since "giving" in this context always comes with some expectation for receiving-in-return, true giving loses its very capacity to exist. In contrast, Cixous sees the multiplicity and abundance of the feminine economy as birthing open the wonder of "giving"—understood in its true sense as "gifting," the "please have" that expects no "give to me" in return. Ironically, it is only when one is devalued that one can really give purely, since it is only when one is devalued that one has no real assurance—or hope—of getting back in return.

In fact, we are invited to a glimpse of this gifting economy in our Torah portion, a few passages before the fee schedule with which we are wrestling. In the context of Divine Blessings and Punishments, Leviticus 26 teaches us about the ultimate cosmic gifting in the image of rain's own fluid abundance—the flow that gives of itself en-tirely and without recompense of any sort:

> If ye walk in My statutes, and keep My commandments, and do them; then I will give your rains in their season, and the land shall yield her produce, and the trees of the field shall yield their fruit. (The Blessing, Leviticus 26:3–4)

> And if ye shall reject My statutes . . . And I will break the pride of your power; and I will make your heaven as iron, and your earth as brass. And your strength shall be spent in vain; for your land shall not yield her produce, neither shall the trees of the land yield their fruit. (The Punishment, Leviticus 26:15, 19–20)

On the face of it, these texts are perfect examples of the masculine economy, illustrat-ing, as they seem to, a dualistic and phallocentric theology-of-reward-and-punish-ment ("you do good, you get good; you do bad, you get bad"). But notice how these very texts choose to exert themselves through the imagery of rain, a clear cosmic marker of the feminine economy of gifting ("I give of myself, and I do not get in return"), an image that stands in stark contrast to the masculine "iron heavens" of Leviticus 26:19–20.

Like any strong deconstructive reading, we look for openings within the text that invite us to unravel the surface and find new voices. Faced with a parasha ostensibly about a masculine economy of divine reward and punishment, might we not use the opening image of rain at Leviticus 26:3–4 as exactly this sort of aperture—an invita-tion on the part of the text itself to reexplore the Leviticus 27:3–4 chart of valuations?

(Notice how it is even the same verses that we are asking ourselves to play up against one another: verses 3 and 4 in each of the parasha's two chapters, a tantalizing mirror for discoveries.)

Looking to *Behukotai's* opening image of rain, we find a symbol par excellence of the feminine economy of pure-gifting—a gifting and laughter that breaks apart the masculine economy of "reward and punishment" and of "I promise this, so you have to give me that." With the image of rain—that which always gives with no expectation of return—we are immediately brought to the feminine economy. Finding in the image of rain precisely the flowing, overabundant, nondual qualities of Cixous's "desire-that-gives," we have found an invitation in the margin of the text itself "to smash everything, to shatter the framework of institutions, to blow up the law"—we have found an invitation to explode open the very foundation of the surface narrative of a dual, rigid, "tit for tat" economy of divine reward and punishment.

We have found, too, an invitation to "break up . . . with laughter" the surface implications of our starting fee schedule. Now, through the invitation of the rain-as-marker-of-the-spirit-of-gifting, we have found a subtle but strong reminder that "less is more," a subtle but strong reminder that it is the Othered—the only ones able to truly give/gift—who are the victors. In this spirit, it is precisely the fact that woman is given a lower valuation on our Levitical fee schedule that we find her strength. For it is only in the undervalued that we find the explosive power of gifting, of laughter, and of every other kind of full, abundant, multifaceted, open living that is impossible within the space of the "privileged." Here, being valued "high" by society invites you into the trap of the mainstream, pulling you outside the explosive and overflowing play of the margin (and with it, into the humorless sway of the "heaven of iron").

In this spirit, we read the *Behukotai* text as an invitation to the power of the undervalued and the gift-giving attitude that separates it from the masculine economy of remuneration and debt. In the very context of a text about the gift of rain alongside a fee chart for vows of debt (i.e., "If God does X for me, I owe him a debt equivalent to the valuation of person X") we have found an invitation to reflect on the spirit of gifting and laughter. Here, we have found an invitation to cross on over to the Other(ed) side.

NOTES

1. See *The Torah: A Modern Commentary, Revised Edition*, edited by W. Gunther Plaut and David E. S. Stein (New York: Union for Reform Judaism, URJ Press, 2005), 876.

2. Simone de Beauvoir, *The Second Sex*, translated and edited by H. M. Parshley, introduction by Dierdre Bair (New York: Vintage, 1989), introduction to book 2, p. xxxvi.

3. Hélène Cixous, "The Laugh of the Medusa," reprinted in *French Feminism Reader*, edited by Kelly Oliver (Lanham, MD: Rowman and Littlefield, 2000), 269.

4. On this term, see Cixous's essay "Coming to Writing" (originally published in 1977 as *"La Venue à l'écriture"*) in *"Coming to Writing" and Other Essays*, edited by Deborah Jenson and translated by Sarah Cornell, Deborah Jenson, Ann Liddle, and Susan Sellers (Cambridge, MA: Harvard University Press, 1991).

PART IV

BEMIDBAR

The Book of Numbers

THIRTY-FOUR

How to Construct a Community
Parashat Bemidbar (Numbers 1:1–4:20)

DAVID GREENSTEIN

Parashat Bemidbar ("in the wilderness") opens the fourth book of the Torah and gives us a record of God's Word to Moses "in the wilderness of Sinai, in the Tent of Meeting" (Num. 1:1). This juxtaposition of the open wilderness with the enclosed Tent signals that in this parasha, we will experience a series of seeming opposites—exposure and sheltering safety, openness and consolidation, precariousness and strength. Thirteen months have passed since the Exodus from Egypt, and as the Israelites continue their journey to the Promised Land, God serves as their guide and protector, addressing their many fears and desires. The Israelites' anxieties, borne of their sense of vulnerability while traversing immense and forbidding spans of desert terrain, coexist alongside a growing sense of community fostered by their very isolation and dependence on God and one another.

Responding to this dual sense of community building and simultaneous vulnerability, God instructs Moses to conduct a census of the Israelites, "according to their families, according to their fathers' household" (Num. 1:2), counting all the Israelite males eligible for military service. By enumerating the Israelites' numbers, the collective is reassured of its might and of its organizational coherence. After presenting the results of the census, each of the twelve tribes is assigned a fixed location around the central shrine, the *Mishkan*, three tribes on each of four sides. Reinforcing the image conveyed by the military census, the Israelites are portrayed as a strongly disciplined marching machine that is both blessed with the Divine Presence, concentrated in the Tabernacle, and also entrusted with the solemn duty of guarding that fragile sanctuary.[1]

This tightly closed configuration of twelve tribes produced a well-defined communal space. For those within it, this was a positive factor in their daily lives, reinforcing their sense of belonging and security. But the establishment of boundaries also makes it possible to determine what and who may be regarded as out of bounds—as "other." Thus, for example, creating a bounded camp made it possible to send lepers outside its borders. The Torah reports that when Miriam was temporarily stricken with *tzara'at* (a skin condition commonly translated as leprosy)[2] she, too, was sent out of the camp. But "the nation did not travel until Miriam was brought back in" (Num. 12:15). Is the implication, then, that in cases of less important people, the Israelites broke camp and moved on while the other lepers, nameless in the Torah, were left behind?[3]

This tension between insider and outsider existed within the encampment as well. The camp is really shaped like a kind of rectangular donut, bounded on the outside by inhospitable wilderness, and with the *Mishkan* at its center—an inaccessible inner core of sacred space. The sanctuary had to be protected, not only from desert marauders but from trespassing Israelites within the camp as well. So the Tabernacle is encircled by an inner ring of guardians, the families of the Levites. They are sentries watching lest an Israelite draw too near to the Holy Space, cross the sacred boundary line, and incur the penalty of death. Left unexplained is why any Israelite would want to try to step over the line, given the severity of the consequences. But, perhaps, that is the point: boundaries are made to be crossed.

The mutability of boundaries and locations continues as a theme in this parasha, and throughout the Torah. The structure established among the twelve tribes in the years of wandering is completely reshuffled once the Israelites enter the Promised Land. For example, the tribe of Levi, once given the privileged position of inner proximity to the Tabernacle, is later dispersed throughout the land, in scattered cities far from the central shrine, without any tribal territory, as was given to the other tribes. And the tribes of Judah and Benjamin, placed at the front and back of the desert camp, historically become intertwined and establish their territory as the new inner core of the people's physical and spiritual geography.

A more striking case of the fluidity of this structure involves the role and place of the tribe of Dan. Dan is assigned to march along the northern flank of the camp. Yet this tribe is also charged with the task of collecting the stragglers (and the lepers left behind?) who cannot keep up with the pace of the rest of the nation. Dan is "the one who takes back in [*m'asef*—the same verb used to describe Miriam's retrieval from outside the camp] everyone for all the camps" (Num. 10:25). This means that the Danites had to march at the back of the traveling camp, picking up stragglers. But the back of the camp was not the northern side but the western side (the Israelites were moving from Egypt to Canaan, so from west to east, with the "front" of the camp on the eastern side). Thus, the Danites had to move out of their assigned place in the north, breaking the orderly structure of the camp. They would assemble in the north and, as the marching proceeded, go against the flow of the marchers in order to circle back behind them. This move was necessary precisely in order to rectify the problem created by the camp's rigid structure—a structure unable to accommodate those Israelites who could not fit into their normatively assigned places in the marching machine of Israel.

Thus, the efforts to establish a clearly delineated and bounded community are defeated by other efforts to maintain and promote the very values that the community holds dear—a sacred connection to Divinity and a compassionate connection to one another. But if these assignments could not be met and the structure of the encampment could not be maintained for long, why does the Torah go to such great lengths to record them? Can we discern from this ancient "community rule" the glue—binding and yet flexible—that can work to hold communities together so that they can realize their central values?

We return to consider the census that is this parasha's opening subject. What function did it play in constituting the community? Earlier I suggested that it was important to build the morale of a people who would soon be tested by the challenges of war. But perhaps, beyond addressing the needs of that historical moment, what we have here is a text that has ratified for all eternity a fundamental human need, the need that we all desperately require to be satisfied, if even for only a fleeting moment: recognition. Andy Warhol's messianic vision of a time when everyone would be famous for fifteen minutes was thus somewhat anticipated and partially fulfilled by the Torah's insistence on recognizing every tribe, counting every able-bodied soldier and recording every census detail. For a moment, if not for a quarter hour, these people and groups were given a place to stand and be recognized. If we conceive of this census and its textual record as gestures toward recognition, we may gain a new appreciation for this seemingly boring exercise in bureaucracy.

The need for recognition is the need to be accepted in terms of one's own self-identification. Can a community satisfy that need? On the one hand this question is clearly a challenge posed to every community, touching on the tension discussed earlier between the individual and the collective, between boundary definition and self-definition. For those like queer Jews who have been rendered outside the community either by *halacha* or by a community's social norms, these questions of the needs of the individual and the community become even more important. And the story of Miriam shows that even the most important, most "normative" member of a community could, at any point, be rendered temporarily as an outsider.

It might also be that the Torah is teaching that the willingness of a group to engage in acts of mutual recognition is actually the surest foundation on which to build a community, for it is the most resilient. Since the act of recognition is simultaneously an act of inclusion while it is also an act of affirming difference, it has the chance of co-opting the self-contradictions of community building instead of being defeated by them. Such a dialectical notion of community, one that simultaneously includes and affirms difference, is the kind of community for which feminists and more recently queer Jews have been advocating.

But we need to probe a bit further. Although the glue of mutual recognition has the power to bind a community together in a way that exerts cohesive force as it simultaneously allows for flexibility and mutability, the necessary ingredient in such a cohesive compound is that the recognition be truly mutual. If recognition is a power that resides only in the hands of the authorities or the normatively privileged, it will become brittle and break under the stress of the antithetical demands of community building. Thus, the census undertaken in the wilderness, if it is only conceived as a process driven by the Israelite elite for the purpose of bestowing recognition on "the fighting masses," would have been simply another exercise in power on behalf of the established hierarchy.

Another understanding of the census is opened for us by the subtle reworking of a midrash cited by *Yalkut Reuveni* (a 17th-century compilation of kabbalistic and midrashic commentaries) at the beginning of its treatment of this Torah portion. It comments on the requirement that Moses and Aaron also include the tribes' chieftains as a committee to administer the census:

> "And with you there shall be one person from every tribe. . . ." (Num. 1:4)—
>
> "And the chieftains of Israel made offerings. . . . [They were the ones supervising the census.]" (Num. 7:2)—For they regretted what they had done earlier. . . . for they were the ones assigned over the Israelites in Egypt, "and the officers of the Children of Israel were beaten." (Ex. 5:14) Now they were the supervisors of the census.

The midrash identifies the tribal leadership involved in administering the census with the officials appointed by the Egyptian oppressors who enslaved Israel. They administered that process as well. That administrative class was caught in a very difficult position, for it served as a buffer between Israel and its oppressors. While the officials tried to protect the Israelites when they were slaves in Egypt and even absorbed blows on their behalf, they also served as agents of the regime, enforcing its edicts and learning to "look askance" at the Children of Israel who could not or would not meet their daily labor quotas (see Ex. 5:19).

The midrash imagines that the chieftains are overcome with remorse. But what did they have to regret? An earlier version of this midrash (as found in the compilation *Bemidbar Rabbah* 12:16) is part of a discussion about the offerings brought by the chieftains at the dedication of the Tabernacle. That midrashic text explains that they regretted their insufficient participation in the communal efforts devoted to designing and building that shrine. But the version in *Yalkut Reuveni* has, like the tribe of Dan that strayed from its assigned marching position in order to collect community members left behind, relocated itself to another place in the text, changing its textual encampment, so to speak, and thereby opened another possibility for our imaginings. The midrash identifies these chieftains as the very officials responsible for running the Egyptian slave system. With that in mind, we may wonder whether what they regretted was not perhaps their complicity (albeit coerced) in the oppression of their fellow Israelites. If that were the case, then their involvement in the counting of each individual may have served as an expiatory offering. But what they offered was not a set of wagons to transport the Tabernacle paraphernalia (see Num. 7:3). Instead, what they offered was their own presence in a community-sponsored encounter, a mandatory meeting of mutual recognition.

The census was not simply an act of recognition bestowed by the princes of Israel on those who were enumerated. The act of recognition worked both ways. As each able-bodied man, who had formerly been pressed into slavery by these very officials, passed, one by one, before them, those who were doing the counting were also recognized for who they were and what they had done. By facing their brothers, whom they had helped to enslave and oppress just a short time ago, the chieftains and the people they counted were pushed into a process of "truth and reconciliation." Such a process was, from an outsider's perspective, a boring, bothersome, and bureaucratic headache. It is not very exciting to read. But, from the inside, one must imagine the electricity in the air as each person came before his chieftain, his erstwhile oppressor, looked him in the eye, and compelled that official to count him and recognize him as a brother. The Torah seems to suggest that without that quiet drama the Children of Israel would never have been able to take a single step forward through the wilderness.

As our encampments, Jewish and general, struggle with our emerging awareness of the oppression of queers and others that we have facilitated in the name of protecting and enforcing community norms and boundaries, we can mull over the lessons of this Torah portion for guidance as we yet strive to continue to build a stronger, more caring, and more sacred community.

NOTES

1. There are different terms used in the Torah to refer to the Israelite desert shrine: *mishkan* (Tabernacle), *mikdash* (sanctuary), and *ohel* (*mo'ed*) (Tent [of Meeting]). Scholars tend to see these terms as derivative of different literary sources. In this commentary, I use these terms interchangeably.

2. Barukh Levine, introducing the main Biblical section dealing with this disease, in Leviticus, writes, "The identification of biblical *tsara'at* with 'leprosy' is unlikely, if by 'leprosy' is meant Hansen's disease, for the symptomology provided in chapter 13 [of Leviticus] does not conform to the nature or course of the disease. Undoubtedly, a complex of various aliments was designated by the term *tsara'at*." *The JPS Torah Commentary: Leviticus* (Philadelphia: Jewish Publication Society, 1989), 75.

3. Besides lepers, other people who had to go outside the camp included those suffering from gonorrheal genital emissions and those who had come in contact with a corpse (Num. 5:1–2). One person was required to leave the camp to defecate (Deut. 23:13). Executions and certain priestly functions were also carried out outside the encampment (e.g., Num. 15:35, 19:3).

THIRTY-FIVE

From Impurity to Blessing
Parashat Naso (Numbers 4:21–7:89)

TOBA SPITZER

A number of years ago, LGBT Pride Weekend in Boston fell on the Shabbat of *Parashat Naso*. Preparing my *d'var Torah* for Shabbat morning services that week, I wondered, what might this portion have to teach about LGBT pride?

At first glance, there was not much. *Naso* seemed to consist of a series of wholly unrelated themes. Sandwiched between a census of Levite clans and a repetitive listing of tribal gifts for the dedication of the wilderness Sanctuary, we read about the following:

- The removal from the Israelite camp of anyone in a state of *tum'ah*, ritual impurity, caused by bodily discharge, skin eruptions, or defilement by a corpse (Num. 5:1–4).
- The restitution and ritual required for someone who realizes he or she has wronged another through fraud or theft (5:5–10).
- The ordeal of the *sotah*, the woman suspected of adultery by her husband (5:11–31).
- Regulations pertaining to the temporary Nazirite, an ordinary Israelite who would dedicate him- or herself to God for a particular period of time by taking on certain abstentions (including refraining from cutting the hair or drinking any grape products) (6:1–21).

What could ritual impurity, unintentional theft, the suspected adulteress, and the laws of the Nazirite possibly have to say about gay pride? So I asked again. The first words of the portion were promising: "*Naso et rosh*," "Lift up the head" (Num. 4:22)—as good a euphemism for pride as any! But how to account for what follows?

On second reading, I realized that despite the surface dissimilarity of these four sections, each deals in some way with social deviance and the attempts by the community to deal with that deviance. Read with a "queer eye," these sections then unfolded before me as a successive—and progressive—understanding of what it means to be queer in relation to the larger society.

Outside the Camp

Naso begins with a census of the Gershonite and Merarite clans of the tribe of Levi and their respective duties in transporting the components of the portable Tabernacle, which sat at the center of the Israelite camp. The following chapter begins with instructions from God to Moses to remove from the camp "anyone with an eruption or a discharge and anyone defiled by a corpse. Remove male and female alike; put them outside the camp so that they do not defile the camp of those in whose midst I dwell" (Num. 5:2–3).[1] This state of "defilement" is called *tum'ah*, a kind of ritual impurity that can be conveyed from one person to another and that precludes the "impure" person from having any contact with the realm of the holy—most specifically, the Tabernacle and its environs.

The person in a state of *tum'ah* can be likened to the most disturbing—and still far too common—understanding of what it means to be LGBT: a subversive, potentially contagious condition that is a threat to society. Accordingly, those with this condition must be "put outside the camp," banished from "normal" society. In this paradigm, those who suffer this condition are antithetical to God's presence and, by definition, are outside the realm of the holy.

Wrong and Restitution

The following verses deal with a very different kind of social deviance. Here, the instructions pertain to a man or woman who realizes that he or she has wronged another (through fraud or theft), "thus breaking faith with the Lord" (Num. 5:6). In order to right the wrong, a series of steps must be followed: confession of the sin; restitution to the wronged party, consisting of the principal amount plus one-fifth; and a sacrificial offering to God.

The violation here is a behavioral aberration, not a state of being. This status corresponds to the view of homosexuality as a correctable deviance, essentially an error of judgment or a failure of will. With realization of one's error, confession, and proper rehabilitative action, the queer person can get back on track and can rejoin normative society, including a reconnection to God. The issue here is having the proper level of penitence and a commitment to changing one's behavior, in order to come back inside "the camp."

The "Bitter Waters"

The case of the *sotah*, the suspected adulteress, is a bit more complicated. The situation involves a husband who suspects his wife of adultery, without witnesses or proof. Without either, he has no legal recourse against her. In such a case the woman would be brought to the priest, who would make her drink a concoction of water, dirt from the floor of the Tabernacle, and the words of a curse written and then rubbed off into the water. According to the words of the curse, if she was innocent, nothing would happen; if guilty, she would be unable to conceive or perhaps suffer a miscarriage.

However shameful or traumatic this ordeal was for the woman, the focus here is ultimately not on her behavior but on her husband's jealousy. The ritual appears to have been a mechanism for assuaging the husband's jealousy and anger, in order to restore some measure of peace to the couple's home.

In this segment, the issue is not primarily the wife's "deviance" per se, as there is doubt as to whether she has done anything wrong. Read queerly, the parasha has something to say about queer "deviance." Reading the *sotah* in a queer context, the focus begins to shift away from assumed abnormality or wrongdoing on the part of an LGBT person and onto the fears, hidden desires, and shame of those around him or her. The question is raised as to whether the problem is deviant behavior or the projected fears and desires of those who are presumably acting according to social norms. Yet even if this segment represents a step forward from the two previous examples, it is still the queer person who suffers, who is made to undergo an ordeal intended to calm the fears and doubts of others. This ordeal is reflected for many LGBT people in the ordeal of the closet, in keeping aspects of one's selfhood and one's life hidden out of fear of the reactions of those around oneself. It is the ordeal of living in a society that constantly and consistently needs to reaffirm the "normalcy" of heterosexuality and to reassure those in the straight world of their own masculinity and femininity. It is the ordeal of needing to "normalize" homosexuality by making same-sex relationships as analogous as possible to straight paradigms. In all of these ways, the potential threat of LGBT identity and activity is neutralized, contained, and controlled.

Separating Oneself for God

The final case of "deviance" is that of the person who makes a vow to become a Nazirite, in order to "set himself apart for the Lord" (Num. 6:2). The Nazirite was definitely outside the social norm—separating him- or herself both through appearance (having uncut hair) and behavior (abstaining from wine, avoiding all contact with the dead). But unlike the person in a state of *tum'ah*, the transgressor, or the *sotah*, the Nazirite proclaimed his or her difference for him- or herself and willingly took on an outsider's status as a path to holiness.

Although some later rabbinic and medieval commentators were uncomfortable with the Nazirite's path, the Torah itself does not display the same ambivalence. It was possible not only to take on the Nazirite vow for a period of months or years but to be dedicated as a Nazirite for life, as did the judge Samson and the priest Samuel. Using the Nazirite model, queerness is not bad, and deviant does not mean diseased or evil. Quite the opposite: it is a self-proclaimed path to holiness, a claim of difference that is socially sanctioned and perhaps even exalted.

Intriguingly, what immediately follows this segment on the Nazirite is God's instruction to Aaron and his sons to bless the entire community of Israel:

Thus shall you bless the people of Israel. Say to them:
> The LORD bless you and protect you
> The LORD deal kindly and graciously with you
> The LORD bestow favor upon you and grant you peace. (Num. 6:23–26)

What are we to make of this abrupt transition from the laws of the Nazirite to the priestly blessing? Perhaps this: the dedication of the Nazirite's claiming of his identity for himself by taking the "queer" path as a path to holiness leads to blessing for the entire community. The priest—who in the earlier segments is the enforcer of norms and the gatekeeper between the deviant and the larger society—here becomes a vessel of blessing, not judgment. *Parashat Naso* has led us on a path from viewing queer status as an impurity or transgression to the blessing of self-proclaimed difference as an avenue of holiness and connection to the divine.

Unique and Equal Gifts

It may not be a coincidence that this progression in understanding queerness is framed by segments that deal with the construction and consecration of the *mishkan*, the Tabernacle in the wilderness. The *mishkan* can be understood as a physical corollary to the social structure that the Israelite community has been commanded to create, a covenantal community in which the Godly attributes of *tzedek* and *chesed*, love and justice, can become manifest in the world.[2] Thus, the detailed narrative of the construction of the *mishkan* contains clues for our understanding of what it means to build such a community or society.

Parashat Naso ends with Moses anointing and consecrating the *mishkan* and "all its furnishings, as well as the altar and its utensils" (7:1). Once he has done this, the heads of each of the tribes bring an offering to be used by the Levites in their service of the sanctuary.

Chapter 7 recounts, in detail, the gift of every Israelite tribe, each brought on a successive day. What is remarkable is that each tribe's gift is exactly the same. What is even more remarkable is that the Torah text, usually so economical in its prose, repeats word for word the details of every gift.

How are we to understand this repetition? In the introduction to the listing of the gifts, the text reads literally, "YHWH said to Moses: one chieftain per day, one chieftain per day, shall bring close their offering for the dedication of the altar" (7:11). Like the repetition of the gifts, this doubling of "one chieftain per day" seems extraneous and unnecessary—an indication that there is something noteworthy here that calls our attention. Each gift, the text seems to be saying, is both absolutely equal and absolutely unique. Each tribe's gift is set off on its own day, so that it cannot be confused with any other. Yet every gift is, at the same time, exactly equal in value.

In building our communal *mishkan*, the full embrace of queerness means the ability to welcome and affirm the equal value of the gifts of every segment of the community, of every "tribe," in all its uniqueness. In moving from the ostracization and expulsion of the deviant "other" to the dedication of difference as sacred service, we allow the blessings of *shalom*, of wholeness, to flow to the entire community. *Parashat Naso* encourages us to "raise up our heads" and celebrate LGBT identity by rejoicing in difference even as we affirm the equal value of each of our gifts.

NOTES

1. All translations, unless otherwise noted, are from the *Etz Hayim Torah and Commentary*, translated by the Jewish Publication Society.

2. For a more complete discussion of this understanding of the *mishkan*, see Toba Spitzer, "And I Shall Dwell among Them," *Reconstructionist* 69, no. 1 (Fall 2004): 12–20.

THIRTY-SIX

Setting the Stage for Pluralistic Judaism
Parashat Beha'alotecha (Numbers 8:1–12:16)

STEVE GUTOW

The Torah is not a text that generally extols and promotes "the power of the people" over the established hierarchy. G-d usually wins arguments. When G-d is not involved, Moses and his chosen few are generally the ones whose power rules over the Israelites. However, this is not always the case. The religious and political control of the Torah establishment and its hierarchy of G-d, Moses, Aaron, Miriam, and the priests is not static. Sometimes those in power create a more populist power arrangement. As rare as that occurs, when the hierarchy actually desires populist change, it tends to be successful. There is no clearer example of that than in this parasha.

In *Beha'alotecha* Moses himself insists that *everyone* should have the opportunity to speak for G-d. If everyone has the chance to prophesy, then certainly, at least in *Beha'alotecha*, everyone in the community can lead. There is remarkable reach in such an idea. If the reader carries the concept to its fullest extent, then certainly the text supports a call to permit LGBT and women the rights of communal integration and leadership.

A more detailed look at the text shows how inclusive and populist the portion is. In chapter 11, Moses, weary of the constant complaining of the Israelites, asks G-d why he has this burden of leadership. He says that the burden is too great and in particularly dramatic and idiosyncratic Jewish guilt-invoking parlance asks G-d to take his life rather than force him to continue as leader. G-d is unusually sympathetic to this guilt-laden appeal and asks Moses to gather seventy elders to whom G-d grants the spirit of prophecy. Prophecy is the most intimate relationship between G-d and humanity because G-d and the prophet become so close that they actually become, for a time, a single voice and spirit. In this relationship G-d's spirit and will actually can be imbued in the words of the prophet. Two men, Eldad and Medad, who had been designated to be with the seventy but did not choose to join the gathering of elders begin prophesying in the camp. Joshua, Moses's lieutenant and in this portion the voice of the established order, asks Moses to restrain them.

In one of the most democratic verses anywhere in the Torah, Moses responds to Joshua, "Are you wrought up on my account? Would that all the Lord's people were prophets, that the Lord put the Lord's spirit upon them." This idea goes beyond the inclusion of Eldad and Medad, who had the right to be among the elders. Moses's revolutionary words include everyone. He goes beyond the idea of any limitation in number or qualification. He simply says that all of G-d's people should be granted the most exalted status in Judaism, the status of prophets.

Similar sentiments are expressed by the prophet Joel (3:1) when he says, "And it shall come to pass afterward, That I will pour out my spirit upon all flesh; And your sons and your daughters shall prophesy, Your elders shall dream dreams, and your young shall see visions." Shimshon Raphael Hirsch, the great German Torah scholar, commenting on the *Beha'alotecha* verse wrote, "We are shown that there is no monopoly on spiritual leadership. The spiritual powers granted by G-d are not the privilege of any particular office or status. The lowliest of the nation shares with the highest the opportunity of being granted divine inspiration." Contrary to the normative voice of the tradition, which extols and protects the power of the hierarchy, here Moses reaches out and includes everyone. If Moses wishes that all of the Jewish people were prophets, certainly women and LGBT people are included.

The full meaning of this populist impulse of Moses is more completely fleshed out in chapter 12 when Aaron and Miriam lead a rebellion against Moses because of his marriage to a non-Israelite, a Cushite, possibly, according to scholars, a black woman—someone very different from a traditional member of the Israelite tribe. In responding to the rebellion, the Torah then states that Moses is "the most humble person in all the world." Moses not only would like everyone to have an intimate relationship with G-d; he himself is able and willing to have an intimate relationship with one of those the Torah would refer to as a *stranger*. The Moses of *Beha'alotecha* seems to have no boundaries as to whom he wants to include in the spheres of his life or the life of the Israelite nation. Humility in its purest form is not a practice that mandates putting "oneself down" but rather the practice of lifting everyone up to a place of equality in society and before G-d. Here Moses is doing exactly that.

It appears not only that G-d approves Moses's relationship but also that G-d chastises Miriam and Aaron for disapproving of it. When they complain that they too speak the word of the Lord, G-d tells them that Moses has a special place, a place above that of any other prophet, in G-d's house. Even though everyone can be a prophet, Moses's humility and leadership cause him to relate to G-d in the closest way possible. Even prophets can ascend to higher levels of prophecy if they do the right thing in their lives. In a powerful and symbolic verse, G-d states that Moses and G-d speak "mouth-to-mouth," an expression of utter intimacy. G-d then punishes Miriam by afflicting her with white scales, and it is left to Moses to plead with G-d to heal Miriam.

In this portion Moses's message is that everyone has the right to equality and leadership in G-d's world. If the great prophet-leader attests that all of G-d's people could be prophets, if he is given G-d's affirmation when he marries outside the tribe, then surely the field is open to everyone to be a part of the Israelite nation regardless of his or her sex or sexual inclinations. Homosexuality is not a reason to limit access to religious leadership or to sexual intimacy even in the time of the Torah. In this portion Moses's statements and victories are messages of acceptance and inclusion. And God's rebuke to Aaron and Miriam suggests that G-d too envisions a pluralistic world.

THIRTY-SEVEN

Ruach Acheret—Ruach Hakodesh/ Different Spirit—Sacred Spirit
Parashat Shelach (Numbers 13:1–15:41)

CAMILLE SHIRA ANGEL

Parashat Shelach tells the story of twelve scouts, one man from each ancestral tribe, who were sent forth to survey the land of Canaan, the land God promised to the Israelite people. The scouts return with a mixed message. While they are enraptured by the possibilities that the land holds for them, "it does indeed flow with milk and honey," they are also terrified by the seemingly insurmountable obstacles.

Ten of the twelve spies describe the land as a place that devours its settlers and its people. The Anakites, often translated as "giants," appear enormously threatening. *"V'chen hayinu b'neichem"*—"and we must have looked like grasshoppers in their eyes, too." Scouting the landscape, the ten naysayers are filled with despair as they perceive the resident population as unconquerable. Sizing up their enemies, the Israelites feel minuscule in comparison. The idea of making this foreign land their own becomes impossible to fathom. Even as God has long promised the Israelites that they shall overcome, the spies succumb to doubts and consequently suffer a failure of nerve. Their mission becomes self-defeating.

For many of us, as we considered coming out and living our lives as gay, lesbian, bisexual, or transgender, it was as if we too were facing an ordeal of epic proportions, a territorial battle for autonomy and self-definition. Likewise, we too were faced with the imposing, if not threatening, dominant culture, the gigantic power and privilege of mainstream thinking.

In this passage of Torah, the contrast between the giants and the spies represents a duality between the Normative versus the Other, the Dominator versus the Dominated. The heavy residue of slave mentality veils the spies' ability to see their own strength and the Divine shield. We do not know what the Anakites think of the Israelites, only what the insecure Israelites think of themselves. Feeling small and powerless, they internalize this deprecation, and it takes a whole new generation before they are able to realize their power.

There are many problems when we judge ourselves through the eyes of others, especially those with an agenda for suppression. *"V'chen hayinu b'neichem"*—"and we must have looked like grasshoppers in their eyes, too." In the Hasidic commentary *Itturai Torah*, the rabbis say that it was a sin for the spies to use those words.

Why? The rabbis continued, if you look at imposing people and say that you feel like a grasshopper, that is a reasonable thing to say because it is based on your feelings. But when you say, "We must have looked like grasshoppers in their eyes," the *Itturai Torah* chides, "What difference should it make how we appeared to them?" What possible good is there in being concerned about how you appear in others' eyes?

But among the twelve, there were two people, Joshua and Caleb, who filed a minority report. Caleb said, "Let us by all means go up, and we shall gain possession of it, for we shall surely overcome it." "We're not paying attention to how we think we might be perceived in others' eyes. Yeah, they're big and we're about to embark on a task that is huge, but" *"yachol, nuchal la,"* "we know that we are able to do it." Seeing ourselves through others' eyes will not chart the direction that we need to take.

Perhaps the "sin"—*"avon,"* of the ten spies was to acquiesce to fear and lose sight of their authentic power. Internalizing a sense of inferiority, the Israelites lost confidence and became vulnerable to the inner voice of self-doubt and denigration. They felt paralyzed to move forward. After all, these people had been slaves descended from slaves. Their slave mentality, an overwhelmingly arresting sense of insecurity, grossly distorted their sense of being created in the image of the Divine; they felt incapable of creating new identities. This feeling is evidenced by their reaction to the spies' message; they are initially inclined to return to Egypt upon hearing this news. Paradoxically, it is this sense of insecurity that does indeed reflect our being made in the image of God, and once they recognize this fact, they are able to transcend their insecurity and move forward.

Unable yet to come to this realization, the ten spies collude in blaming themselves for not having the necessary attributes to overcome the forces that they perceive as keeping them suppressed, whereas, truly, it is not the giants but their own insecure selves, in the shadow of this perceived threat, that are keeping them suppressed. By referring to themselves in dehumanizing terms, as "grasshoppers," they allowed their own insecure, fear-based projections of themselves, represented by the ruling class, to define them. In reality, their world was not as dangerous as it appeared to be. Likewise, LGBT folk sometimes make assumptions that the world is more dangerous than it is, whereas in reality, it may only appear to be so due to our own depleted confidence.

In contrast, Joshua and Caleb demonstrated hopeful resistance. Together they challenged the dispiriting impressions of their peers. They recognized that they could not advance their cause, their conquest of the Anakites, if the people had a diminished sense of hope, pride, and faith in themselves. Recognizing that their whole selves were made in the image of the Divine, insecurities and all, Joshua and Caleb were able to reveal this realization to the Israelites and rally them to conquer their fears and, in turn, the Anakites.

Like the Israelites, who were damaged by the effects of the negative reports, so we LGBT people have absorbed and internalized the historical, pervasive, and deeply embedded negative messages of homophobia, transphobia, and heterosexism. It is no wonder that many of us worry about being abnormal or would choose invisibility and try to pass as heterosexual—and that many Jews consider "fixing" their noses, taking on anglicized names, and making efforts to pass as gentiles. We have received a strong message, that it is dangerous to be like our own people and therefore different from the norm.

It is also very difficult to be true to ourselves and our uniqueness when the ways we are different from the dominant culture have been labeled as deviant, disgusting, and dangerous. When literature, history, books, art, movies, and television show a multifaceted, positive vision of the dominators and a single, negative vision of the dominated, then a person growing up female, of color, lesbian or gay, and the like has to work against the entire culture in order to develop a sense of pride and wholeness.

That is why it is so meaningful that our text has Caleb's otherness recognized and rewarded by no less than the Divine, Godself. God is countering the negative self-image and engendering pride in its place. Therefore, we need to honor the different ways we see, feel, and understand, leading toward diversity and away from homogenization.

This is the greatness of Caleb—which merits him a comparison with Abraham. In chapter 14, verse 24, God says that God will single out Caleb and bring him into the Land—"*ve 'avdi Caleb 'ekev hayita ruach acheret 'imo . . .*"—"And my servant Caleb, BECAUSE [*'ekev*] there was a different spirit within him . . ." This word—*'ekev*—is the word with which God uplifts Abraham at the Akeidah, granting him an eternal covenant "BECAUSE [*'ekev*] you listened to my voice."

Ibn Ezra understands Caleb as an individual who had the ability and "spirit" to take on new tasks, even in the face of adversity and opposition. "My servant Caleb, because he was imbued with a different spirit and remained loyal to Me, shall see the land that I promised on oath to their fathers; none of those who spurn Me shall see it" (Num. 14:24). His "*ruach acheret*," literally "a different spirit," empowered Caleb to enable nation building. I sense this tremendous spirit within our community as we express our different spirit, our spirit informed by the empathy of knowing what it is to be treated as Other, while never losing sight of our Divine imprint. This identification with the Other and this Divine fuel is what enables us as Jews and queers to move forward with our justice and equality agenda.

Caleb and Joshua were the two optimistic spies who God determined each had a *ruach acheret*, a "different spirit." As long as queers are not grasshoppers in our own eyes, we can use this passage to cultivate within ourselves "a different spirit," the spirit that brings with it the intrinsic qualities of compassion, courage, and perseverance.

As Jews, we take inspiration from our primary narrative about crossing the boundary between slavery into freedom. As queers, our experiences of wrestling the giants without and within help shape not only our memories of the past but also our actions in the present and our visions for the future. We celebrate the certain knowledge that our *ruach acheret, our different spirit,* coupled with our inherent *ruach hakodesh,* our sacred spirit, can be our guide on the individual and collective journey toward transformation.

THIRTY-EIGHT

Torah and Its Discontents

Parashat Korach (Numbers 16:1–18:32)

JANE RACHEL LITMAN

I sit in the retro-modern kitchen of a suburban Los Angeles home, the off-avocado appliances proclaiming distress in almost equal volume to that of my twelve-year-old cousin Adam struggling to master tropes and write his drash as he prepares for his bar mitzvah. According to my aunt, he needs some help, and I, the family rabbi, have been summoned to the rescue. This is pretty funny, because it is a well-known family "fact" that I cannot carry a tune or sing on key. But the rabbinic mojo is powerful, and it is hoped that perhaps my general familiarity with the Torah might do the trick. Indeed, as soon as my aunt and uncle retire to the sunken dual entertainment and rumpus room, I reach over and press the stop button on Adam's cassette-tape player. "Let's just talk about the portion," I suggest.

Adam looks guiltily at the kitchen door, as if expecting the Torah police to burst through and place him under religious arrest. He fidgets a bit, sizes me up, glances at the door again, and says, "I hope you won't get upset, but I like Korach. I think he's in the right. He is being very reasonable. Moses is a big bully, not to mention God." My young cousin Adam is the first, but not the last, bat/bar mitzvah student to hesitantly disclose to me an inner personal dissent from the object lesson intended in this parasha—a disclosure I hear not only from the mouths of twelve-year-olds; adults as well often tell me of their discomfort with the dramatic struggle for power and brutal resolution recounted in the tale.

The tense showdown in *Parashat Korach* is presented in high relief. Moses is both the symbol and substance of authority, chosen and favored by God. Korach is the rebel, challenging the existent chain of command. The parasha opens with a dramatic description of the confrontation; Korach and his co-conspirators accuse Moses: "You have gone too far! All of the people are holy. . . . Why do you raise yourself above Adonai's congregation?" (Num. 17:3). Moses responds in kind, using similarly aggressive language: "The man who Adonai chooses, he is the holy one. You have gone too far!" It is high noon in the *midbar* (Sinai): the terms set out, pistols drawn; a duel to the death.

This clash over authority has its paradoxes, even in the Torah's own terms. Moses is leader of the Hebrews by virtue of having led a successful rebellion against Pharaoh, the supreme political authority figure of Egypt. Moses's previous encounters with human authority show anything but restraint. In a fit of rage, he kills an Egyptian slave overseer, and he repeatedly overtly threatens Pharaoh. Moses—to his core—represents the virtue of resistance against arbitrary power and domination. Yet, in the eyes of Korach, now Moses himself has become the seemingly willful and arbitrary leader. Korach envisions himself as the idealistic rebel. No wonder young cousin Adam is confused; the Torah has gone too far!

The Pharisaic Sages, in their approach to this text, are aware of the complexity of their interpretive task. Like Moses, the ancient Rabbis do not have a simple relationship to authority. Though they are the Jewish authority figures of their times, in terms of Jewish religious history, the Rabbis are profoundly revolutionary. If anything, Rabbinic Judaism is the fulfillment of Korach's claim that "all of the people are holy." In the period of its emergence, Pharisaic Judaism—the precursor of Rabbinic Judaism—was but one sect of many. Its core practices stemmed from the religious strategy of relocating worship from the ancient Temple into the home and synagogue. As a result, study, prayer, and good deeds replaced showy public sacrifices, and religious leadership shifted from the hereditary priesthood to the populist rabbinate. Rabbinic literature justifies this profound change by citing prooftexts from the Torah, which it understands as the direct word of God. The Rabbis often cite Exodus 19:6, "You are a kingdom of priests," to illustrate the rightness of their way. That sounds very close to Korach's accusation against Moses.

In addition, during the time of the Rabbis, the real political authority and power lay with the much-hated Roman occupation force. The Sages were morally incensed by the cruel and arrogant nature of the Roman government. The Rabbis have not only a natural tendency to support the righteous rebel but also a vast political and religious context for the support. But, unlike my modernist cousin Adam and his ilk, the Rabbis are constrained from siding with Korach the rebel against God/Moses. For the Rabbis, God is the unquestionable ultimate source of truth, and the Torah is God's direct revelation. So, just as the Rabbis reinvent Jewish theology, they recast the nature of Korach's conflict to suit their moral sensibilities and resolve their dilemma.

The Rabbis view Korach as a villain. They debate whether Korach and his followers will have a portion in the world to come or will be condemned to eternal oblivion (*Sanhedrin* 109bff.). The Sages explore Korach's sins in great detail, including the wrongdoings of his wife (who is not mentioned in the Torah). The Korach of rabbinic midrash is not the Korach of the Torah.

The Sages' midrashic re-creation of Korach emerges from three key suppositions. The first is that God is always good and right and that God is ultimately on the side of the Rabbis. The second is that the Torah is the word of God. The third is that Korach's basic argument about universal holiness is correct. Thus, according to rabbinic midrash, Korach's transgression cannot be rebellion against authority. So then, what is it?

The Sages paint Korach not as an idealistic conscientious dissenter but as a manipulative greedy hypocrite. The midrashic Korach is a man of extreme wealth: "the keys of Korach's treasure house were a load for three hundred white mules" (Rabbi Levy on *Sanhedrin* 110). He cynically and disingenuously stages the confrontation with Moses in order to replace Moses with himself. This midrashic Korach is creating spin about equality and universal holiness, but in actuality he is a power-hungry corrupt politician.

The Rabbis are at pains to show that it is Moses who is actually looking out for the welfare of the masses. The midrashic Moses is humble, conciliatory (hearing that some of the Levites have concerns, he goes out to look for them to discuss the problems), responsible and fair. He is anything but authoritarian or arbitrary. He is a true populist whom the Sages call Moshe Rabbeinu. If anything, the Talmudic persona "Moshe Rabbeinu" is even holier than the Torah's Moses. The midrashic Korach, on the other hand, is avaricious and scheming. No wonder God chooses Moses and dooms Korach! The Rabbis use midrash to change the sacred record and thus reframe the nature of the conflict from one about authority to one about values.

This is a moral strategy worthy of some comment. Ostensibly, it seems that the Rabbis could have found a way to support the Moses of the text. They might have justified Moses by making an argument of ethical relativism. They could have said that Moses's situation excused totalitarianism in order to maintain security. The Sages could have acknowledged that Korach might have had a good point about equity during times of political stability, but in a situation of transition and chaos, Korach and his followers were straining the social resources. But the Sages do not make this argument, because they simply do not support that perspective. For them, Korach's claim is not relative to a certain social situation but is absolute. The Sages agree with Korach's assertion that "all of the people are holy" whether the social order is solid or whether times are chaotic. Therefore, the problem cannot be in Korach's claim of universal holiness. Nor is it his power position relative to Moses; the Rabbis are sympathetic to those with less power. The Rabbis resolve the conflict by asserting that the transgression must be one of unethical personal character.

What is the queer lesson in all of this? We tend to look at the Torah from a modernist "realistic" perspective; that is, we tend to take the story at face value and move on from there. In the showdown between Korach and Moses, our queer identification tends to favor Korach. Korach represents the (relatively) disenfranchised. Korach seems the less violent, though to be fair, the savagery seems more at the hand of God than of Moses. Lastly, Korach makes a very appealing moral argument, the same one that queers make—that holiness resides in everyone. One possible interpretive strategy is for us to follow young cousin Adam's approach, counterread the Torah and side with Korach.

The Rabbis employ another hermeneutic methodology. They feel perfectly comfortable interpreting the "truth" of the Torah by adding material in a way that we might initially define as rewriting history. But the Torah is not history; it is sacred mythos. The approach of the Sages is similar to that of renowned feminist theorist Monique Wittig: "There was a time when you were not a slave, remember that. You walked alone, full of laughter. . . . You say there are no words to describe this time, you say it does not exist. But remember. Make an effort to remember. Or, failing that, invent" (*Les Guérillères,* trans. and ed. David Le Vay [Urbana-Champaign: University of Illinois Press, 2007], 89).

Discontent with the face-value narrative, the Sages dehypostasize the Moses and Korach presented in the parasha to "invent" two new opponents, a different kind of dramatic conflict, and thus a new ethical teaching. In the Torah, Moses and Korach fight over authority; in the midrash, their dispute is over moral integrity. This rabbinic teaching is a powerful one for contemporary queers. The Rabbis teach that the core issue is not power but ethics.

What does this teaching mean to the queer community? Some contemporary gay people frame our struggle as one of equal access to power and to social institutions. Can we get married? Can we join the army? Can we make a decent living without job discrimination and harassment? These are important questions. But the Rabbis use *Parashat Korach* to ask a deeper question: do I want equality just for me and mine or for everyone? The former concerns are about power, the latter about moral values. The rabbinic teaching on *Parashat Korach* asks the gay rights movement to think seriously about the depths of inclusion. Do we really mean it when we say that everyone has a spark of holiness, or do we want to supplant one privileged class with another? Does "everyone" include the less socially acceptable members of our community: trannies, butches, queens, the leather clubs, and AIDS survivors? And beyond our community, the broader world: what would it mean politically to believe that every single person has a spark of holiness?

If the Talmud's message emphasizing ethical leadership and universal holiness is profound for the queer community, its methodology is even more so. Beyond the substance of the rabbinic teaching, the rabbinic (Wittig) process opens opportunities to queers. Reading the Torah on its own creates a dichotomy: either we affirm the text as it stands or we counterread it in dissent. But the Rabbis created a system of ongoing revelation through creative interpretation. The Sages give queer people (and all the unvoiced) an opportunity to enter the mythos and thus change it. We are not so much rewriting history as amending it. Thus, as the Jewish people grow and change through maturation over time, the Torah can as well.

There in the suburban Los Angeles kitchen, sitting on red-vinyl-covered dining chairs pulled up to a drop-leaf, oddly patterned Formica table, I explain all of this to my cousin Adam. Initially he seems unconvinced. "Pretty hard on Korach," Adam tells me. "First the Torah has him swallowed up by the earth, and then the Rabbis diss his character. But I like that Wittig quote. Could you say it again?" I repeat the part about inventing. "Yeah," says Adam, "that makes sense. About using your imagination and own moral values to find the meaning. I think I'll write my own midrash, in which Moses and Korach reunite in the World to Come, make peace, and become friends."

"That's great," I reply, "and I think I'll write a drash that ends with your tone-deaf cousin Jane helping you chant Torah." I reach over and punch the start button on his cassette player.

THIRTY-NINE

The Healing Serpent: Recovering Long Lost Jewish Fragments

Parashat Hukkat (Numbers 19:1–22:1)

JACOB J. STAUB

When Ezra returned to Jerusalem from the Babylonian exile, he brought a version of the Torah virtually identical to the one we have today. All subsequent Jewish reflection on the text was recorded as commentary. Ezra and the scribes who edited the final version of the Torah out of other texts, however, did not preserve earlier versions. They intentionally sought to create the impression that the Torah has always spoken with one, normative voice. They did a masterful but imperfect job of editing out diverse strands of the tradition. Queering the Torah thus involves more than questioning the received text; it also involves digging beneath it for echoes of suppressed ancestors. One such echo is the copper serpent story in *Parashat Hukkat*.

The Israelites in this parasha complain, as they do throughout the book of Numbers. Who can blame them? By now, their dramatic rescue at the Sea of Reeds and their receipt of the Torah at Mount Sinai are distant memories. They find themselves wandering in the wilderness without a reliable source of water (Num. 20:2), attacked by the Canaanite king of Arad (Num. 21:10), and detouring around Edom (Num. 21:4). With no end to their trek in sight, they want to return home, even to Egyptian slavery. They believe, understandably, that they are going to die in the desert, before reaching the Promised Land. Moses loses his temper, striking the rock in anger and frustration at the people's impatience, and he himself is punished for his unseemly behavior (Num. 20:6–13).

God, too, loses his temper and punishes the Israelites for their faithlessness by sending serpents whose bites are lethal, causing many Israelites to die. Thus, the people are induced to acknowledge their sinful murmuring and to beg Moses to plead for God to rescue them. At God's instruction, Moses makes a copper serpent and mounts it high and visible on a standard; suffering snakebite victims who look at the serpent do not die.

This narrative is problematic for those who believe that the Torah consistently reflects uniformly exalted values and that immediately following the revelation at Mount Sinai, the Israelites did not engage in totemic, magical practices.

Repeatedly in the stories of Israel's wilderness trek, we may feel the urgent need to question the narrative's basic underlying premise: that God is a tyrannical tribal chieftain who requires absolute, unambivalent loyalty, who has a quick temper and punishes insubordination in extreme ways, and who is oh-so-merciful in being willing to relent when the sinners confess and repent. We are heirs to a heritage whose formative narratives demand, on pain of death, absolute obedience and conformity to the norm, leaving precious little space for multivocality or diversity. The Golden Calf episode is the classic example of this worldview; the narrative in *Parashat Hukkat* is but a minor echo. Both stories of "insubordination," however, can be read as accounts of Israelite practices that were condemned only in later centuries by those who wrote the stories down.

The narrator of the copper serpent episode leaves some seams exposed. We are able to peer beneath the normative, monotheistic façade that contemporary Bible scholars tell us was constructed in 8th-century Jerusalem. Traumatized by the fall of the Northern Kingdom in 721 BCE and Jerusalem's narrow escape from the Assyrian siege, Judean leaders blamed the catastrophe on the allegedly idolatrous practices of the North. That is, the North *must* have done something to deserve its fall. They warned the people of Jerusalem (including many refugees from the North) not to repeat those mistakes, lest Judea fall as well.[1]

This is the context in which the Pentateuchal documents were edited into their final form, and we can assume that the editors were interested in condemning traces in the narratives of older practices and beliefs that were current and acceptable but that they now viewed as deviant and worthy of punishment. In the wake of the Assyrian destruction of much of the Judean countryside, they were centralizing and normalizing the cult in the Jerusalem temple, where they could control practices. These condemnations thus reveal more about their contemporary concerns than about the age-old stories themselves.

If queering the text means questioning the norms that it sets, then we must begin by questioning the assumption that all Biblical voices had the norm-setting agenda of late–First Temple editors. If they are admonishing the people not to act like the exiled people of the Northern Kingdom, then they must have been addressing an audience who they thought were inclined to engage in the practices they were now condemning. Thus, not all Judeans were piously inclined to eradicate diversity. Similarly, in centralizing the cult at the Temple in Jerusalem, they condemned heterogeneous practices that until that point had been current in the local high places outside Jerusalem and that had never before been made homogeneous. Contrary to the assumption of the prophets, the practices that they condemned were not idolatrous deviations from pristine older rituals; rather, they were older, accepted practices that were being newly condemned.

The literary counterpart to these leaders was a group of Biblical historians often called the "Deuteronomist," who edited the book of Deuteronomy as well as the historical books called First Prophets and who lived in the 8th and 7th centuries BCE; these editors present Israelite history through a repeating cycle: we sinned, we were punished, we repented, and we were saved. Having witnessed the destruction of Samaria and the near destruction of Jerusalem and Judea, they urged the people to change their sinful ways and ward off further destruction, and they read this theology back into earlier narratives: three thousand were slaughtered by the Levites after the sin of the Golden Calf; many were killed by the serpents after the Israelites complained. But then, the rest of us were delivered when we repented. So let us now repent and be saved. A queer perspective questions whether the pressure to conform to a monolithic norm, developed as a posttraumatic response to the catastrophic Assyrian invasion, need be regarded as the only authentic strand that we inherit from our Judean ancestors.

Queering our text also means imagining the voices that were silenced by the redactors. The seams in the façade of the edited text are the ancient narratives that remain. They are cast in the text as illustrations that support the editors' agenda, but they nevertheless give us a glimpse into our ancestors' narratives before those stories were edited into moralizing fables. The Israelite men are healed from their venomous snakebites by *looking* at the copper serpent. They whine, having lost their virility in their inability to stand fast and firm in their faith. Moses built what sounds like a very impressive phallus. Just looking at it heals them, restoring their masculinity. The story probably survived as a warning against lack of faith, but it preserves a snapshot of other Israelite beliefs that were becoming unacceptable in the 8th century.

Freud had something to say about looking at snakes. In his 1922 essay "Medusa's Head," he identifies the terror of Medusa as the fear of castration, linked to the sight of female (mother's) genitals, surrounded by hair, minus a penis. Medusa's hair is often represented as snakes. Frightened at the thought of castration, men see phalluses everywhere. The sight of Medusa's head turns the terrified (male) viewer into stone, stiff with terror—terrified yet erect once more. Displaying the male genitals—whether on Medusa's head, as a giant copper serpent, or in a locker-room pissing contest—is a way of defending oneself against the terror of castration with bravado.[2]

The Israelites are certainly terrified, not to mention bitchy. Listen to their words as they address God and Moses: "Why did you make us leave Egypt to die in the wilderness? There is no bread or water, and we have come to loathe this miserable food" (Num. 21:5).[3] Assailed by lethal serpents, they are cured by gazing upon a copper serpent, erect and larger than life. As per Freud, the serpent is both lethal and redemptive.

The sequence of our questions might proceed as follows: Could it be that earlier Israelite traditions included a narrative in which Moses, at God's instruction, uses a phallic totem to heal the sick? Does pure monotheism allow for that? Had they always believed uniformly in the One God who did not need magical props? The copper serpent narrative reveals a layer of primal Israelite symbolism that is illumined by Freud's analysis.

Subjecting Numbers 21:4–9 to Freud's analysis of the Greek Medusa myth also allows us to learn from Hélène Cixous's criticism of that analysis.[4] Addressing the phallocentric tradition of writing, Cixous argues,

> For what [men] have said so far, for the most part, stems from the opposition activity/passivity from the power relation between a fantasized obligatory virility meant to invade, to colonize, and the consequential phantasm of woman as a "dark continent"

to penetrate and to "pacify." . . . Conquering her, they've made haste to depart from her borders, to get out of sight, out of body.[5]

Men do not want to linger. They do not want to view the phallusless woman. Men's fear of looking at the Medusa is their fear of castration. Women remind them of this primal fear, so they avert their gaze. Looking itself is lethal.[6] Cixous exhorts women to refuse to play the roles assigned to them in this phallocentric psychodrama. Women need not continue to be passive, dark, and therefore threatening. "Too bad for them if they fall apart upon discovering that women aren't men, or that the mother doesn't have one. . . . You only have to look at the Medusa straight on to see her. And she's not deadly. She's beautiful and she's laughing."[7]

Moses in *Parashat Hukkat* wants the stricken Israelites to look and be healed. The feminist Cixous exhorts men to look at women in order to transcend their fears. But the overwhelming weight of rabbinic tradition commands us not to look at the physical world lest we be tempted. As an example, I choose the early-16th-century Italian Biblical commentator Rabbi Obadiah Sforno because he represents the culmination of the medieval (hence "traditional") approach to Bible commentary and because his allegorical reading is so clear and precise in its separation of body and spirit. Here are his comments on the word "serpent" in Genesis 3:1:

> *And the serpent.* "He is Satan; he is the evil inclination (*yetzer hara*)."[8] [That is,] he does great damage while being barely visible. . . . Our text refers to the evil inclination, the cause of sin, as a "serpent," in that it resembles a serpent, whose utility is slight, while its damage is great and its visibility is small.
>
> The rabbis said that "Samael rode upon him."[9] That is, the power of desire leads us to sin by means of the power of the imagination, which brings to it images of material pleasure that deflect it from the path of perfection intended by God, may God be blessed. . . . The rabbis taught that the eye and the heart are the agents of sin, just as [the Torah] warns us, "Do not follow your heart and eyes [after which you go lusting]" [Num. 15:39].[10]

According to Sforno and so many of his predecessors, we (at least, we men) should not *look* at anything. Our eyes provide the pleasurable views that fuel the imagination and that feed desire and lead us to go a-whoring. Look instead at the *tzitzit* (fringes) on your *tallit* (prayer shawl) so that you do not think about material things, thereby feeding your lust with your imagination. The threat of castration for the murmuring Israelites in *Parashat Hukkat*, as for mind-wandering, prayer-shawled men at prayer, comes from God the Almighty. Do not complain, do not fantasize, do not lust, or you will be dealt with most severely. Images of material pleasure thwart God's intention and will. According to Sforno, God frowns not only on pleasure but on fantasies of pleasure.

How can this narrative be told in a way that helps us to avoid reinscribing the message that the Other is dangerous and should be subjugated—whether it is the other gender or the other, imaginative impulse or the body and its pleasures or lust?

Here is at least one place in which we are given a precedent for looking—and for its healing power. The Israelites look at a totemic phallus and are healed. They look because God commands them to look. Numbers 21:4–9 does not have the weight to counterbalance the third paragraph of the Shema ("Do not follow your own heart and eyes" [Num. 15:39]), but it is a start, one small step toward embodiment, toward celebrating physical pleasure as divine. To be healed, you must look.

But it is not only desire-inducing material images at which we are forbidden to look. Moses is also commanded not to look at God's face. Looking at God's face is lethal (Ex. 33:20). Traditionally, the explanations of these two different prohibitions are worlds apart. One can wonder, nevertheless, whether at some earlier period, it was an embodied God at whom one could not look—the One with an outstretched arm and flaring nostrils, the One who occupied a very definite physical space in the Temple's Holy of Holies, the One seen by Isaiah in robes and Ezekiel in flight, the One whose physical measurements were calculated and recorded in the *Shiur Komah* literature. You do not look into the eyes or at the groin of a father or a chieftain and leave undamaged.

Imagine, then, that we could travel to Judea at a time prior to the Assyrian invasion, before the two Israelite kingdoms had been ravaged by a brutal imperial power, before Judean leaders feared for their survival and sought to fend off additional divine punishment by suppressing what they now regarded as sin. Imagine a society in which the cult was not centralized and diverse customs flourished at local shrines, where nobody thought it idolatrous to bake cakes to the Queen of Heaven or to cast bronze calves or bulls to represent the seat of an invisible but very embodied God, and where serpent totems healed. Without necessarily embracing these ancient beliefs as credible in the 21st century, we can be liberated by their diversity to see that norms were imposed then, just as they are today, by those who seek power and make dubious claims to ancient authority.

Once we free ourselves from the censors, we can look where we have been forbidden to look. Unafraid that "copper serpents" are idolatrous, we might be freer to explore symbols and rituals that are, after all, Jewishly authentic. Understanding that we need not accept the portrayal of God as an autocratic, vindictive tribal chieftain, we might discover benign, supportive, nonjudgmental aspects of God that we had never noticed. And rediscovering God's body, we might reclaim the blessedness of our own bodies, affirming that materiality and physical pleasure are divine gifts rather than temptations.

NOTES

1. For a review of the current literature, see Jason Radine, "The Book of Amos and the Development of Judean Political Identity" (Ph.D. diss., University of Michigan, 2007).

2. Sigmund Freud, *Sexuality and the Psychology of Love* (New York: Simon and Schuster, 1963), 202–203.

3. Translation from *Tanakh* (Philadelphia: Jewish Publication Society, 1999).

4. Hélène Cixous, "The Laugh of the Medusa," translated by Keith Cohen and Paula

Cohen, in *New French Feminisms: An Anthology,* edited by Elaine Marks and Isabelle de Courtivron (New York: Schocken Books, 1981), 245–264. I thank Dr. Lori Lefkovitz for sending me to Cixous.

5. Ibid., 247n. 1.

6. Ibid., 254–255.

7. Ibid., 255.

8. B. *Baba Batra* 16a.

9. Pirkei de Rabbi Eliezer 13.

10. My translation. For the complete comment, see Sforno, *Commentary on the Torah, Volume 1,* translated by Raphael Pelcovitz (Brooklyn, NY: Mesorah, 1989).

FORTY

Between Beast and Angel: The Queer, Fabulous Self
Parashat Balak (Numbers 22:2–25:10)

LORI HOPE LEFKOVITZ

Parashat Balak is replete with boundary crossing and ambiguous identity categories: a beast talks; angels walk among us; the protagonist-prophet Balaam, who ultimately blesses the people Israel, is himself a gentile and in the Bible and later commenting tradition, he is characterized as both friend and foe, an ambiguous hero. Interrupting the well-ordered regulations of Temple worship and stories of Moses, Aaron, and the priesthood, which are more typical of the book of Numbers, this narrative intrudes and is distinctive in its failure to observe the conventions of Biblical realism. Instead, we are treated to a fabulous story—indeed, a fable—with some of the upsidedown, and therefore subversive, features of carnival. One might read this story as a countertext: possibly comic, a corrective vision that challenges the rigid definitions of Biblical categories. This dream-work, populated by anomalous beings, reminds the reader that the identity categories to which people are assigned—especially categories of gender and sexuality—are, after all, optional to the extent that their borders are arbitrarily drawn and must be rigorously policed.

Parashat Balak presents as a fable. An ill-intentioned, powerful, and wealthy king, Balak, twice offers riches to the skilled diviner Balaam to curse the Israelites in the hope of ridding them from the land. The protagonist prophet, in possible need of moral strengthening, reluctantly agrees to travel to see these Israelites but insists that he can only say the words that God puts in his mouth. A journey (the road of life, where knowledge is acquired) is interrupted en route by a sharp-talking, sword-brandishing angelic presence who can choose to whom he manifests himself. A loyal donkey protectively avoids the angel, who is invisible to Balaam, and so provokes her master's violent reaction (he beats her three times). When the talking donkey objects to this mistreatment, she finds support in the formidable, threatening angel, suddenly and terrifyingly visible to Balaam. The angel secures Balaam's promise of obedience. Still, in an effort to influence fate, Balaam has Balak offer three hill-top sacrifices, each with seven altars, seven bulls, and seven rams (magic numbers), but the will of Heaven will not be thwarted. Including the famous lines preserved in Jewish liturgy, "How goodly are your tents, O Jacob, your dwellings, O Israel!" the people are blessed in a clear, poetic conclusion that affirms the unyielding power of fate and definitively supplants the evil king's intended curses with the abiding blessings from Heaven.

A second, darker ending (beginning with Numbers 25) in which the fickle, idolatrous people cease to deserve these blessings, a functional postscript rife with illicit sex and murder, breaks from the genre of the fable and restores the more usual conventions of Biblical narrative.

I want to look a little more closely at how the story leapfrogs identity boundaries; but first, let us pause over the figure of the angel. Insofar as angels are asexual (non-carnal) men or ambiguously-sexed fantasies, the angel's presence reinforces our sense of a world in which identity is not what it seems. The angel's careful decision about when to reveal himself—to "out himself," as it were—further enforces the message of a ubiquitous unknowable, hidden population. Even a great seer cannot tell where an angel may be. The power (and threat) of the closet is that one can never be sure before whom one stands. This story is about power and perception and, ultimately, about the power of perception. What the seer sees governs the fate of a nation. The reader, through identification with Balaam, receives a small education in human limitation and the life-and-death consequences of interpretation.

If the Great Chain of Being goes from the lowliest of creatures to the loftiest, from bugs and fish up through four-legged beasts to humanity, angels, and God, then the donkey and the angel are situated outside the extremes of humanity, which is, at its best, angelic and, at worst, beastly. In this story, there is a brief alliance formed between beast and angel against the main human character, Balaam, who would more conventionally be in relationship with either of them than they with each other.

First the angel stands in the way of the donkey, who is beaten; then the angel backs the donkey into a wall, squishing Balaam's foot and earning the donkey another beating; and finally, the angel forces the beast to lie down altogether, earning the donkey not just a beating but the murderous threat that if Balaam had had a sword, he would have done away with his incorrigible ride. When the poor donkey protests and asks her master if she has not been loyal all her life, the angel manifests himself in the donkey's defense. Wielding a sword of his own, the angel exchanges Balaam for the donkey as the object of threatened violence. Indeed, Balaam might imagine here that his having conjured a sword to be used against the donkey produced the vision of a sword that could be used against Balaam himself. The power relationship between master and beast is reversed by an unseen force that stands, as a corrective, on the donkey's side of the scale of justice. And to the extent that the sword represents a hypermasculinity that Balaam wishes for but does not have, the angel—who has no carnal or material needs or appetites himself—uses his sword to keep Balaam from misusing such power as he has. Even though Balaam has already made this commitment, the angel forces Balaam to promise yet again that he will only say what he is told to say, will function, essentially, as dummy to the divine ventriloquist.

If Balaam has limited autonomous power, the human king has even less. The king, Balak, and the prophet, Balaam, represent classes of people who possess different kinds of power, material and spiritual, respectively. The king, despite his wealth and authority, requires the skills of the diviner if he is to effectively curse the Israelites and end their obnoxious reproduction on the land. Balaam is in turn dependent on God to earn the riches promised by the king, and so Balaam sets about instructing

Balak on the sacrificial offerings that might turn things his way: three times with seven altars, prophet and king work together to influence God, and three times, Balaam delivers blessings "though Balak had ordered curses" for which he was prepared to pay handsomely. The king is irate.

The king's anger signals the frustration of authority without power. Indeed, a recurring phenomenon in the story is frustrated anger with those less powerful, on the one hand, and a complementary fear of the anger of those with greater power, on the other. The frustration of authority leads to the fable's theme of acceptance, resignation to God's will.

The king is an angry guy: first at the Israelites and ultimately at Balaam. Balaam is afraid to provoke God's anger, but he has no problem expressing anger against his loyal ass. But in this fable, all threats are idle, and anger at thwarted desire proves futile and fizzles. After Balaam's lesson from the angel, he says nothing further to the ass. Balak rails weakly and impotently against Balaam, and Balaam ventures not a syllable against God. King and diviner have no choice but resignation. Although neither resigns his lofty post, both must be resigned to self-limitations. In this story, the strict boundaries of Biblical order are violated, the rules of the world are upturned, power is reversed and restored, wishes are thwarted, anger is diffused, and bullies are put in check.

The Biblical angel is echoed in two of the late 20th century's most powerful American dramas that attend to the triumphs and tragedies of queer America. Jonathan Larson's award-winning musical *Rent* and Tony Kushner's *Angels in America* feature sexually transgressive, boundary-crossing Angels who function to tame rage and exemplify the joy of loving self-expression. Tony Kushner's Angel is a comic and powerful revision of the Biblical prototype. She warns, "You can't outrun your occupation, Jonah. / Hiding from me in one place you will find me in another. / I I I I stop down the road, waiting for you" (179). And in her triumphant conclusion, the angelic voice yells, "for this age of anomie: a new law! / Delivered this silent night, this silent night, from Heaven, / Oh Prophet, to You" (182).

When Balaam blesses Israel, he blesses the good tents of Jacob, and Israel is identified in this story repeatedly as "Jacob," named for the patriarch who saw angels ascending and descending a ladder and who famously wrestled an angel, from whom he wrested a blessing and who left him marked on the thigh. These encounters with fighting personal angels in ambiguously homoerotic engagements (Balaam's angel wields a sword; Jacob wrestles him in the night, and Jacob will not release him) also expose the psychic dream-work beneath Biblical narrative.

Parashat Balak concludes by departing from the other world outside Israel, with its envious kings, gentile prophets, talking donkeys, and sword-brandishing angels. Back in those goodly tents, the story becomes grimly realistic. The people sin and worship Baal-peor. The men whore with Moabite and Midianite women. God's anger is serious, and the punishing plague visited on the Israelites is checked only by the public murder of two flagrant sinners. It is as if the reading's conclusion aims to reverse its earlier effects: it ends by putting an end to the comedy, refusing permission to cross ethnic or sexual boundaries, and planting us firmly in a world with God and sinners, one without angels and talking donkeys, a world with dangerous, consequential anger.

But it is too late. This countertext has worked its magic, surprised our expectations, and subverted the categories on which the Torah often insists with too much protest. In *The Politics and Poetics of Camp*, Moe Meyer writes that "what 'queer' signals is an ontological challenge that displaces bourgeois notions of the Self as unique, abiding, and continuous while substituting instead a concept of the Self as performative, improvisational, discontinuous, and processually constituted by repetitive and stylized acts" (2–3). In this sense, *Parashat Balak* is a "queer story," with king and prophet desperately and rather futilely enacting their life-roles, and angel and beast disrupting their self-assessments. In the fashion of all carnival texts, this parasha reminds us that because each of us improvises a Self, the Self is queer, by definition.

WORKS CITED

Kushner, Tony. *Angels in America: A Gay Fantasia on National Themes*. New York: Theater Communications Group, 1995.

Meyer, Moe. *The Politics and Poetics of Camp*. New York: Routledge, 1994.

FORTY-ONE

Pinchas, Zimri and the Channels of Divine Will
Parashat Pinchas (Numbers 25:10–30:1)

STEVEN GREENBERG

After forty years of circling the desert, the Israelites are a stone's throw from Jericho. They arrive at the Transjordan and are thrown together with their future neighbors, the Midianites and the Moabites. Social introduction leads to shared celebration and, very quickly we are told, to sex with the local women and idolatrous rites with their pagan god, Baal of Peor. This is the setting that introduces us to a bold and potentially rebellious prince of Israel and a zealous priest who acts on his impulses. The story actually begins in the previous week's portion and then introduces the portion of Pinchas. Here is the text:

> and the people began to go whoring with the daughters of Moab and they called the people to the sacrifices of their gods and the people ate and bowed down to their gods. And the people attached themselves to the Baal of Peor so the wrath of God flared up against Israel: The Lord said to Moses, "Take the chiefs of the people and impale them before the Lord in broad daylight, so that the Lord's wrath may turn away from Israel." Moses said to the officials of Israel: "Let each man kill those of his men who yoked themselves to the Baal of Peor!"
>
> Just then, a man of the Children of Israel had come and brought near to his kinsmen a certain woman of Midian before the eyes of Moses and before the eyes of the whole community of the Children of Israel while they were all weeping at the entrance to the Tent of Meeting.
>
> When Pinchas, son of Elazar son of Aaron the priest, saw this, he left the assembly and, taking a spear in his hand, he followed the Israelite into the chamber and stabbed both of them, the Israelite and the woman, through the belly and the plague against the Israelites was checked. . . .
>
> And the Lord spoke to Moses saying, Pinchas, son of Eleazar son of Aaron the Kohen, turned back my wrath from upon the children of Israel, when he zealously avenged me among them, so I did not consume the Children of Israel in my vengeance. There say: Behold! I give him my covenant of peace. The name of the Israelite who was killed, the one who was killed with the Midianite woman, was Zimri son of Salu, chieftain of a Simeonite ancestral house. The name of the Midianite woman who was killed was Cozbi daughter of Zur. (Num. 25:1–8a, 10–15)

Phineas, or *Pinchas* in Hebrew, is the Bible's most celebrated zealot. After the violent event he is awarded, with a certain irony, a "covenant of peace." Despite the Bible's praises of Pinchas's vigilante initiative that practically assuaged God's anger, however, the successive traditions of interpretation of these passages are ambivalent about him. Moreover, the occasion of this encounter between a public sexual menace and his vigilante assailant leads not only to discussions of how far one may take the law into one's own hands but also to a very surprising Hasidic portrayal of sexual desire.

First, from Pinchas's perspective, what did he see? He saw the Israelites for the second time succumbing to idolatry in a dangerous repetition of the episode of the golden calf. The last time such an outbreak occurred was just after the revelation of Torah, and now it was reoccurring just before their entry into the promised land. In response, a plague begins, and to make matters worse, in a public display of rebellion, a prince of Israel, Zimri, takes a princess of Midian, Cozbi, into a marital tent and perhaps, as some suggest, into the Tent of Meeting itself and begins to have sex with her. Pinchas, embodying divine wrath, enters the tent and impales them both and, in doing so, stops the plague.

Among the ancient and medieval interpretations of this story, one finds praise of Pinchas's daring alongside a deep suspicion of vigilante justice. No doubt worried by the dangerous precedent the text sets, the rabbis insist on the most narrow frame for this sort of action. Not anyone can take such extralegal initiative. Only a person of the purest motives might be trusted to act outside the system. Moreover, the zealous can respond only *in flagrante delicto*, literally "while the fire is blazing." Had Zimri separated from Cozbi for a moment, then Pinchas would have been guilty of murder. Had Zimri, in an attempt to protect himself, turned the tables and killed Pinchas, it would have been considered a legitimate act of self-defense (TB *Sanhedrin* 72a).

The Talmud reminds us that had Pinchas asked the court for permission, he would have been prohibited from action and instructed in the due process of the law. One does not get permission in advance of vigilante justice. The rabbis say that Moses was ready to excommunicate Pinchas for his behavior and would have, had God not intervened with his blessing of peace (ibid.).

Lastly, Ibn Ezra is patently uncomfortable with Pinchas. He does not want vigilante justice to be included in the divine praise, so against the plain sense of the text he suggests that Pinchas was indeed acting as an executioner, on the basis of the already-given testimony of witnesses, and so fully within the framework of the law.

And what was Zimri's motive for this public show of sexuality? From the Biblical story it could be that Zimri was simply caught up in the lusty excitement. Some Biblical scholars suggest that Zimri was engaged in an act of ritual intercourse to appease Baal Peor. Perhaps Zimri's act was actually politically motivated, challenging Moses's harsh demand for execution of all those who had worshiped at Baal Peor. The midrash adds the telling detail that Moses himself was married to Zipporah, the daughter of a Midianite priest. If so, then one might read Zimri's sexual insolence as a protest to what could look like a double standard.

The most radical rabbinic reading of the story, however, explores Zimri's motives and finds not political challenge but profound love. Rabbi Mordechai Yosef Leiner of

Izbica, Poland (referred to as the Ishbitzer), an early-19th-century Hasidic rebbe and thinker, read the story in a way that marks not Pinchas but Zimri as the unlikely hero of the episode. These are his words:

> Behold there are ten levels of sexual passion. The first is one who adorns himself and goes out intentionally after a sinful liaison, that is, that he himself pulls toward him the evil inclination [*yetzer hara*]. After that there are another nine levels and at each level another aspect of freedom is taken from him so that increasingly he cannot escape from sin until the tenth level. At that [level] if he distances himself from the *yetzer hara* and guards himself from sin with all his power until he has no capacity to protect himself further and still his inclination overpowers him and he does the act, then it is surely the will of God. . . . For Zimri in truth guarded himself from all wicked desires, and when he understood that she [Cozbi] was his soul mate, it was not in his power to release himself from doing this deed. . . . The essence of the matter is that Pinchas thought Zimri was an ordinary adulterer . . . and the depth of the matter eluded him regarding Zimri that she was his soul mate from the six days of creation.

Of course, the key to this interpretation is that Zimri's subjective experience—fought and denied, guarded against and so purified ten times—is at the end God's will. The depth of Zimri's love for Cozbi, his repeated attempts to thwart his desire, and his failure ultimately to do so reveals a love that is destined from on high. This is among the most antinomian religious texts anywhere in the Hasidic tradition. Reb Mordechai was not widely supported in his understanding of the conflict between powerful personal emotional experience and the law. Moreover, this interpretation, like the one that justifies vigilante justice, is dangerously open to abuse. Still, the text is there, and it invites us to explore how the fullness of subjective experience, tested repeatedly against the demands of the law, might, in surprising ways, reveal the will of God.

For Reb Mordechai, when it comes to sexual prohibitions, strong desire, desire that cannot be overcome with great effort, introduces us to another frequency of divine will. What ordinary Israelites were doing was indeed whoring. But what Zimri did with Cozbi was not. It was the act of uniting with a passionately desired but formally unacceptable soul mate that was beyond Zimri's ability to refuse and so beyond the law.

One is required to wage a great spiritual battle in order to arrive at such a conclusion. One must fight to resist temptation through ten levels of struggle before accepting a prohibited sexual urge as a divine will. Zimri did the hard work of *birurim* (clarification), but Pinchas could not fathom these workings of the soul. He was a typical "true believer," spiritually unsophisticated and dangerously sure of himself. Like other zealous defenders of public morality, Pinchas pours his wrath on a man whom he does not understand. Zimri's proof of innocence, the story of his tenfold resistance and final surrender to God, was never shared.

Although God may have willed this match made in heaven between star-crossed lovers from different sides of the tracks, there is no protection offered them in the story from brutish zealots like Pinchas, who rise up in righteous indignation ready to punish those who defy the rule. Even worse, God's promise to Pinchas of a covenant of peace is hard to square with Reb Mordechai's take on the story. God seems forced to live with simplistic religious leaders who are beyond nuance, who have idealized the ordinary and think of every difference as an essential danger. For Reb Mordechai, God comes out torn between the structures of nation-building defended by Pinchas and the lives of those individuals whose unconventional love is also God's will.

To be sure, Rabbi Mordechai of Izbica has not provided a path for halakhic change. The law itself is not challenged, just its relevance to a set of particulars. Still, the story of Zimri's hidden love for Cozbi, his repeated attempts to deny and resist it, and his failure itself ultimately becoming a discovery strikes a resounding cord for many gay and lesbian people. Many of us have spent years going through clarification after clarification only to discover that our desire was neither debased nor changeable.

Moreover, the question of desire in the context of idolatry is no accident. Whereas the Israelites burned with desire for Midianite women, for Zimri, sex with Cozbi was not a palliative, a diversion, or game of conquest. Zimri is not a man in heat but a man in love. For a 19th-century Hasidic rabbi to paint such a dramatic picture of the category-defying power of romantic love is truly amazing. Without tampering with the system, the rabbi from Ishbitz has given us a unique vision of queer love that lives at the margins of a much larger divine plan and that, being at the margins, can rightly claim to obey a different set of rules.

FORTY-TWO

Going Ahead
Parashat Matot (Numbers 30:2–32:42)

LISA EDWARDS

The peculiar relation between Camp taste and homosexuality has to be explained. While it's not true that Camp taste is homosexual taste, there is no doubt a peculiar affinity and overlap. Not all liberals are Jews, but Jews have shown a peculiar affinity for liberal and reformist causes. So, not all homosexuals have Camp taste. But homosexuals, by and large, constitute the vanguard—and the most articulate audience—of Camp. This analogy is not frivolously chosen. Jews and homosexuals are the outstanding creative minorities in contemporary urban culture. Creative, that is, in the truest sense; they are creators of sensibilities. The two pioneering forces of modern sensibility are Jewish moral seriousness and homosexual aestheticism and irony.

—Susan Sontag, "Notes on Camp"

In the early years of resettlement in prestate Palestine, *khalutzim,* "pioneers," founded the first kibbutz, Degania, in 1912 just east of the Jordan River.[1] They borrowed the word *khalutzim* from our *Parashat Matot* (Num. 32) and, more significant to them, from its reappearance in the book of Joshua. In Joshua, the *khalutzim*—men of fighting age belonging to the tribe of Reuben, the tribe of Gad, and half the tribe of Manasseh—make good on the promises they had made to Moses at the end of the book of Numbers: to be the vanguard troops, who go in front into the battles after the Israelites cross the Jordan. Once the conquering has happened, Joshua in turn makes good on the promises Moses made to these two and a half tribes: he lets them keep the rich allotments of land east of the Jordan, just outside the Promised Land, where they have already settled, raising their families and their cattle (see Num. 32 and Josh. 13).

This high-powered negotiation happens in our parasha. As the book of *Bemidbar* (Numbers) nears its end, we find the Israelites encamped in the steppes of Moab, at the Jordan near Jericho, assessing their damages, booty, and captives after fighting against the Midianites. The forty years in the wilderness is also drawing to a close, as is the life of the Israelite leader Moses, though readers know that more battles await once the Israelites enter the Promised Land. With this lull in the action, the Gadite and Reubenite leaders come to Moses and other community leaders and ask to stay where they are rather than go to the Land: "it would be a favor to us if this land were given to your servants as a holding; do not move us across the Jordan" (32:5). Moses immediately suspects them: "Are your brothers to go to war while you stay here?" (32:6). The condemnation, threats, warnings, promises, and negotiations go on in some detail for most of the chapter, but an agreement is eventually reached. Moses does not live to see it fulfilled, but readers do, if we read beyond Torah and cross into the Promised Land ourselves by reading the book of Joshua, the first book of the next section of the Hebrew Bible, the Prophets.

The Zionist pioneers/*khalutzim,* inspired by the Reubenites, Gadites, and half the tribe of Manasseh, take their story one significant step further. Though they too served as a vanguard, helping to protect settlements elsewhere; when they crossed the Jordan, they stayed in the Promised Land and helped to settle it instead of opting for the suburbs/diaspora as their ancestors had done.

Bible scholar Robert Alter, among others, opts to translate the Hebrew *khalutzim* as "vanguard," rather than the more familiar "shock-troops" or the more Israeli "pioneers." Vanguard summons up more questions for us, coming as it does from *avant-garde.*[2] Who are these people who lead the way, who push the boundaries—sometimes violently—making it safer for those who come after? How interesting that this vanguard only agreed to serve after Moses yells at them. Presumably they wanted to stay outside the Land, as many do, to remain in their "comfort zone."

All people need comfort, but there are times when we are—sometimes unwillingly—pressed into service. Just by being who we are, we may find that we are leading society in a new and necessary direction.

Take the reluctant fighters of the Stonewall Rebellion, for example, who, legend has it, fought back only when their comfort zone was infringed upon, only when their well-being, and that of their community, was endangered. Once engaged in battle, though, they became fierce fighters indeed and helped change a culture and a community in the process.

Scholars tell us that the war of conquest did not happen quite the way it is described in the book of Joshua (the book of Judges suggests a more gradual process of settlement), but the process of becoming Israel was, in any case, a long, hard struggle. Had the *khalutzim* of *Matot,* the men of the tribes who wanted to stay behind, argued with Moses to stay out of battle, who knows how differently the story might have unfolded? As played out in *Matot,* not just a majority but *"all* the vanguard to the battle" (Num. 32:29) must take part in the struggle (32:30).

In 1988, Rob Eichman and Jean O'Leary declared October 11 as annual National Coming Out Day, a year after the Second National March on Washington for Lesbian and Gay Rights, in which an estimated five hundred thousand people marched down the streets of Washington, D.C. Noting that marching on a Sunday down the streets of our nation's capital resulted in very little media attention and very small numbers of onlookers, the organizers of National Coming Out Day events aimed at raising awareness of the LGBT community among the general populace in an effort to give a familiar face to LGBT people.[3] The theory is simple: if all queer people declare themselves queer on one day, every homophobe in the world would discover they know someone queer. And as we encounter over and over again, often all it takes for someone to overcome homophobia is to discover that someone they know or love or like or respect is queer. It can be world-changing, and most especially if everyone—the whole vanguard—takes part.

Beyond Torah and Stonewall and marches and National Coming Out Day, other examples present themselves of the ways Jews and queers both often serve as vanguards—and perhaps queer Jews all the more so.

How appropriate that Susan Sontag in the passage quoted in the epigraph uses both terms: "vanguard" and "pioneering." Whereas we often see what Jewishness and queerness have in common—the "otherness," the boundary crossing, the tradition of "passing," to name a few—Sontag, while giving both credit as "creators of sensibilities," makes a clear distinction between the two sensibilities created. One is moral seriousness; the other, aestheticism and irony—perhaps they are even opposites: "Camp is a solvent of morality. It neutralizes moral indignation, sponsors playfulness," Sontag writes in the next note on Camp (#52).[4]

So what happens when the Jews and queers come together? Perhaps the contemporary equivalents of the vanguard that clears the way into the Promised Land are the many queer Jews learning and reviving Yiddish, for example, or queer Jewish theater that is both serious, moral, and playful such as the juggling queer Jewish performance artist Sarah Felder or the cross-dressing "storahteller" Amichai Lau-Lavie.[5] In these instances, the queer Promised Land is Jewishness itself, at least an engagement with Jewishness that moves beyond convention.

Maybe the other common translation of *khalutzim* works best here: "shock-troop." In military terms, the front soldiers absorb the shock of entering battle, and so protect those behind them. In our context, the vanguard who shocks "the enemy" by their entrance into "battle," provides a safer environment by paving the way for those more ordinary folks in the back. When internalized homophobia surfaces, say, against the "outrageous" floats at a Pride Parade, we would do well to remember that their pushing at the boundaries has made more room for those who are tame by comparison. Sometimes just living with honesty and integrity turns us into a vanguard. Sometimes, just by being who we are, we may find that we are leading society in a new and necessary direction.

As the tribes of Gad, Reuben, and half of Manasseh lead the way into the Promised Land, the book of Joshua presents a dramatic, and often forgotten, event: as soon as the feet of the priests bearing the Ark of the Covenant dipped into the water of the Jordan, the waters piled up on either side, and "the priests who bore the Ark of God's Covenant stood on dry land exactly in the middle of the Jordan, while all Israel crossed over on dry land, until the entire nation had finished crossing the Jordan" (Josh. 3:15, 17).

Wondrous events can happen more than once, and in more than one way. Whether the vanguard remains in the Promised Land like the *khalutzim* of Kibbutz Degania or returns to the other shore like the tribes of our parasha; whether they volunteer to lead the way or find themselves pushed to do so; whether they take their assignment with moral seriousness or with a sense of campy fun, it turns out that vanguards, *khalutzim*, pioneers, shock-troops can part seas, opening new possibilities to those who lead the way and to those who will follow.

NOTES

The epigraph to this chapter is drawn from Susan Sontag, "Notes on Camp" (1964), in *Against Interpretation: And Other Essays* (New York: Picador, 2001), 290.

1. Facts about Degania come from Rachel Havrelock, "My Home Is over Jordan: River as Border in Israeli and Palestinian National Mythology," *National Identities* 9:2 (2007): 105–126.

2. *The American Heritage Dictionary of the English Language: Fourth Edition*; Robert Alter, *The Five Books of Moses* (New York: Norton, 2004).

3. "National Coming Out Day," Wikipedia, http://en.wikipedia.org/wiki/National_Coming_Out_Day.

4. Sontag, "Notes on Camp," 290

5. Members of the Klezmatics or Irwin Keller of the Kinsey Sicks are two examples of many queer Yiddishists. See, among others, http://www.klezmatics.com, http://www.kinsey-sicks.com, http://www.sarafelder.com, http://www.storahtelling.org. See also David Shneer, "Queer Is the New Pink: How Queer Jews Moved to the Forefront of Jewish Culture," *Journal of Men and Masculinity Studies* 1:1 (2007): 55–64.

FORTY-THREE

Hearing Ancient, Courageous Voices for Justice and Change
Parashat Masei (Numbers 33:1–36:13)

AMBER POWERS

Parashat Masei, the final portion in the book of Numbers, begins with an extensive summary of the travels of the People Israel after their redemption from Egypt. As their forty years of wandering draws to a close, they stand at the Jordan River near Jericho, and Moses instructs them about the boundaries of the Promised Land and how the land will be divided among the tribes.

Parashat Masei includes an important postscript to a narrative told in the book's twenty-seventh chapter, the story of the daughters of Zelophekhad and their challenge to the Jewish inheritance laws, which follow male hereditary lines. Following their father's death, the five daughters, Mahlah, Noah, Hoglah, Milkah, and Tirzah, stand before the entire community and argue that they should inherit their father's portion of land since they have no brothers to perpetuate their father's name. Moses brings their request to God, and God declares that their request is just and orders that the daughters should inherit their father's share of the land. This victory establishes a precedent, and it becomes Biblical law that any woman in that situation has the right to inherit. In the midrash *Numbers Rabbah,* the daughters are praised for their intelligence and righteousness, and it is said that their role in promoting the addition of this law to the set of laws received at Mount Sinai is a source of merit for them and their descendants.[1]

This story represents an important affirmation of justice and equality. Although the daughters are part of a thoroughly patriarchal system, they have the courage to speak up and challenge their exclusion. Their victory does not overturn the gender inequality inherit in the system but does mark a very important, moral step toward widening the rights of women in specific circumstances—when a woman's father has died, and she has no living brother. By successfully arguing for their right to inherit in this situation, the daughters open the door for others to similarly fight for their inclusion and reject the notion that Biblical law is forever fixed and protected from any and all challenges.

Unfortunately, the postscript to this narrative told in *Parashat Masei* is a troubling one. The male leaders of Zelophekhad's daughters' family clan argue that if the daughters inherit their father's portion of land and then marry men from other tribes, their tribe's total portion will be diminished because their husbands would be entitled to take control of the land the daughters inherited. Moses declares that the men's concern is also just and modifies the new law with an additional stipulation. Zelophekhad's daughters will still inherit their father's land, but their choice of whom they may marry is restricted to only the men within their father's tribe, so that the total amount of land assigned to each tribe remains unchanged. The daughters are placed into what is clearly a compromised position. In order to receive what is rightfully theirs, they must restrict their choice of a mate or choose to remain unmarried. The unfair choice they faced between their freedom to partner as they wished and their need for economic security is one that countless queer persons of all faiths have faced throughout the generations. This choice has caused great suffering. The Torah states that the daughters complied with the additional restriction on which their inheritance depended, and they each married one of their cousins.

This chain of events raises important questions about how change occurs. First, an individual situation was brought forward to call attention to an inequality in the system. Through its merit, a new law was created that would create equality and protection for anyone in a parallel situation. Once the new general law became public, another group voiced concerns that this new right could lead to their own privilege, the right of each tribe to inherit a fixed portion of land, being diminished. In response, they acted to protect the privilege they held. Their fear of inequality and their resistance to any collective loss ultimately leads to others' freedom being restricted. The men benefited greatly from the patriarchal system and were unwilling to accept any modification that would reduce their privileged position. For those of us involved in any type of queer advocacy, this story is an ancient example of a challenging pattern we still face today.

The daughters' initial success in advocating for their right to inherit is often touted as a feminist victory. Vanessa Ochs describes the first story as "a happy story of women who succeeded when they join together to protest an unjust social order and bring about dramatic change without much ado."[2] Other scholars have noted that other ancient Near Eastern law codes included inheritance rights for women, and so the daughters' request may not have been especially radical.[3] Adding this law to the Torah might have been an attempt simply to restore a missing piece of legislation or to rectify an unjust omission, enabling the ancient Israelites to adjust to the more inclusive model used by their neighbors. Nevertheless, the daughters' choice to bring their cause before the community is a tremendous act of courage. In the midrash, it is taught that the daughters had to wage quite a fight, for each authority they approached to argue for their right to inherit deferred to the next. In the end, only God was willing actually to make a decision. The daughters persevered because they were confident in God's wisdom:

> When the daughters of Zelophekhad heard that the Land of Israel was about to be divided among the tribes—but only among the males, not the females—they consulted together as to how to make their claim. They decided that the compassion of God is not like human compassion. Human rulers favor males over females but the One who

spoke and the world came into being is different. Rather, God shows mercy to every living thing, as it is written in Torah "The Lord is good to all and God's mercy is upon all
God's works" (Psalm 145:9).[4]

It is often the case that we can do our best advocacy work when we speak from our
own experience and bring to light the exclusion we have faced, but doing so requires
overcoming our own sense of vulnerability. When my partner and I were looking for
a preschool for our son, it was important to us to look for a school that was welcoming to different types of families. We were pleased with the messages we heard from
the staff members at the school we chose. It came as quite a surprise when, a couple
of weeks into the school year, a note was sent home to all the families in the class addressed to "dear mom and dad." Though this issue was a minor one, I was hurt and
irritated—the teachers knew that our son has two moms, so why would they be so
careless with their words or, worse, dismissive of our equal roles as parents? I debated
whether I wanted to say something to the head teacher because I had just recently
met her and I did not want to risk establishing an adversarial relationship, which
might negatively affect our son's experience in her classroom. I had not yet decided
when, a few days later, I found another copy of the note in my son's backpack, with
"dear mom and dad" crossed out and replaced with "dear parents" and a note that
read, "oops—sorry about that!" I was happy that the teacher caught the error, and
I felt reassured that our family was seen and accepted. I was also ultimately disappointed in myself for failing to speak up when I first got the note. I realized that by
not wanting to rock the boat by drawing attention to our exclusion, I also was not
speaking up for the other families that were also excluded—including a single mom
and a child being raised by an aunt. When we choose not to advocate for ourselves
and to allow ourselves to continue to be excluded, we fail to bring justice for others
for whom the exclusion may be even more critical or who may be unable to speak on
their own behalf.

As human beings, Jews, and as members of queer communities, we each have an
obligation to follow in the footsteps of the daughters of Zelophekhad and be a *dover
emet*, a speaker of truth. In *Pirkei Avot* 5:7, it is written that one of the characteristics
of a *hacham*, a wise person, is the willingness to concede the truth, as God does in
declaring the daughters' claim just.[5] At times the truth we speak will grow out of our
own experience, and at other times we will be speaking up to end injustice against
others. Though not all exclusion or discrimination is intentional, we still must have
the courage to confront it when we encounter it because, more often than not, others
will be affected positively too. We also must speak out because full engagement in
community and in relationships requires openness, honesty, and striving for truth,
even when the system is tilted against us, even when we are afraid, and even when we
know we may not yet succeed in our efforts.

The fight for justice and equality is ongoing and not a linear path. There are often
real conflicting values that must be acknowledged and negotiated. I view Moses's ruling in favor of the heads of the clan requiring the daughters to marry within their
own tribe as his attempt to balance the right of women to inherit and the custom of

continuing hereditary lines through land ownership. Like Moses, there will be times when we are in a leadership role and it may feel as if no solution will meet the needs and demands of all those individuals and groups in our communities. Like the heads of the family clan in this Torah portion, there may be times when we personally stand in a place of privilege and we would risk losing something if we supported another's fight for change. Like the daughters of Zelophekhad, there are times when we will submit to a less than fully just solution as a compromise, a temporary measure, or because we have no choice. Nevertheless, we must remain clear about our visions of justice and equality and continue to work for their fullest expression in our communities and our practices.

There is a natural tension between accepting compromise and pushing for full equality. In our own society, some people believe that civil unions are a helpful and important step toward full marriage equality,[6] while others point out that most civil union legislation creates a system in which same-gender couples not only remain separate but also receive only partial rights. I imagine that the five daughters of Zelophekhad may also have disagreed about exactly how hard to push and when to accept that they had done as much as they would be able to do. These conversations within our communities, even when we passionately disagree, are important because they keep us talking about our visions for justice, what our particular role is in achieving our vision, and how to move forward strategically and with integrity. Our tradition and our values challenge us to be brave and continually join in the chain of courageous change-agents who spoke out against inequality and helped create a more just society for themselves, for others in their communities, and for future generations.

NOTES

1. See *Numbers Rabbah* 21:11 and BT *Baba Batra* 119b.

2. Vanessa L. Ochs, *Sarah Laughed: Modern Lessons from the Wisdom and Stories of Biblical Women* (New York: McGraw-Hill, 2004), 41.

3. Tal Ilan, "The Daughters of Zelophehad and Women's Inheritance: The Biblical Injunction and Its Outcomes," in *Exodus to Deuteronomy: A Feminist Companion to the Bible*, ed. Athalya Brenner (Sheffield, UK: Sheffield Academic Press, 2000), 179.

4. *Sifre Numbers* 133.

5. *Avot De Rabbi Natan*, 37:17.

6. For more information on the effort toward marriage equality in the United States, visit www.marriageequality.org.

PART V

DEVARIM

The Book of Deuteronomy

FORTY-FOUR

From Whom Do We Learn History?
Why Queer Community Needs Texts
More Than Other Communities
Parashat Devarim (Deuteronomy 1:1–3:22)

DAVID SHNEER

Eile ha-devarim asher diber moshe el kol yisrael be-ever hayarden.
[These are the words that Moses said to all of Israel on the other
side of the Jordan.]

In this portion the Israelites and the now very elderly Moses have reached the Jordan River, the physical and metaphorical boundary between before and after, between wandering in the desert and being a Jewish nation, between a generation marked by the scars of slavery and one that only knows slavery as a memory told through the stories of the community's elders—what some people in the context of the Holocaust would call the "second generation." The Jordan River, mentioned no fewer than six times in this portion, serves as the political and military boundary between Jewish sovereignty and power, on the one hand, and the wandering and powerlessness of the Israelites, on the other, and also as a metaphysical boundary between the Israelites' past and the Jews' future. In the books of Joshua and Nehemiah (both are beyond the scope of the Torah), the Jordan takes on added significance in an emerging Jewish collective identity, the boundary between home and diaspora, between here and there.[1]

Devarim ("words" or "matters"), the portion that opens Deuteronomy, the last book of the Torah, has Moses recounting a history of the Jews' experiences over the past forty years. Moses speaks to "all of Israel," which some scholars interpret to mean both those inside the community and those many "outsiders" attached to the community, such as non-Jewish spouses, slaves, and others. He tells the story of the Israelites' Exodus from Egypt, the gaining of the commandments, and then the many struggles of their sojourn in the desert. It is not always a glorious history—despite a few miracles and triumphs, the wandering in the desert was largely marked by struggle, failure, and disappointment. Still, this is the history of this people.

Moses does not simply recount a litany of facts, place names, and conquests. His history is peppered with admonitions, laments, and lessons for the future. In some ways this at times depressing narrative is Moses's *tsavuah*, or "ethical will," to his community. As the elder, he has the responsibility to tell the Israelites their own story and to *give meaning* to the past in order to shape how the Israelites will live in the future. The recitation of past disappointments and failures is meant to instruct the Israelites how to do things better as they prepare to enter the land.

The ability to recount a history illustrates that a community has reached maturity. Group stories and histories are, in fact, the very foundation of a community. They enable the birth of a collective memory, often retold by elders as oral history, and these collective memories include the painful recollections of struggle and loss. Delineating the hardships of a nascent community is one of the key ways of *defining* a community.

Moses's words are spoken to "all of Israel," suggesting two things. First, as much as it might be a series of acts, rituals, places, and people that define the community, it is also a series of words, stories, and memories that unite the Jewish people. The word *devarim* also means "things" in modern Hebrew, reminding us that words can become tangible. In some ways, words can mark and define our world more concretely than inanimate objects can. And second, if it is true that words and stories define community, "all of Israel" is anyone connected and committed to those words and stories. This is a more expansive notion of the community than one defined by lineage.

Moses spends quite a bit of time in his speech on the geographic details of where "all of Israel" finds itself at the moment of telling and also where they have been. The portion opens, "These are the words that Moses spoke to all of Israel, on the other side of the Jordan, concerning the Wilderness, concerning the Aravah, opposite the Sea of Reeds, between Paran and Tophel, and Laban, and Hazerot, and Di-zahab; eleven days from Horeb, by way of Mount Seir to Kadesh-barnea" (Deut. 1:1). It is a pretty long list of obscure places and landmarks covering the collective experiences of the community. The Israelites have a history, a history that includes struggle, failure, and disappointment, but nonetheless a forty-year history rooted in time and place.

Moses, the elder, is not just passing on Israelite history and showing, as the portion ends, that "it is the Lord your god who will battle for you" (Deut. 3:22). Moses is, like elders in other communities, *creating* that history. This opening portion of Deuteronomy shows the importance of both historical text (the first four books of the Torah) and oral history (the fifth book) to communal identity. Text alone is not enough. In other words, history only becomes such when someone takes the fragmented stories of the past and gives them shape and meaning. Moses is only retelling those events of the past that he remembers, that he thinks are important. Is he telling "objective" history, or is he recounting his own selective memory, framing these stories of the struggle in the desert into a cohesive, and therefore coherent, purposeful narrative?

This tension between history and memory is dynamic, and it is this tension that has defined Jewish consciousness since Biblical times.[2] Most Biblical scholars agree that history telling began, even before the Greek historians Herodotus and Thucydides, with the establishment of the Davidic monarchy, whose story is told in the next section of the Bible, known as the Prophets.[3] And these stories of kingly glory (and royal hubris) are referred to as "the book of the deeds of Solomon" or the "book of the deeds of the kings of Israel." The Hebrew word used for deeds is *davar* or *deva-rim*. Thus, it is *devarim*—deeds, actions, and words—that define historical narrative. With the textual echo of *devarim,* we must look back to Deuteronomy, Moses's original telling of all "deeds," which laid the foundation for future forms of communal power, authority, and historical memory.

In our own time period, this desire to have communal histories that lay out key dates, people, heroic struggles, and myths has shaped the way history has been taught in the United States. In the beginning, the young American nation needed a single, master history to unite people in opposition to those from whom they had been freed, the nasty British. For many years, histories of women, slaves, working classes, queer people, and others were not widely told as part of American national history, because the presence of multiple histories suggested the presence of many kinds of Americans.

But since the 1960s, new kinds of histories, histories of particular groups, have been added to the curricula at universities, and sometimes in high schools, junior highs, and even elementary schools. We now have African American history, women's history, queer history, and a myriad of other particular or group-oriented narratives. I teach a class called Queer in America, Now and Then, a history and sociology course that takes Moses's challenge seriously and blends history and memory to create a narrative of a particular community—that of lesbian, gay, bisexual, and transgender Americans—but we study this tension between history and memory self-consciously, asking where one ends and where the other begins.

Each of these histories needs both the texts and the memories of their respective communities to carve out particular communal identities. Some historians have criticized this trend in history, calling it the splintering of history, the destruction of a history common to all Americans. Some of my colleagues claim that "queer history" is too much about identity and not enough about history. "Do you have to be queer to take your class, David?" I have been asked on more than one occasion. Such questions force us to reflect on the purpose of telling history. Some historians might say the purpose is simply "to know the facts," but as we have seen, it can also be about creating community. And this tension between history and memory is precisely what historians today have to wrestle with when they teach and write history. For Jews, whose historical consciousness goes back further than almost anyone's, history never has been and never will be simply about knowing the facts.

So, then, we can go back to Moses and ask why Moses was telling "all of Israel" the story of the desert. He suggests that the primary purpose of history and memory is the making of community, and an expanded notion of community that includes those who might not identify as Jews but who are connected to Jews through common stories and experiences (like wandering through a desert together). Moses shows that one needs both history and memory, both text and voice, to create collective memories of events, places, and people.

Historical consciousness, which Jews understand as a religious and divine obligation, is something queer community needs more of. But queers are at a disadvantage. Most groups of people receive some kind of collective memory and historical consciousness from their families and schools from the earliest years of life. In fact, when public schools were born in the 19th century, one of their primary purposes was to instill a sense of citizenship and national pride in the future of the nation. That is why American public school children recite the Pledge of Allegiance and have to learn civics and the workings of government in school. For collective groups smaller than the nation, families are the primary bearers of national consciousness. That is how Jewish, African American, and other collective memories have been passed along for generations.

If schools and families are the primary institutional bearers of history and memory, how are queers supposed to generate a historical consciousness when family members at best usually do not identify as part of the community and at worst create a hostile environment for queer identity, and when schools render queerness invisible? The lack of family, elders, and affirming institutions is one of the key factors that make queers a minority unlike almost any other, lacking in the basic tools for creating a collective consciousness.

Deuteronomy, which comes from the Greek for "second telling" or "retelling," reminds us that communities need oral history and memory. For queers, that means making the effort to write books, tell stories, and codify histories that can be passed on. It means following in Moses's footsteps and producing ethical wills to future generations. Because queers do not have family members passing on queer community with traditional recipes from the home country, stories about grandma and grandpa, or old photographs of ancestors, queers must find the story of their "deeds" elsewhere. This lack of inherited queer consciousness makes books and community elders all the more important. They, rather than family, become the bearers of historical consciousness.

NOTES

1. On the Jordan River's place in Jewish, Israeli, and Palestinian national identities, see Rachel Havrelock, "My Home Is Over Jordan: River as Border in Israeli and Palestinian National Mythology," *National Identities* 9:2 (2007): 105–126, or her forthcoming book *River Jordan: The Mythic History of a Dividing Line*.

2. On the tension between history and memory in Jewish consciousness, see Yosef Yerushalmi, *Zakhor: Jewish History, Jewish Memory* (Seattle: University of Washington Press, 1982). On the notion of historical consciousness as a mediating force between history and memory, see Amos Funkenstein, *Perceptions of Jewish History* (Berkeley: University of California Press, 1993).

3. See among others James Williams, "History-Writing as Protest: Kingship and the Beginning of Historical Narrative," *Contagion: Journal of Violence, Mimesis, and Culture* 1 (1994): 91–110; John Van Seters, *In Search of History* (New Haven, CT: Yale University Press, 1983); Robert Alter, *The Art of Biblical Narrative* (New York: Basic Books, 1981).

FORTY-FIVE

Rethinking the Wicked "Son"

Parashat Vaetchanan (Deuteronomy 3:23–7:11)

JULIE PELC

When I was sixteen years old, I made an appointment with my rabbi to ask about the Jewish tradition's seemingly cruel response to homosexuality, an identity, I argued, not within the control of the individual to alter. My rabbi, not knowing my reasons for asking this question or pausing to reconsider his own biases, replied that resisting homosexual urges "is like choosing not to eat a cheeseburger. I may want to eat a cheeseburger, but I know that it is forbidden." I was stunned. Even as a young teenager, I knew him to be wrong. I later told a friend (who unbeknownst to me was deeply conflicted about his own homosexuality in relationship to his traditional conservative Jewish upbringing), "It's not like choosing not to eat a cheeseburger; it's like choosing not to eat at all!" More than any other moment in my formative Jewish education, this interaction taught me that knowledge and truth must be constantly evaluated and reevaluated in light of new information and deeper understanding in successive ages and generations.

I did not know it then but later discovered (to my delight) that there are texts and ideas embedded in the tradition itself that acknowledge my realization about the relativity of knowledge and truth. I found that even in texts read year after year, new insights and interpretations lay waiting for the fresh perspective of a new generation. In the book of Deuteronomy, in *Parashat Vaetchanan*, we find a text that, when read anew, can encourage us to open doors of inclusion and acceptance previously assumed to be permanently closed and locked.

The parasha consists of the final pleas from Moses to the children of Israel preceding Moses's impending death and the people's departure into the Promised Land without his leadership as a guide. As might be expected, the parasha is replete with reminders about the people's special relationship with God, their history together, and the laws the people must obey so as not to incur God's wrath against them. The parasha includes famous passages such as the opening section of the traditional *Shema* prayer (in its original context) and also a repetition of the Ten Commandments.

But the parasha also includes a selection that may seem at first glance to be completely out of place: a story later reinterpreted by the rabbis of the Babylonian Talmud to be the words of the "Wicked Son" in the litany of the Passover seder.[1] Interestingly, though, in this context, there is no such judgment made on the child, his question, or his identity as a Jew. Additionally, the child is not gendered male; in fact, the text reads "children," which essentially allows for a much more generalized interpretation including many different kinds of children and many different kinds of challenges and questions. The verse reads,

> When, in time to come, your children ask you, "What mean the decrees, laws, and rules that the Lord our God has enjoined upon you?" you shall say to your children, "We were slaves to Pharaoh in Egypt and the Lord freed us from Egypt with a mighty hand. . . . Then the Lord commanded us to observe all these laws, to revere the Lord our God, for our lasting good and for our survival, as is now the case. It will be therefore to our merit before the Lord our God to observe faithfully this whole Instruction, as He has commanded us." (Deut. 6:20–25)

The text in Deuteronomy does not react with anything resembling the anger implied in the Passover Haggadah to the question(s) raised by the younger generation; it acknowledges that these children did not experience the Exodus firsthand and so must ask their predecessors about both their experience of slavery and their subsequent liberation.

The Passover Haggadah, in quick judgment of the boy and his question (plus the seamless switch from "children" to "son," assigning both gender and singular, individual responsibility to the questioner), deems the appropriate response to be, "because of what God did to me, in taking me out of Egypt," explicitly reminding seder participants that the wicked son "distances himself from the service [by saying "to you" and not "to me"],"[2] and so generations of Jews performing the rite of the Passover seder are explicitly instructed to exclude him in the reply, admonishing him by telling him if he had been present during that time, he would not have been freed.[3]

Looking at the original text and again at the liturgy of the Passover seder, it is not difficult to see how the biases of the rabbis completely altered a simple question into a boundary of acceptability and inclusion in the Jewish people and its story. The rabbis, in interpreting the text of Deuteronomy, essentially determine (seemingly arbitrarily) lines of communal acceptability that thereby limit and judge the very questions they seem simultaneously to want to encourage in the next generation of Jewish children.

The story of the "Four Sons" comes just after the "Four Questions" in the seder. In fact, the idea of the "Four Questions" strongly encourages (actually, *mandates*) the asking of essential questions, imploring the youngest children to participate in the seder even amid their own struggles, their lack of Judaic knowledge, and their lack of familiarity with the rituals.

This rabbinic move from "children" to "son," from a presumed harmless question asked by a younger generation to its elders to the labeling of both the question and the child as "wicked" is hardly innocent. In addition, the biases and rejection of the "wicked son" reflect the myriad ways in which the normative Jewish community has traditionally (and unfortunately) dealt with difference over generations after the codification of Deuteronomy. In fact, the book *Respecting the Wicked Child: A Philosophy of Secular Jewish Identity and Education* uses the "wicked son" as a metaphor for secular Jewish identity.[4] Haggadot throughout different countries, cultures, and eras depict the "wicked son" as whatever culturally specific "enemy" or "opposition" functions in that place and time. The "wicked son" has come to represent any force that the normative power system wishes to oppose, systematically and publicly. Some Haggadot in Israeli *Haredi* (Ultra-Orthodox) communities depict the "wicked son" as a soldier in the Israeli army;[5] many American-edited Haggadot depict the wicked son as an assimilated youngster dressed in that generation's fashionable clothing.

Passover is heralded as contemporary Judaism's most celebrated holiday: more Jews hold a Passover seder than participate in any other Jewish rite or ritual. How interesting that so many different Jews in such diverse communities practicing divergent Jewish lives all participate in some version of exclusion by reading (or believing) that tradition labels a child (or children) as "wicked" for asking essential questions of relevance and meaning.

LGBT communities may lead the Jewish world in a reexamination of this question and its questioner(s) in their original context in Deuteronomy. Looking again at Deuteronomy, the question is simple: it comes from a new generation that does not know the slavery of the past (if only we could imagine a comparable future in which future generations of queer kids cannot imagine the horrible persecution known so intimately by their predecessors); they ask the generation that came out of Egypt to describe it to them, asking (appropriately), "What does all of this mean to you?" The answer that comes should reflect the integrity and sensitivity of the question, indicating that it is precisely "because of what God did for me that I must obey the guidelines established for my spiritual, social, and physical well-being."

The very presence of this passage in *Parashat Vaetchanan* should indicate its importance in our spiritual, intellectual, and religious heritage. It is nestled in the parasha containing Moses's final acceptance that he will not accompany the people into the Promised Land; he wishes to impart a few lasting words to remain in their hearts and minds as they travel forward into the Jewish future. It is accompanied by two of our tradition's most sacred and oft-recited texts: the Shema and the Ten Commandments. We recite, "Hear, O, Israel, God, our God, is One," and we are reminded of the ten most essential laws by which we must live our lives just as we learn of the primary importance of coming to understand our collective past, our role within the context of our ancestors' history, and the deeply held value of asking questions when we are confused or wish to understand another's experience more fully.

In the context of a volume titled *Torah Queeries*, it seems appropriate to acknowledge specifically what a renewed look at these verses in Deuteronomy might mean for the LGBT communities:

Four Answers to Questions We Should Be Asking:
- When a queer child asks a parent, "What does all of this mean to you?" that parent should see inside the question a genuine desire to understand the experience of another (namely, what does my sexual or gender identity mean to

you? What implications might my identity have for you in your life?) and try to answer the questions as honestly and nonjudgmentally as possible.

- When LGBT Jews want to join Jewish communities and find that the membership forms ask questions that do not apply to their lives or their families, the Jewish community has a responsibility to learn from the question and the questioner, welcoming both them and their concerns into the fabric of the community and shifting communal norms when possible and appropriate.

- When Jewish professionals (teachers, rabbis, cantors, and others) encounter Jews who do not seem to fit or who ask questions that seem to challenge the authority of the system, it is important to pause before responding in anger and try to evaluate the context of the question and the real emotions underlying the inquiry. And, further, when we write Haggadot or lead Passover seders, we can eliminate labels and simply acknowledge the importance of and divinity within each of the questions and the questioners themselves.

- As people who have struggled to leave slavery behind, it is our sacred obligation to tell our stories to the next generation. We must be diligent in recording our experiences of liberation and be open to sharing these tales with those who may (God willing) come into a world in which freedom is normative.

Parashat Vaetchanan teaches us to look anew at our tradition and, most especially, at texts we assume to have been appropriated and interpreted by benevolent sages without biases we do not share. Therein lies the key to unlocking the theology of oppression and exclusion: our insistence in looking again with our own eyes at rites and liturgies we have inherited in order that we may see things in them that were previously unseen by the preceding generations.

In this case, more specifically, what the rabbinic tradition has deemed the legacy of the "wicked son" is actually Moses's instruction to the people about how to educate future generations about experiences and places that helped to shape the communal narrative contributing to their cultural and religious identity. The "wicked son" is, actually, not a "son" at all but a group/collective/generation simply called "children" in Deuteronomy.

At my family's Passover seders, we always rotated leadership of the seder around the table, enabling each participant to read aloud in turn. The kids all wanted to read the "Wise Son," as we assumed that doing so meant that we, ourselves, embodied values and traits valued by our tradition. I now see that, perhaps, we should have each been vying to read the part of the "Wicked Son," as "his" question is the only one quoted directly from the Torah and is placed poignantly in the same parasha as the Shema, indicating that it has a crucial role to play in the story of our tradition.

May we have the wisdom and courage to ask questions of ourselves, our predecessors, and the texts we hold dear, and may we listen carefully as we try to answer the questions asked by others.

NOTES

1. In the traditional Passover seder, there is a recitation of the story of the Exodus from Egypt, including a section entitled "The Four Sons" (one is "wicked," one is "wise," one is "simple," and one "does not yet know how to ask"), each of whom needs to hear the story of the Exodus told differently, according to his own personal needs and biases.

2. In the section of the seder known as "The Four Sons," tradition teaches us that the "wicked son's question" ("What is this service to you?") differentiates him from his ancestors and, therefore, isolates himself from the Jewish people. He is rebuked by the explanation that "it is because God acted for my sake when I left Egypt." (The Haggadah explicitly states that the seder is not for him because he, had he been present at that time in Egypt, would not have deserved to be freed from slavery.)

3. Traditional Haggadah: *Haggadah Shel Pesach.*

4. Mitchell Silver, *Respecting the Wicked Child: A Philosophy of Secular Jewish Identity and Education* (Amherst: University of Massachusetts Press, 1998).

5. Although Israel has mandatory conscription, most *Haredim* in Israel do not serve in the army, in order to prevent the secularizing influence of performing military service with non-religious Jews and because of fundamental disagreements with the nature and purpose of the Israeli government.

FORTY-SIX

Bind These Words
Parashat Ekev (Deuteronomy 7:12–11:25)

ARI LEV FORNARI

Therefore impress these My words upon your very heart: bind them as a sign on your hand and let them serve as a symbol on your forehead.

—Deuteronomy 11:18

Chest Binder: an undergarment worn by female-to-male (FTM),[1] transgender,[2] genderqueer,[3] and gender-variant[4] people, and by anyone else who chooses to flatten the appearance of their chest.

Tallit Katan: An undergarment traditionally worn daily by observant Jewish men that has knotted fringes tied to its four corners as a reminder of the 613 mitzvot.

There are four knotted strings that hang from the corners of my chest binder. "Speak unto the children of Israel, and bid them that they make them throughout their generations fringes in the corners of their garments" (Num. 15:38). Standing in front of the full-length mirror in my room, I unfold the *tallit-katan*-as-chest-binder and inspect the *tzitzit* to make sure they are properly knotted.

"*B'shem mitzvat tzitzit u'mitzvat hityatzrut*. For the sake of the *mitzvah* of ritual fringes and the *mitzvah* of self-formation."[5]

I say this *bracha* quietly to myself, as I bind these words, as I tighten the Velcro fabric that presses my chest flat. I pull the fabric tight, knowing it will leave marks on my flesh. Micah Bazant explains in his Trans Jew Zine *TimTum*, "Alterations of the flesh engage the spirit. Fasting, cleansing/immersion (as in the *mikvah*), and binding (as with *tefillin*) are familiar Jewish physical vehicles for intense psychological shifts into a mental state that could be designated sacred."[6] The thick, sweaty fabric is uncomfortable, making it difficult to breathe and making my sternum ache. I struggle to find God beneath layers of dark clothing and the self-conscious slouch of my shoulders. I struggle to find God in choices that cause physical pain to my body. How can I make my gender sacred? How can I make my gender a sign of my covenant with God?

240

Parashat Ekev foregrounds the concept of *brit*, a covenant between God and Israel. This covenantal relationship is binding together a community through mitzvot. The *brit* is made tangible through the actions of the *V'ahavta*, the paragraph of the *Shema*[7] that commands Jews to lay tefillin as an *ot*, a sign, of the covenant between God and Israel (Deut. 11:18). However, rereading the concept of *brit* and the words of the *V'ahavta* through trans experience obligates us to transform the mitzvot.

> INSTRUCTIONS: *There are sixteen strands in a pack—four long ones and twelve short ones. Separate these into four groups with one long one and three short ones in each. The longer one is called the* SHAMMASH *and is the one used for the winding.*

It is not easy to learn Jewish rituals traditionally reserved for nontrans men. Patriarchy isolates people who do not benefit from Jewish gender privilege—namely, women, trans people, and gender-variant folks who do not have access to teachers who can transmit the how-tos of halakhic observance. In addition, most histories of how gender-variant people have maneuvered and moved through the world have been erased. Since we do not have records of how our gender-variant ancestors reclaimed Jewish ritual, we are forced to invent it for ourselves all over again. In the Jewish world *tallit* and *tefillin* are still privileged as markers of masculinity and Jewish authenticity. In light of this fact, it is necessary to appropriate symbols of Jewish masculinity so that women and gender-variant people can feel whole and seen in Jewish tradition. In *Life on the Fringes*, Haviva Ner-David, one of the first Orthodox women ordained as a rabbi,[8] asks, "What does it mean to be a Jew and at the same time wonder if I am a full member of the covenant?"[9] Her response is, "I strive to find beauty in the *mitzvot*, even when it means assigning new meanings to them."[10] She speaks directly to this history of feminist appropriation as a way to navigate Jewish patriarchy in asking, "Why choose to make this mitzvah my own? Why not create a new ritual, a female reinterpretation of this commandment?"[11] Ultimately, Rabbi Ner-David and I choose to make the existing mitzvot our own; it is powerful to weave tradition in with our many identities—literally to bind them together and affirm, "this is mine too." Rabbi Ner-David recounts, "I commissioned a seamstress friend of mine . . . to design and sew special *tzitzit* just for [my daughter] and me."[12] The actual intention of creating "special *tzitzit*" affirms our creative expression, existence, and legitimacy. Thinking of the similarities between Rabbi Ner-David's reappropriation and my own drives one to ask, What ritual objects can be appropriated? What is the significance of women and gender-variant people wearing a *kippa* and wrapping tefillin? Does transfeminist[13] Judaism require transformation of the rituals themselves? If it does mean participating in traditionally male rituals, how do we engage with traditional forms without idealizing the Jewish man? How can transmen take on obligations, rituals, and roles that have been traditionally associated with male privilege, in a way that increases gender participation and expression for everyone?

> *Even out the four strands at one end and push the group through one*
> *of the corner holes in the* TALLIT KATAN. *Even up seven of the eight*
> *strands (the four being doubled) and leave the extra length of the*
> SHAMMASH *hanging to one side.*

I try to enter Jewish traditions from a place of textual knowledge, learning what they are about and then figuring out how I can connect with their intention in my own life. In *Man's Quest for God*, Abraham Joshua Heschel writes, "Our problem is how to live what we pray, how to make our lives a daily commentary on our prayer book."[14] He asks us to reconsider what it means to be observant. What does an observant Jew look like, act like, pray like? Although the words of the Shema and the *V'ahavta*, which we receive in this Torah portion, are commonly used to describe the practice of laying tefillin, for me they resonate with the practice of wearing a chest binder. For me a chest binder signifies part of my relationship to my body and my gender, in much the same way as a *tallit katan* is a daily reminder of my relationship to God. By integrating the two practices, I have created a new ritual object that deepens my understanding of my gender, my Judaism, myself, and my relationship to the divine. The *tallit katan* chest binder is a way for me to mark my body and sanctify my gender. "I keep trying to integrate my life. I keep trying to make all the pieces into one piece."[15]

Ukshartam l'ot al yadecha,[16] I wrap the leather tightly around my arm seven times, using my palm as a spool for the remaining leather. *V'hyu l'totafot bein aynecha*,[17] I place the tefillin on my forehead. I unwrap the remaining leather on my left hand and carefully rewrap it to form a *shin*. *L'shem yhud*,[18] I mark my body, literally leaving marks on my body where the tefillin and my chest binder lay, seeking integration of my own self-understanding. With the tefillin tight around my left arm, I place my right hand over my eyes and prepare to recite the Shema prayer: *Shema Yisrael Adonai Eloheinu Adonai Echad*. "Hear O Israel, the divine abounds everywhere, and dwells in everything. The many are one."[19] I hold these words close in my prayers as I recite the second paragraph of the Shema. I kiss the *tzitzit* tied to the edges of my chest binder. I am learning to listen to my own divinely inspired sense of my gender. I am learning to love myself, and simultaneously unlearning my internalized transphobia.[20]

> *With the four strands in one hand and the other four in the other hand,*
> *make a double knot near the edge of the material. Take the* SHAMMASH
> *and wind it around the other seven strands in a spiral—seven turns. Be*
> *sure you end the winding where you began—otherwise you may end up*
> *with seven and a half or six and a half winds. Make another double knot*
> *at this point (four over four).*

In light of liberal Judaism's relatively open relationship to halakha, I have been trying to decipher what Jewish "thickness"[21] looks like. What binds us as a community? What is our *brit*? There are many meanings for the word *Ekev*; one translation is "on the heels of"—referring to Ya'akov emerging "on the heels" of Esau. Thus, transfeminism is emerging on the heels of Jewish feminist thinkers who have carved space for this work. Judith Plaskow boldly states in her groundbreaking book *Standing Again at Sinai*, "Halakha . . . supports a patriarchal order. Those whom the law benefits may see it as God-given, but the outsider, the Other, knows it differently."[22] As trans and gender-variant people, we are both outsiders and insiders, and we have the capacity to do things differently—to continually transform rituals, squirming and wiggling and creating more space, not only for ourselves but for people of every gender. The *tallit katan* chest binder is one attempt to do it differently. I think part of doing it differently is reclaiming traditional rituals and making them relevant to our own lives. In this way we can sustain our connection to Jewish tradition, as we unravel and embrace a deeper sense of ourselves.

Accessorize!

Transfeminist Kate Bornstein writes, "Anyone who knows fashion will tell you that the operative word is *accessorize!* That's how I dress in the morning. That's how I shift from one phase of my life to the next—first I try on the accessories."[23] *Kippot, payot, tallitot, tefillin*—there are many fun accessories for Jewish men. And I have been playing with all of them![24] These accessories help me to feel whole and seen. And sometimes they help me to pass.[25] In *Nobody Passes*, Mattilda, a.k.a. Matt Sycamore Bernstein, writes, "I am hoping to reveal the ways that we're all caught in a passing net, even in our attempts to challenge, subvert, and dismantle this tyranny."[26] Although it is affirming to reclaim how people name me and perceive my gender, my desire to pass as a boy, as male, is inevitably tangled with a tradition that privileges men in the eyes of the law, a tradition that is deeply gendered in language, clothing, and ritual obligation.

Perhaps the first step is to untangle Judaism, patriarchy, and masculinity. Wearing a *tallit* or wrapping tefillin is not inherently sexist. The rituals themselves are not problematic, but rather the culture and customs that surround and sustain them are. Just as femme-identified women have reclaimed and "queered" many traditional markers of femininity (such as lipstick and high heels), trans people have the potential to liberate rituals and traditions from their oppressive boxes and binaries. Binding my chest is as much about being visibly trans in queer community as it is about being passed[27] as a boy in an Orthodox Judaica shop. Like all performance, it caters to its audience.

Wearing a *tallit katan* chest binder is simultaneously observing and reclaiming Jewish tradition. It is reclaiming what observance looks like on the heels of feminist Jewish thinkers who have challenged me to do it differently and inspired me to accessorize along the way. Observance is a commitment to engage with Jewish texts and traditions and actively seek transformation of the text and oneself through that engagement. I want to fulfill the commandments, both in light of and in spite of my attempt simultaneously to subvert gender norms and to transgress gender boundaries. I bind the words of Torah close to my heart, bringing the intention of the Shema into my daily life, making my gender an *ot*, a sign of my covenant with God, "when I stay at home and when I am away, when I lie down and when I get up" (Deut. 11:19).

Spiral the SHAMMASH *eight times around. Double knot.*
Spiral the SHAMMASH *eleven times around. Double knot.*
Spiral the SHAMMASH *thirteen times around.*

The *tallit katan* chest binder empowers me to be active in the formation of my gender, my Judaism, and my connection to the divine. It helps me to transform my own internalized transphobia into a powerful affirmation of the presence of God and holiness in my body and in my gender. "*Vayivra Elohim et-ha'adam b'tzalmo.* God created human beings in God's image" (Gen. 1:27). For me, in this moment, binding my chest brings me closer to knowing God's image, *b'tzalmo.*[28]

"And it shall be unto you for a fringe, that you may look upon it, and remember all the commandments of the Lord, and do them and be holy unto your God" (Num. 15:39).

Final double knot.

NOTES

Thank you Max K. Strassfeld and Rachel Brodie for cofacilitating the TransFeminist Ritual Roundtable, a program of Jewish Milestones. Infinite gratitude to Andrea Guerra, Andrew Ramer, Joseph Berman, Margot Meitner, Rahel Smith, and Stefan Lynch for attending the roundtable and volunteering their time, energy, and insight. Many of the thoughts espoused in this chapter were initiated and developed in conversation with these fabulous people.

1. FTM stands for female-to-male and usually refers to a person who is assigned female early in life but later identifies as male and/or transgender. Similarly, the term MTF stands for male-to-female. Some FTM and MTF trans people choose hormonal and/or surgical treatment in order to live more comfortably in society, although these options are not accessible or desirable to all trans people.

2. The word *transgender* is an umbrella term often used to describe individuals whose gender expression and/or gender identity differs from conventional expectations based on the physical sex they were assigned early in life.

3. Rocko Bulldagger writes in *Nobody Passes*, "My own personal definition of gender-queer . . . Someone who identifies with the effort to subvert oppressive power dynamics by undermining traditional gender expectations." Rocko Bulldagger, "The End of Genderqueer," in *Nobody Passes: Rejecting the Rules of Gender and Conformity*, ed. Mattilda, a.k.a. Matt Bernstein Sycamore (Emeryville, CA: Seal, 2006), 139.

4. *Gender-variant* refers to a person who, either by nature or by choice, does not conform to gender-based expectations of society.

5. Blessing written by Rabbi Elliot Rose Kukla employing a play on the word *Yatzar.*

6. Micah Bazant, *TimTum: A Trans Jew Zine.*

7. The Shema, a central prayer in Judaism, is recited daily and includes quotations from Deuteronomy 6:4–9 and 11:13–21 and Numbers 15:37–41.

8. Unlike the Reform, Conservative, and Reconstructionist communities, the Orthodox world does not maintain a single governing body to ordain new rabbis. Mimi Feigelson studied under Shlomo Carlebach and received private ordination from a *beit din* (rabbinic court)

of three Orthodox rabbis shortly after his death. Eveline Goodman-Thau was ordained in 2000 by Rabbi Jonathan Chapman. Haviva Ner-David does not publicly define herself as an *Orthodox* rabbi.

9. Haviva Ner-David, *Life on the Fringes: A Feminist Journey towards Traditional Rabbinic Ordination* (Needham, MA: JFL Books, 2000), 21.

10. Ibid., 64.

11. Ibid., 34.

12. Ibid., 48–49.

13. Transfeminism asserts a vision of gender justice that accounts for the ways the gender binary system and patriarchy continue to oppress us all. Transfeminism understands third wave feminists' goals to be in alignment with transgender liberation. It confronts the ways that male supremacy subjugates women, as well as trans and intersex people, and limits the full expression of everyone's humanity. Transfeminism builds an analysis from the understanding that systems of oppression are intricately linked and must be dismantled simultaneously.

14. Abraham Joshua Heschel, *Man's Quest for God* (Santa Fe, NM: Aurora, 1998), 94.

15. Kate Bornstein, *Gender Outlaw* (New York: Routledge, 1994), 1.

16. "Bind them as a sign upon your arm" (Deut. 6:7).

17. "And let them be tefillin before your eyes" (Deut. 6:7).

18. "For the sake of the unification," the introductory words one recites as a declaration of intent before putting on tefillin.

19. Marcia Falk, *The Book of Blessings* (Boston: Houghton Mifflin, 1999), 24.

20. *Transphobia* is the irrational fear or hatred of gender-variant people.

21. The term *thickness* for me connotes a certain depth in one's relationship to a belief system, in this case Jewish tradition. My search for thickness is a desire to understand what my covenantal relationship is as a liberal religious Jew.

22. Judith Plaskow, *Standing Again at Sinai: Judaism from a Feminist Perspective* (New York: HarperOne, 1991), 71.

23. Bornstein, *Gender Outlaw,* 4.

24. Thank you to my femme friends, who have been such important role models.

25. Passing in its broadest possible sense—passing as the "right" gender, race, class, sexuality, age, ability, body type, health status, ethnicity—describes a pass/fail situation, in which there are (largely unspoken) standards for societal acceptance and authenticity that erase the possibility of ambiguity and complexity.

26. Mattilda, "Reaching Too Far: An Introduction," in Mattilda, *Nobody Passes* (see note 3), 13.

27. "In this context, 'passing' refers to trans people being perceived as non-trans members of their correct gender category. While this is a goal for most trans people, I think it's important to stay aware of the systemic power imbalance that is implicit in this term. I prefer the term 'being passed,' because it emphasizes the fact that trans people do not have total control over how we are perceived, and that the power in the equation of passing lies completely with the non-trans person who 'passes' us. It is something done to us, not something we are able to control." Micah Bazant, *TimTum: A Trans Jew Zine.*

28. The broader category of *trans* encompasses a universe of different gender expressions, just as the categories of *women* and *men* contain individuals of a million subtle and vast gender differences. For each trans person, in each moment in time, the ways we express our gender carry personal meaning and social connotations.

FORTY-SEVEN

Neither Adding nor Taking Away

Parashat Re'eh (Deuteronomy 11:26–16:17)

GREGG DRINKWATER AND DAVID SHNEER

In the opening lines of *Parashat Re'eh,* Moses shares both a blessing and a curse with the Israelites. "The blessing: if you obey the commandments of the Lord, your God, which I command you today. And the curse: if you do not obey the commandments of the Lord, your God, and you stray from the path that I command you today" (Deut. 11:26–28).

But what does "obey the commandments" actually mean? Who is blessed and who is cursed? For Orthodox Jews, to "obey the commandments" means keeping all of the 613 mitzvot found in the Torah,[1] following halacha essentially to the letter, and living a life embedded in Jewish tradition. For most Jews who approach Judaism liberally (Reform and Reconstructionist, but also Conservative Jews, to a degree), to "obey the commandments" is interpreted a bit differently. Many progressive Jews are deeply committed to Jewish tradition and the Torah but approach the mitzvot and Jewish law with varying degrees of skepticism and modification. In some cases, progressive Jews are comfortable with outright rejection of those precepts that seem to violate competing ethical standards or that do not easily conform to the realities of contemporary society.

In *Parashat Re'eh*, there are plenty of such commandments that strike the modern reader—liberally and strictly interpreting alike—as problematic: "You must destroy all the sites at which the nations you are to dispossess worshiped their gods, whether on lofty mountains and on hills or under any luxuriant tree. Tear down their altars, smash their pillars, put their sacred posts to the fire, and cut down the images of their gods, obliterating their name from that site" (12:2–3). We cannot imagine finding too many Jews who would support obliterating cultural and religious artifacts today, although this verse seems tailor-made for Afghanistan's former Taliban government, which in a fit of religious zealotry dynamited the historic towering stone Buddhas of Bamyan in 2001 (the famed fifteen-hundred–year-old monuments were situated in "lofty mountains," no less).

Given the complications of following the law to the letter, can we dismiss this concern over blessings and curses and safely say that all Jews are cursed for not completely following the laws laid out in *Parashat Re'eh* and elsewhere in the Torah? Or perhaps all are blessed because we each interpret these Biblical commandments differently and feel correct in our own perspective. The followers of the various Jewish movements, then, can all feel eligible for the blessing and reserve Moses's curse for someone else, somewhere else. We are all Lake Wobegon Jews—each of us above average.

But before readers leave themselves feeling too secure in using our powers of interpretation, the text adds a rejoinder: "Be careful to observe only that which I enjoin upon you: neither add to it nor take away from it. If there appears among you a prophet or a dream-diviner and he gives you a sign or a portent, saying, 'Let us follow and worship another god'—whom you have not experienced—even if the sign or portent that he named to you comes true, do not heed the words of that prophet or that dream-diviner" (13:1–4).

Now we have a problem. What does it mean when Moses tells readers that they should "neither add to it nor take away from it"? How are readers to know if someone is a prophet and dream-diviner, tempting Jews away from God, or a textual interpreter helping Jews understand a truer or deeper meaning of Torah? Does the phrase "neither add nor take away" simply mean that we cannot edit the Torah by adding or subtracting verses, something that would have been going on in the years before the Torah was canonized sometime in the 6th or 5th century BCE? What about the Oral Law? Is that included when Moses references "that which I enjoin upon you"? For our purposes, does the prohibition of adding or taking away restrain our ability to read queerly, to reinterpret and possibly *add* some kinds of meanings and take others away?

Rabbi Moshe Sofer (1762–1839) of Bratislava, who was known as the Chatam Sofer, was a fierce opponent of change. He famously responded to the *Haskalah* (Jewish Enlightenment) and early German Reform Judaism by ruling "*hadash asur min ha-Torah*" (anything new is forbidden by the Torah). This concept, which invites a deeply conservative reading of *Parashat Re'eh*, had a profound impact on what we today call Ultra-Orthodox, or Charedi, Judaism, and it helps explain the traditional dress and habits of most Charedi Jews. According to the Chatam Sofer, all change is forbidden. Thus, he might say that anyone creating LGBT-inclusive space, rereading text, and advocating for the revision of halacha is a prophet or dream-diviner trying to encourage Jews to follow a false God.

But what if we use the Chatam Sofer's seemingly reactionary response to innovation in the name of innovation? Can the Chatam Sofer's edict support liberatory strategies of rereading texts that have been classically used to oppress LGBT people? Traditionally, rabbis have interpreted Leviticus 18:22 and 20:13 *expansively* to ban any kind of sex, sexual relations, or expressions of intimate desire between people of the same sex. Most Jews think, incorrectly as David Brodsky shows in this volume, that Leviticus bans homosexuality broadly and not just a particular type of male-male sex. Lesbians are not referenced directly in the Torah at all, although there are two and a half Talmudic discussions that are commonly understood to prohibit sex between two women. Yet most contemporary Orthodox rabbis come down harshly on women who love women. But *Parashat Re'eh*'s command neither to add nor take away suggests that halacha, and rabbinic textual reasoning more generally, may need to rein itself in and keep to the text. "*Hadash asur min-Torah*," said the Chatam Sofer, and "neither add to it nor take away from it," says *Parashat Re'eh,* yet no where in the Torah does it say anything about lesbians or homosexuality in general. This phrase in *Re'eh* then can be used to support projects of textual reinterpretation, such as those of Steven Greenberg, David Brodsky, and others,[2] which attempt to bring people *back* to the text, to remove that which the rabbinic tradition, in an attempt to create an elaborate "fence around the Torah," has added.

As for transgender Jews, the commandment in Deuteronomy that prohibits cross-dressing and the prohibitions on modifying the body are, once again, commonly understood to forbid living a transgendered life. However, *Parashat Re'eh* encourages modern interpreters to get back to the original text and take back overly loose bans on transgender lives that are not actually explicitly grounded in the text. Ironically, then, if we follow the Chatam Sofer, we need to move backward from rabbinic prohibitions to the essence of Biblical mitzvot, undoing in some cases that which halacha has erroneously added. In this way, the Chatam Sofer's call against innovation can actually liberate queers from homophobic legislation that has accreted over time in the Jewish tradition.

In contrast to the goal of undoing halachic or rabbinic innovation, Joseph Albo, a 15th-century scholar, wrote in his *Sefer Ha-Ikkarim* (Book of Principles) that "it does not necessarily follow that a divine law cannot be changed. . . . The Torah merely warns us not to add or to take away from the commandments *on our own account.* But what can there be to prevent God's self from adding or diminishing as God's wisdom decrees?" (emphasis added). Albo is not suggesting that we should rewrite Jewish law as we see fit. He also does not call on people to reject all interpreters of text but only those prophets and dream-diviners out for their own motivations. Rather, he says that prophets may come along from time to time, and we should remain open to their insights, and that the ideal prophet is someone *not* advocating on behalf of him- or herself.

Albo allows for a different kind of queer reading of *Re'eh,* for opening up textual space for prophecy without violating the commandment against following prophets and dream-diviners. Albo would call on us to open our hearts to prophets acting for justice, not for self-interest. And here, Albo throws down a challenge to modern queer interpretation: when is queer interpretation an act of self-interest?

For those of us who are ourselves queer, the act of rereading text is about social justice and textual hermeneutics, but it is also about ourselves. We want space in Judaism. We want to have our relationships and families sanctified. We want to become rabbis. Are we acting out of self-interest in making Judaism more expansive?

Albo might say that the most effective prophet for LGBT inclusion would be the person who has the least to gain from such inclusion—straight allies. He would applaud those in this volume who write on behalf of the other, who support a cause from which, at least directly, they do not gain. Yes, all forms of oppression are interconnected, so the inclusion of LGBT Jews in Jewish life benefits everyone, straight allies included. Albo's point is that we should not reinterpret Torah *on our own account.*

Like the Chatam Sofer's conservative approach, this reading of Albo suggests that only those already with power can effectively and honestly advocate for those without it, not the most satisfying conclusion to draw from *Parashat Re'eh*. But if we read Albo's quotation to the end, we see that the true prophets are not simply those with the least to gain (i.e., those who already have power and privilege and thus do not need to gain). Prophecy is about social justice and divine, creative inspiration, because as Albo says, how can one "prevent God's self from adding or diminishing." And queer Jews advocating for rereadings of text also recognize that their hard work today benefits the next generation more than it does themselves, thus holding up Albo's command to be working on account of others.

A rabbi in Jerusalem recounted to us that Sir Jonathan Sacks, England's chief rabbi, once said, "Judaism never changes, but halacha does." The rabbi went on to explain that at Sinai, God gave us truth. This is Judaism. The Jewish people seek a world returned to absolute peace through the coming of *Moshiach* (the Messiah)—pure goodness. Halacha and tradition, then, help us on our journey from truth to goodness, from Sinai to *Moshiach*, bringing us closer to *tikkun olam*. Along the way, halacha and our tradition changes as society changes, allowing us to keep and celebrate the core values given at Sinai. "Observe only that which I enjoin upon you," or as Hillel once said, "That which is hateful to you, do not do to your neighbor. That is the whole Torah; the rest is commentary."[3]

NOTES

1. The distillation of the 613 mitzvot in the Torah by the Rambam in his *Mishneh Torah* is the most widely accepted list. Although many of the mitzvot, particularly those related to the Temple and sacrifices, cannot be observed today, Orthodox Jews still generally reference adherence to all 613, understanding that many are not currently applicable.

2. For this interpretive strategy, see Steven Greenberg's *Wrestling between God and Men: Homosexuality in the Jewish Tradition* (Madison: University of Wisconsin Press, 2005) and David Brodsky's essay on Kedoshim in this volume, along with the essays by Jay Michaelson, David Greenstein, and Elliot Dorff.

3. Babylonian Talmud, tractate *Shabbat* 31a.

FORTY-EIGHT

Setting Ourselves Judges
Parashat Shoftim (Deuteronomy 16:18–21:9)

JULIA WATTS BELSER

One of the most stirring calls for justice-seeking in the Torah comes near the beginning of *Parashat Shoftim*: "Justice, justice shall you pursue" (Deut. 16:20). A longstanding rallying cry for socially engaged Jews, this verse has been an important buttress for queer folk and allies who call for the creation of a Jewish community that includes and celebrates queer experience, as well as Jewish activism for LGBT justice in the wider world. Yet just before this classic phrase, the Torah offers a verse that is just as resonant for queer Jews, but often overshadowed. *Parashat Shoftim* opens, "Judges and officers shall you give yourselves, in all of your gates which God has given you, for your tribes, and they shall judge the people with right justice" (Deut. 16:18). In the verses that follow, the Torah teaches that these judges must not take bribes or judge unfairly. They must judge righteously, for it is their discerning judgment that will ultimately inspire the larger community to pursue justice.

Though the message seems outwardly straightforward, the opening verse of *Parashat Shoftim* has an odd grammatical structure that caught the attention of classic interpreters. The phrase "for your tribes" protrudes from the otherwise seamless sentence—a dangling clause full of potent meaning for contemporary gay, lesbian, bisexual, and transgender Jews. According to Rashi's medieval commentary, this phrase teaches that the Torah obligates each of the twelve ancestral tribes to appoint its own judges. The twelve tribes of Israel represent the mythic organization of Jewish genealogy that links us back to one of the twelve sons of Jacob. In Rashi's reading, the verse's mandate to establish judges "in all of your gates" and "for all of your tribes" means that each of these ancient tribes must appoint a judge to serve in every place and every city. Whereas Rashi reads this verse as an instruction on the establishment of an actual system of judges and understands the tribes as Judah, Reuben, Gad, and the rest of the "official" twelve, a contemporary queer reading reminds us of the other tribes in our midst: dykes, gender queers, fairies, and more. Read through a queer lens, this verse calls to gay, lesbian, bisexual, and transgender folk as a tribe within the whole—a tribe bound by spiritual kinship and mythic memory, a tribe with an obligation to honor our own particular history, and a tribe that also carries the responsibility for self-governance, moral stature, and right justice.

Whereas Rashi speaks of a judge as one who wields legal authority and probably imagines these judges as traditional deciders of Jewish law and practice, a contemporary queer reading must wrestle with the power and danger of the judge. We queers have suffered others' harsh judgment. We are a people who struggle for a voice in the legislative bodies of this country, who struggle for protection from the courts and the law, who must all too often struggle for a generous hearing from our families. We have known so much judgment and so little justice. In the face of this history, we might well be tempted to eschew judgment altogether, to turn away from the idea of ethical authority, to fear the power of the judge and the moral weight he or she carries. With the vibrant diversity of queer families and queer life paths so often derided and maligned—or overlooked and silenced—by the judgers of this world, we might give up on encountering a judge who recognizes our face, who listens for our story, who hearkens with interest to the intimate texture of its own unfolding.

But the Torah obligates us to raise up judges from our own ranks. Reading again the opening verses of *Parashat Shoftim* from a queer perspective, we hear a call for *our* tribe to appoint judges and officers for ourselves. Whereas Rashi read these judges as the linchpins of a formalized legal system, a contemporary queer reading sees the judge as a metaphor for leadership and ethical authority, manifest in a variety of forms. Our judges are the ones whose discerning righteousness inspires us toward the pursuit of justice. They are the ones who will see us truly, who will speak hard truths and carry high expectations, who will call forth our own decency and goodness. We are asked to find judges who recognize the landscape of our lives, who have lived in similar terrain and can help us navigate its cliffs and fissures. We are expected to come before judges who expect holiness within us and consequently find it—who know our goodness and consequently call it forth. *Judges and officers shall you give yourselves, in all your tribes.*

But what is a judge and what an officer? Rather than reading these two words as synonyms, the classic commentators maintained that every word of Torah has its own particular nuance and interpretation. Judges, Rashi suggests, "pass judgment" and determine the law, whereas officers "force the people to follow their command, until they accept upon themselves the judgment of the judge." On the face of it, that is not a particularly liberating remark. The idea of an officer who imposes authority—the verb Rashi uses in his comment can also be used to mean oppressing or punishing—sounds like the same old story: agents of an external authority who lord it over us and force us to do their will. Yet Rashi's distinction between the role of a judge and the role of an officer draws attention to an important difference between imposed authority and authority that an individual accepts for him- or herself. Rashi's judge passes judgment, whereas his officer uses external force to see that judgment carried out. Yet ultimately, the officer strives to have a person "accept upon himself the decision of the judge."

Rashi's comment exposes a disjuncture between the structural power that can demand obedience to the will of a judge and the more subtle, internal shift that occurs when a person resonates with the teachings of a true judge. A queer, feminist reading of this verse casts a critical eye on the structures of power and authority that have allowed officers to impose their will and judges to divorce their authority from their responsibility to the people. Though the powers-that-be may subjugate and oppress us, our power lies in our ability to accept upon our own selves the authority of a judge—and to reject that authority when it is unjust. Just as a true judge must "judge with justice" (Deut. 16:18), "not judge unfairly" (Deut. 16:19), and inspire people to "pursue justice" (Deut. 16:20), liberatory, justice-seeking officers cannot simply force others to their will. Instead, they must draw their people to find a response to the judge within themselves.

In this queer frame, Rashi's "officer" need not be a dominating figure. The real power of the officer lies in his or her ability to transmute an external obligation into an inner yearning—to help people "accept upon themselves" the right justice that the judge embodies. Rashi's officer operates in the potent space between the word of the judge and the soul of the individual. The officer mediates between outside and inside, between obligation and responsibility. The officer helps translate the judge's concept of justice into an authentic, livable, and accessible reality. Through the figure of the officer, the judge's example becomes something we each accept for ourselves. The officer prods, inspires, and ultimately facilitates a kind justice that comes from within. Through the teaching and action of the officer, we find a way to translate the judge's wisdom into our own idiom. The moral authority of the judge sinks inexorably into our own skin. We take justice into ourselves—and we make it a force of our own.

Judges and officers shall you give yourselves, in all your tribes. Turn it again, and the verse unfolds with a slightly different twist: we shall give *ourselves* as judges and officers. We queer Jews have an obligation to make ourselves into true judges and righteous officers, so that justice becomes a force that rises up within us. The responsibility of discerning judgment and right justice is not only an external expectation but an internal yearning. To meet that yearning, we kindle the discerning judge within us and strengthen our own righteous officer. We fashion ourselves into judges we can trust, into officers on whom we can rely. To do so, we seek out our own moral wisdom and ethical discernment, bridging the hard-won lessons and celebrations of our own lives with the insights and spiritual resources of the rest of the Jewish community.

This call to seek our own moral wisdom does not mean setting ourselves apart from the larger fabric of the Jewish people. But it does require attention to the particulars of queer insights. By requiring a judge from each tribe, the opening verse of *Shoftim* reminds us that these "tribal" differences matter. The Jewish community requires judges from all its tribes, in order to meet its obligation to judge with justice. In other words, the community needs judges that will honor and preserve the particulars of queer insights—and the particulars of the other tribes in our midst. To actualize our work for justice, we must strive for a radical connectivity to *all* our tribes. Our race and class complicate our queerness. Our bodies and disabilities and genders shape our truth. Elevating the question of how a single life refracts Torah, I ask how my life as a bisexual Jewish rabbi with a disability shapes the justice I long for and the wisdom my bones know. I ask how my white skin and my wheels and my Jewishness intersect—and not only listen for the cleanest answers but also interrogate the silences and uncertainties. To pursue this complicated, contextual discernment, I seek out the right judgment of those whose lives are different from my own—listening to the moral authority of those who offer correctives and rebukes to the unobserved and unconscious injustice in my own life. We queers are one tribe—and we are more than one tribe. And all of us as queers have kinship ties to many communities.

Judges and officers shall you give yourselves, in all your tribes. Our tribes are manifold, and Jews need judges from them all. Let us seek out and nurture the right justice of queer Jews of color. Let us affirm the moral wisdom of queer interfaith couples. Let us raise up judges steeped in the possibilities of ethical polyamory. Let us strengthen our judges who speak for the earth, for the Goddess, for the hidden faces of holiness in our lives. Let us affirm and empower the Torah emerging out of radical Jewish queer creativity—finding in the multiplicity of these voices new possibilities for authentic justice and righteous action. No single judge will hold all our answers, and no single officer will provide us with a perfect map. Just as each of us can alchemize the truth of our own lives into Torah, so too we must each seek out the judges and officers who illuminate our paths and strengthen our capacity for holiness—within our tribe, within our communities, and within ourselves.

FORTY-NINE

To Wear Is Human, to Live—Divine
Parashat Ki Tetse (Deuteronomy 21:10–25:19)

ELLIOT KUKLA *and* REUBEN ZELLMAN

For all of us who have ever struggled with how to discipline unruly children, *Parashat Ki-Tetse* offers an easy answer—stone them to death.

We read in the Torah: "[Parents of a stubborn and rebellious son][1] should say to the elders of the town: 'This child of ours is disloyal and defiant; he does not heed us. He is a glutton and a drunkard.' Thereupon the people of the town shall stone him to death" (Deut. 21:20–21). Thankfully, Jews today do not follow this verse literally. Indeed, if we did, rather few of us would have survived the occasional poor behavior of adolescence.

This verse of Torah seems fairly straightforward in its instruction. And yet, for two thousand years, Judaism has not carried out the extremely harsh practice that the Torah would seem to require. Rather, this verse has been read by Jewish sacred tradition to yield a much more complex message. We learn in the Mishna that a rebellious son can only be a child who has at least two pubic hairs (but not a full "lower beard") and who has flagrantly eaten an excess of meat and guzzled wine in public, but not at a religious festival. If he eats nonkosher foods or drinks any beverage other than wine, he does not meet the qualifications of being a proper "glutton and a drunkard." Furthermore, a rebellious son is only a person who steals food from his father's house and eats it in the house of another. Finally, he must have been simultaneously accused by both his parents, warned in the presence of three witnesses, and tried by a court of twenty-three judges (Mishna *Sanhedrin* 8).

In fact, it is so difficult to determine that someone qualifies as a genuine "rebellious son" that we learn in the Talmud, "A stubborn and rebellious son—there never was and there never shall be" (*Sanhedrin* 71a). Jewish tradition recognized that stoning children is an unacceptable solution to a common problem. Indeed, commentators read and reread this Torah portion to find a different, more compassionate way to understand this troubling passage. Our Sages refused to understand the verse literally. They would not accept that the Torah would command us to harm children, because this mandate would conflict with their understanding of the holiness and value of each and every human life.

Keeping in mind the evolution of the "rebellious son" in Jewish thought, let us read another verse in this action-packed parasha: "A man's clothes should not be on a woman, and a man should not wear the apparel of a woman; for anyone who does these things, it is an abomination before God" (Deut. 22:5). This verse is familiar to many of us, because it has long been understood as a ban on "cross-dressing." It is often invoked to condemn queer and transgender lives and used to "prove" the idea that everyone needs to stay within a rigid definition of gender. This portion has been used for hundreds of years against seven-year-old tomboys and sixty-year-old drag queens alike. Along with the infamous verses from Leviticus that appear to deal with sex between men, this short verse is probably the most common teaching of Torah that is used as a weapon against the LGBT community.

And yet our Sages have *never* read this verse as a literal ban on cross-dressing. Just as classical Jewish scholars narrowed the scope of the commandment to stone to death rebellious children to yield very different, and more compassionate, practical outcomes, they also read this portion's apparent ban on cross-dressing and drag to yield a very different kind of teaching.

In the Babylonian Talmud (*Nazir* 59a), the Sages argue that it is not plausible to read the verse in Deuteronomy literally, since wearing the clothes of another gender could not possibly be seen as an abomination. Instead, the Talmud understands the Torah prohibition this way: wearing clothes of another gender *in order to falsify your identity*, and infiltrate spaces reserved for the "opposite" sex, is what is forbidden. The key point here seems to be that cross-dressing is only prohibited when there are ulterior motives involved—in this case, the violation of another person's space and therefore trust. When it comes to cross-dressing in and of itself, the Talmud is crystal clear: "There is no abomination here!"

The great medieval commentator Rashi follows the Talmudic lead. He explains that this verse is not a simple prohibition on wearing the clothes of the "opposite gender." Rashi writes that such dress is prohibited only if it is done with the intent to commit adultery. Rashi's interpretation further narrows the prohibition: one must not falsify one's identity in order to seduce someone. Here Rashi further clarifies the point that clothing in and of itself is not the central issue. According to him, the term "abomination" used in this Torah verse refers to the acts that might arise from costumes used for tricking others into unethical sexual relations—and not to the clothing itself.

Rambam (Maimonides) claims that this verse is actually intended to prohibit cross-dressing for the purposes of idol worship. (Sefer haMitzvot, *Lo Taaseh* 39–40). Rambam—like Rashi and the Sages in the Talmud—argues that the problem of wearing the clothing of another gender is that it might *lead* to other forbidden practices.

In all these classical commentaries, wearing clothes of "the wrong gender" is proscribed only when it is done for nefarious purposes. The problem with idolatry and adultery is not the acts in and of themselves—Jewish tradition views both the acts of sex and worship as positive acts—the problem is the betrayal of our most intimate loving partnerships with a loved one or with God. In both cases the acts come out of a lack of integrity and result in damage to our relationships or the exploitation of another human being.

This view is made explicit in an unusual legal reading of this portion by Moses Isserles, the primary Ashkenazi commentator on the medieval Sephardic Jewish legal code, the *Shulchan Aruch*. This code is still seen as an authoritative compendium of Jewish law in many communities. Joseph Caro's *Shulchan Aruch* (Orach Chaim 696:8) explains that the custom of men dressing as women on Purim—a common custom to this day—is permitted under Jewish law. Isserles, in his supplementary comments, explains why: the purpose of cross-dressing on Purim is to increase the joy of those who are celebrating the holiday. For Isserles, promoting happiness and rejoicing is a worthy goal. Indeed, Judaism understands it as a religious obligation.

Isserles's commentary provides an interesting balance to the commentaries of his predecessors that we just examined, including the Babylonian Talmud, Rashi, and Rambam. These earlier commentaries offer scenarios when cross-dressing is done for unacceptable purposes: when it is for purposes of violating a relationship with people or with God. Isserles offers an example of cross-dressing being done for a good purpose: the promotion of happiness.

This idea can be understood as a significant teaching in the context of transgender and cross-dressing communities. If we follow Isserles's thinking, then choosing to wear clothing that is traditionally designated for a different gender from the one in which we were raised is acceptable if we are doing it because it makes us happy. And if we are permitted to dress in these ways because it makes us happy, then all the more so is it appropriate to wear the clothes that express our authentic selves. For some of us, the truth of who we are is better revealed when we wear the clothes of another gender than of the one we were assigned at birth. When we allow others to see our honest identities, it increases our comfort, helps to bring internal reconciliation, and promotes real fulfillment. Nothing promotes joy as much as the freedom to be who we are meant to be.

According to our Sages, then, the prohibition that we learn from this verse in *Ki Tetse* is very specific: we must not misrepresent our true gender in order to cause harm. Otherwise, wearing clothing of another gender is not prohibited.

So what does this verse mean for us today? In order to understand it in our own context, we need to examine two questions: First, what does it mean to us to wear clothing of a gender we are not? And second, what does it mean to cause harm?

Many people feel like their true gender is not (or is not only) the gender that was assigned to them at birth. The Torah is asking us not to misrepresent our gender, which we can understand as using external garments to conceal our inner selves. Unfortunately, many people today feel forced to hide in exactly this way. In our society the penalty for gender nonconformity is often severe and can include verbal, sexual, and physical abuse, employment discrimination, and an inability to access education, health care, and other critical services. It is no overstatement to say that gender conformity in our society can be a matter of life or death.

Gender rigidity affects people from all walks of life: the seven-year-old boy sent home from school for wearing "girl's clothes," the female employee who is fired for refusing to wear makeup to work, the multitudes of butch lesbians who are harassed and kicked out of women's restrooms all over the country. Much of this mistreatment comes from those who insist that wearing the clothes of the "other gender" is wrong "because it says so in the Bible."

Classical Jewish scholars did not accept such a justification for narrow-minded-ness. Neither should we. Rather, we can flip mainstream understandings of this verse on their head and understand the central verse from this parasha (Deut. 22:5) as a positive *mitzvah*: a sacred obligation to present the fullness of our gender as authentically as possible. Unfortunately, not everyone is able to fulfill this *mitzvah* without endangering their life or livelihood, and the protection of human life always comes first in Judaism. But the Torah wants us to be able to be true to ourselves, whoever we are: in all our sequined, buttoned-down, spikey-haired, or bow-tied glory.

Next, we come to the second part of our prohibition: that we must not cover up our gender in order to cause harm. Transgender and genderqueer[2] people who hide under the clothing of the gender they were assigned—rather than expressing themselves as they really are—suffer terrible harm. Among transgender people, rates of depression, suicide, and destructive self-medication are astronomical.[3]

Each and every soul is created in the multifaceted image of the Creator. When we try to conceal that uniqueness, we cause ourselves pain. And when we ask others to obscure themselves, we cause them harm. The great majority of our parasha is concerned with the minute details of preventing harm. The verses just before the infamous verse teach that if we find a lost object, we are obligated to restore it to its owner, and if we see that someone's donkey has fallen down, we are required to help that person lift the animal up. The verse immediately following instructs us never to hurt a mother bird as we are collecting her eggs. And the very next verse commands us to build a guardrail around the roof of our houses to prevent anyone from falling off. The verse about what to wear is nestled among mitzvot that guide us toward exquisite levels of empathy, gentleness, and responsibility toward all of creation.

One of the Hebrew words that is used in these verses is unusual—it is often translated to say that we should "not ignore" a fallen animal or a lost object. However, the Hebrew word in this verse, *hitalam*, does not actually mean "do not ignore" but rather "do not hide yourself." When we ignore the demands of the difficult process of finding the owner of a lost object, we are hiding ourselves from the truth of that object and causing harm and hurt to its owner (objects can be powerful things that are imbued with our most precious feelings). Likewise, when we hide ourselves from the demand for truth of our own souls that ask us to express the fullness of our complex gender, we cause ourselves pain and hurt.[4]

Like the return of lost objects, expressing gender diversity is countercultural. Our society asks us to ignore the ethical demand made on us by the common sight of stray property, but the Torah speaks in a different voice and asks us to engage in the lengthy and difficult process of finding and restoring property to its true owner. Likewise, the modern world asks us to ignore the parts of ourselves that are not neatly contained within the gender we were assigned at birth. But the Torah asks us to engage in the long and complex process of restoration—revealing the fullness of our gender and our souls. And when we engage in this sacred process ourselves, and live as who we truly are, then we support others to do the same. To enable wholeness and truth in those around us is certainly a mitzvah from the Torah.

Modern readers tend to read the verse on "cross-dressing" out of context of the passage of Torah within which it falls, but Jewish Sages have read it within its Biblical context to yield a subtle message about integrity, care, and concern. As our Sages realized, a sacred tradition that commands us not to cause pain to a single mother bird must not be asking us to stone to death small children or to conceal our true gender. Jewish tradition asks us to safeguard each unique being created in the image of God by preventing harm. When we cover up our true souls and muffle our divine reflection under clothes that feel "wrong," we are harming God's creation. And that is what our Torah prohibits.

NOTES

1. The relevant texts on the "stubborn and rebellious son" make it clear that they are specifically referring to a son, and not to a son or daughter or to a child in general. Although the word for "son" (*ben*) can refer to a "child" without specific gender, in this case the child is clearly male. For this reason, we have translated this phrase accordingly.

2. The term *genderqueer* is used by a wide range of people to identify themselves or refer to others as people who do not, in a great variety of ways, fit into traditional molds of gender conformity. Genderqueer people are not necessarily transgender; they can be of any gender identity or sexual orientation.

3. For statistics, please refer to the Sylvia Rivera Law Project: www.srlp.org.

4. "My Phranc Mother," drash by Rabbi Lisa Edwards, Beth Chayim Chadashim, Los Angeles, August 31, 2001.

အၥ: အၥ:

FIFTY

In a New Country

Parashat Ki Tavo (Deuteronomy 26:1–29:8)

SHIRLEY IDELSON

> I proclaim this day unto the Lord thy God, that I am come into the
> country which the Lord swore our ancestors to give us.
> —Deut. 26:3

Indeed, I am grateful—for I belong to a generation that has entered a new land where many of us were, not so long ago, excluded. Within the liberal Jewish world today, many of us in the LGBT community find ourselves for the first time in history able to participate openly in synagogues, seminaries, schools, organizations, and communities accessible in the past only to those who hid their identity. We have gained powerful Jewish institutional allies in our battle for healthcare and adoption rights, and though civil marriage rights are not yet broadly won, marriage *rites*—religious recognition of our relationships—have become commonplace. The liberal Jewish world has largely embraced the principle of inclusion and effectively attempted to welcome lesbian and gay Jews into the mainstream. We now find our lives reflected in new liturgy, we serve on the pulpit, and we share the pews openly with our partners. We have become equal players—even powerful—in organizations that once excluded and feared us. Many of us who share in the Jewish community's wealth, living middle-class lives, are acutely aware of the liberation we have experienced.

Yet every day that I traverse the byways of this new land, I am conscious of my immigrant status. The Old World I left feels never far away. And as I enjoy the great promise of the *goldeneh medineh* in which I live, I am ever cognizant of the tenuous nature of good fortune. Jewish historical consciousness precludes the possibility of taking societal acceptance for granted, and so we live with the uncertainty of fate, and the possibility that progress made rapidly in one generation may unravel in the next. For the time being, however, many liberal American Jews—not all, to be sure— find themselves rather comfortable, and while some of my younger colleagues view this comfort, this *equality,* as expected, I continue to experience it as miraculous.

Ki Tavo, which spells out the actions God commanded the Jewish people to fulfill upon entering the Land of Israel, offers instruction for our generation and for all who have entered this new land. The bringing of the first fruits and the obligation to tithe—both elucidated in this Torah portion—teach that with comfort and access comes obligation. Those of us who have the good fortune of experiencing possibility in our lives—possibility inconceivable to our predecessors—bear a unique responsibility.

Upon bringing the first fruits, the Israelite was commanded to thank God for having been delivered from slavery into freedom and for the privilege of entering the Land of Israel. Though the Israelites entering the Land of Israel were a generation away from the experience of slavery in Egypt, nonetheless, regardless of the degree to which they personally shared the experience of bondage, they were commanded to proclaim their deliverance. The commandment resembles our own reading of the Passover Haggadah, when we, too, acknowledge our gratitude to God for having been personally rescued. We, too, proclaim, "I have crossed from narrow straits to enter a land of expansive opportunity I never dreamed possible."

The ancient Israelites, bringing their first fruits, were to acknowledge publicly their immigrant status by uttering the words "*Arami oved avi.*" The meaning of these words is not self-evident, and the rabbinic commentators offered various interpretations. Among these, that of Ibn Ezra stands out. According to Ibn Ezra, *oved* is an intransitive present-tense verb that effectively functions as an adjective meaning "lost" or "impoverished." *My father,* the phrase suggests, *was a lost* or *an impoverished Aramean.* According to Ibn Ezra, and other commentators as well, *my father* refers to Jacob and his travails in Aram, where he was a fugitive on the run, possessing little and vulnerable to the abuse of others. The ancient Israelite, upon offering his first fruits to God, expressed his gratitude to God for liberation from slavery by recalling the lowly status, as well as the suffering and distress, of his forbear Jacob. What can the LGBT community learn from this? How are we, today, to acknowledge our ancestry?

The men and women who fought for our freedom were, like Jacob, fugitives. We who now find ourselves comfortable owe our ease of existence to a band of outcasts who dared defy powerful—and narrow—prescriptions of sexuality. Many of us no longer have to hide our identities because, not long ago, a cadre of radicals quite literally risked their lives to challenge core societal assumptions regarding family structure and gender roles. Our predecessors did not experience acceptance in the liberal Jewish world that today embraces us; rather, they incurred lowly status and ostracization. Each generation, Judaism teaches, must remember and identify with the journey taken by our ancestors. So let us never forget those who risked their well-being and their lives for the sake of women's liberation and gay liberation. Our matriarchs and patriarchs include extraordinary individuals who fought in the public realm, people such as Audre Lorde and Adrienne Rich, Harvey Milk and Larry Kramer. And they also include thousands more who fought daily for their right to participate in synagogue and Jewish organizational life, to work in Jewish schools and summer camps, and to enter and serve in Jewish education and in professions such as the rabbinate and the cantorate. Only because of their courage and willingness to risk loss of livelihood, loss of parental rights, and physical attack can we live our lives openly today.

And so, one generation after Stonewall, let us identify our ancestry publicly: *My father was a fugitive Aramean.* Dare we say to our straight colleagues, those with whom we share a mainstream existence, "My forebears, my patriarchs and matriarchs, were lesbian feminists and gay activists"? Dare we say, "My brothers and sisters today include those who remain far outside the norm"? At this time, the debt we owe our ancestors can be paid only by risk-taking ourselves, by identifying with and sharing in the struggle of those who still face the choice of living in hiding or placing themselves in peril for challenging contemporary prescriptions of family structure and gender.

In addition to acknowledging our past, we must *give of our first fruits*. Why? Maimonides, commenting on *Ki Tavo*, warns against the complacency that can come with comfort: "Those who amass wealth and live in comfort are more prone to fall victim to the vices of insolence and haughtiness, and abandon all good principles."[1] Therefore, not only must we who live in comfort recall our people's history of suffering and oppression, but we must bring the first of all we produce to God. By doing so, Maimonides teaches, we learn to be generous, we temper our greed, and we cultivate a sense of humility. For ultimately we are not responsible for our good fortune; we are indebted to our ancestors for the risks they took on our behalf, and to God, for bestowing blessing upon us. Let us be mindful of this always, lest we succumb to arrogance.

Finally, for the ancient Israelites, *tithing* was the logical extension of publicly recognizing an impoverished ancestry and of cultivating a spirit of generosity. Symbolic and ritual acts must lead to change in the material world in which we live, and for this reason the ancient Israelites were commanded to give away a significant portion of their own produce to the Levites (who owned no land), the orphan, and the widow. Might we, having entered a land of promise, create a system of tithing for the LGBT community today? It is time that we consider doing so, looking not only to ancient Israel for a model but also to more recent Jewish history. The American Jewish immigrant community at the end of the 19th century established the first federations of Jewish charities in order to provide for the needy. Eventually these grew into a national philanthropic model that served Jews as well as non-Jews, reflecting and exemplifying the Jewish values of communal responsibility, *tzedakah,* and social justice. United Jewish Communities (UJC) federations support Israel; offer aid to Jews everywhere who are in need; support Jewish education, family, and children's services; care for the elderly; and play a central role in mediating inter- and intracommunity relations. The LGBT community has a similar obligation to provide for those in need, and like the Jewish community, we too would benefit from building a philanthropic model based on a shared value system. With the legacy we have inherited from our own "fugitive" ancestry, we inherit, too, a singular responsibility to work for the redemption of those who remain on the margins and those in need.

Such an endeavor would require that we articulate a shared value system, a difficult task—but if the Jewish community, with all its competing internal interests, could do this, then the LGBT community can as well. We need to articulate an agenda that goes far beyond the demand for marriage rights. Just as the American Jewish community did a century ago as a huge wave of Jewish immigrants entered this country, we too need to make central to our political and philanthropic agenda the provision of education, family, and children's services, care for the elderly, and aid to the poor—both within and extending beyond the LGBT community. We need to turn our philanthropic efforts, as well as our activism, to helping the uninsured gain access to health care, providing services for runaway gay youth living on the streets, supporting those who live in nontraditional family structures, and advocating for the transgendered as well as others who cannot or refuse to bend to the still narrow bounds of acceptable gendered practice. Although many individuals and organizations participate in these efforts now, their visibility has been eclipsed at the most public level by the movement for marriage rights. The LGBT community can far more effectively articulate and demonstrate how communal responsibility and social justice lie at the core of our own value system, and we who have been fortunate owe it to our people—past, present, and future generations—to do so.

Ki Tavo provides important instruction for those of us who, like the ancient Israelites, have experienced liberation and entered a new land: we must always acknowledge our ancestry and our indebtedness to the many who fought and risked all they had so we can enjoy the rights and privileges they never experienced. We must recognize that the gains we have made warrant gratitude to God, generosity to others, and constant vigilance—not complacency. Finally, we, as immigrants into a new land, must create structures that will enable us to be true to our past, to embody the best of our values, and to ensure a secure future for the many who are not yet free.

NOTE

1. *Guide for the Perplexed, 3, 39,* as quoted in Nehama Leibowitz, *Studies in Devarim* (Jerusalem: Ahva, 1980), 258.

FIFTY-ONE

Embodied Jews

Parashat Nitzavim (Deuteronomy 29:9–30:20)

SUE LEVI ELWELL

Parashat Nitzavim, like many parshiyot, is named for the first verb in the portion: *nitzavim,* "stand" (Deut. 29:9). As we approach the conclusion of both the book of Deuteronomy and the Torah, we read Moses's sense of urgency as he reframes and recasts his message to the Israelite people. This portion, which is read both as part of the yearly cycle of readings on the Shabbat immediately preceding Rosh Hashana and as the Torah reading on Yom Kippur morning, has particular power and nuance when read through LGBT eyes, from the opening challenge to stand to the concluding verses that challenge us to choose life (Deut. 30:19).

This portion opens with Moses's final exhortation in Moab:

> You stand this day, all of you, before your God—you tribal heads, you elders, and you officials, all the men of Israel, you children, you women, even the stranger within your camp, from the woodchopper to water drawer—to enter into the covenant of your God, which your God is concluding with you this day, with its sanctions; in order to establish you this day as God's people and in order to be your God. . . . I make this covenant, with its sanctions, not with you alone, but both with those who are standing here with us this day before our God and with those who are not with us here this day. (Deut. 29:9–14)

The first and fourth words fuel the first verse: *atem* (you, plural) and *culchem* (all of you). The repetition of these intentionally inclusive terms sets up, and extends, the explicit designations that follow. The use of merism, the linking of two nouns that implies the inclusion of subjects between those named, opens the way to all who read these words. Wherever we see ourselves on the spectra specified here—communal roles, gender, age, and profession—all are included in Moses's charge. The final phrase, "those who are standing here with us this day . . . and those who are not with us here this day," can be read as reaching toward the temporal future, those who are literally not yet here, that is, yet alive, and also connecting with those who may be present yet are not now revealed as who they will become. So each of us who see ourselves as continuing to evolve, we too are embraced in the emerging spiritual collective addressed in the opening of *Nitzavim.*

The portion continues, and one verse calls to us, "Concealed acts concern our God, but with overt acts, it is for us and our children ever to apply all the provisions of this

Teaching" (Deut. 29:28). This verse is particularly challenging to LGBT readers. Many LGBT folks have lived at some point in our lives in the shadows, on the margins, in secret, concealed. And certainly, our "acts" do not define our selves. The concealed/revealed, divine/human polarities suggested here call for our attention. First, let us consider the translation of *hanistarot* and *haniglot* as "hidden and revealed things," not acts.[1] This more accurate translation enables us to consider a difference between matters that only the Holy One may understand and things that are the reach and realm of human understanding. Many of us might agree that the source of our sexuality and gender identification is a mystery. Indeed, reading "hidden things" as the purview of the Holy One actually reflects the insights of hundreds of years of Jewish mysticism. Who, other than God, is concerned with matters that are inaccessible to mortals? Our concern, and the concern of our communities, should be on that which is here, in our present, in our reality.

The second half of this verse calls for interpretation because of the unusual diacritical marks on top of the words translated as "and our children." As Dalit Rom-Shiloni writes in *The Torah: A Women's Commentary*, "Traditionally these two Hebrew words (*lanu ulvaneinu*: it is for us and for our children) . . . are written with extraordinary dots over the letters, a scribal phenomenon that occurs in fifteen places throughout the Bible."[2] For LGBT folks, this unusual emphasis has particular power: each reader, including each of us, is explicitly linked here with our children. As biological and adoptive parents, and as those whose very families often take by surprise other Jews and some Jewish communities, we are also those who nurture the next generation of LGBT folks. We may face particular challenges in welcoming and keeping ourselves and our children in relationship with God and with the many communities of which we are a part. When we claim this welcome, and see ourselves and our children as part of God's covenantal community, we are encouraged to rededicate ourselves to work tirelessly "*ad olam*: ever to apply all the provisions of this teaching" (Deut. 29:30).

Just as we are challenged to reread and rethink the dichotomy between concealment and revelation, so too must we reconsider that between blessing and curse. When LGBT readers confront the phrase "the blessing and curse that I have set before you" (Deut. 30:1), we may not immediately think of the blessing of drawing near—and the curse of distancing ourselves—from God. Such a reading may open the way to a fresh understanding of the invitation "then your God will restore your fortunes and take you back in love." The text continues, "Even if your outcasts are at the ends of the world, from there your God will gather you" (Deut. 30:3–4).

Throughout this portion, Moses senses the pain of those who have left, or have been marginalized, and felt themselves to be on the periphery of the community. With words that reiterate a community with permeable boundaries, Moses intentionally employs the language of love to encourage his listeners to draw closer and to return. For many LGBT folks, love has been our blessing, yet we, and others, may have interpreted love as our burden, indeed, our curse. The intentional repetition of God as One who "will open up your hearts and the hearts of your offspring—to love your God with all your heart and soul, in order that you may live" (Deut. 30:6) makes the link between love and life. The literal inscription of the covenant on the heart is explored here: "The metaphor of the circumcised heart exemplifies the profound internal transformation of each and every person. God needs to act upon the heart where the recognition of sin develops (v. 2) and where full obedience and devotion reside (vv. 3, 10)."[3] The text continues, "For God will again delight in your well-being, as in that of your ancestors" (Deut. 30:9). As we were previously linked to our off-spring, here we are explicitly connected with our ancestors. For LGBT folks, reading ourselves into the tradition of the past is as essential, and as transformative, as reading ourselves into the future. Moses's words invite us to claim this opportunity and to open ourselves "with all [our] heart and soul" to this teaching (Deut. 30:10).

The portion concludes with nine verses that echo an earlier choice, presented in Deuteronomy 11, between blessing and curse. Here each individual is presented with the choice between life and death.

> Surely, this Instruction which I enjoin upon you this day is not too baffling for you, nor is it beyond reach. It is not in the heavens, that you should say, "Who among us can go up to the heavens and get it for us and impart it to us, that we may observe it?" Neither is it beyond the sea, that you should say, "Who among us can cross to the other side of the sea and get it for us and impart it to us, that we may observe it?" No the thing is very close to you, in your mouth and in your heart, to observe it. (Deut. 30:11–14)

We may read this passage as an answer to the previous distinction between concealed and revealed "things"; truth, here, is revealed in a palpable way, as close as one's own mouth and heart.

Jews often think of themselves as people of the book, as people of the word. In the past two decades, an increasing number of Jewish scholars and teachers including Rebecca Alpert, Howard Eilberg-Schwartz, Judith Plaskow, Daniel Boyarin, and others have reminded us that Jews are also people of the body.[4] "The thing is very close to you, in your mouth." The mouth is a primary opening of our bodies. The daily prayer that is called by some people "Asher yatzar" thanks the Holy One for the openings that should be open and the closed places that should be closed (*n'kavim n'kavim, chalulim chalulim*). Those powerful verses from Deuteronomy remind us of the immediate accessibility of this teaching, which we can inhale, ingest, and welcome into our very bodies. We learn that opening ourselves to Torah in the most intimate, immediate sense is how we choose life. Claiming the body as where we— and God—dwell is our path to affirmation of life. Too many LGBT folks have spent years claiming our bodies, making peace with our bodies, celebrating and embracing our bodies. *Nitzavim* invites us to embrace Torah that celebrates these our bodies as God's dwelling place.

As the portion concludes, the challenge is reiterated: "Choose life—if you and your offspring would live." Again, we are linked with those who follow us, and to the land, as we are shown, one final time, the path to life: "by loving your God." If we read the Torah with an open heart, the path of life is revealed. May we remember the inclusive words that begin this portion as we choose a journey that sees us as a link between past and future, standing between our ancestors and future generations. Through this portion, we discover new meanings of the concealed and the revealed, embrace anew the power of love, and stand proudly as part of the community, in all our diversity, claiming and celebrating our bodies, our spirits, and all our blessings.

NOTES

1. See Robert Alter, *The Five Books of Moses* (New York: Norton, 2004), 1026; and Richard Elliott Friedman, *Commentary on the Torah* (San Francisco: Harper, 2003), 657.

2. Dalit Rom-Shiloni, commentary on Nitzavim, in *The Torah: A Women's Commentary*, edited by Tamara Cohn Eskenazi and Andrea L. Weiss (New York: Women of Reform Judaism/Union for Reform Judaism Press, 2008), 1224.

3. Rom-Shiloni, commentary on Nitzavim, 1225.

4. Rebecca Alpert, *Like Bread on the Seder Plate* (New York: Columbia University Press, 1997); Daniel Boyarin, *Carnal Israel* (Berkeley: University of California Press, 1993); Howard Eilberg-Schwartz, ed., *People of the Body: Jews and Judaism from an Embodied Perspective* (Albany: SUNY Press, 1992); Judith Plaskow, *The Coming of Lilith: Essays on Feminism, Judaism and Sexual Ethics* (Boston: Beacon, 2005).

FIFTY-TWO

"Be Strong and Resolute"
Parashat Vayelech (Deuteronomy 31:1–30)

MARTIN KAVKA

The Covenant of the Dishwasher is forever written on my heart. Water glasses can only be placed on the right half of the upper rack, and mugs can only be placed on the left half, wine glasses in the second row from the left, champagne flutes in the silverware compartment. All plates must face toward the center. Pots are not to be placed in a manner that minimizes the number of plates that can be fit in the dishwasher. Once the dishwasher is full, all dishes that do not fit are to be washed by hand immediately.

These are only the most introductory of the mitzvot of dishwashing given by Dan, my partner of almost fourteen years. If I obeyed them, I would be blessed with cleanliness and order at all seasons; if not, there would be incomprehensible muttering while I watched him rearrange the dishes in the dishwasher ("What did I do wrong?" "grumble grumble [clash of dishes]"). Of course, there are many other covenants that constitute the fabric of the relationship—both ones that are as importantly ridiculous as these and ones that are far more private. Yet all are equally intimate, ours and ours alone. At times, there are objections to their terms. But the renegotiations and expansions that then take place—in the case of the Covenant of the Dishwasher, decisions as to when Tupperware should be washed by hand or which sets of silverware should be washed handle-up—are always, in the end, peaceful. And then, with two huge convulsions and a final slump downward in an easy chair, all this came to a halt.

What has been most surprising to me is the difficulty of sustaining memories of Dan. Although at times they can be a solace, most of the time they come unbidden, fast and furious, and only enervate. This has meant that even thinking about mourning, much less actually doing it, is often the last thing I want to do. I go on as normal. Or I stare into space. Or I do both at the same time: I try to go on as normal while colleagues and students remark about the catatonic look in my eyes.

I have looked at so many photos for so long that I have sucked them of all their power. Conversations with friends are dotted with awkward silences or flashes of anger, and I have never been as thankful for the fakeness of the customary "How are you?" But when alone, I am surprised to find myself loading the dishwasher with renewed fastidiousness. (Water glasses can only be placed on the right half . . .)

In those moments, a warm connection to the past is forged, despite there no longer being four hands in the vicinity of the dishwasher.

Still, not all covenants are the same. What does my Covenant of the Dishwasher have to do with the texture of the covenanted life of Jews?

Certainly there are thematic similarities between my life at present and that of the people of Israel in *Parashat Vayelech*. Moses, having just been told that he is about to die, tells the people that they are to be strong and resolute without him. In his absence, what gives strength is divine presence: "Be strong and resolute, be not in fear or in dread of them, for the Lord your God himself marches with you. He will not fail or forsake you" (Deut. 31:6).

But what gives divine presence is the people's observance of the mitzvot. Otherwise, God will absent God's self from their history and hide God's face from them if they "forsake me [God] and break my covenant that I made with them" (31:16).

The narrative of *Parashat Vayelech* seems to realize that it is difficult to maintain observance of the mitzvot after the loss of someone integral to the community. And so it provides for a regular recitation of Moses's words; even without the original speaker, the text still has motivating power: "Every seventh year, the sabbatical year, at Sukkot, when all Israel comes to appear before the Lord your God in the place that He will choose, you shall read this Torah aloud in the presence of all Israel. Gather the people—men, women, children, and your strangers in your communities [*ve-gerekha 'asher bisha'areykha*]—so that they may hear and learn to fear the Lord your God and that they may faithfully observe all the words of this Torah" (31:10–12).

The argument that the Torah is making here, then, is that there is no possibility of strength and resoluteness without having some routines of life through which one remembers a relationship by continuing to engage in the practices that were the components of that relationship. At a time of loss, this is the most difficult and most important thing to keep in mind. Only through bringing the past into the present in one way or another can one hope to depart from the space of mourning that is discontinuous with everything the mourner has known and realize that one is still the same person one had been before becoming a mourner.

But who is to say that this parasha speaks of my loss now? It is not simply an issue of having the Bible speak to someone mourning a same-sex partner. It is also an issue of having a Biblical text about a covenant between God and a people speak about a covenant between two individual persons. Perhaps when I assert that I hear something in this text that speaks to me now, I am simply getting too big for my britches. Perhaps I am butchering the parasha, profaning it by claiming too little difference between the dignity of the human being and the dignity of God. Yet *Parashat Vayelech* faces me now and means something different. And so perhaps it is time to accept my status as a stranger in the Jewish community (*ger 'asher bisha'areyhem*).

Deuteronomy 31:12, which speaks of the gathering of the people, is a strange verse. It is notable in scholarship primarily by its frequent comparison to another verse in the Torah about the community being gathered to hear the covenant, Exodus 19:15. In that verse, the command "do not go near a woman," so as not to incur impurity before the theophany at Sinai, implies that the covenant is valid only for men. This implication was famously pointed out by Judith Plaskow in the opening pages of *Standing Again at Sinai*.[1] The verse in Deuteronomy, on the other hand, makes it clear that the entire people of Israel, regardless of gender, is a covenanted people. But the suggestive feminism of this verse still leaves unaddressed the question of who precisely these *gerim*, these strangers in the communities, are. The verse's presupposition that the *gerim* are to follow every commandment of the Torah implies that an individual *ger* is a convert to Judaism (what the rabbis later described as a *ger tzedek*), a "proselyte" who has taken on the ways of the Jewish communities in which he or she lives and has been recognized as a full convert by the leaders of those communities.

Yet if this interpretation were to be the case, it would be the only example of *ger* having this meaning in Deuteronomy. Elsewhere in Deuteronomy, *ger* clearly has the sense of what the rabbis later called a *ger toshav*, a "stranger-sojourner" or a "resident alien." In the Tanakh, this term refers to an unlanded person who, in order to survive, made a covenant with a landowner and became something like a serf. (The most obvious example of this use is in Deuteronomy 29:10, in which the exemplars of *gerim* are wood-choppers and water-carriers.) In rabbinic literature, the *ger toshav* is the nonidolator who obeys the seven Noahide laws that rabbis understood to be binding on all humans, gentile or Jew.[2] Which of these categories is at stake in Deuteronomy 31:12?

If *ger* here were to refer to the proselyte, there would be no reason for the verse to talk about *gerekha*, "*your* strangers." Proselytes have equal legal status in the community with native-born Israelites and would neither be another's possession nor subordinate to others in the community. Yet if *ger* here only refers to the resident alien, it is puzzling why the *ger* is expected to observe every word of this teaching, especially to those readers who want to affirm the cohesiveness of the Jewish tradition and thus the rabbinic understanding of the *ger toshav* as one who is only bound by seven commandments.

The *ger* in Deuteronomy 31:12 is in the strange situation of being both apparently legally equal to and socially different from the Israelite. That means that we cannot once and for all answer the question of who the *ger* is in this verse. And that in turn means that we cannot answer the question of what commandments are or are not binding on the *ger*. All we can say is that the *ger* must "observe all the words of Torah" *without* practicing the totality of the halakhic life; the *ger* must live a commanded life, but that life must be different from other Jews' commanded lives. For the *ger* to fulfill this obligation requires the most strenuous exercise of imagination.

All queer readers of Torah are strangers, *gerim*, either in our communities or in the broader fabric of Judaism. When queer congregants are not taken as equal members of a community but still show up at services and are active in congregational life, we have a class of *gerim*. When nontraditional marriages are not recognized, we have a class of *gerim*. And although queer Jews may be the most visible *gerim* in Jewish communities, we are not the only ones. When our straight friends who converted at marriage are seen as fake Jews by people down the pew or in other congregations, we have a class of *gerim*. When our straight friends who converted and proceeded to learn more about the Jewish tradition than those who were born Jewish become objects of unjust resentment, we have a class of *gerim*. Whenever any Jew is judged to be not Jewish enough (to marry, to share food with, to teach children, to serve on committees), we have a class of *gerim*.

It is tempting to address this situation by broadening the category of "Jew" by saying that all these marginal Jews are no less Jewish than any other Jew. But I hope instead that the identity of *ger* is cherished by those who are estranged from the tradition. Why? Because if Deuteronomy 31:12 teaches us that the Jewish tradition has no set answer to the question of what the rights and responsibilities of the *ger* are, it becomes a question that we *gerim* have to answer for ourselves as we hear the Torah. Those texts offer little guidance, and so *we* must become *their* guides, making of them what we will, hopefully with the respect and love and support of those in our local communities (congregations, community and advocacy groups, universities, etc.).

If queer Jews were to do this—to remain in their communities but remain in them as *gerim*—it would no longer matter whether certain sex acts between men are characterized as abominable in Leviticus or whether Maimonides sanctions lashes for "women who rub against each other" in the *Mishneh Torah*. We are *gerim*, and as soon as we take on an identity that forces us to hear Torah in a different way, we gain the freedom to make something else of those passages in the tradition and find ourselves in the Jewish tradition once more. It would no longer matter whether queer relationships are judged to be sanctifiable by denominations' law committees or other institutional bodies or whether they are sanctifiable as marriages or as covenants for which names have not yet been invented. We are *gerim*, and we and our local communities and spiritual leaders can sanctify them ourselves, even if we have to form new communities and find new leaders to do so.

Maybe if we were to do this, queer Jews could be at the forefront of putting an end to the tired who-is-a-Jew debate that seems to bedevil every Jewish community. We who are strangers, in and through that identity, gain power to get the tradition to meet our needs, even and especially in moments of personal crisis. But we can do this only by seeing ourselves as *gerim*. Nevertheless, as we guide the texts back to us, we will become *gerim* in the full sense of the word, simultaneously both strangers and proselytes. At that moment, the answer to the question "Who is a Jew?" will be as banal as the answer to the question "Who is a *ger*?"

For these reasons, I, as a *ger*, declare with confidence that *Parashat Vayelech* is about the Covenant of the Dishwasher and about my responsibilities to remember it and to observe faithfully its terms. In so doing, I find the strength and resoluteness that I have been commanded to have and take one small step forward in my desire to observe faithfully all the words of this Torah.

Water glasses can only be placed on the right half . . .

NOTES

1. Judith Plaskow, *Standing Again at Sinai* (San Francisco: HarperSanFrancisco, 1990), 25ff.

2. See T. H. Meek, "The Translation of Gêr in the Hexateuch and Its Bearing on the Documentary Hypothesis," *Journal of Biblical Literature* 49:2 (1930): 172–80; S. B. Hoenig, "New Light from the Prophets?" *Jewish Quarterly Review* 62:4 (1972): 233–45; David Novak, *The Image of the Non-Jew in Judaism* (Lewiston, NY: Edwin Mellen, 1983), chap. 1; Shaye Cohen, *The Beginnings of Jewishness* (Berkeley: University of California Press, 2001), 120–21.

FIFTY-THREE

Dor l'Dor

Parashat Ha'azinu (Deuteronomy 32:1–52)

JHOS SINGER

Ha'azinu, the Torah's penultimate parasha, brings us to the end of the Israelites' forty-year journey in the wilderness. Those who tasted the bitterness of slavery in Egypt have all but died out (Num. 14:26–35). A nomadic generation born in freedom is on the verge of leaving the desert to settle down in the land they have been promised. The degradation of slavery and their parents' bones will be left in the sands behind them. This new breed will cross the river Jordan to enter the Promised Land with only two living remnants of their past: the spy Caleb and their new leader, Joshua. Moses, his death imminent, is making his final speech.

The Israelites' break from Egypt and their four-decade-long desert adventure bears striking resemblance to the first forty years of lesbian, gay, bi, trans, intersex, and queer (LGBTIQ) liberation. Like Moses, queers' drag-queen/butch-dyke forebears stood up in anger and passion to defy the pharaohs of New York City's Christopher Street.[1] Queers traversed and battled their way across the badlands of homophobia, leaving in our wake *La Cage aux Folles, Torch Song Trilogy, Angels in America, The L-word, Brokeback Mountain,* and *Queer Eye on the Straight Guy* in Netflix queues all across mainstream America and beyond. Forty years after a ragtag bunch of gender-variant and homosexual folks threw off the yoke of homophobia, rose up against queer oppression, performed miracles, marched in parades, and said, "Let my people go!" their children stand on the brink of a new era. Like the Israelites, we lost many of our forebears on the way. Homophobia infected us with depression, alcoholism, and drug abuse; poverty claimed many; AIDS devastated an entire generation of our men; and there continues to be a large mixed multitude imprisoned in closets all over the world. Nevertheless, forty years after the Stonewall rebellion, GenQ is poised to go forth into a land flowing with the courage, wisdom, and influence of Harvey Milk and Honey Labrador. The question is, will they go alone, or will they bring the memory of the first-wave leadership with them?

Parashat Ha'azinu is a pivot point. The old guard, Moses, is stepping down. He will not accompany the Israelites into the next book (Deut. 32:52). *Ha'azinu* is Moses's valedictory address. Visually and stylistically this parasha is distinctive. The calligraphy is uniquely laid out: the text is written in two distinct, parallel columns in the space that would normally house a single column. One can look at this section of a Torah scroll from across the room and see that it is *Ha'azinu*.[2] The text is also surprising on a literal level. Moses, who four decades prior described himself as "a man with uncircumcised lips" (Ex. 6:12), is now a poet, a bard, a troubadour, a preacher. Like the text, Moses is presented in a different form. No longer a reluctant orator needing either a spokesman (Ex. 4:10–16) or a chorus (Ex. 15:1) to back him up, solo he speak-sings his swan song "into the ears of the people" (Deut. 31:30, 32:44). His poem is passionate, blunt, and eloquent. He is not the least bit held back—gone is the foreskin of his lips. As an orator, Moses has finally found the perfect synthesis of his gifts of poetry and prophecy. His unfettered opening lines are astonishing and poignant:

> Give ear, O heavens, that I may speak.
> And let the earth hear my mouth's utterances.
> Let my teaching drop like rain,
> My saying flow like dew,
> Like showers on the green
> And like cloudbursts on the grass. (Deut. 32:1–2)

And although the poetry, lyricism, and singing may be new to the Children of Israel, the fundamental message is not: they have been selected for a special role in God's plan for humanity (Deut. 32:8, Ex. 19:4), and they should be grateful; if they do not behave themselves and prove themselves worthy, they will be assailed by their enemies without God's protection, but if they are good they will be rewarded (Deut. 32:19–25, Ex. 20:5–6); they must remember their deliverance from Egypt and remain vigilant in their identity as God's children (Deut. 32:6, 10–12, Ex. 20:2–3). And just for good measure, Moses calls them crooked, twisted, base, and witless (Deut. 32:5–6) and warns them that God finds them terribly irritating (Ex. 32:17–21).

Since the content is a rehash of what has come before, let us look for significance beyond the plain meaning of the verses, in the graphic and literary structure. The two columns of text might represent two different voices. One voice is that of the generation who left Egypt, and the other is the generation who was born in freedom and who will enter the Promised Land. Visually there is no bridge—the two parallel columns of text are separated by empty space. But the graphic layout is not merely a visual metaphor. The text itself can read either as one very emphatic poem or two reflexive poems.[3] The *sofer*, the scribe, who laid out this text literally split the text into twins. Each line contains two versets (which are pretty hard to miss with that gaping empty space between them) that are repetitive but not redundant. Robert Alter describes this technique:

> Far more prevalent in biblical poetry than incremental repetition is what might be characterized as "hidden" repetition—that is, the very common maneuver of ellipsis in which a word in the first verset, usually a verb, governs the parallel clause in the second verset as well. . . . It is used to introduce an increment of meaning.[4]

In this instance, however, it is blatant, not hidden at all. You cannot miss it: are you following me, right there in front of you, get it? Alter notes that the second verset usually sharpens the meaning of the material introduced by the first (Deut. 32:9–10). But our Biblical graphic designer tweaks the formula by taking some liberties with the line breaks (creating a brilliant example of ancient intertextuality).[5] By visually shifting the first verset to the second column, a third of the way through the poem the columns alternate between which one is introducing the material and which is enhancing the idea.[6] Although the second verset tends to intensify the drama by bringing in more possibilities and creativity, if one is reading each column as a poem unto itself, intercutting the versets allows both poems a complete range of expression. Each one is whole, entire in itself, yet separated by a gaping rift—two generations with parallel experiences but no visible means of connection.

Establishing and sustaining a movement (especially one that has to do with sex or religion) that aims to topple the dominant paradigm while eradicating prejudice, injustice, ignorance, and intolerance is slow work. There is often a catalyzing big-bang type of event, and from there it can take a few decades just to get the new idea to stick. Leadership and membership get built up over time, and slowly a group identity forms. It is easy, once momentum builds, for factionalism to rise. One of the places that the LGBTIQ community is clearly fractured is by age. This is why *Haʾazinu* has so much value. Because buried in the redundant message and the repetitive style is the text-seed of one of Judaism's "Big Ideas"[7]—the connection of the generations—while, paradoxically, the text is showing us that there exists a great divide.

Moses introduces the Hebrew phrase *dor v'dor* (literally meaning "a generation and a generation")[8] in his final ode:

> Remember the days of old/Have understanding of the years of generation and generation
> Ask your father, he will inform you/Your elders, they will tell you.   (Deut. 32:7)

Part of Moses's final teaching to his tribe is that they must not lose their connection to their elders, their parents, and their history. Perhaps, then, there is yet another layer of meaning to the pervasive repetition in his song. Maybe he is cautioning them against repeating the mistakes of the past by reiterating the consequences they might face. Perhaps he is aware that if they remain caught up in the pioneering experience, the Israelites might be less interested in their forebears' foibles. Maybe he feels he just has to bang them over the head with this one last time, and he pulls out all the stops to do it—he sings, he opens his mouth, and he pours out his heart, again and again, because he knows everything he has worked for is riding on this generation's ability to formulate some way of establishing a sense of continuity in their group identity.

I share his concern. There is a gulf separating GenQ from what is left of the Stonewall generation. I worry that we will not have enough sense of our history to navigate the next part of our journey wisely. We need bridges to our past, we need queer sages and elders, and we need to build on their experience and knowledge. When the Israelites left Egypt, they crossed the sea by way of a miracle. With no bridge, and no way to retrace their steps, they repeatedly romanticized their past. "We are sick of Manna! Let's go back to Egypt! At least we had onions, garlic and cucumbers back there, at least we had meat and fish!" (Num. 11:4–5, 14:3, 20:5). If it was so easy for the survivors of slavery to forget their oppression, then for those who never even lived through it, well, how much more so. Fortunately, Moses recognized, just in the nick of time, that he could be a link between the generation that left slavery and the generation that would enter the Promised Land. His ability to overcome his old impediments, even at the end of his life, is inspiring. What a gift he left queers and Jews as a role model, a poet, a teacher, an activist, and a pioneer. In the eleventh hour of his life, he still searched for and found the subtle language needed to establish the concept of *dor v'dor*.

The importance placed on Jewish group identity through Jewish continuity remains one of our guiding principles. Judaism holds tremendous value and respect for our elders, despite an increasing worldwide emphasis on youth culture. I love the intergenerational aspect of Jewish communal life. I love joking around after services with the *alte kockers* who stay for the *oneg*. I love seeing grandparents who haul across the country to listen to their progeny's progeny reading from the Torah for the first time. I love the Jewish kids and the babies and the baby boomers and the crinkly wrinkly old yidd'n and the cool-hip-young-multiethnic-pierced-and-tattooed Jews and the secular Israelis who will gather to celebrate, commemorate, or commiserate at the drop of a *kippah*. I love that the whole spectrum of the Jewish world continues to show up, creating richness, diversity, and an incredible sense of history. When I weigh the value of this multigenerationalism in Judaism, I feel that need for more intergenerational contact in the queer world is pressing. But there will need to be an attitude adjustment in queerland before this will happen.

> Our rabbis taught:[9] "You shall rise before the aged." Rabbi Yose the Galilean says: "The word 'aged' means only one who has acquired wisdom. . . ."
>
> Isi the son of Yehudah says: "'You shall rise before the aged' implies any aged person," and Rabbi Yohanan says: "The law is as Isi the son of Yehudah." Rabbi Yohanan used to rise before the heathen aged, saying, "How many troubles have passed over these."
>
> "The elder among them says before them words of admonition."
>
> Our Rabbis taught: "If there is an elder, the elder speaks. And if not, a Sage speaks. And if not, a man of [imposing] appearance speaks."
>
> But is the elder whom we mentioned [chosen] even if he is not a Sage? Abaye said: "He says thus: If there is an elder who is [also] a Sage, the elder who is a Sage speaks. And if not, a Sage speaks. And if not, a man of [imposing] appearance speaks."[10]

The opinion of our rabbis, *z"l*, that being an elder trumps being a sage and that being a sage trumps being attractive, is shocking by today's standard. The dominant paradigm today reverses the order. Elders are the chaff of our society, often ignored and shunted out of sight until a gust of deathwind simply blows them away. Our culture bends over backward to segregate the generations and holds youth and beauty above all. We have got Boomers, Yuppies, Gen X, Gen Y, Millennials, and the GWs (George W. and Global Warming). Most of our intergenerational interaction occurs in our families, while most of our socializing is with people within a five-year radius of our own age. LGBT folks, who may find themselves estranged from their family of origin as a reaction to being queer, are even more likely to live "homo-generational" lives. This leaves us learning most of our life lessons from peers. Certainly very few of us in the LGBTIQ community have queer parents or grandparents who could guide, initiate, or explain life's mysteries to us through a queer lens.

The chasm between LGBTIQ generations is even wider than it is for the general population. Ironically, the changes and advances in the social and political position of queerfolk have sometimes caused GenQ to look back and down on the ways and choices of the pre-Stonewall generation. Similarly, some of our elders never adjusted to life beyond the closet and passing.[11] Just as there were many Israelite slaves who did not follow Moses in the Exodus from Egypt, many homosexuals, either out of habit, fear, or a lack of belief, remained closeted; many of our people did not jump on the "gay liberation" bandwagon that started rolling after Stonewall. Without them, the queer generation gap is even wider.[12] Standing on the banks, ready to enter a postmodern promised land with loosened up attitudes toward gender and sexuality, it is easy to forget that to live as a queer person in America in the 1960s was to be in survival mode all the time. The closet was a foxhole, the binary gender system provided nifty disguises, heterosexuality was still compulsory, and the remains of the McCarthy witch hunts were still smoldering. Not everyone came out, true, but those who did surely have a lot to teach us.

We often look back with judgment and embarrassment at the lives of our forebears. They were stereotypical, cliché; they aped heterosexual behavior and presentation. They seem fundamentally different and therefore irrelevant to us. But we must remember that the difference between coming out in 1968 and now is staggering. Despite enormous advances, coming out is still a wrenching experience for many; the torment our forbears went through (before there was a Harvey Milk Institute, before Honey Labrador left modeling and became a lesbian-mom poster girl) is unimaginable. How long will we stand apart, like the columns of our Torah text, despite our shared message and common goal? Without our elders to bridge the gap, how are we going to really know ourselves, take our place at the table, and become elders ourselves? Will we spend our time repeating their mistakes, or will we draw from the well of their hard-earned pioneer wisdom? Now is the time to connect, to realize that we really are riding directly on the shoulders of our forerunners, to feel their strength beneath us, and to get ready for the next episode, *dor v'dor.*

NOTES

1. On June 27, 1969, a spontaneous protest to a routine vice-squad raid of the Stonewall Inn (a Greenwich Village gay bar) was led by homosexual and transvestite patrons. This event is widely accepted as the one that led to the formation of the gay liberation movement, which provided the foundation for the establishment of the global LGBTIQ community of the early 21st century.

2. Interestingly, the bookend to this text is *Shirat HaYam*, the Song of the Sea (Ex. 15:1–19),

which begins our sojourn in the desert. That text is also calligraphically distinctive, but it is laid out like overlapping bricks and is sung by Moses and B'nei Yisrael. It visually has the appearance of the beginning stages of cell division, whereas *Ha'azinu* appears as two distinct units.

3. For a scholarly treatment of this literary convention, see Robert Alter, *The Art of Biblical Poetry*, chap. 1: "The Dynamics of Parallelism," 3–27.

4. Ibid., 23.

5. Julia Kristeva coined the term *intertextuality* in 1966 to refer to the use of one piece of text to shape or influence another piece of text.

6. The first shift occurs at Deuteronomy 32:15; here the first verset is actually in the second column:

So Jeshurun grew fat and kicked/
You grew fat and gross and coarse—   He forsook the God who made him/
And spurned the rock of his support.   They incensed Him with alien things/
Vexed him with abominations.

7. "Big Ideas" is a term coined by Max Kiddushin to refer to core Hebraic values or concepts.

8. Exodus 3:15 uses the redundant phrase *L'dor dor*, literally "to generation generation," and similarly in Exodus 17:16 *mi'dor dor*, literally "from generation generation," both taken to mean "eternally" or "throughout time." The exact phrase *dor v'dor* with the conjunction "and" does not occur until this seminal moment at the end of both the Torah and Moses's life.

9. Babylonian Talmud, Tractate *Kiddushin* 32.

10. Babylonian Talmud, Tractate *Ta'anit* 16a.

11. For a fascinating presentation of first-person pre-Stonewall accounts, I highly recommend Dana Rosenfeld, *The Changing of the Guard: Lesbian and Gay Elders, Identity, and Social Change* (Philadelphia: Temple University Press, 2003).

12. For example, some who did not engage in the political struggle for gay rights did not feel a connection to the next generation, as exemplified in the following anecdote:

I have a nephew that's gay in Montreal, a college kid. And he came out to his mother and father when he was in college. I went home, and the mother said, "Manny, call Josh. Manny, call Josh." I said, "OK, I'll call Josh." So I'm leaving Montreal and I didn't call Josh. So Josh calls me: "Uncle Manny? You're leaving—I'm gay!" So I said, "What do you want me to do?" You know? (Manny—77 years old).

Ibid., 158.

FIFTY-FOUR

This Is the Blessing: The "First Openly Gay Rabbi" Reminisces

Parashat Zot Ha'bracha (Deuteronomy 33:1–34:12)

ALLEN BENNETT, *as told to* JANE RACHEL LITMAN

The thing about being a social pioneer is that when you are young, you are the "first," but when you are old, you are the last. This thought came to me as I squeezed in around a very large and crowded table of queer rabbis at a convention dinner. Putting aside the future shock of sitting with dozens of LGBT rabbis and their spouses, the strangeness of meeting in a public restaurant as an official body of the rabbinical organization (back in the old days, all of us could easily fit in someone's small hotel room at a secret late-night gathering arranged by word of mouth), the topper of the event for me was the round of introductions, as each rabbi—one after another—happily introduced his husband or her wife to the group. My friend Allen Bennett, "the first openly gay rabbi," whispered in my ear, "I'm so tickled, I could pee in my pants." I chuckled in assent. I could picture Allen and I sitting in rocking chairs on the porch of the Jewish Home for the Aged, the last queer rabbis in the world to use the words "lover" and "partner." Before that eventuality came to pass, it seemed appropriate to write a piece about Allen's gay rabbinical life, how it happened and the years that followed. This drash on the final parasha of the Torah, *Zot Ha'bracha*, which recounts the close of the life of Moses, is the result.

I am not comparing Allen Bennett to Moses, but the life stories told in Torah are powerful starting points for reflections about the life of the Jewish people, and the life of each Jew. The Torah's brief closing parasha asks the question, when does the central Jewish formative tale of oppression, liberation, wandering, and promise reach its conclusion? After this parasha, the narrative more or less continues in the book of Joshua, but it is a fundamentally different tale. The life of Moses and his Hebrew community is that of rebels and pioneers; Joshua and the emerging Israelite nation have other distinct stories and roles. From the present, looking back across the desert and forward to the promised land, the recent history of queer Jews mirrors the Torah's tale of oppression, liberation, and wandering, not (yet?) the early prophetic stories of conquest, settlement, and nation building. Each of us who has been part of this peculiar and powerful Jewish queer movement is a little bit Moses. Each of us who has been marching and writing and praying for all or part of these wandering desert years of struggle has learned about Torah and *bracha*. Perhaps Allen Bennett, from his unique position as the first, has learned just a bit more.

Allen Bennett's personal life story is a metaphor and a microcosm of the Jewish queer odyssey, just as Moses is the personification of the Jewish people's extraordinary religious journey of Exodus and Sinai. From his complex childhood to his last moments, laconically described in this last parasha, Moses represents what is best—and what is flawed—about the Jewish people in their transition from slavery to freedom. Similarly, Allen's story is bigger than he, and it epitomizes what is both the blessing and the curse of being Jewish and queer in our time.

No one really applies for the "first openly gay" mission. Jews have a long tradition of reluctant advocacy. When Allen was five, he knew he wanted to be a rabbi. On Sunday mornings, his friends playacted "temple" in religious school, and he was the rabbi. Always. But he never wanted to be a *gay* rabbi, and certainly not a pioneer or a leader. In the days of Moses's youth, there was no such thing as a free Jew. The very idea was a contradiction—slavery defined the Jewish experience. Reluctantly, Moses became the first free Jew and thus created possibilities for the entire Hebrew people. Similarly, in the 1950s there was no such thing as a gay rabbi. Heterosexuality was a definitional component of the rabbinate. Reluctantly, Allen Bennett changed that.

Allen heard the call to his gay identity in Jerusalem in 1970, the year after the Stonewall riots, that watershed event that marked the beginning of a widespread gay rights movement in the United States. For Allen, Jerusalem was Midian, far away from family and the American Jewish community, a place ripe for reflection and post-adolescent existential liberation. But unlike Moses, Allen's Jewish American parents came to visit. Allen responded by coming out to them. Allen's mother had always told him that "honesty was the best policy," but when Allen revealed his new sense of self, his mother replied, "You didn't have to be that honest." Allen's father, a Republican, worried about the social impact of having a gay son and threatened to have Allen "locked up."

Torah teaches us that becoming free is a lengthy struggle. In the '70s, the gay world and Allen's rabbinical world were completely separate. Earlier in Hebrew Union College's history, a student had killed himself after being outed. Being gay was considered a psychological aberration, and any known gay student would have been quickly asked to leave. Allen lived those student years in the closet, his own personal Egypt. He never looked for gay sex, but he found it anyway. Many years later, reflecting over a cup of tea, he confides to me that he could not have survived without those furtive physical contacts.

But there are also expansive moments as the Exodus approaches, the miracles, large and small. "Of course," Allen smiles, half hiding behind his teacup, "that said, there was the incident of the swimming pool." Moving toward freedom is a complex passage; in some way it allows for considerable risks, the risks needed to stay whole. Hebrew Union College in Cincinnati had an indoor swimming pool. Allen managed to procure a master key to the building that housed the pool. So Allen invited all his young gay male friends to a nude swim party at the seminary's gym. They were having a blast—this was during the pre-AIDS early 1970s—when there was a rap at the door. Allen hurriedly donned a towel and peeked out. It was the campus Matron of Dormitories. "Are you boys okay?" she asked. "Everyone's fine," replied Allen reassuringly.

Allen was ordained and began working as a congregational rabbi. He became engaged to a woman and, even then, expected that everything would "somehow" work out. At his prenuptial party, there was an informal "gay table." But relatively soon, Allen's marriage began to unravel. His wife was looking for a father figure, not a husband. Allen continued his semi-secret gay life. When his wife found out, she was hurt and angry and told his parents. Allen felt confused and betrayed but was also relieved to stop hiding. In that paradoxical unfolding of life, this betrayal of trust gave Allen the opportunity to become whole. Allen filed for divorce and moved to the San Francisco Bay Area, "Gay Mecca," as it was then called. This was Allen's passage through the Red Sea. It was no longer possible to return to the slavery of silence.

But Allen was still wandering in the desert. He took graduate classes with a vague idea of eventually teaching religion, and in the meantime, he worked at McDonald's. In 1978, the gay rights movement in California was galvanized by the Briggs Initiative, a ballot measure that would have outlawed the hiring of gay teachers. Several organizers against the initiative came to Allen and asked him to come out publicly to show the human face of homosexuality. Allen's out status became undeniable when *Time* magazine decided to run a piece about "the first openly gay rabbi" and sent a photographer to Allen's little apartment.

After the article appeared, Allen wondered if his ordination would be rescinded. He heard nothing for months. Then, students began to call. In the early years after Allen came out, perhaps two hundred students and rabbis contacted him for help. They were in dire straits—afraid of losing jobs and relationships, fearful of public humiliation, jail, blackmail. Like Moses in this portion, Allen found words of wisdom for the next generation. He told them, "*Asei l'cha chaver,* find yourself a friend. There is someone in your setting, probably straight, someone who can and will be an advocate for you. And there is always somewhere you can turn; you can always call me." This went on for about ten years, perhaps more, though an official response from the powers that be never materialized.

I am surprised when Allen tells me that no one calls him about these issues anymore. (I still get calls—not as many—and mostly from rabbinical students involved with non-Jews but occasionally from newly bisexual lesbians and every so often from transpeople). Allen does relate to me that sometimes a student or younger rabbi will meet him and say, "Oh, I've heard of you—weren't you lovers with Davey Crockett?" Allen looks at me and laughs: "When I was the first guy and they needed me, that was extraordinary. Talk about a calling! I got a calling every day. I'll tell you; I never felt abandoned by God. Sometimes I would tell God, 'Listen, it wouldn't have killed you to give me a better sense of how to cope with certain difficult situations.' But I always knew that God was there. If I ever felt abandoned, it wasn't by God but by people."

That first year of being a public gay figure, Allen decided to attend the Reform movement's annual rabbinical convention (the same convention of the restaurant dinner some twenty-seven years later). The then-president of Hebrew Union College took Allen aside and told him, "If I had known then what I know now, I'd have made certain that you would never have been ordained." The director of placement, the person in charge of finding jobs for rabbis, loudly proclaimed that Allen was a major embarrassment to the Reform movement and a danger to the future of the Jewish people. But not every rabbi was hostile. Jacob Rader Marcus, the dean of American Jewish historians, stood in the lobby watching his fellow rabbis arrive and waved Allen toward him. Marcus kissed Allen on both cheeks; "Bennett," he declared, "you've got balls. And you're going to need them."

Allen peeks out over his cup and laughs again:

You're pretty confident, Jane, with this Toraitic idea of coming to the promised land. It hasn't been forty years for us; for me we're still wandering in the desert. I don't count it from Stonewall the way you do. I don't even count from 1985, when Deborah Brin was ordained as an out lesbian at the Reconstructionist Rabbinical College. It took the Reform movement four more years after that, and the Conservative movement is still struggling. Its Israeli seminary won't ordain LGBT students. We're not at forty years, not even at twenty, not even halfway through the wilderness. We have an immense amount of work to do. Sexual-minority rabbis mostly undergo tremendous emotional agony, dealing with complex issues about authenticity and appropriate boundaries. People are still afraid to tell the truth about their lives, about their relationships, about their feelings. Just because we've made some progress doesn't mean we're there. When God takes Moses up that mountain, Moses doesn't say a thing, not a word. That doesn't mean he's disappointed because he won't be going to Israel. He's at the age where you look forward and also backward. He's quietly looking back and reflecting on all he's seen.

I ask, "Allen, when you look back to the desert and out to the Promised Land, what reflections do you have?"
He responds,

If I were at the border of the promised land, knowing I couldn't get in, which at this point would be fine, what would I say to the folks who are going to make it? I'd say, "Be true to yourself." I don't say it glibly; it's one of the most difficult challenges any of us face. It doesn't matter what our sexual identities are or if we're in a despised minority or if we're in a majority—it's still the biggest challenge. Whatever it costs you to live a life of integrity, you have to do it. Rabbis are role models, even if we don't choose it. I haven't always lived with integrity, and I regret that—but to live with myself, I need more integrity, not less. Queers aren't paranoid; there are people who are out to get us, I don't know why. It's hard. And we still need to enjoy ourselves when we're doing the best we can, even if we're not perfect. I'd say, "Make us proud of you. Let it be that everything we did was worth the effort."

Allen smiles at me one more time, "You know, Moses died through God's kiss. It's very romantic. His last exhalation was into God's mouth."

Amen.

PART VI

HOLIDAY PORTIONS

FIFTY-FIVE

The Parade of Families
Rosh Hashanah

JOSHUA LESSER

My family tended to arrive at Rosh Hashanah services early. We usually were not early enough for the red velvet cushioned seats, which were probably held for major donors anyway, but we were always in time to snag prime seats for the Rosh Hashanah catwalk. I used to call it the "Parade of Families." We did not belong to one of the more posh synagogues in Atlanta, but we still had what seemed like a fashion show every year on this one day when every family in the community would be in attendance. Contrary to the spirit of the holiday, we would make fun of outrageous outfits, especially the rare few who would show off their furs in the Indian summer of Georgia autumn.

As I got older, what became more interesting were the comments that would be made about families entering the sanctuary. People seemed inclined to disregard that the Yom Kippur contrition was only ten days away. I heard the juiciest gossip when tuning out the *chazzan* and listening really closely to those around me.

"Silverman, there, is filing for bankruptcy, and his wife next to him will certainly be leaving him soon, poor bastard."

"Jane hasn't been able to give birth. I think they are going to try adoption. So sad."

"Alex is here with the boys; Barbara left him for her OBGYN."

"Amanda and Ilan have their hands full; their twin girls are out of control."

Predictably, there was commotion over one couple's daughter coming out as a lesbian, and sadly people spoke with false sympathy about the grieving parents whose son was one of the first to die of AIDS in the Atlanta Jewish community. It dawned on me that it was unlikely that anyone was spared the parade critique, including my own family. It was at Rosh Hashanah as much as anywhere else that I learned a sense of shame and a need to hide what might not be normative about our family. Even if we were not a perfect Jewish family, I was determined that we could look like one in this parade.

Ironically, in the background of the Rosh Hashanah liturgy is the introduction to "the First Family of Judaism." Abraham, Sarah, and their miracle-child, Isaac, were introduced to me as an idealized Jewish family early on in my Orthodox upbringing. Our patriarch and matriarch were presented through midrashim, stories, and explanations, as the pinnacles of faith, hospitality, wisdom, goodness, and generosity. To question anything about them was heresy. This picture of perfection that was ingrained in me was so compelling that it took many years before I was able to de-construct these messages and connect to what the text actually says about them. I was taught that Abraham was the "perfect *tzadik*," the exemplar of righteousness, or so claimed Rashi in his commentary on *Parashat Noach,* when he compared Abraham's righteousness to Noah's righteousness. This idea was continuously expanded upon by rabbis and leaders in my Jewish world. Growing up in day school, I was taught mes-sages such as the following weekly e-teaching called *Parsha Parenting*:

> Such was the path of Avraham Avinu. He succeeded in saving not only his family, but brought tens of thousands of people to knowledge of HaShem, not through polemics or politics, but by following the ways of HaShem through abundant and abiding *chessed* (kindness). Therefore, he and Sarah are seen as true partners of HaShem in creation, as the Torah states, *hanefesh asher asu beCharan,* the souls that they made in Haran. This is true righteousness, which serves all of humanity.[1]

But once you read Genesis more closely and with open and critical eyes—partic-ularly the portions that lead up to the dramatic Rosh Hashanah readings—you find a complex family set with challenges. Abraham and Sarah have, using contemporary terminology, a non-normative family structure. For queer people this is promising. By letting the text speak for itself, rather than single-mindedly seeking evidence to prove what incredible spiritual parents Abraham and Sarah were, interesting and sur-prising models for family and parenting emerge.

Before I detail those models, I want to shed light on how the text is misread in the first place. Conservative theologians often accuse their progressive counterparts of the self-indulgence of "eisegesis," particularly in the Christian world. In James White's book *Pulpit Crimes: The Criminal Mishandling of God's Word*, he identifies eisegesis as one of the worst crimes of hermeneutics after the word crimes and defines the term as "the reading into a text, in this case, an ancient text of the Bible, of a meaning that is not supported by the grammar, syntax, lexical meanings, and over-all context, of the original. It is the opposite of exegesis, where you read out of the text its original meaning by careful attention to the same things, grammar, syntax, the lexical mean-ings of the words used by the author (as they were used in his day and in his area), and the over-all context of the document."[2] A prolific author and debater, White and others like him charge that people who try to justify pluralism, egalitarianism, and especially homosexuality textually are guilty of eisegesis by projecting their opinion or desire onto the text.

Although this charge may be true, it may not be a bad thing to read the Bible with contemporary needs and context in mind, especially if we think Biblical texts can evolve and need not remain static. More important, everyone—conservative clergy, academic scholars, and queer activists—reads the text through his or her own lenses, which makes conservative criticism all the more ironic, since it all too often simplistically reads monogamy, patriarchal gender conformity, heterosexuality, and idealized family structures into the texts of Genesis—interpretations that do not have integrity with a simple reading of the text. Whether it is the denial of the complex gender dynamics of the two creation stories and the possibility of Adam's being created intersexed as "male and female" or the interpretation of these Rosh Hashanah texts that claim Abraham and Sarah's superiority, conservative clergy tend to ignore the simplest readings. Doing so upholds much more rigid ideas about sex, partnership, and family then the text dictates. When we let the text guide us, we are open to more possibilities.

Immediately preceding the Rosh Hashanah text in the Torah, Abraham bemoans to God his childlessness and seeks to bestow the promised inheritance onto Eliezer, his servant (Gen. 15:2–3). He asks God to make Eliezer his heir, indicating that Eliezer is already like a son to him. Although in our Jewish story, Eliezer does not become the heir, it does not change the emotional relationship that Abraham feels for Eliezer, whom he refers to as faithful, like a family member. I do not think that it is a stretch that Eliezer appears to be an adopted family member or, stated less definitively, that the relationship they share opens up the possibility of adoption.

God's response also reminds us that adoption comes with complications. For queer people, for whom a family model based on adoption is often explicitly chosen, the connection between Eliezer and Abraham clearly resonates. Just like Abraham and Eliezer, many queer families are formed with ethnic or "tribal" differences between the adoptive parents and the children, and they establish a familial bond despite that difference. Too often, though, we pretend that such cultural and racial differences do not exist. Instead, we must find ways to integrate this diversity so that our families are comfortably dealing with the reality. Too often, queers do not enter into adoption prepared to address the complexities, hoping that the love they have for their children is enough. Unfortunately, our world is not yet a utopia, so ethically we cannot ignore the challenges of how society and, in our Rosh Hashanah story, God privileges biology over adoption, and we must strengthen the support of our families and prepare our children and families to be well equipped in the world to address the bias.

Another diversion from today's traditional model of family is that Abraham and Sarah choose a concubine. Sarah, by allowing her servant Hagar to have sex with Abraham so she would conceive and allow Sarah and Abraham to raise the child as their own, tries to create family another way. Children of concubines under Babylonian law were equivalent to slaves, but according to Biblical Jewish law, they hold equal status to their siblings from a legitimate wife.[3] This fact provides textual grounds for today's surrogacy, another queer avenue for creating family that we find embedded in our Rosh Hashanah text.

Although the text contains this option for family planning, it is not without its complications. Sarah is jealous of Hagar, and Hagar exploits Sarah's discomfort with her own infertility, causing tension to build until Hagar's expulsion. Although some readers may point to this outcome and say that it is reason for this alternative to be discouraged, I suggest that it is instead a lesson for anyone considering surrogacy: he or she should understand that there can be complications with this alternative if not handled well; unlike Abraham and Sarah's mishandling of surrogacy, we have the opportunity to look at the ethics and challenges of these situations.

Finally, though many people assume that Abraham and Sarah then procreated through the normal channels of marital intercourse, a closer reading of the text suggests something quite different. Just before the Rosh Hashanah reading, Genesis 17:11 notes Sarah's infertility, so when Sarah hears God's messengers saying they will return when Sarah gives birth, she laughs. God reproves her to Abraham, saying, in verse 14, "Is anything too wondrous for Adonai?" When the Rosh Hashanah portion begins a few chapters later, it opens with the ambiguous verb *pakad*, which people translate variously as "visited," "remembered," "took note of," or "fulfilled a promise." The first sentence of the portion harks back to God's earlier promise in Genesis 21:1, which says, "Adonai *pakad* Sarah as was promised; thus did Adonai as was spoken." She conceived and bore a son.

The *Jewish Daily Forward*'s "Philologos" column about language once addressed what *pakad* might mean:

> A repeated motif in the Bible is that of the woman who is unable to conceive until there is divine intervention on her behalf, after which she gives birth to a son who grows up to be a spiritual hero. This is the story of Sarah, of Rebecca, of Rachel and of Hannah. . . . Their pregnancies are divine miracles nonetheless—Sarah's even coming after menopause! Furthermore, the Hebrew verb used for God's intervention in such cases is pakad, as in va-adonai pakad et Sarah—a word that can be translated either as "remembered" or "visited," and that in the post-biblical Hebrew of the early Christian era even has the occasional sense of "had sexual intercourse with."[4]

Thus, we have God serving as an infertility specialist and even a hint of divine conception—yet another unconventional model for creating family. Today we have physicians serving as godly agents who have been sources of comfort as they have provided solutions for people seeking alternative ways for insemination. Although God serving as the donor is not one of them, we do have a potential reading of a Biblical precedent for alternative insemination.

Clearly, this First Jewish Family looks nothing like our so-called traditional or typical family. Were we to explore the Rosh Hashanah text further, we would see examples of rivalry between Sarah and Hagar and sibling rivalry between Ishmael and Isaac. Parental abandonment is found as Sarah and Abraham expel Ishmael along with Hagar. We then have the story of the Akedah, the binding of Isaac, involving attempted child sacrifice. If Abraham and Sarah walked down the aisle in my childhood synagogue, they would not have been spared the harsh light of "Families on Parade."

There are two lessons I take from this reading. First, if we emphasized the humanity and complexity of our First Jewish Family, perhaps more Jews would feel less shame and discomfort over the complexities of their own families, queer people especially. Second, we must highlight the different ways that Abraham and Sarah attempt to create families rather than project a reading of normalcy that the text does not bear out. Ironically, then, a literalist Biblical reading of the Jewish First Family gives us artificial insemination, surrogacy, multiethnic adoption, and other routes to finding complex family formations. In the Bible, the nuclear family *is* an alternative family. Furthermore, as Sarah's and Abraham's lives detail, family is complicated no matter how it is formed. Queer people need to be on the forefront of raising those complications, promoting education on alternative families, and preparing ourselves and others for the ethical issues that arise. That way the "Parade of Families" can celebrate diversity, not castigate or shame difference.

NOTES

1. Rabbi Shlomo Goldberg (the spiritual leader of *Yeshivas Ohr Eliyahu*), Commentary on *Parashat Noach* from the weekly *Parsha Parenting* column of Rabbi Goldberg hosted at www.torah.org.

2. James White, *Pulpit Crimes: The Criminal Mishandling of God's Word* (Vestavia Hills, AL: Solid Ground Christian Books, 2006), 3.

3. Louis M. Epstein, *The Jewish Marriage Contract: A Study in the Status of the Woman in Jewish Law* (New York: Jewish Theological Seminary, 1937), 123.

4. "Virgin Legend: On Language," Philologos, *Jewish Daily Forward,* August 27, 2004, www.forward.com/articles/5221/.

FIFTY-SIX

What Is Atonement?
Yom Kippur

DAVID GREENSTEIN

Traditionally, the annual cycle of Torah readings in the Jewish world operates according to two principles. The main organizing structure is the continuous reading (in one or three years' time) of the entire Torah from start to finish, and then back to start again. This system is all-inclusive, omitting nothing from the sacred text, with no concern for applicability or relevance to the season.

The other principle is the opposite of the first. It is selective, noncontinuous, and primarily determined by the timely relevance of the text chosen, even if that relevance is not immediately apparent. That principle is put into effect for the Torah portions publicly read during the holy days of the year—the Days of Awe, the Festivals, and other special days in our calendar. The interaction of these two principles guarantees that Torah portions read during a holy day will also be read during the regular cycle as well. Such a portion is thus read twice, at least, once in its set place along the continuous scroll of the Torah and again during a particularly relevant occasion.

This structure raises the question of the special relevance of the traditional Yom Kippur readings for this most sacred day—the annual Day of Atonement, a time of Divine forgiveness, purification, and reconciliation. This moral and spiritual cleansing applies to every individual and to the nation as a whole.

We should notice that any number of other texts that might have been deemed relevant to the themes of Yom Kippur were not chosen. We do not read the Ten Commandments, for example, or the declaration of God's mercy and forgiveness that, the rabbinic tradition teaches, was first uttered on Yom Kippur. Instead, on Yom Kippur morning we read the description of the High Priest's temple ritual for Yom Kippur (Lev. 16), and on Yom Kippur afternoon we cover the listing of forbidden sexual relations (Lev. 18).

The morning reading, which describes how Aaron, the High Priest, entered the sanctuary to seek atonement from God in a murky cloud of incense, is a bit arcane for modern readers and listeners. But it must be conceded that it is connected with Yom Kippur. In Temple times it was read out loud by the High Priest right after he had finished performing all the rituals delineated therein (Mishnah, *Yoma* 7:1). At that time, the reading could have served as a confirmation and guarantee of Divine atonement, since all the rules had been followed. Even after the destruction of the Temple, our liturgists clearly felt that the Temple rite of Yom Kippur was essential to the nature of the day, for they insisted on incorporating the reenactment of the priestly rites—the *Avodah*—into the synagogue service. Still, its continued relevance today is up for discussion. Is it simply a memento of times past, or does it have more urgent significance?

But a far greater problem for modern Jews is the assignment of Leviticus 18 as the afternoon reading. The problem here is twofold. First, it is not immediately clear why this whole topic is chosen for this public reading. It certainly lacks the inspirational quality we would prefer. In addition, this section includes the key verse (18:22) used for millennia by Christians and Jews as a scriptural warrant to condemn homosexuality.

This problem has impelled some communities (including most Reform, Reconstructionist, and Renewal congregations, along with many independent and some Conservative congregations) to substitute other readings for this selection. The most popular practice is to replace the afternoon reading of Leviticus 18 with another section of the Holiness Code, Leviticus 19:1–18, which contains a listing of ethical and ritual precepts beginning with a call for the people of Israel to be holy and concluding with the verse "Love your neighbor as yourself; I am God" (19:18). Other congregations maintain the ancient practice of reading the Levitical sexual prohibitions but adopt a method of reading reminiscent of how we read the two versions of the "Admonition," the Torah's horrific catalogue of curses and sufferings visited on Israel. In the order of the traditional yearly cycle, one version, Leviticus 26, is read shortly after Passover. The other version, Deuteronomy 28:15ff., is read shortly before Rosh Hashanah. We read the verses in a self-consciously hushed and hurried undertone. In this way we may follow tradition and simultaneously express our pain and our protest. This approach can be a powerful expression of outrage, but it leaves the content of the text unexplored. Is it possible to engage the text in a way that promotes its appropriateness as a reading for the Day of Atonement?

I have offered elsewhere a detailed argument for an alternative understanding for Leviticus 18:22,[1] the classic verse used to condemn homosexuality. I explain that standard Biblical terminology and usage allow us to read that verse in an entirely new way. In this reading, the verse has nothing to do with prohibiting homosexual intercourse. The prohibited act, "*mishk'vei ishah*," actually refers to heterosexual intercourse. The prohibition is against one male engaging in sexual relations with a woman (*v'et*) "along with" (*zakhar*) another male. The prohibition is against two males forcing themselves on a woman.[2]

Now this reading is hardly the common understanding within the Jewish community. So, if one were to choose to read the traditional text in this new way, one would have to use the reading as a platform for discussion and teaching, for *targum*—public translation and explication of the text. What are some of the elements that would be part of that discussion? The new reading suggested here, while it denies any stigma with regard to homosexual intercourse, leaves the larger issue of sexuality and sexual practices before us. And that is as it should be. For the mysterious entry of the High Priest into the Holy of Holies is very much a sexually charged drama. The entire rite is punctuated over and over by the priest's bathing of his body. To enter the holy chamber he must divest himself of the garments of the High Priest, entering with only the simplest linen coverings. Inside he will sprinkle drops of blood with his finger.

We often think of atonement—the central element of Yom Kippur—as a gift bestowed on us by God. It is a gracious gift that flows from the Divine toward us. But this text alerts us to a reciprocal aspect of this act. When atonement happens, we are not the only ones acted on. Something happens to God as well. The act of atonement is, at least in part, an act of permitted penetration. The atonement of Israel is assured because God has allowed the Divine "insides" to be entered and bloodied. Atonement is attained through at-one-ment. This parsing of the word *atonement* into its Old English components reminds us that the process of forgiveness and purification is for the purpose of uniting—"at-one-ment"—with one's beloved, human or Divine.

It is no wonder, therefore, that this solemn day was also a day of erotic celebration in ancient times. The daughters of Jerusalem, usually cloistered away in their patriarchally controlled homes, would, on this Day of Atonement, dance outside and invite the young men to choose their mates (Mishnah, *Ta'anit* 4:8; Babylonian Talmud, *Ta'anit* 26b).

Atonement is to be celebrated; but it is not to be assumed. The afternoon reading warns us all—however we experience our sexuality—that our sexuality must be sanctified through discipline and limitation. The new reading suggested here, as it cancels the prohibition on homosexual activity per se, inserts into the Torah a set of concerns hitherto neglected by traditional readings—the need to grant permission for sexual activity. As our traditional readings stand now, the Torah never explicitly prohibits or punishes forced intercourse between people who are not married.[3]

This new reading moves in the direction of establishing a different set of Torah criteria for the sacred process of achieving at-one-ment.

This connection between the morning reading and the afternoon reading manifests itself in the seemingly offhand reference that opens the morning Torah portion. The Yom Kippur instructions are given to Aaron "after the death of the two sons of Aaron, as they drew near before God and died" (Lev. 16:1). In some unexplained way, these two young men die as they try to penetrate the Holy. In their case, entry was denied. The new rituals that are outlined in the Torah after this introductory verse are designed to allow entry into the Divine space without further death and loss.

If we imagine the process that Aaron had to undergo in order to accept and perform these rituals, we may also gain a model for our own engagement with these readings. Aaron hears these words after suffering a terrible tragedy. His reactions, as recorded by the Torah, follow these steps: First, he is silent (Lev. 10:3). Then, he insists on his right to mourn, even in defiance of God's demands, for God had demanded that Aaron partake of a festive meal to celebrate the dedication of the Sanctuary. Aaron, in his grief, refuses to do so. When an angry Moses decries his failure to follow God's instructions, Aaron firmly replies that he cannot imagine that God does not accept his decision regarding what is required in the Divine service. He overturns Moses's original understanding of what God requires because he knows that his feelings are sacred in themselves. And Moses acquiesces (Lev. 10:16–20). And now Aaron is ready to assume new functions on behalf of Israel, to enter the holy precincts and achieve atonement "for himself, for family and for the entire congregation of Israel" (Lev. 16:17).

Similarly, the LGBT community can hardly hear these readings without an initial sense of mourning and loss. How many have suffered and, yes, died, as their efforts to enter the holy failed or were denied? The next step is to ground a new understanding of God's Will on that very sense of pain and outrage. And then the community must undertake the task of reentering the sacred text so as to achieve a more genuine reconciliation and healing—unforced, reciprocal, forgiving, and finally exuberant—a true fulfillment of the goal of the Day of Atonement.

NOTES

1. For a concise version, see David Greenstein, "Parashat Aharei Mot and Parashot Kedoshim: On Gaining Access to the Holy," available online at Jewish Mosaic's Torah Queeries project at http://www.jewishmosaic.org/torah/show_torah/72; for the full essay, see David Greenstein, "Open the Gates of Righteousness for Me," *Journal of the Academy for Jewish Religion* 3, no. 1 (2007), available online at http://www.ajrsem.org/uploads/docs/article_greenstein.pdf.

2. For more detail on this verse, and to explore other interpretations, see the essays in this volume by Elliot Dorff (*Acharei Mot*), David Brodsky (*Kedoshim*), and Jay Michaelson (*Metzora*).

3. See David Brodsky's essay on *Parashat Vayishlach* in this volume.

FIFTY-SEVEN

Strength through Diversity
Sukkot

LINDA HOLTZMAN

It was 1979. I had just graduated from rabbinical school and moved to the small town where I would serve as rabbi. For Sukkot, I had decided to build a sukkah (for the first time) and invite my congregation to have Kiddush in it following Shabbat morning services. I was thrilled. As a closeted lesbian, I rarely gave my congregation glimpses into my personal life, and this felt like an important opportunity. I decorated; I baked; I prepared every detail. I went to sleep on Friday night looking forward to the next morning. When I awoke and looked outside, I was crestfallen. The fierce winds that had sprung up during the night had broken apart the entire sukkah, which now lay in pieces on my front lawn. This was not surprising: I was a novice builder, the winds were strong, and the sukkah was fragile. Yet it felt as if something more had occurred, a deeper message was implicit within the collapse of my sukkah.

Sukkot is a grand holiday: celebrating the harvest, confronting us with the tenuous nature of our mortality, placing us in the ancient Israelites' long journey through the desert, reminding us of God's sukkah of peace. Yet there is even more hidden within Sukkot. The sukkah is a fragile reminder of the breadth and diverse nature of our harvest. We decorate with gourds, grapes, pumpkins, and corn, with cranberries, apples, squash, and flowers. Into this mix of natural diversity, we invite human diversity. The custom of *Ushpizin*, of welcoming guests and visitors from the past into the sukkah, is a custom that grew out of the desire of medieval mystics to welcome in our ancestors who embodied the qualities that form the essence of our character: we invite Abraham, Isaac, Jacob, Sarah, Miriam, Deborah, Joseph, Moses, Aaron, David, Avigail, Hannah, Huldah, and Esther. These characters embody kindness and strength, justice and compassion, patience and determination, wisdom and spiritual depth. Within them are the qualities that we need in order to be whole.

Yet they are not enough. If Sukkot is a time of celebrating the diversity in the natural world, it must also be a time of celebrating all of us diverse humans. We add to our *Ushpizin*, our visitors list, those people who have lived but have not always been included in a Sukkot celebration. We invite LGBT people of previous generations who were not welcome in their families' Sukkot. We invite everyone who has worked toward a more accepting, more open world. We invite all who have challenged our society's "traditional" family structure, all whose courage has enabled them to make a difference. And we invite the parts of ourselves that are queer, that are not easily accepted in our world, that challenge us to live outside the box. The sukkah is always open to the elements and to everything that surrounds it. A sukkah has no doors. All the parts of ourselves can find room within its walls; indeed, it is the strength from this diversity that lets the sukkah stand.

Once we invite everyone into the sukkah and once we invite all of ourselves into the sukkah, we are ready to perform the ritual that is at the heart of Sukkot: we wave the *etrog* (citron) and *lulav* (palm, willow, and myrtle branches tied together). An automatic response to the etrog and lulav upon seeing them is to think of the lulav as a male symbol and the etrog as female. The lulav is long and thin and reaches straight up when one holds it. The etrog is the size and approximate shape of a large lemon. As they are waved, the lulav extends outward, the palm branch making a potent statement, while the etrog is closer to the waver's body, less outer-directed. If we put the two together, one might say, there are both male and female represented. Yet that would be a limited understanding of the symbolism of the lulav and etrog.

An etrog is not just round and lemony. Its fragrance is bold, and it is the only one of the four items that is waved to stand independently; the others are tied together. The etrog is bright and dramatic in its presentation, scrutinized closely for any possible imperfections by those who purchase it. If a leaf is removed from any of the other items, the item can still be used; if the tip is broken off the etrog, it is rendered unusable. In Jewish symbology, the etrog is often seen as representing a person's heart, the vital center of an individual. By virtue of its strong taste and fragrance, it is seen as a person who is steeped in learning and who also performs good deeds. The etrog is a complex being.

A lulav is complex as well. It is three very differently shaped leaves tied together. There is an enormous range: from the long, pointy palm frond to the almost round tiny myrtle leaves to the slim, floppy willow leaves. When a lulav is waved, the scent is not great, but the sound of one leaf rustling against another coupled with the sight of a long, graceful palm branch waving creates a powerful impression. The lulav symbolizes the spine (palm), the eyes (myrtle), and the mouth (willow). Held together with the etrog, essential parts of a human body are represented: that which keeps it alive and enables it to stand, to see, and to speak. Each leaf on the lulav represents a different kind of person: the willow has neither taste nor smell, so it is a person who has no learning and who performs no good deeds; the myrtle has smell but no taste, thus learning but no good deeds; and the willow has taste but no smell, so good deeds but no taste. Together with the etrog, everyone is represented in the waving.

It seems clear that the etrog and lulav represent all the people in the world in very different ways. Together, they represent people with diverse sexualities and genders, lesbian, gay, bisexual, transgender, questioning: all queer people and those who are not queer coming together to wave in the sukkah. It is necessary for all kinds of people to be represented to keep the sukkah standing. As a house, the sukkah is a fragile one, not too sturdy and not able to remain standing in a storm unless it gains its strength from the energy generated by the waving within its walls.

The etrog stands alone. It is a queer person who resists blending in with the community, who never follows the community's norms. Everyone notices the etrog and appreciates its vibrancy but hopes it can be held close enough to the rest of the community to get support and nurturance from it. The etrog needs to feel whole to accomplish what it strives for in the world, and once it is broken, the etrog can never fully heal. However close the etrog may be with the parts of the lulav, it is always somewhat apart. The etrog could be the heart of the community, but it is always on its own. Its sense of pride stems from its individuality.

The lulav is a bustling, lively community of diverse types of people. Though tall and sedate, the palm is surrounded by frilly branches. It is a variety of people, all finding different roads to fulfillment, different life choices, different ways of being. When the lulav is waved, it is a celebration of all the diversity possible within the world. Its sense of pride stems from its community. Together with the separate, individualistic etrog, the lulav makes a strong statement: *only together can they keep the sukkah standing.* My sukkah did not stand, which metaphorically reminded me of my closeted identity. I could not yet bring together all the parts of myself. I could not yet fully celebrate openly as a Jew and a lesbian. Sukkot is a holiday of welcome, of openness, and of diversity. It would not be the same if the etrog or any part of the lulav were left out. It would not be the same if they were not all fully celebrated. And it would not be the same if in opening up our Sukkot to the people to whom we look back for inspiration, we left out those LGBT people whose very lives gave us the courage to live our own lives fully and freely.

When I put up my sukkah this year, I expect it to remain standing for the whole week of Sukkot. As we wave the etrog and lulav, I will give thanks to all who made it possible for my life to take the shape it has. I will give thanks to all who have taken unexpected paths, unusual journeys into uncharted waters. Each Sukkot, we are thankful for the harvest that they have given us and for the beauty and diversity that they brought into the world. Sukkot is known as "the time of our rejoicing." It is the great variety of people who enter the sukkah each year who make it a time of real joy.

FIFTY-EIGHT

Ad de'lo Yada: Until We Don't Know the Difference
The Book of Esther and Purim

GREGG DRINKWATER *and* ELLIOT KUKLA

> All Prophetic Books and the Sacred Writings will cease to be recited
> in public during the messianic era except the Book of Esther. It will
> continue to exist just as the five books of the Torah . . . will never
> cease.
>
> —Rambam[1]

Why does the book of Esther—the source of the Purim story and the text read aloud
on the holiday—warrant such special status that it figures in the rabbinic dream of a
perfect Messianic future?[2] After all, it is the most secular Biblical book, with no reference to prayer, Jewish rituals, the Temple, or even God's name.[3] And why will the
significance of Esther, an uppity intermarried Jewish woman, last in an era when the
writings of the mighty prophets—including Isaiah, Ezekiel, and Jeremiah—will have
faded away into irrelevance?

These questions ask us to look beneath the surface of this deceptively simple text.
In the world of the book of Esther, and in the carnivalesque traditions of the holiday of Purim, everything (including our preconceptions of Judaism) is turned upside
down. The book of Esther—and indeed Purim itself—is about the holiness of transgression and the redemptive potential of masquerade.

The story begins with Esther hiding her Jewish identity to become the wife of the
Persian king Ahasuerus. She disguises herself by performing (in a kind of Near Eastern drag) as a non-Jewish Persian woman, to win the king's favor and ultimately to
save her people from an edict of destruction orchestrated by the story's villain, the
scheming Haman. In this text, disguise and the transgression of social norms lie at
the heart of redemption, teaching us that the hidden self can be the true hero of the
story and that masquerade can save the entire people. This is why the vision that the
book of Esther communicates is so compelling for the ancient Sages and for contemporary queer folk alike.

The blurring both of personal identity and of social boundaries, as embodied by
Esther, is the key to the significance of Purim and helps us understand why the book
of Esther is connected to rabbinic dreams of Messianic redemption. As any student
of Talmud or other classical Jewish texts soon learns, in the Jewish sacred imagination the realm of the possible is constantly expanding, and there is rarely a yes or no

answer to any question. The book of Esther and so many of Judaism's other sacred texts seem to be reminding us to expect the unexpected, to search for the hidden meaning, and do not be so quick to assume that what you see before you, the literal or *peshat* level of understanding, is ever the ultimate truth (or even that an "ultimate" truth exists).

Traditions have developed to help us focus on this lesson every Purim in an experiential way. Our Sages teach that on Purim, we must drink "*ad de'lo yada*" (until we do not know)—until we are so drunk that we do not know the difference between the blessed Mordechai (who, along with Esther, is the story's other hero) and the cursed Haman. The point of this exercise is not simply to release our inhibitions but to free our mind-set from its rigid socialization—to see for ourselves that there is no such thing as opposites but rather infinite diversity.

As the Rebbetzin Hadassah Gross noted in a special Purim essay that launched the online Torah Queeries project in 2006 (www.jewishmosaic.org/torah), "Purim is dedicated to the courageous peeling away of labels, unmasking the safety of the familiar and entering the delicious territory of the unknown." She goes on to encourage us "to piously observe the important laws of Purim—especially the ones that ask us to go beyond the law, peel the label, turn the table, and drink the night away. Yes. Drink, *kinderlach*, or whatever it takes to blur the differences until you don't know the difference between . . . Mordechai or Haman, Jew or Gentile, man or woman, straight or gay, *meshugena* or *mentsch*. From this upside-down folly, taken seriously, much redemption is born to the soul!"[4]

We learn in the Talmud that Yom Kippur, the most solemn day of the year, is the most spiritually alike to Purim, the silliest day of the year. Our Sages read the name of the Day of Atonement as "Yom Ha-Ki-Purim," which literally means "A Day like Purim." At first glance, no two holidays could be more different, but when we look closer there are surprising similarities. Both holidays ask us to suspend our daily behaviors and step out of our realities: Yom Kippur through abstaining from food, drink, and sex; Purim by reveling in these worldly pleasures. By placing these two holidays together our tradition once again teaches us to release the idea of binary opposites and embrace a more complex reality. Redemption comes when we are ready to blur the boundaries of social norms, question the limits of our own minds, and expand our vision of the possible.

It is true that the Sages often seem obsessed with boundaries and generally tried to sort the world into binaries. But they also acknowledged that not all parts of God's creation can be contained in orderly boxes and struggled to find ways to sanctify what lies in between. Distinctions between Jews and non-Jews, Shabbat and the days of the week, purity and impurity are crucial to Jewish tradition. However, it was the parts of the universe that defied human categories that interested the rabbis of the Mishna and the Talmud the most. Pages and pages of sacred texts are occupied with the minute details of the moment between fruit and bud, wildness and domestication, innocence and maturity, the twilight hour between day and night.

For example, we read in the Babylonian Talmud, "Our sages taught: As to twilight, it is doubtful whether it is part day and part night, or whether all of it is day or all of it is night."[5] We might have thought that the blurriness of twilight would have made it forbidden within Jewish tradition. But in fact our Sages determined that dawn and dusk, the in-between moments, are the best times for prayer. Jewish tradition acknowledges that some parts of God's creation defy categories, and these liminal people, places, and things are often the sites of the most intense holiness. After all, the word for *kedusha*, "holiness," in Hebrew literally means "set apart" or "out of the ordinary." It should come as no surprise, then, that the Hebrew Bible is filled with characters, such as Esther, who have transgressed boundaries and crossed over apparently rigid lines to help the Jewish people and the Jewish tradition continue to grow.

As in our sacred texts, those in our contemporary world who live at the borders are often the ones who expand the boundaries of our society. The individuals who are not easy to fit into our categories of race, class, religion, ethnicity, religion, ability, sexual identity, and gender are the ones that help us question our narrow assumptions and challenge the limited imaginations that keep us from embracing the true abundantly diverse potential of being created in God's image. When we focus on surface appearances and refuse to look deeper, we limit ourselves and fail to heed the lesson of Purim. We miss the hidden gem, the profound truth of our diversity, and the prophetic gifts that boundary crossers bring to our world.

The author(s) of the classic Jewish mystical text the Zohar teaches that when angels wish to descend from the upper world, they put on earthly garments. As with angels, the Zohar suggests, how much more so of the Torah itself—the narratives of the Torah are its garments.

> He who thinks that these garments are the Torah itself deserves to perish and have no share in the world to come. Woe unto the fools who look no further when they see an elegant robe! More valuable than the garment is the body which carries it, and more valuable even than that is the soul which animates the body. Fools see only the garment of the Torah, the more intelligent see the body, the wise see the soul, its proper being.[6]

The story of Esther is one of those "garments" that shrouds a deeper meaning, and the traditions of Purim—the drink, the costumes, and the revelry—help us peer beyond the surface, even if only for a day. By so doing, we cross boundaries, encounter the hidden, and come one step closer to redemption.

A queer approach to Torah has redemptive value for all people, regardless of gender or sexuality. We read in the Psalms, "The rock that the builders rejected has become the cornerstone" (118:22). The term "cornerstone," *rosh pina*, refers to the foundation of the Temple that will be rebuilt in a more perfect Messianic age. In other words, those that have been thrown away, misread, ignored, or discounted can become the base of a society reborn. By opening our doors, eyes, and hearts to those that are falling between the cracks of the rigid lines we draw, we can renew and rebuild our Judaism. When the rock that has been rejected becomes the cornerstone of a more open society, we will be able to express our full human potential in infinite expressions of our uniqueness.

"*Ad de'lo yada*," our Sages tell us. Look beyond the boundaries, celebrate the hidden, and be blessed by the abundant diversity of our world.

NOTES

1. Mishneh Torah, *Megillah* 2:18, Maimonides (Rambam), as translated by Philip Birnbaum in his abbreviated Hebrew/English edition of the Mishneh Torah published in 1967.

2. The most often cited reason for the Sages' vision of the book of Esther's staying power is its focus on Jewish continuity against all odds. Just when the Jewish people faced another grave threat to their very existence, a Jewish heroine, Esther, saved the day. As Rabbi Yitzchak Etshalom notes in his online essay "The Days of Purim," in the messianic era, the "essential miracle of Jewish existence [recorded in the book of Esther] which will have made Messianic redemption possible will never be forgotten." Yitzchak Etshalom, "The Days of Purim," Torah.org, http://www.torah.org/learning/rambam/special/mt.sp.purim.html.

3. Adele Berlin, "Esther," in *The JPS Bible Commentary* (Philadelphia: Jewish Publication Society of America, 2001).

4. Rebbetzin Hadassah Gross (the alter ego of Amichai Lau-Lavie), "High Healing: A Purim Message," Jewish Mosaic, http://www.jewishmosaic.org/torah/show_torah/6.

5. Tractate *Shabbat* 34b.

6. Zohar, iii, 152, as cited by Joseph Jacobs and Isaac Broyde, "Zohar," in *The Online Jewish Encyclopedia*.

ლლლლლლლლლლლლლლლლლლლლლლლლლლლლლლლლლლლ

FIFTY-NINE

Liberation and Transgender Jews
Passover

AYELET COHEN

Jews prepare for the holiday of Passover in their kitchens and in their liturgy like little else in the Jewish year. The holiday is preceded by weeks of special Shabbat readings, building up to the festival, and the traditional dietary requirements of the holiday require intensive spring cleaning. Yet ironically, all the Passover preparation that Jews do is intended to help them remember the last-minute rush that was the Exodus from Egypt.

The Israelites left Egypt in such tremendous haste that the Torah had to create a word for it. Nothing before had ever happened in such a hurry, with such trepidation, and with such fear. The Children of Israel were leaving everything they knew for the promise of something completely unknown—and their lives depended on it. The Torah introduces the word *chipazon* for this intense combination of hurry and fear. This is how the Israelites first tasted freedom. "This is how you shall eat it," they were told, "your belts fastened, your sandals on your feet, and your walking stick in your hand; and you shall eat it hurriedly, *bechipazon*" (Ex. 12:11).

Passover is known as "the Time of Liberation." The Jewish festival of spring, it celebrates the rebirth of the Israelites as a free people after the Exodus from Egypt and their liberation from slavery. The Haggadah, the telling of the Passover story that is the guiding text of the Passover seder, takes participants through an experiential journey from slavery into liberation. Its unusual rituals, interactive atmosphere, and special foods that evoke the taste of oppression and the taste of freedom are all intended to spark questions and inspire conversation about the Israelites' history of slavery and the nature of freedom. "Why do we carry out all these rituals?" participants will be moved to ask. The Haggadah gives the simplest and most fundamental answer:

Avadim Hayinu l'Pharoh b'mitzrayim. Veyotzieinu Adonai Eloheinu misham b'yad chazakah u'bizroa netuyah.

We were slaves to Pharaoh in Egypt. And God brought us out from there with a strong hand and an outstretched arm.

The Passover Haggadah reminds us that in every generation all Jews are obligated to see themselves as if they had personally left Egypt. Jews know Egypt. Jews in every generation have too often experienced "Egypt," or *mitzrayim,* narrow places in which they have been enslaved—physically or metaphorically—and silenced for being who they are.[1] Gay, lesbian, and bisexual Jews are particularly well suited to fulfill the commandment to remember and personally identify with the experience of the Exodus, for everyone who has left the closet has known Egypt and has left Egypt in his or her lifetime.

But what if *mitzrayim* was not a place or not even a set of expectations or societal norms or religious prohibitions or legal limitations? What if *mitzrayim* was your own body? And every time you looked at your reflection, every time someone called you by your name, you knew that you were imprisoned, enslaved in a body that was not your home? What if like the generations of Israelites born in Egypt, you were born into that narrow place? And even though you had never known anything else, you knew in your heart of hearts that you did not belong there?

For so many transgender people, that is the experience of the world. Every day they are called by names that do not describe them and dressed in clothing that feels foreign to them. Forced by birth or by society to inhabit a body that does not belong to them, they must move through the world betraying their knowledge of themselves or transgressing the definitions and roles of male and female that this culture holds so sacred.

Avadim Hayinu l'Pharoh b'mitzrayim.

We were slaves to Pharaoh in Egypt.

There is no one transgender experience. Each transgender person is coming from a different place, and each chooses a different journey. For no one is that journey easy. For a transgender person every moment can be complicated, and even the most mundane can become dangerous. Which bathroom to choose? Which will be safer, and where will you be less likely to get harassed? There is no one right answer. Every moment might require a different reaction and a different response.

Judaism, for better or for worse, loves categories. It likes to know what things are, to name them, and to keep them separate. The sacred is separated from the ordinary, *Shabbat* from the six days of creation, dairy from meat, woman from man. The priestly system of the Israelites, the origins of which are found in Leviticus, created a whole system of holiness around these separations. Trying to create order in a world they did not always understand, the priests tried to legislate holiness through separation, believing that was the surest means of carrying out divine will. These distinctions were further developed in Rabbinic Judaism, which cemented the bifurcated gender roles in the religious sphere. Men and women were seen as having different spiritual needs and a different connection to the divine. Only men were full spiritual adults, with women subject to fulfilling their husbands' or fathers' needs before they could turn to their own religious obligations.

Just as men and women sit separately in Orthodox synagogues, separated by a *mechitzah*, Orthodox women and men say different blessings every morning. In

Orthodox communities to this day, every morning men say, "*Baruch atah adonai shelo asani Ishah* / Blessed are You, God . . . that I was not created a woman." And women say, "*Baruch atah adonai sh'asani kirtzono* / Blessed are You, God . . . for making me according to your will."

In egalitarian Jewish communities, such separations make little sense, and many of them have been dissolved. In these communities, everyone sits together in the synagogue, and every adult is counted as a full participant in religious services and may take part in leading the community in prayer. The morning blessings in progressive, and egalitarian communities have long since been amended so that men and women both recite the same blessing, praising God for having been created in the divine image. Progressive Judaism does not rely on upholding the Levitical categories of separation in order to achieve holiness. Holiness is sought through individual and communal connection to God, through prayer, study, and action. But despite these equalizing measures, egalitarian Jewish communities have not actually collapsed traditional gender boundaries, nor have most gay and lesbian communities done so. Although these gender categories are no longer seen to have communal value or spiritual or Jewish legal significance, they still hold tremendous emotional weight.

An astounding poem by the Israeli poet Yehuda Amichai, Israel's poet laureate, expresses a little boy's despair at being trapped on the wrong side of those categories, on the wrong side of the *mechitzah*.

> I studied love in my childhood synagogue
> In the women's section with the help of the women behind the partition
> That locked up my mother with all the other women and girls.
> But the partition that locked them up locked me up
> On the other side. They were free in their love while I remained
> Locked up with all the men and boys in my love, my longing.
> I wanted to be there with them and to know their secrets
> And say with them, "Blessed be God who has made me
> According to His will." And the partition—
> A lace curtain white and soft as summer dresses, swaying
> On its rings and loops of wish and would,
> *Lu-lu* loops, lullings of love in the locked room.
> And the faces of women like the face of the moon behind the clouds
> Or the full moon when the curtain parts: an enchanted
> Cosmic order. At night we said the blessing over the moon outside, and I
> Thought about the women.[2]

Amichai's child is on the wrong side of the *mechitzah*. And it is not funny and it is not tragic and it is not grotesque. It is deeply Jewish and deeply personal and profoundly real. We need to understand that this child is nowhere else but in the depths of *mitzrayim*.

Avadim Hayinu l'Pharoh b'mitzrayim.

The fact that gender is complicated is not a new idea for the Jews. As much as they liked categories, the sages of Jewish tradition were aware of a certain fluidity of gender. Although they were limited in their understanding of gender by their focus on biology and sexual acts, we know from the Mishnah that the Rabbis were aware of at least four genders—male, female, *tumtum,* and *androginos,* a theme explored in the essays in this volume by Charlotte Fonrobert, Margaret Wenig, and Rachel Biale.

But are we more highly evolved today? Even within the gay and lesbian community transgender people often face ignorance and discrimination. And in the straight world every day they are subjected to ridicule and targeted for discrimination and are too often victims of horrific violence. Again and again transgender people are denied legal protections even as gay men and lesbians are finally achieving them.

Avadim Hayinu l'Pharoh b'mitzrayim.

We have a great deal of work to do. Although individual transgender people have pursued their own liberation, the transgender community is still very much experiencing *mitzrayim.* Michael Waldman, a transgender member of Congregation Beth Simchat Torah in New York, shared with me what liberation might look like for him:

> Liberation from society's expectations and assumptions, and liberation to become who you are. It's definitely a journey. And you don't quite know where you're going to end up, even if you know that you have to move/change. It's about having trust that if you follow that internal voice, you will be led to a better place, where you don't have to think about killing yourself quite so often.

Avadim Hayinu L'Pharoh b'mitzrayim

The Israelites in Egypt ate the Passover sacrifice, their first taste of freedom, in *chipazon*—in haste and in fear. Today, Jews eat matzah on Passover to remember their flight from Egypt, their *chipazon.* The Torah tells us that for seven days "you shall eat unleavened bread, bread of distress—for you departed from the land of Egypt hurriedly—*bechipazon*—so that you may remember the day of your departure from the land of Egypt as long as you live" (Deut. 16:3). The Israelites ate the Passover sacrifice in such a hurry because they knew they were on the cusp of liberation. Their lives depended on their leaving. They ate with their bags packed and their sandals on, ready at any moment to begin the flight from Egypt, to leave behind everything that they had ever known. They did not know when exactly the moment would come. They knew that Pharaoh still might pursue them. It was for this reason that they had no time to wait for the bread to rise.

But let us not make the mistake of confusing their haste for a lack of readiness. To say they did not prepare is to deny the extreme readiness of the Israelites for freedom. To say they did not prepare is to deny the generations of enslavement in Egypt. The time for liberation had more than come.

The journey of a transgender person, like the journey of the Children of Israel, involves leaving everything known for the promise of something completely unknown. Their lives depend on their leaving. Leaving is terrifying, even if what is being left, the place that is known, is *mitzrayim*. The time for liberation has more than come.

Still, even when they are ready, they still must contend with Pharaoh, who does not want to let them go: the Pharaoh of the progressive world that is still deeply attached to binary notions of gender; the Pharaoh of gay and lesbian communities that still do not embrace transgender people and transgender rights as an essential element of queer identity, queer activism, and queer community; the Pharaoh of fear, the Pharaoh of the body. . . . There is no shortage of Pharaoh.

Jews in every generation are commanded to eat matzah on Passover, so that they will always remember that they too were slaves in Egypt. They are commanded to eat matzah so that they will remember the day they departed from Egypt and experience that feeling of *chipazon,* the haste and fear that comes with leaving. They are commanded to eat matzah so that they will remember that although they have already experienced liberation, there are others who are still enslaved.

Avadim Hayinu l'Pharoh b'mitzrayim. Veyotzieinu Adonai Eloheinu misham b'yad chazakah u'bizroa netuyah.

We were slaves to Pharaoh in Egypt. And God brought us out from there with a strong hand and an outstretched arm.

It takes God's outstretched arm and it takes all of us together raising our hands to fight injustice within our own communities and beyond. Only then can we say that we remember leaving Egypt. Only then can we imagine creating a path through the sea so that we may rejoice together on the other side.

NOTES

1. The Hebrew word for Egypt, *mitzrayim,* can also be translated literally to mean "narrow places," from the Hebrew word *tzar,* lit. "narrow."

2. Yehuda Amichai, excerpt from poem number 21, in *Open Closed Open* (New York: Harcourt, 2000), 46–47. Translated from the Hebrew by Chana Bloch and Chana Kronfeld.

SIXTY

Trance and Trans at Har Sinai
Shavu'ot

RACHEL BIALE

Shavu'ot is consecrated in the Torah as a pilgrimage festival, the offering of the first fruit of the wheat harvest at the Temple: "And a Festival of Weeks you shall make for yourself, first fruits of the harvest of wheat. . . . Three times in the year all your males shall appear in the presence of the Master, the Lord God of Israel" (Ex. 34:22–23).[1] The first reference to Shavu'ot as *Hag Matan Torah*—the Holiday of the Giving of the Torah—appears in the book of Jubilees (2nd century BCE). The association is based on the rather vague timing that opens the chapter, describing the giving of the Torah: "On the third moon of the Israelites' going out from Egypt, on this day did they come to the Wilderness of Sinai" (Ex. 19:1). The celebration of Shavu'ot as Matan Torah became the predominant feature of the holiday after the destruction of the Temple and with the evolution of Jewish life in the Diaspora. It is this aspect of Shavu'ot that is my focus in this commentary, and thus I turn to the description of the giving of the Torah in Exodus 19 for a gender-lensed reading.

Three major gender-related issues come to the fore:

1. What is the meaning and function of the only specific reference to gender differences in the chapter, namely, Moses's admonition to the people, "Do not come near a woman"?
2. Is there a way to read the imagery of the revelation with a "queer eye"?
3. Does the scene of the giving of the Torah and the subsequent conceptualization of the Torah in feminine terms shed light on categories of gender and sex?

The description of Matan Torah begins with two sets of instructions to the people on how to prepare for the encounter with God, including directions for purification and separation. God's instructions make no gender distinction, as He calls on the people to "wash their cloaks," "ready themselves for the third day," and "watch yourselves not to go up on the mountain or to touch its edge" (19:9–12). But Moses, when relaying God's instructions to the Israelites, introduces a new idea: "Do not go near a woman" (*al tigshu el ishah*; 19:15). Why the innovation, and what are its implications?

God's prescription of consecration through washing of the garments has no gender bias, no presumption that doing the laundry is "women's work." Likewise, the following days of preparations emphasize setting a boundary and separating the people from the mountain, not men from women. The people may not approach the mountain or touch its side, on pain of death (*ha'noge'a bahar mot yumat*). This separation from the mountain appears to apply equally to men and women, with no distinction drawn between them in receiving the revelation.

The word prohibiting approaching the mountain surprisingly does not come from the root *karev*, the typical term used in Biblical references to trespassing on the territory of the divine presence ("And the stranger who draws near [*hakarev*] [the Tabernacle] shall be put to death" [Num. 1:51 et al.]). Nor does the text use another likely option, "to come" (*lavo*), a term that would carry a double entendre, as it is also used for approaching a woman sexually (both coming physically near and having intercourse). Thus, we might say that Moses's introduction of the injunction not to go near a woman and the implied gender distinction is man-made, not divinely mandated.

How are we to understand Moses's addition of the separation of men and women and the placement of men as subject, women as the object to be shunned for three days? On the simplest narrative level, Moses decrees a moratorium on sex during the preparation period. This is easily understood as a reflection of the same notions as those that underlie the laws in Leviticus 15, which rule all genital fluids, including semen, as agents causing a state of impurity that bars one from entering the Temple grounds.

> And the Lord spoke to Moses and to Aaron, saying, "Speak to the Israelites, and you shall say to them, 'Should any man have a flux from his member, he is unclean. . . . And a woman who a man had bedded with emission of seed—they shall wash in water and be unclean until evening. And a woman who has a flux of blood, her flux beginning from the genitals, seven days she shall be in her menstruations.' . . . And you shall set apart the Israelites from their uncleanness lest they die through their uncleanness by making unclean My sanctuary which is in their midst." (Lev. 15:1–2, 18–20, 31)

The separation of men and women at Sinai is needed to bar any chance of sexual relations and "emission of seed." As we learn from the rest of Leviticus 15, other bodily contacts and states cause impurity (*tum'ah*), which bars one from entering the Temple: contact with a corpse, certain illnesses, and touching certain "creepy crawly things." But no other moment of revelation stands in parallel to this text in requiring sexual abstinence.

On a deeper level, the separation prepares the people for a spiritual and sensual union with God and the mountain that holds God's presence. The phallic Har Sinai practically explodes with an ejaculation of sights and sounds that overwhelm all senses:

> there was thunder and lightning and a heavy cloud on the mountain and the sounds of the ram's horn, very strong and all the people who were in the camp trembled. . . . And Mount Sinai was all in smoke because the Lord had come down on it in fire, and its smoke went up like the smoke from a kiln, the whole mountain trembled greatly. . . . And all the people were seeing the voices ["sounds" or Alter's translation,

"thunder"] and the flashes and the sound of the ram's horn and the mountain in smoke. (Ex. 19:16, 18)

God's presence is at once terrifying and enveloping. The blurring of senses expressed through the paradoxical "seeing the voices" is evocative of the experiences of mystical and sexual union. The barrier separating the people from the mountain on threat of death may be needed to prevent them from a closer embrace with the divine presence. At the same time, the period of abstinence might incline the people (presumably both men and women) toward sexualized desire for union, making the spiritual moment more potent and more engulfing.

While "the people" includes both men and women, the target audience is clearly framed as men, who must not approach women. There is no word about women approaching men or women (or, for that matter, possible male homosexual liaisons). Although, as we shall soon see, the encounter with God is rife with homosexual and transgender possibilities, the frame of reference of the earthly gender separation is thoroughly heterosexual.

Rabbinic reflections on this scene complicate matters. On one hand, the Rabbis render this moment of receiving/embracing the Torah as quintessentially heterosexual, since they so frequently portray the Torah in feminine terms and the people of Israel as its male suitors. On the other hand, the Rabbis generally imagine God in male terms, and thus their vision of the moment of revelation at Har Sinai is of a homosexual fusion of the male entities of God and the men of Israel.

Imagining the Torah as feminine is most pronounced in the Rabbis' understanding of Proverbs, which is replete with references to wisdom as a woman, in constant battle to lead men away from the "other woman"—the personification of wickedness and temptation (e.g., Proverbs 6:18–20, 8:22–30). The Rabbis easily elide "Wisdom" with the Torah. They amplify this image with sayings such as "Anyone who does not have a wife has no happiness, no blessings, no goodness . . . [and lives] without Torah, without a protective wall" (Babylonian Talmud, *Yevamot* 62b) and "How good is a good woman [or wife—the word *ishah* in Hebrew means both]—the Torah is likened to her" (Babylonian Talmud, *Yevamot* 63b). Even more poignantly, the Rabbis do not shy away from sensual and sexual images: "Behold the doe, her womb [womb and vagina are fused into one] is narrow and she thus gives pleasure to her possessor every time as if it were the first, so the words of the Torah are pleasing to its student every time as if it were the first. . . . Why are the words of the Torah likened to a breast? Just like with the breast, when the infant fondles it he draws milk, so the words of the Torah—as long as a man contemplates and studies them, he finds new flavor and meaning in them" (*Eruvin* 18b).

Thus, rabbinic midrash portrays the people, imagined as male, as united at Sinai with the male God in a homosexual fusion. Two conceptions enrich the giving of the Torah with sexualized images: God, a male entity, gives birth to the Torah; the people of Israel receive it, becoming impregnated with the Torah. Altogether we find a fluidity of heterosexual images of sex, conception, and gestation. Ezekiel amplifies this latter image of gestations with a vivid picture when he imagines the revelation of the word of God as a scroll he is ordered to swallow. He ingests the revelation, impregnating himself with God's message.

> He said to me, "Mortal, eat what is offered to you; eat this scroll, and go speak to the house of Israel." So I opened my mouth, and He gave me this scroll to eat, as He said to me, "Mortal, feed you stomach and fill your belly with this scroll that I give you." I ate it, and it tasted as sweet as honey to me. (Ezekiel 3:1–3)

Ezekiel is orally inseminated and becomes pregnant with the word of God, blending, and thus blurring, his male identity with female attributes. He clearly adds a new layer of meaning and imagery to the dramatic description of the revelation at Sinai that we find in the Torah.

To complicate the gender boundaries even more, we need to remember that it is God who embodies the ultimate gender fluidity. In several Biblical depictions, God is endowed with feminine qualities, including through the name *El Shadai* (which some scholars have argued should be understood literally as "the God with breasts") and where he is described as carrying, birthing, and suckling the people of Israel. At the same time, other verses depict God as Israel's groom, a masculine role, which then casts the people of Israel as the bride and frames the collective identity of *am yisrael* as feminine. Again, gender identity and sexualized roles are slippery. The people of Israel are female to God's maleness as lover and husband, but male to the Torah as their beloved. The complexity grows with other texts that portray the Shabbat as a bride, making the nation male in its love and devotion to it. All in all, at Har Sinai and elsewhere in the Torah and rabbinic imagination, male and female identities blend and fuse in the image of the people of Israel and its God, creating a thoroughly multifaceted and fluid gender identity.

Of course, the very first manifestation of this gender blending within God's image is in the creation of Adam, the first human, as a dual-sexed creature made "in the image of God" (*betzelem Elohim*; see full discussion in the commentary on *Parashat Bereshit*, Gen. 1:27). The text poses the radical idea that the first, most perfect, and most pristine human being, who was a direct embodiment of God, was a hermaphrodite. It seems to suggests that trans- or intersexuality may be the ultimate state of human and divine perfection. It also appears to question the division of male and female into binary opposites. The intriguing possibility of transsexuality seems to be behind the rabbinic categories of *androginos*, *saris*, *aylonit*, and *tumtum*, which fill in the space between male and female (in numerous references in the Mishnah and Talmud, e.g., Mishnah *Bikkurim*, chapter 4). These gender categories that occupy the space between "male" and "female" do not even include the homosexual man and lesbian woman, who combine "traditional" gender identities coupled with "nonnormative" (for hetero-centered Jewish law and tradition) sexual preferences.

In complex reasoning, the Rabbis delineate under what circumstances other-gendered people are treated as men and when as women. They fine-tune their distinctions by making gender identity circumstantial. Depending on the context, they allow that a person with mixed sexual features, or one with no clear ones, may function as a man or as a woman, thus stretching their binary gender conceptions to accom-modate a multifaceted reality. Try as they might, they ultimately find circumstances in which their categories fail, so that Rabbi Yossei declares, "Androginos is a creature unto itself" (ibid.).

We return to Sinai, having enriched its meaning with prophetic voices, Wisdom Literature, and rabbinic interpretations, endowed with a larger palette of gender va-rieties. Clearly, some were not on the horizon of the Biblical imagination, but the foundation for options beyond only male or only female is there. The encounter at Sinai is the drama of a triad—God, Israel, and Torah—with fluid gender boundaries within and between them.

If, as the midrash says, all Jewish souls were present at the giving of the Torah in the first celebration of Shavu'ot at Sinai, it is incumbent on us to reimagine and retell its story for Shavu'ot in our generation. We have, among many other challenges and opportunities, the momentous task of understanding the contours of a society and its individual members who transcend binary gender identities. Let us hope it will take less than forty years of wandering in the desert.

NOTES

1. All Torah translations are from Robert Alter's *The Five Books of Moses* (New York: Nor-ton, 2004), unless otherwise noted.

The New Rabbis
A Postscript

BENAY LAPPE

The visionaries who picked up the pieces of a shattered Judaism two thousand years ago, after the destruction of the Second Temple and the crashing of Biblical Judaism, were courageous, creative, out-of-the-box-thinking, fringy radicals. Queer, if you will. Not in the sense of sexuality or gender, perhaps, but in what *being* those very kinds of people usually makes you: courageous, creative, out-of-the-box-thinking, fringy, and radical. And deeply attuned to that still, small voice inside and confident of the truth it is telling you even when the whole world is telling you something else. These guys called themselves Rabbis. Teachers. They were the architects of a Judaism that would have been virtually unrecognizable to those practicing the Judaism of the Temple era.

Their Judaism, like ours, was crashing. Theirs, in many ways, was no longer physically possible. Ours, in many ways, is no longer morally plausible. They had a new take on what it could mean to be a human being and took a shot at playing it out. Their radically transformed Judaism survived, and we are its descendants. In a way, it was easier for them than it is for us. The Judaism they knew was over. They had nothing to lose. No one could pretend that sitting in (the) Temple was "working for them" anymore—there *was* no more Temple. It is harder for us. We have a lot to lose. But much of what we are afraid to lose is illusion, the illusion that Judaism today is working for us all even when it is not working for most of us. And it cannot work for most of us until it understands *all of us.*

Queer people (along with women, the deaf, the disabled, and people of color, among many others) have important—*essential*—things to say about what life is really like that the Tradition needs to hear. And although the Rabbis may have delegitimated the God-spoke-to-me kind of prophecy as a source of new Jewish law two millennia ago, they elevated our informed internal ethical impulse to the status of Torah itself and called it *svara.*

Those queer Rabbis took their outsider insights—their sensitivity to those marginalized and oppressed by the Torah itself, their courage to stand up for them and mess with the Tradition to incorporate them—and declared their informed internal ethical impulse an authentic source of God's will. They deemed it a source of Jewish legal change as authoritative as a verse in the Torah itself—so much so that a law that they created out of *svara* has the same status as one that appears verbatim in the Torah itself—*d'oraita*. And they went even further than that. They declared that one's *svara* could even trump a verse in the Torah when the two conflicted.

Svara is a term and a concept that has been kept virtually secret—certainly in its far-reaching implications—for over fifteen hundred years. It is not taught even to rabbis or rabbinical students today. In my six years of rabbinical school at the Conservative Movement's flagship, the Jewish Theological Seminary, the word was never uttered. Not once. We were never assigned a text that contained it—though hundreds do. Instead, we were taught, as if it were Jewish dogma, the lie that our leaders have succeeded in conveying to most Jews: that when it comes to certain verses in the Torah, "There's nothing we can do," "Our hands are tied," "If we could change it, we would." Understanding the Talmudic concept of *svara* exposes these excuses as the untruths that they are.

That is why queer Jewish learning must begin with an understanding of the game-changing concept of *svara*. Yet it is understandable that *svara* would not be taught in seminaries. Seminaries (particularly movement-affiliated ones) are typically in business to perpetuate the status quo of an era long gone—not to teach mechanisms of potentially radical change. *Svara* allows *any* change—even to the point of uprooting the entire Tradition itself—to create a system that better achieves that Tradition's ultimate goals. It is a mechanism of change that arguably should be entrusted only to those who are committed stakeholders in the Jewish enterprise. My reading of Talmud also tells me that the Rabbis who came up with this potentially dangerous and potentially chaos-creating source of change required its practitioners to be learned in the Tradition. This cannot be overstated. They did not believe that *svara* was merely one's uneducated "gut feeling" but that it was one's moral impulse that was deeply influenced by having been steeped in the intricacies of the values, principles, and concerns of the entire Jewish Tradition as well as by a broad exposure to the world and its people. Menachem Elon, the former deputy chief justice of the Israeli Supreme Court, defined *svara* as "legal reasoning that penetrates into the essence of things and reflects a profound understanding of human nature. [It] involves . . . an appreciation of the characteristics of human beings in their social relationships, and a careful study of the real world and its manifestations."[1] In other words, you cannot be a Jewish ignoramus and claim that "what I think is right" is *svara*. It is not. And neither can you have never met a queer person and presume to legislate on matters of, well, just about anything in Jewish law. The Rabbis of the Talmud were explicit, though, that exercising one's *svara* to upgrade the Tradition—to play the game, as it were—did not require rabbinic ordination. It did not for them, nor should it for us. But it did require learning.

Like that small band of queer Tradition-changers and inventors two thousand years ago, most of the new Tradition-changers and inventors of this next era of Judaism may not be ordained. They will, though, like their predecessors, have to possess learning and *svara*. The queer Jews who take up the challenge will be Judaism's new Rabbis.

The fact that each queer person is still alive is a testament to a willingness to heed the truth of one's inner voices when the world would have queer people silence them, and to do so at great personal cost. Queers have been willing to face inconvenient truths to live fuller, more human lives. The prophetic insight of queer Jews is ultimately less about sexuality and gender than it is about the imperative to live by one's *svara*. And that, it turns out, is a very old Jewish idea.

My dream is that when every queer Jewish kid comes out, he or she or ze will know—having already learned the concept of *svara* in Hebrew school—that the voice that they are choosing to listen to not only does not place them *outside* of their Jewish tradition or in conflict with God's will but is the most authoritative manifestation of both. The authors contributing to this book are, likewise, speaking not from outside of the Tradition but from the place most respected by it, from the place that, two thousand years ago, our founding Rabbis determined was actually the most authoritative source of God's will—more authoritative than the Torah itself. Though most are probably unfamiliar with the term, the authors in this book are utilizing the Tradition's mandate to each of us to become learned and to allow our informed *svara* to push the Tradition beyond its current boundaries to become a truer, more humane vision of what it means to be a human being.

I challenge those who read these essays—queer or not—to accept upon themselves the implicit charge of *svara* that animates every chapter of this book: go and learn, refine and develop your *svara*, and use it to make Judaism, or your own traditions, places where we are all freer to live more *fully human* lives.

NOTES

1. Menachem Elon, *Jewish Law: Cases and Materials* (Albany, NY: Matthew Bender, 1999), 97.

Contributors

CAMILLE SHIRA ANGEL has been the spiritual leader of Congregation Sha'ar Za-hav, San Francisco's all-inclusive LGBT synagogue, since 2000. She is author of *Intimate Connections: Integrating Human Love with God's Love*, a curriculum that sensitizes students to the lesbian/gay experience using Jewish values.

CARYN AVIV is a sociologist and Academic Director of the Certificate in Jewish Communal Service at the University of Denver. Aviv, along with David Shneer, is the author of *New Jews: The End of the Jewish Diaspora* (also available from NYU Press). Aviv and Shneer also coauthored *American Queer, Now and Then* and coedited the anthology *Queer Jews*. Caryn Aviv is a cofounder and the director of research for Jewish Mosaic: The National Center for Sexual and Gender Diversity.

JULIA WATTS BELSER is Assistant Professor of Religious Studies at Missouri State University, where she teaches courses in rabbinic literature, Jewish history, religion and ecology, and world religions. She received her rabbinic ordination from the Academy for Jewish Religion, California, and her Ph.D. in rabbinic literature from the Joint Doctoral Program in Jewish Studies at the University of California, Berkeley, and the Graduate Theological Union.

ALLEN BENNETT is the rabbi at Temple Israel in Alameda, California, and President of the Board of Rabbis of Northern California.

RACHEL BIALE is Bay Area Regional Director of the Progressive Jewish Alliance. She is the author of *Women and Jewish Law* and two books for parents and children, *My Pet Died* and *We Are Moving*.

MARLA BRETTSCHNEIDER is Professor of Political Philosophy at the University of New Hampshire. She is founder and past Coordinator of Queer Studies at UNH and currently serves as Coordinator of Women's Studies. Her most recent book is *The Family Flamboyant: Race Politics, Queer Families, Jewish Lives*—winner of a 2007 IPPY (Independent Publishers) Award in the GLBT category. Her earlier books include *The Narrow Bridge: Jewish Views on Multiculturalism*, winner of the Gustavus Meyers Human Rights Award.

RACHEL BRODIE is the cofounder and Executive Director of Jewish Milestones (www.JewishMilestones.org) and coauthor of *Jewish Family Education: A Casebook for the Twenty-first Century*, with Vicky Kelman.

DAVID BRODSKY is Assistant Professor and Co-chair of the Department of Rabbinic Civilization at the Reconstructionist Rabbinical College. He teaches courses on Talmud, midrash, and other aspects of rabbinic literature and civilization.

AYELET COHEN is Associate Rabbi of New York City's Congregation Beth Simchat Torah (CBST), the world's largest synagogue serving the LGBT community, family, and friends.

MENACHEM CREDITOR serves as rabbi of Congregation Netivot Shalom in Berkeley, California. He is founder of ShefaNetwork: The Conservative Movement Dreaming from Within (www.ShefaNetwork.org), cofounder of Keshet-Rabbis: The Alliance of Gay-Friendly Conservative/Masorti Rabbis (www.KeshetRabbis.org), and author of *The Tisch: A Jewish Spiritual Commentary*.

ELLIOT N. DORFF is a rabbi and Rector and Distinguished Professor of Philosophy at the American Jewish University, and coauthor of the rabbinic ruling that permitted commitment ceremonies and ordination of gays and lesbians in the Conservative Movement. His books that articulate his thinking on homosexuality include *Matters of Life and Death* (on medical ethics) and *Love Your Neighbor and Yourself* (on personal ethics). He earned a Ph.D. in philosophy at Columbia University.

GREGG DRINKWATER is Executive Director of Jewish Mosaic: The National Center for Sexual and Gender Diversity, an organization dedicated to helping Jewish institutions become more welcoming of lesbian, gay, bisexual, and transgender Jews and their families. Drinkwater, with the help of the World Congress of GLBT Jews, launched Torah Queeries as an online project on Purim in 2006 (www.JewishMosaic.org/Torah). He earned his B.S. and M.A. degrees at the University of California, Berkeley, where he also devoted several years to a Ph.D. in history.

NOACH DZMURA is Online Projects Consultant for Jewish Mosaic and since spring 2008 has edited Torah Queeries (online). He is editor of an anthology about gender-variant Jews and is a founding member of Kol Tzedek's Gender Variant Task Force, a Bay Area initiative to give voice to gender-variant Jews.

LAURENCE EDWARDS serves as the rabbi of Congregation Or Chadash in Chicago. For twenty-two years he was a Hillel Director, first at Dartmouth College and then at Cornell University. He was ordained at Hebrew Union College–Jewish Institute of Religion in New York and received a Ph.D. from Chicago Theological Seminary. He is the brother of Lisa Edwards.

LISA EDWARDS has been the rabbi of Beth Chayim Chadashim (BCC) in Los Angeles since 1994. She holds a Ph.D. in literature and lives in Los Angeles with her wife, Tracy Moore, editor of *Lesbiot: Israeli Lesbians Talk about Sexuality, Feminism, Judaism and Their Lives*.

DENISE L. EGER is the founding rabbi of Congregation Kol Ami, West Hollywood's Reform synagogue. She has served as the rabbi of the LGBT community in Los Angeles since 1988. Eger is President of the Board of Rabbis of Southern California and

President of the Pacific Association of Reform Rabbis. She has written extensively on LGBT issues and coauthored, with Yoel Kahn, the official liturgy of the Reform Movement for gay weddings and commitment ceremonies.

DAVID ELLENSON, a rabbi and President of Hebrew Union College–Jewish Institute of Religion, is the author of *Tradition in Transition: Orthodoxy, Halakhah and the Boundaries of Modern Jewish History, Rabbi Esriel Hildesheimer and the Creation of a Modern Jewish Orthodoxy, Between Tradition and Culture: The Dialectics of Jewish Religion and Identity in the Modern World,* and *After Emancipation: Jewish Religious Responses to Modernity.* He received a Ph.D. from Columbia University in 1981.

SUE LEVI ELWELL, is a Worship Specialist for the Congregational Consulting Group of the Union for Reform Judaism and has served as rabbi for congregations in California, New Jersey, and Virginia. A Senior Rabbinic Fellow of the Shalom Hartman Institute in Jerusalem, she is the editor of *The Open Door,* the CCAR Haggadah, and served as one of the editors of the acclaimed *The Journey Continues: The Ma'yan Haggadah.* Elwell also served as editor, with Rebecca Alpert and Shirley Idelson, of *Lesbian Rabbis: The First Generation* and as Consulting Poetry Editor of *The Torah: A Women's Commentary.* She earned her doctorate at Indiana University.

KAREN ERLICHMAN is the director of Jewish Mosaic's San Francisco Bay Area office and a licensed clinical social worker in private practice in San Francisco.

CHARLOTTE ELISHEVA FONROBERT is Associate Professor in the Department of Religious Studies and Co-Director of the Taube Center for Jewish Studies at Stanford University. She is the author of *Menstrual Purity: Rabbinic and Christian Reconstructions of Biblical Gender,* which won the Baron Prize for a best first book in Jewish studies of that year. She also coedited the *Cambridge Companion to the Talmud and Rabbinic Literature,* to which she contributed the chapter "Rabbinic Legal Discourse and the Making of Jewish Gender."

ARI LEV FORNARI is a rabbinical student at Hebrew College in Newton, Massachusetts, and a member of the TransTorah collective.

MARK GEORGE is Associate Professor of Hebrew Bible at the Iliff School of Theology. He is the author of a forthcoming book, *Israel's Tabernacle as Social Space,* that examines the social nature of the Tabernacle.

STEVEN GREENBERG is an Orthodox rabbi, ordained at Rabbi Isaac Elchanan Theological Seminary. Since 1985 he has served as a senior educator for CLAL, a think tank, leadership training institute, and resource center. Rabbi Greenberg is the author of *Wrestling with God and Men: Homosexuality in the Jewish Tradition,* which won the 2005 Koret Jewish Book Award. He is currently rabbi-in-residence at Hazon, a leading Jewish environmental organization, and Keshet, a grassroots organization dedicated to LGBT inclusion in the Jewish community.

DAVID GREENSTEIN is the rabbi of Congregation Shomrei Emunah, Montclair, New Jersey He was formerly Rosh Ha-Yeshivah of the Academy for Jewish Religion

(AJR), New York. He has published essays on Jewish thought and culture, exploring possibilities for rethinking Jewish tradition. He holds a Ph.D. in Kabbalah and Rabbinics from New York University.

STEVE GUTOW is a rabbi, an attorney, and President of the Jewish Council for Public Affairs. He served a pulpit in St. Louis, and as an adjunct professor at the St. Louis University Law School, and as Founding Director of the National Jewish Democratic Council.

JILL HAMMER is a rabbi and Director of Spiritual Education at the Academy for Jewish Religion. She is also Director of Tel Shemesh, a website and community celebrating Jewish traditions connected with the earth, and the cofounder of Kohenet, a program in Jewish women's spiritual leadership. Rabbi Hammer is the author of two books: *The Jewish Book of Days* and *Sisters at Sinai: New Tales of Biblical Women*. She holds a Ph.D. from the University of Connecticut.

LINDA HOLTZMAN is the senior rabbi at Mishkan Shalom. She has served as Director of Practical Rabbinics at the Reconstructionist Rabbinical College and has worked closely with the Philadelphia LGBT and progressive Jewish community.

SHIRLEY IDELSON is a rabbi and Dean of the New York campus of Hebrew Union College–Jewish Institute of Religion. She is coeditor, together with Rebecca Alpert and Sue Levi Elwell, of *Lesbian Rabbis: The First Generation*, and a Ph.D. candidate in history at the CUNY Graduate Center.

YOEL KAHN is the rabbi of Congregation Beth El in Berkeley, California. He has served on the Central Conference of American Rabbis' Responsa (Law) Committee and on the Editorial Committee for *Miskhan Tefilah*. His forthcoming book *The Three Blessings* looks at identity, censorship, and boundaries in Jewish liturgy over time. He received a Ph.D. through the Center for Jewish Studies at Berkeley's Graduate Theological Union.

TAMAR KAMIONKOWSKI is Vice President for Academic Affairs and Associate Professor of Biblical Studies at the Reconstructionist Rabbinical College. She is the first woman and lesbian to hold the senior academic-administrative position at a rabbinical seminary. Kamionkowski is the author of *Gender Reversal and Cosmic Chaos: Studies in the Book of Ezekiel* and numerous articles on prophetic and priestly literature and feminist readings of Biblical texts.

MARTIN KAVKA is Associate Professor in the Department of Religion at Florida State University in Tallahassee. He is the author of *Jewish Messianism and the History of Philosophy* and coeditor of *Tradition in the Public Square: A David Novak Reader* and *Saintly Influence: Texts for Edith Wyschogrod*.

GWYNN KESSLER teaches at Swarthmore College. She is the author of *Conceiving Israel: The Fetus in Rabbinic Narratives*, "Let's Cross That Body When We Get to It," and "Bodies in Motion: Preliminary Notes on Queer Theory and Rabbinic Literature" in *Mapping Gender in Ancient Religious Discourses*.

JASON GARY KLEIN currently serves as the director of Hillel at the University of Maryland, Baltimore County (UMBC) and Campaign Chair of the Reconstructionist Rabbinical Association.

ELLIOT KUKLA is a rabbi at the Bay Area Jewish Healing Center in San Francisco, offering spiritual care to those struggling with life-altering illness or grief or dying. Throughout the United States, he has lectured and led workshops on gender and sexual diversity in sacred texts, spiritual care at the end of life, and Judaism and mental illness. His articles are published in numerous magazines and have been anthologized widely, and his prayers and rituals for new life-cycle moments have been used by synagogues across the country.

BENAY LAPPE is a rabbi and Executive Director and Rosh Yeshiva of SVARA, a traditionally radical queer yeshiva. She was ordained by the Jewish Theological Seminary in 1997 and holds three additional advanced degrees, in teaching and rabbinics. An innovator in combining Talmud study and queer theory, she currently serves as Professor of Talmud at the Hebrew Seminary of the Deaf, in Chicago, Visiting Professor of Talmud at the Richard S. Dinner Center for Jewish Studies at the Graduate Theological Union, at the University of California, Berkeley, and is an Associate at CLAL, a think tank in New York City.

AMICHAI LAU-LAVIE is the founder of Storahtelling, Inc. and is an Israeli-born performer and teacher of Judaic literature, hailed by *Time Out New York* as a "Super Star of David" and an "iconoclastic mystic" and by *New York Jewish Week* as "one of the most interesting thinkers in the Jewish world." Lau-Lavie is a 2008 Jerusalem Fellow, a consultant to the Reboot Network, and the recipient of a Joshua Venture Fellowship award 2002–2004.

LORI HOPE LEFKOVITZ is the Sadie Gottesman and Arlene Gottesman Reff Professor of Gender and Judaism at the Reconstructionist Rabbinical College, where she directs Kolot: The Center for Jewish Women's and Gender Studies. She is Executive Editor of the website ritualwell.org, and her publications include *Shaping Losses: Cultural Memory and the Holocaust.*

JOSHUA LESSER is the rabbi of Congregation Bet Haverim in Atlanta, a Reconstructionist community founded by gays and lesbians. He is also the founder of the Rainbow Center, a resource, information, and educational center addressing the needs of LGBT people and their families.

SARRA LEV is chair of the Department of Rabbinic Texts at the Reconstructionist Rabbinical College. She has taught courses on Judaism for a range of programs and institutions including Jewish Alive & American, the Feminist Center of the American Jewish Congress, New York University, and Bat Kol: A Feminist House of Study, which she cofounded. Lev received her rabbinic ordination from the Reconstructionist Rabbinical College and a doctorate in rabbinic literature from New York University.

JANE RACHEL LITMAN is Western Regional Director of the Jewish Reconstructionist Federation and serves as the rabbi of Kolot Mayim Temple of Victoria, Canada. Widely published in the fields of gay rights, Jewish women's history, and contemporary theology, Rabbi Litman is the coeditor of the award-winning *Lifecycles 2* anthology. Her recent writing on the politics of gender expression appears in the anthology *New Jewish Feminism*.

JAY MICHAELSON (www.metatronics.net) is a writer, scholar, and activist. He is the executive director of Nehirim, a nonprofit organization for GLBT Jews, partners, and allies; a columnist for the *Forward* newspaper and *Reality Sandwich* magazine; and a contributor to the *Huffington Post, Zeek, Tikkun,* and *Slate.* His books include *Everything Is God: The Radical Path of Nondual Judaism, Another Word for Sky: Poems,* and *God in Your Body: Kabbalah, Mindfulness, and Embodied Spiritual Practice.* A recent visiting professor at Boston University Law School, Jay is completing a Ph.D. in religious studies at the Hebrew University of Jerusalem.

AYALA SHA'ASHOUA MIRON was born and raised in Tel Aviv, Israel. Miron was ordained as a rabbi at Hebrew Union College–Jewish Institute of Religion in Jerusalem in November 2005. She is the founding rabbi of Bavat Ayin Congregation in Rosh HaAyin, a thriving Kehila of the Israeli Movement for Progressive Judaism (IMPJ) established in September 2004.

JULIE PELC is a rabbi, Assistant Director of the Kalsman Institute on Judaism and Health, and Director of the Berit Mila Program of Reform Judaism. She is coeditor of the anthology *Joining the Sisterhood: Young Jewish Women Write Their Lives,* and she contributed to *The Torah: A Women's Commentary* and *Celebrating the Jewish Year: The Winter Holidays.*

SARAH PESSIN is Associate Professor of Philosophy, the Emil and Eva Hecht Chair in Judaic Studies, and the Director of the Center for Judaic Studies at the University of Denver.

JUDITH PLASKOW is Professor of Religious Studies at Manhattan College and a Jewish feminist theologian. She is author of many books and articles, including *Standing Again at Sinai: Judaism from a Feminist Perspective* and *The Coming of Lilith: Essays on Feminism, Judaism, and Sexual Ethics, 1972–2003.*

AMBER POWERS serves as Dean of Admissions and Recruitment at the Reconstructionist Rabbinical College. She previously served as the rabbi of Temple Menorah Keneseth Chai in Northeast Philadelphia and as Mid-Atlantic Regional Director of the Jewish Reconstructionist Federation.

DAWN ROSE is the rabbi of Temple Emanuel of the Merrimack Valley, in Lowell, Massachusetts. Forced from the Rabbinic Program at the Jewish Theological Seminary because of her sexual orientation, Rose cofounded the Incognito Club, JTS's first lesbian/gay organization while she completed a Ph.D. there in Jewish philosophy. Rabbi Rose has taught theology and ethics at JTS and the Reconstructionist

Rabbinical College, where she was also Director of the Center for Jewish Ethics. Currently, Rose is working on a novel about the search for faith in an era of religious extremism.

DAVID SHNEER is Associate Professor of History and Director of the Program in Jewish Studies at the University of Colorado at Boulder. His most recent books include *Yiddish and the Creation of Soviet Jewish Culture, New Jews: The End of the Jewish Diaspora* (coauthored with Caryn Aviv and also available from NYU Press), and *American Queer, Now and Then* (also coauthored with Caryn Aviv). Aviv and Shneer also coedited the groundbreaking anthology *Queer Jews*. Additionally, Shneer is a cofounder of Jewish Mosaic: The National Center for Sexual and Gender Diversity.

JHOS SINGER serves as the maggid/rabbi for the Coastside Jewish Community in Half Moon Bay, California, which has put up with his trance/gender approach to Judaism's profound, paranormal, and paradoxical practices since 5760.

TOBA SPITZER is the rabbi of Congregation Dorshei Tzedek in West Newton, an affiliate of the Jewish Reconstructionist Federation. President of the Reconstructionist Rabbinical Association from 2007 to 2009, she was the first gay or lesbian to serve as the president of a denominational rabbinic organization.

JACOB J. STAUB is a rabbi and serves as Professor of Jewish Philosophy and Spirituality at the Reconstructionist Rabbinical College, where he directs the program in Jewish Spiritual Direction. He is a member of the Nehirim faculty and directs Shalshelet, the Nehirim queer Jewish mentoring program. He is coauthor, with Rebecca Alpert, of *Exploring Judaism: A Reconstructionist Approach*.

MARGARET MOERS WENIG is Rabbi Emerita of Beth Am, The People's Temple, and Instructor in Liturgy and Homiletics at Hebrew Union College–Jewish Institute of Religion.

REUBEN ZELLMAN will complete his rabbinical studies at the Hebrew Union College–Jewish Institute of Religion in 2010. He currently serves at Congregation Sha'ar Zahav in San Francisco and Congregation Beth El in Berkeley, California.

Index